Becoming an Enterprise Django Developer

Discover best practices, tooling, and solutions for writing and organizing Django applications in production

Michael Dinder

BIRMINGHAM—MUMBAI

Becoming an Enterprise Django Developer

Copyright © 2022 Packt Publishing

All rights reserved. No part of this book may be reproduced, stored in a retrieval system, or transmitted in any form or by any means, without the prior written permission of the publisher, except in the case of brief quotations embedded in critical articles or reviews.

Every effort has been made in the preparation of this book to ensure the accuracy of the information presented. However, the information contained in this book is sold without warranty, either express or implied. Neither the author, nor Packt Publishing or its dealers and distributors, will be held liable for any damages caused or alleged to have been caused directly or indirectly by this book.

Packt Publishing has endeavored to provide trademark information about all of the companies and products mentioned in this book by the appropriate use of capitals. However, Packt Publishing cannot guarantee the accuracy of this information.

Publishing Product Manager: Pavan Ramchandani
Senior Editor: Mark Dsouza
Content Development Editor: Divya Vijayan
Technical Editor: Simran Udasi
Copy Editor: Safis Editing
Project Coordinator: Ajesh Devavaram
Proofreader: Safis Editing
Indexer: Manju Arasan
Production Designer: Shyam Sundar Korumilli
Marketing Coordinator: Anamika Singh and Marylou De Mello

First published: June 2022

Production reference: 1240622

Published by Packt Publishing Ltd.
Livery Place
35 Livery Street
Birmingham
B3 2PB, UK.

ISBN 978-1-80107-363-9

www.packt.com

To my father, Joe Dinder, and uncle, Tom Dinder, who continuously encouraged me throughout the long journey of writing this book, I thank you very much. To my many other friends and family who supported me throughout this journey, thank you very much. To some of my colleagues, past and present, such as Micah Mangione and Adam Straub, and others who are not mentioned, who allowed me to interview them prior to writing this book, thank you for all the knowledge you shared with me. The knowledge they shared helped me to decide which content to include in this book. Thank you very much, everyone!

Contributors

About the author

Michael Dinder works as a senior backend developer at Cart.com, Inc. Michael has helped to develop projects for large enterprises such as PayPal and other companies such as Corcoran Pacific Properties, and countless more either directly or indirectly. He has been programming for more than 15 years with a number of different languages and frameworks, with a focus on Python/Django for the past 5+ years.

About the reviewer

Luca Bezerra has been working with software development for over 12 years across a very diverse set of technologies, be it professionally, as a hobby or during the course of his Master's degree. With experiences ranging from .NET to Unity3D to Python, Luca enjoys finding out about new technologies and the feeling of starting a project from scratch. He also loves to give talks, having presented on DjangoCon US, PyGotham, PyBay, Python Brasil and a few others over the years. Finally, Luca believes bios can sometimes make a paper plane sound like a fighter jet, so he suggests people should read them with a grain of salt.

Python and Django have always held a special place in my heart, so reviewing this book served a personal goal to keep in touch with these technologies. I also feel that the Python community has always been very welcoming and eager to help, so being able to contribute back to it in some way is very rewarding. I'd like to thank Packt for the opportunity and especially the people close to me for enduring my lack of availability during this project.

Table of Contents

Preface

Part 1 – Starting a Project

1
Undertaking a Colossal Project

Technical requirements	4	Visualization and interpretation	18
Building an enterprise	6	Hosting and deployment	27
Reasons to choose enterprise-level applications	6	Creating and configuring a Heroku plan	28
Types of enterprise systems	7	Configuring Heroku environments	30
Why Python/Django?	10	Custom repositories	35
Types of APIs	12	Advanced deployment	41
		Domain Name System	44
Designing and planning	14	Summary	46
Requirements gathering	14		

2
Project Configuration

Technical requirements	50	Creating a virtual environment	60
Choosing development tools	51	Configuring the requirements.txt file(s)	62
Text editors	52	Using the IDE	63
Integrated development environments	53	Using the command line	67
Starting a project	57	Project configuration	71
Using the IDE	57	Django settings.py file	71
Using the command line	59	Creating an environment file	73
		Creating a Procfile	76

Django static files	77	PostgreSQL	89
Django media files	78	**Preparing PostgreSQL for Heroku**	**90**
Creating a .gitignore file	79	Installing PostgreSQL	90
Creating a Django app	81	Using the PgAdmin tool	93
Using basic database settings	**84**	Environment connection settings	96
SQLite	85	Building initial table structures	97
MySQL	86	Remote data migrations	99
MariaDB	87	Heroku database push/pull operations	100
Oracle	87	**Summary**	**102**
SQL Server	88		

3
Models, Relations, and Inheritance

Technical requirements	**104**	Decorators	131
Preparing for this chapter	**104**	**Extending models**	**132**
Writing model classes	**105**	Extending basic model classes	133
Standard field types	106	Extending the Django User model	136
Third-party field types	112	**Using the Django shell**	**138**
Model field validators	115	Running basic Python scripts	139
Working with model field relationships	**117**	Generating a SECRET_KEY variable	140
Field arguments	117	Saving data	141
Field type – ForeignKey	119	Loading the chapter_3 data fixture	145
Field type – ManyToManyField	121	**Performing queries**	**146**
Mutable versus immutable objects	122	Model method – all()	146
Using the Meta subclass	**124**	Model method – get()	147
Meta options – verbose_name and verbose_name_plural	124	Model method – filter()	147
Meta option – ordering	124	Aggregates	148
Meta option – indexes	125	**Writing model managers**	**151**
Meta option – db_table	127	**Summary**	**153**
Customizing models	**129**		
Writing methods	129		

Part 2 – Django Components

4
URLs, Views, and Templates

Technical requirements	158	Processing trailing slashes	191
Preparing for this chapter	159	**Resolving absolute URLs**	**192**
Configuring URL patterns	**160**	Creating a context processor	192
Basic path functions	160	From the request object	195
Redirecting patterns	170	From within a model class	197
Using path converters	172	**Working with complex views**	**199**
Mapping URL patterns	**176**	Class-based views	199
Using simple views	176	Extending class-based views	203
Using kwargs in views	178	Asynchronous views	204
Working with conditional responses	182	**Working with templates**	**204**
Linking models to views and templates	184	Template tags	205
Resolving URLs	**186**	Template filters	209
Naming URL patterns	186	Custom tags and filters	210
Using the reverse() function	187	Error page templates	212
Using the {% url %} template tag	189	**Summary**	**213**

5
Django Forms

Technical requirements	216	**Cleaning forms**	**225**
Preparing for this chapter	217	Method – clean_{{ your_field_name }}()	226
Types of forms	**218**	Method – clean()	228
Form class – Form	218	**Creating custom form fields**	**229**
Form class – ModelForm	219	Field class – Field	230
Using form fields	**219**	Using a custom field	232
Common field arguments	220	**Working with form views**	**234**
Field widgets	222	View class – FormView	234
Field validators	223	HTTP request methods	237

Rendering forms in templates	240	View class – UpdateView	252
Render form – as_p	242	**Adding inline formsets**	**256**
Render form – as_table	243	Formset function – formset_factory	256
Render form – as_ul	243	Using inline formsets in the view class	258
Render form – using template_name	244	Rendering inline formsets in	
Render demo	246	the template	260
Linking a model to a form	**247**	Dynamic inline formsets	262
View class – CreateView	248	**Summary**	**265**

6
Exploring the Django Admin Site

Technical requirements	**268**	Method – get_form()	302
Preparing for this chapter	269	Method – save_model()	304
Using the Django admin site	**269**	Method – delete_model()	304
Activating the Django admin site	270	**Writing custom admin**	
Logging into the Django admin site	271	**form classes**	**305**
Writing admin classes	272	Initializing an admin form	305
Registering models	274	**Using the Django**	
Configuring admin class options	**276**	**authentication system**	**307**
Changelist view-related options	277	Adding a seller	307
Change/add view-related options	286	Granting permissions	309
Add view-related options	299	Permission groups	310
Adding admin class methods	**301**	**Summary**	**311**

7
Working with Messages, Email Notifications, and PDF Reports

Technical requirements	**314**	Enabling the Django	
Preparing for this chapter	**315**	messages framework	318
Creating a Mailtrap account	315	Creating a message	323
Using the Django		Displaying messages	329
messages framework	**318**	**Configuring email notifications**	**331**
		As plain text emails	331

As HTML emails	334	For HTML emails	342
As HTML emails with a plain text alternative	335	Providing template context	344
With file attachments	337	**Generating PDF reports**	**347**
That fail silently	339	As template-based PDFs	348
		Adding context	353
Writing custom email templates	**340**		
For plain text emails	340	**Summary**	**355**

Part 3 – Advanced Django Components

8
Working with the Django REST Framework

Technical requirements	361	Writing custom API endpoints	386
Preparing for this chapter	362	Creating the view	386
Installing the Django REST framework	362	Building the template	389
		Modifying the JavaScript	390
Serializing objects	**364**	Mapping the URL pattern	391
The serializer classes	366	Second demo	392
The viewset classes	369		
Using URL routers	371	**Authenticating with tokens**	**396**
		Project configuration	396
Using the Browsable API	**373**	Creating the view	398
Building SPA-like pages	**376**	Building the template	401
Creating the view	376	Modifying the JavaScript	401
Building the template	378	Mapping the URL pattern	402
Writing the JavaScript	379	Third demo	403
Mapping the URL pattern	383		
First demo	383	**Summary**	**406**

9
Django Testing

Technical requirements	408	Getting started with unit testing	413
Preparing for this chapter	409	Basic unit test script	413
Understanding automated testing in Django	411	Testing Django models	415
		Testing HTTP view requests	**419**

Testing method-based views 419
Testing class-based views 422

Testing authenticated view requests 425
Using the Client() class 425

Testing Django REST API endpoints 429

Creating an object test case 429
Updating an object test case 431

Using the DjDT 434
Installing the DjDT 434
How to use the DjDT 437

Summary 448

10
Database Management

Technical requirements 450
Preparing for this chapter 451
Exporting data into a data fixture 452
Using the dumpdata command 453

Importing data from a data fixture 463
Using the importdata command 463

Using the select_related() method 465
Creating the view 465
Building the template 466

Mapping the URL pattern 468
First demo 469

Using the prefetch_related() method 471
Vehicles view 471
Sellers view 475

Using the Prefetch() class 483
Modifying the view 483
Modifying the template 484
Fourth demo 485

Summary 486

Index

Other Books You May Enjoy

Preface

Django, a backend framework with frontend tools built in, is designed to help developers build apps quickly and easily. It is designed to take much of the hassle out of web development so that developers can focus more on the features they are building and not the problems they are facing. Loaded with dozens of tools and combined with countless third-party Python packages, Django provides many features and components that work right out of the box.

The Django framework has been built with scalability and versatility in mind. As demand and traffic grow, so can your project. This allows developers to build onto an existing system easily. Security is also something that Django takes seriously by building many different security measures directly into its framework. This has been done to help developers avoid common mistakes when it comes to security. It even has its own user authentication system to help manage your users.

In this book, we will learn about the fundamental components of the Django framework and how it relates to web development. From small websites to large, enterprise-level applications, this book will dive in and discuss the essential components for building a website or app of any size.

Who this book is for

This book focuses on full-stack enterprise-level application development. If you are looking to build a web app, API, or website or maintain an existing project, this book is for you. The book assumes intermediate-level knowledge of the Python programming language and it has been carefully fine-tuned for those who are new to the Django framework. Whether you are new to web development or have years of experience working with other technologies, this book is for you.

What this book covers

Chapter 1, Undertaking a Colossal Project, gives you an understanding of how to prepare for a large project.

Chapter 2, Project Configuration, covers virtual environments, hosting, and deployment.

Chapter 3, Models, Relations, and Inheritance, covers database table structures.

Chapter 4, URLs, Views, and Templates, covers rendering HTML with Django.

Chapter 5, Django Forms, covers rendering HTML forms with Django.

Chapter 6, Exploring the Django Admin Site, looks at Django's built-in administration site.

Chapter 7, Working with Messages, Email Notifications, and PDF Reports, covers using Django to send emails and create documents.

Chapter 8, Working with the Django REST Framework, covers building APIs with Django.

Chapter 9, Django Testing, covers writing test scripts with Django.

Chapter 10, Database Management, covers optimizing database queries.

To get the most out of this book

You will need the latest version of Python. All code examples in this book have been tested using Python version 3.9 on Windows 11 using Django 4.0. However, they should work with future version releases as well.

Software/hardware covered in the book	Operating system requirements
Python	Windows, macOS, or Linux
JavaScript/jQuery	
HTML5	
CSS3	
SQL	

Each chapter will provide additional installation and configuration instructions as the book progresses, such as in *Chapter 2, Project Configuration*, when we install an optional integrated development environment software suite, or in *Chapter 9, Django Testing*, when we install a productivity and testing tool.

If you are using the digital version of this book, we advise you to type the code yourself or access the code from the book's GitHub repository (a link is available in the next section). Doing so will help you avoid any potential errors related to the copying and pasting of code.

Download the example code files

You can download the example code files for this book from GitHub at `https://github.com/PacktPublishing/Becoming-an-Enterprise-Django-Developer`. If there's an update to the code, it will be updated in the GitHub repository.

We also have other code bundles from our rich catalog of books and videos available at `https://github.com/PacktPublishing/`. Check them out!

The code provided in this book's GitHub repository includes every example from every chapter. Much of the code is commented out except for the first exercise found in each chapter. If you are using the code provided with this book, it is intended to comment and uncomment code as you progress throughout the book. If you jump ahead, you may need to uncomment the necessary code that was skipped in order for the project to work. Each chapter has been organized into its own chapter app within the project as a whole. Project apps will be introduced and discussed in *Chapter 2, Project Configuration*.

Code in Action

The Code in Action videos for this book can be viewed at `https://bit.ly/3HQDP9Z`.

Download the color images

We also provide a PDF file that has color images of the screenshots and diagrams used in this book. You can download it here: `https://static.packt-cdn.com/downloads/9781801073639_ColorImages.pdf`.

Conventions used

There are a number of text conventions used throughout this book.

`Code in text`: Indicates code words in text, database table names, folder names, filenames, file extensions, pathnames, dummy URLs, user input, and Twitter handles. Here is an example: "Be sure to also include this app in your `INSTALLED_APPS` variable found in the `settings.py` file."

A block of code is set as follows:

```
# /becoming_a_django_entdev/chapter_5/forms.py
from django.forms
import Form

class ContactForm(Form):
    pass
```

When we wish to draw your attention to a particular part of a code block, the relevant lines or items are set in bold:

```
# /becoming_a_django_entdev/chapter_5/forms.py
from django.forms
import Form, ModelForm
class VehicleForm(ModelForm):
    pass
```

Any command-line input or output is written as follows:

```
RuntimeError: Conflicting 'vehicle' models in application 'chapter_3':
```

Bold: Indicates a new term, an important word, or words that you see onscreen. For instance, words in menus or dialog boxes appear in **bold**. Here is an example: " We can see the **chapter_3_engine** and **chapter_3_practice_engine** tables in the preceding screenshot."

> Tips or Important Notes
> Appear like this.

Get in touch

Feedback from our readers is always welcome.

General feedback: If you have questions about any aspect of this book, email us at customercare@packtpub.com and mention the book title in the subject of your message.

Author: If you would like to get in touch with the author directly, you may find and message him on LinkedIn here https://www.linkedin.com/in/mikedinder/.

Errata: Although we have taken every care to ensure the accuracy of our content, mistakes do happen. If you have found a mistake in this book, we would be grateful if you would report this to us. Please visit www.packtpub.com/support/errata and fill in the form.

Piracy: If you come across any illegal copies of our works in any form on the internet, we would be grateful if you would provide us with the location address or website name. Please contact us at copyright@packt.com with a link to the material.

If you are interested in becoming an author: If there is a topic that you have expertise in and you are interested in either writing or contributing to a book, please visit authors.packtpub.com.

Share Your Thoughts

Once you've read *Becoming an Enterprise Django Developer*, we'd love to hear your thoughts! Scan the QR code below to go straight to the Amazon review page for this book and share your feedback.

https://packt.link/r/1801073635

Your review is important to us and the tech community and will help us make sure we're delivering excellent quality content.

Part 1 – Starting a Project

In this part, you will begin by learning what enterprise development is, understanding the requirements gathering process, and creating a free hosting plan with Heroku. You will create a local, development, staging, and production environment for the code to live and run in. You will then create a Django project and push that code to those environments.

We will discuss configuring the project files and settings to work with a Heroku-hosted app. We will also create and configure a database to work with the project we are building. Then, we will build models that relate to the tables within that database. Heroku is not necessary for the rest of the book. The majority of this book can run locally on your machine.

This part comprises the following chapters:

- *Chapter 1, Undertaking a Colossal Project*
- *Chapter 2, Project Configuration*
- *Chapter 3, Models, Relations, and Inheritance*

1
Undertaking a Colossal Project

Considering the increasing complexity of applications and websites these days, this chapter will introduce you to what it takes to tackle a colossal project of your own. We will explore the concepts of enterprise-level development, and then take a peek at the many different paths we could take. We will discuss methods and tools that help us to draft plans for a project, essentially building the blueprints that we will need to get started. Every project also needs hardware for its software to live on, so we will be exploring what service options are available to provide the hardware we need. Of the options provided, we will settle upon one choice for a hosting provider and demonstrate working with that provider throughout this book.

The project itself can be used with any hosting provider or even run on a self-built server; however, keep in mind that certain settings may be configured specifically for the host that we will be using. By the end of this chapter, we will have created a hosting account with the provider chosen and picked the simplest, free plan for use with this book. We will also be creating and configuring multiple working environments on that hosting plan for the code to run in. We will also connect each environment in that hosting plan to a remote repository, keeping the code in a safe place.

In this chapter, we will be covering the following topics:

- Building an enterprise
- Designing and planning
- Hosting and deployment

Most people would suggest using a UNIX- or Linux-based operating system, such as Ubuntu or macOS, when working with **Django**. Django is built to be so versatile that the concepts and code examples that will be demonstrated throughout the course of this book can run on all three major platforms (Windows, Mac, and Linux) and beyond. Personally, I have been using Django on a Windows-based machine ever since I started to learn and work directly with this framework. I did so because I came from a Windows background; about half of my jobs provided the equipment or mandated the use of certain software on a Windows-based machine. Later on, more and more companies started to give developers the choice to work on whatever machine they were most comfortable with. I continued to choose Windows because I was already familiar with it.

Technical requirements

Whether you are using a Windows, Mac, or Ubuntu system, **Python** will need to be installed. Python version 3.9.0 is the latest version available at the time of writing this book. It is highly likely that this code will still work with future versions of Python but there is no guarantee that all of the code will continue to work and there could be some hiccups in future versions. You can find the Python installation files for all platforms on their website here: https://www.python.org/downloads/. For non-Windows users, the most straightforward way of installing Python is with **Homebrew**, which creates for you a symlink to the package that you installed.

For Windows users, an easy way to install Python is through the Microsoft Store. Search for `Python` and select **3.9** from the list. During installation, if you see the **Add Python to Environment Variables** option, select the checkbox to include it! This sets a path to your global library of Python packages/libraries on your development machine. These are different from the packages that are included in your project, which we will discuss in *Chapter 2, Project Configuration*.

A command-line tool is needed to execute commands that interact with and use Django. **PowerShell** is a common command-line shell that comes standard in Windows today. This command-line utility comes packed with some of the coolest features from an assortment of other existing shells, all merged into one. It is also available on the Mac and Linux operating systems. However, **iTerm2**, or the built-in **Terminal app**, is what most developers tend to gravitate toward using. Regardless, PowerShell has become a popular tool used by many developers for automating the management of various systems today.

You will also need to install the **PIP Python Package Manager**, if it was not already installed during your Python installation. Starting with Python 3.4 and after, pip is included by default with the Python binary installers; thus, it is likely it was already installed on your machine. If Python was installed using Homebrew, then pip is not included, and you will need to install it separately. Install pip via the official installation guide found here: `https://pip.pypa.io/en/stable/installation/`. Since this is a package manager, it is likely that any version of `pip` in the future will continue to work with the rest of the code and concepts discussed in this book. However, not every third-party package discussed in this book is guaranteed to be supported in the future by that provider. Regardless, the concepts of using a third-party package and how they would be configured and used in a project are taught in this book and can be used to find a package of your own.

> **Tip**
>
> Whatever operating system you are working on, if you get an error message while working with any command throughout this book, such as **pip/python is not recognized as an internal or external command**, it means that you need to configure environment variables on your system to point to the corresponding file directories. To manually configure your environment variables in any of the three major platforms, visit these links:
>
> - Windows: `https://phoenixnap.com/kb/windows-set-environment-variable`
>
> - macOS: `https://phoenixnap.com/kb/set-environment-variable-mac`
>
> - Ubuntu: `https://help.ubuntu.com/community/EnvironmentVariables`
>
> If a command is not recognized as an internal or external command, you may need to add the path to where that item was installed on your machine. In Windows, this is commonly the `Path` variable. For example, if `python` is not recognized as a command, add the path to where Python was installed on your machine to your global `Path` variable in Windows. The same applies to Linux or Mac but is most commonly a problem on Windows.

All of the code created and used in this book can be found here: `https://github.com/PacktPublishing/Becoming-an-Enterprise-Django-Developer`. This chapter doesn't actually dive into any code at this time. However, for those of you who are already familiar with Django or are new to Django who have already read through *Chapter 2, Project Configuration*, and come back to this chapter, an app called `chapter_1` is included with the code of this book to demonstrate a diagramming package introduced in the subsection titled *Entity relationship diagrams* of this chapter.

Check out the following video to see the *Code in Action*: `https://bit.ly/3OfagBj`.

Building an enterprise

Building an **Enterprise Application Software (EAS)** is not an easy task to tackle. The task requires many different technical specialists all working together with a high level of collaboration and preplanning to complete. Failure to perform adequate planning can result in the project taking far more time and money than anticipated. Important features that your business model relies on could be left out of the equation, resulting in disruptions in everyday flow when a new system turns on.

Enterprise-level software is geared toward satisfying the needs of a business as a whole. EAS takes all of the business logic of an organization and encompasses that into one system, thought of as a collection of many smaller subsystems. The software eliminates the need for paperwork, reduces the steps involved in completing a task, and provides self-automated or even artificially intelligent solutions to all kinds of problems in the world today. The website itself is only a small fraction of what the entire system actually comprises.

Reasons to choose enterprise-level applications

Enterprise-level software is usually thought of as a solution for organizations that already have a system in place and need to improve upon that. Whether or not that system is something digital or a manual process, as in paper in filing cabinets, companies are always searching for ways to simplify everyday tasks. Thus, enterprise-level software can consist of one or a collection of many different consumer-level applications. If you need more than just a website and need a system that also takes on your business management tasks, you will likely need to scale up to the enterprise level. However, Django can still be used for the simplest of websites as well as large-scale projects beyond your wildest dreams. Applications can also be broken down into individual Django projects.

Let's say you have an organization with many departments and many users, all consisting of different permission roles. You need a way to connect them all so that they may generate and share reports, send notifications, store and manage customer/user data, create invoices, and work with other systems. Maybe you found that your organization needs to connect employees working remotely from home to be more productive and efficient at their job. The idea is that each user type will interact with the system in a completely different way and even have different permission levels granting them access to different parts of your system.

Generally speaking, when someone thinks enterprise level, they also think of something that is unique and custom crafted. Such software is termed **proprietary** or **closed-source software** and is not intended to be redistributed to the public by any means. However, not all EAS has to be proprietary; the distribution license can be set to anything you desire it to be. For example, the main system may be branded for one parent company and yet parts of the system may be branded for its subsidiaries, or copies can be distributed and rebranded per your license agreement. It may also be a good idea to speak with a technical lawyer to help write your software license agreement should your project(s) be extremely complex. Inviting the help of a technical lawyer at the beginning is a good way to prevent lawsuits later on.

Next, we will discuss some of the major types of enterprise systems.

Types of enterprise systems

There are many different kinds of enterprise-level systems but we can consolidate them into six major categories, as follows:

- **Customer Relationship Management (CRM)**
- **Enterprise Content Management (ECM)**
- **Enterprise Asset Management (EAM)**
- **Enterprise Resource Planning (ERP)**
- **Supply Chain Management (SCM)**
- **Enterprise Information System (EIS)**

In this book, we will not actually be building any of these systems in their entirety. Instead, we will touch on the key Django programming concepts that, when combined, will get you part of the way to the end zone. Not every concept can fit into this book but Django is fully capable of handling all of the features that each of these types of systems includes. It is really up to your team to take on each of the rest of the concepts discussed in this book and use them as another tool in your toolbox when building your system. Let's discuss briefly what each of these six major types of enterprise-level systems is and what they are primarily used for.

Customer Relationship Management

CRM systems can typically be thought of as lead management, marketing communications, sales and inventory control, retail management, and so much more. The systems can be thought of as everything but the actual selling of products and services. They can even go further to include customer support and data analytics. These systems are designed to develop better relationships with your business partners, customers and potential customers, and anyone else in the equation.

Enterprise Content Management

An ECM system can best be described as a system for people working in fields that deal with creative and other intellectual property in some kind of way. Newspapers, magazines, and other news companies today have a great deal of content that they make available to the internet on a daily basis. A **Content Management System (CMS)** provides a less technical and rapid way to build new pages and enter that content onto the web. Enterprise level just means you are adding more and more tools to your toolbox for your organization to use.

Enterprise Asset Management

In an EAM system, products and inventory of all kinds can be entered into a system in the same way as a CMS. This is often known as an e-commerce or shopping cart website. It's where you make your physical goods and assets available online. These systems allow the tracking of inventory, project management, and document control, such as contracts and other legal documents. These systems may even consist of physical assets, such as real estate, automobiles, and music records.

Enterprise Resource Planning

An ERP system is typically thought of as a way to manage people, the employees of the company, or what is commonly known as the **Human Resources (HR)** department. The system can handle on-boarding and off-boarding procedures and store all personnel records. It could serve as a tool for project management, risk assessment, and record keeping. It can even serve as a knowledge base such as in the form of the **Frequently Asked Questions (FAQs)** area. A knowledge base is often used to point people to and have them find common questions and answers in order to reduce the workload on your staff. These can also be used for training purposes, such as generating quizzes or asking trivia questions and playing tutorials.

Supply Chain Management

SCM systems are similar to CRM and EAM systems. These are systems that manage inventory in every aspect of its development in the supply chain. These systems manage inventory on a national or even a global scale. They communicate with suppliers, connect to buyers, track packages, predict future supply orders, and may even automatically place those orders. One way to look at the difference between a CRM and SCM system is that a CRM is mostly used for sales and marketing while an SCM is mostly used for production and distribution. Both deal with products but in different ways and a large company or a conglomerate would need both.

Enterprise Information System

An EIS is a system that generally combines a CRM and SCM system to handle a wider range of business needs. An EIS may even integrate some or all of an ERP system and act as one giant central nervous system. Depending on the needs, this may consist of numerous databases and even numerous development projects all working together, comprising the brains of everything. These systems are known for storing and processing large volumes of data and connecting many different systems all together into one.

We will now take a look at why people gravitate toward using Python and Django when they are building any of these enterprise-level systems. We'll see why it suits a variety of projects and what features it is best known for.

Why Python/Django?

Python was created in 1991 by Guido van Rossum. He came up with the name Python after reading the script for *Monty Python's Flying Circus*. The language was created primarily for the purpose of code readability and reliability. Python has been growing in popularity as the preferred backend framework for several years now. Python plays an important role in some very popular websites today, such as Google, NASA, Netflix, Spotify, Uber, and Dropbox, just to name a few. The Python language has become desirable among many developers for its ease of use, quickness to learn, and overall adaptability of the code written.

Django came into existence in late 2003 by the newspaper publisher Lawrence Journal-World in Lawrence, Kansas. Similar to Python, it had one goal in mind: to create complex database-driven websites in a simple and easy-to-read way. Along with readability, it was designed with rapid development and a **Don't Repeat Yourself** (**DRY**) code structure in mind. Readability is why Python was chosen as Django's foundation for the framework. Django is best referred to as a backend framework because of how it works to build and manage databases. It comes with many concepts built in surrounding the architecture of websites, which makes it appealing to most web developers.

Many people use Django today for their backend; but the framework can also serve as your frontend. If you have ever used Shopify's Liquid template language, otherwise known as Liquid syntax, or even ASP.NET's Razor syntax and how that is used in conjunction with C# .NET or Visual Basic .NET, you will notice commonalities with the **Django template language**, which is Django's method of using Python to build HTML files. Django uses context when the page is rendered to serve up user-generated content or database-driven data onto that page. The template language syntax is fairly easy to read and quick to learn. Some examples of sites that use Django are Bitbucket, Instagram, National Geographic, Spotify, The Washington Post, and YouTube.

Django's features include the following:

- Caching framework
- Data serialization
- Extensibility
- Form handling and validation
- Scalability
- Security
- Template language
- Testing framework

Of these features, extensibility means that Django is built to allow easy integration of other third-party services. Your developers can spend more time focusing on the specific needs of the project versus trying to figure out how to connect your project to a third-party servicer's system. Django makes it easy to connect to virtually anything that exists today. If a functionality doesn't already come built in, there is usually a pip package for it.

Django does not need to be used to build only websites. It can be used to build an API that stands as the central hub for anything, communicating with a **REpresentational State Transfer** (**REST**) framework, which is a common architecture for standardizing communication between computer systems on the internet. From here, you can use any variety of common existing tools to build an iOS app for iPhones or even Android apps. Depending on your particular business requirements, deciding to tap into smartphones can be beneficial in many ways. With somewhere around 85% of Americans owning a smartphone today, some companies might want to build an app where a user can install that app on their personal phone (`https://www.pewresearch.org/internet/fact-sheet/mobile/`), versus the company having to purchase additional hardware to distribute devices to all of their employees. APIs can be used for many other things as well, from microservices to large-scale external web systems and databases.

Personally, when it comes to using the Django template language and a JavaScript-based framework such as React or Angular together, I would recommend against doing that as it can get far too complex to work with. If you are using React, Angular, Vue.js, or Handlebars.js, to name a few, to work as your frontend, then Django would just serve as your backend where context is served up through your API. You can still keep your frontend and backend files in the same Django project folder.

I have a few recommendations to help you choose. If you want to build an Android or iOS app or a **Single-Page App** (**SPA**) website, use Django as an API on the backend. Then, for the frontend, you can use a common JavaScript-based framework to build mobile apps. For multipage websites, just use the Django template language along with your context to work as your frontend. There are ways to build an SPA website without the use of React or Angular and just rely on Django alone, but even then, you will still need something such as jQuery, AJAX, or vanilla JavaScript to help you process triggers and events that send requests to your API. I often resort to preloading my base `.html` file with jQuery, which I will discuss how to do in *Chapter 4, URLs, Views, and Templates*. Many people prefer to use vanilla JavaScript so that they can write simple tasks without loading the entire jQuery library. When it comes to adding bells and whistles on the frontend of things, in all of the projects that I have worked on, I find that I can pretty much do everything that I need to do with just the Django template language and jQuery. I may be biased on this one but it is really simple to use. However, there are a lot of benefits of using **ECMAScript**, which is actually a set of international standards for building and compiling JavaScript, such as ES8, ES9, or ES10. Using ECMAScript is something I should be focusing on more in my projects.

> **Tip**
>
> When working with Django and Python, ask your developers to adopt the **Python Enhancement Proposal 8** (**PEP-8**) style guide for Python code. This is an officially adopted formatting guide to keep code consistent among developers. This can be strict or relaxed. Personally, I like to choose a more relaxed version where I can make things a bit more broken down and readable. If you are building something proprietary, for internal use, it is not necessary to follow this exactly and you may prefer to choose a style that your team will be happy with. If you are building a package that will be shared publicly with anyone, I would recommend you follow the PEP-8 format exactly. It may actually be a requirement for submitting a package to the **Python Package Index** (**PyPI**) library. You can find out more about the official style guide here: `https://www.python.org/dev/peps/pep-0008/`.
>
> PyPI is the official repository for third-party Python package libraries both public and private. It's a wonderful resource when looking for new packages to play around with and it provides information on how to work with the code as well: `https://pypi.org/`.
>
> A package called Black can be used as a code linter to help developers make sure they are following PEP-8 style formatting. You can learn about Black here: `https://pypi.org/project/black/`.

Next, let's explore what the different types of **Application Programming Interface** (**API**) are and why we might need to know about these when planning for a project.

Types of APIs

An API is a means for two systems to communicate with each other through what are known as endpoints or a URL.

We can categorize APIs into three main categories:

Open   **Private**
       Partner

Figure 1.1 – Types of APIs

In the following sections, we will discuss what each of these API types is and what they are used for. Depending on the requirements of the project, we may need to choose one or the other as a type of system that we want to build.

Open APIs

Open APIs are open to the public and are sometimes referred to as an external API. This typically means there are no restrictions and anyone can be granted access. Sometimes, a simple registration or API key may be required before developers can gain access but they usually have the freedom to do with it as they wish. These APIs can be open bidirectionally as well, meaning the system is open for all GET, POST, PUT, PATCH, and DELETE requests coming to and from your system.

Partner APIs

Partner APIs are commonly found in business-to-business relationships. The general public cannot gain access and permission is only granted to strategic partners who need to use your API in order to do business with you. Limitations can be defined depending on your agreements with each party. These are fairly common in the world today when business mergers occur and your team is tasked with making two external systems communicate with each other. Sometimes, you have to build a central database in between the two existing systems for various reasons, such as your business model is based on granting access to your API in order for companies to sell their goods on your platform. A common example of this is the Amazon **Selling Partner API** (**SP-API**), which is used for selling goods on the Amazon Marketplace.

Private APIs

Private APIs are the most secure; these APIs are locked down because they are intended to be used internally by that company or organization only. Large financial institutions or corporate retail entities may use these to manage any aspect of their internal functions. The public and any other external sources may not be granted access unless a specific need for it is warranted. Common examples are government organizations using APIs to connect to systems that keep legal records and documents. Another example could be a university granting an educational department access to student and class records.

By now, we have brushed up on what enterprise-level software is, in terms of what types of enterprise-level systems exist today and how we can classify them. We also discussed how Python and Django play a role in enterprise-level software. Now that we have learned about these various concepts, let's begin designing and planning for a project of our own.

Designing and planning

Every project, however big or small, needs a clear plan for what it is and how it will be built. The larger the project, the more work should be put into the beginning phase of preparing for development. It is no surprise that enterprise-level development should also require a great deal of preliminary work before actual development begins. Whether you are working for a company or are a company providing a solution to a client, you should have a clear plan of what needs to be done. There is a lot of flexibility here based on factors such as cost, lack of developers, and deadlines. Prepare as much as possible and try to stick to the timelines that are set to keep you on track to completion. Remember that too little planning could come back to haunt you later.

Developers should be given as much information as possible to help them understand what they are building. If your developers are not provided with enough documentation, blueprints, and other materials, then they will be left to make assumptions on their own, assumptions that later on are found in the testing and **Quality Assurance (QA)** phases of development as bugs in your application. When this happens, you may discover that a particular feature needs to be rebuilt, requiring major foundational changes that will take a great deal of time to refactor. If we think about something other than programming for a moment, such as building a house, we all know a foundation needs to be built before a team can frame the house. In turn, that foundation needs to be completed before a team can build the roof, wire up the electrics, install plumbing, and so on. You can't start building a roof without a frame, and you can't build a frame without a foundation to put it on.

Let's discuss how to gather requirements for your project.

Requirements gathering

Gathering requirements is important to help document the build process and to allow both parties, the developer and the owner of the software, to reference it at any time during development. This ability is essential in order to ensure things stay on track until completion and are also completed on time. There should be an initial brainstorming phase to get a feel for the scope of the project. One good trick is to have all the stakeholders get together and debate the needs of the system, while you record any key points raised during the debate and include them in your requirements findings. You should always start by asking questions, and you should ask alternate questions for different sets of people. After you have spoken to stakeholders, move on to directors, project managers, developers, and employees, known as end users. Interview as many different types of users as possible. For extremely large entities, you could create a questionnaire, distribute that questionnaire to a number of users, and then come to a conclusion based on the results.

If there is a legacy system currently in place, even if it's a manual versus digital process of some kind, you should try and get a feel for how it works and identify any pain points within that process. My favorite tactic is **User Observation**, where I watch a user as they go through the flow of an everyday task and then try to identify things that may slow them down. The next thing I would do is try **Role Playing**, which is a method where you jump in and use the system as a user would perform a task. You could also ask two different kinds of users to swap positions and ask them what was easy or hard about doing the other person's task or what they think could improve the workflow. There must be bottlenecks of some kind or else there wouldn't be a need to build something better. These are things that bog down your everyday tasks and end up costing the company a lot of money in terms of time and resources. You need to keep an eye open and identify the pain points that your client could not identify themselves or they will have a difficult time communicating with you. Your client won't always know the best solution to a problem, and they may not even know a particular problem is even a problem until you reveal a way to improve that process for them.

Research and discovery

Find out whether this will be an internal, partner, or public project. If it is a partner project, you may have certain limitations based on the partner's specific needs. This is when we get into the difference between **business requirements** and **functional requirements**. Functional requirements are things such as determining what hosting plan and server to live on, a backend framework, a frontend framework, and a set of pages. Business requirements, on the other hand, encompass the vision, goals, and objectives of the business as a whole. They are specific to the needs of the organization or the partners they are working with. The structure of a set of web pages or API endpoints may be defined by the business model of that company versus some other logical reason that may otherwise be chosen. Do your stakeholders have any goals, suggestions, or requests that you need to consider? Here are 15 common questions that can help you formulate your set of questions. You shouldn't limit yourself to just these questions alone; use them for brainstorming:

- Do you have business-specific requirements?
- Why do you need a new system?
- What does your current system prevent you from doing; are there any bottlenecks?
- What new features would you like to add; do you need any improvements?
- What old features would you like to keep or remove?
- Who will you interact with in the system; what types of users and roles?
- Will you need reporting, email messaging, or any other kind of notification system?

- Will the system connect with any third-party or partner systems in any way?
- What kind of traffic or load on the server are we predicting?
- When does this new system need to be operational?
- What kind of budget have you allocated toward completing this project?
- Will data need to be migrated from the old system to the new system?
- How will development be divided up among the development team members?
- What skills does the development team have; what are the team's strengths and weaknesses?
- How should the **User Interface** (**UI**) flow work; should it be multipage or single page?

Decision making

From the common questions listed previously, you can formulate dozens, if not hundreds, of other questions to fit your unique set of needs. Then, these questions can be grouped into several categories of development, each category with a unique set of requirements and guidelines. You will want to focus heavily on usability, data migration, performance, security, scalability, and reliability. It's good to know this information beforehand so that you can choose the best direction that your development should move forward with.

These will be decisions such as what frontend framework you will choose, who you will go to for hosting, whether you will be building your own servers or renting space at a data center in the cloud, and how your server will be configured. There are countless possibilities to consider. When it comes to the UI, there is a number of questions that need to be asked regarding form field layout, form field validation (server side and client side or both), placeholders, labeling placement, and the flow from start to finish. Flow here refers to whether the user should complete part or all of a form before proceeding and/or whether those parts should be included in a separate form.

Keep in mind that when it comes to form field validation, Django will only validate your data on the server side. Your project does not need both server- and client-side form field validation. However, a healthy website will implement both. So, when a postback error occurs, anomalies will emerge, such as not displaying your form or the field errors that are present, if your form is not visible when the page first loads, for example, when a user needs to scroll down really far on the page or perform several actions before the form becomes visible to the user. Client-side form field validation solves this problem by checking for data to be valid before it is sent to the server, known as **data integrity**. This validation also reduces work for the server to process and provides for event handling, letting you write functions to help you format HTML and CSS on your page. When it comes to decision making, you can choose whether or not field validation will take place on the client side or the server side, or both. If client-side validation will take place, then you can choose what tools will be used, which are usually JavaScript based.

For example, take input attributes such as `required`, `minlength`, and `maxlength`, which can exist in your HTML. These are usually generated by Django when rendering form fields that have specific field arguments set, such as the following example. We will discuss rendering forms in detail in *Chapter 5, Django Forms*:

```
# Demo Code
<input type="text" name="field" id="field-id" class="form-input" maxlength="150" minlength="5" required="">
```

Most browsers will natively restrict a user from submitting a form if these attributes are present and the data does not satisfy them. All browsers will handle and style these error states differently from one another as well, like Mac versus Windows or Chrome versus Safari. The reason for this is that they are developed by separate entities competing against each other in the market and as a result have different branding. This difference hinders the ability of Django to serve up a postback displaying the error message that was defined in your code for that field. If for some reason the user is able to submit a form with invalid data, the postback may not display the form if, as I mentioned previously, the form is hidden from sight on page load. This is why your project may require both client- and server-side form validation.

Handling error state messages between your server-side code where you define your form fields and your client-side implementation can be tricky as well, meaning you have to store the same error message in two different locations within your source code: one for server-side validation and one for client-side validation. Over time, and with many different developers, this will get very messy, especially when someone remembers to change one but not the other when edits, additions, or deletions are made to these messages. If you have a strict need to make sure they are both worded exactly the same, it might be necessary to create a data dictionary that your source files could access, allowing you to put all your error messages in one spot. How you do that will take some thinking. This file will also need to be accessible via both Python and JavaScript.

Visualization and interpretation

When it comes to the actual design of how the UI will look, there is a number of factors involved. Large corporations may have specific branding guidelines that they mandate for marketing and other legal reasons that can restrict the overall design of your frontend. Sometimes, these corporations will have an in-house creative and marketing department or they may outsource to a third-party creative company to mock up a set of Illustrator or Photoshop documents to assist your frontend developers in doing their jobs. For smaller projects, you are free to design something yourself, but that often takes up time and developers often experience a type of writer's block when tasked with actually designing something versus building something.

One big misconception about frontend developers is that everyone automatically assumes they are designers, which is not always the case. Similar to how a construction worker reads blueprints to build a house, someone else usually drafts the blueprints for them. For this reason, you can use open source templates and boilerplates in the form of HTML, CSS/SCSS, or even JavaScript from online suppliers such as Envato Market, formerly known as ThemeForest (`https://themeforest.net/`), or Nicepage (`https://nicepage.com/html-templates`). I have resorted to using design templates from sources such as these in my own Django projects before. Each of these templates and template providers is different. Some are free, while others can be used for a price, and usage licenses vary. Independent research will have to be done on your part before deciding whether any of these sources can work for you. These design templates may also require a bit of digging around in order to make sure they fit in your project nicely, but they can still save a lot of time and provide a stylish-looking site that may be far better than what someone who lacks a creative eye for designing something from nothing could create for you.

Many of these HTML, CSS, and JavaScript templates may resort to the use of the **Node Package Manager** (**NPM**) for you to build source files into production-ready files. Similar to PyPI, NPM is used to store and distribute JavaScript libraries that are used in development. They rely on Node.js to run them. There are even pip packages that you can use within your Django project to help you build source files using an NPM package. I will discuss managing pip packages and dependencies further in *Chapter 2*, *Project Configuration*. There is a number of Python packages that can help you transpile SCSS, auto-prefix, bundle, and minify files. I have played around with a lot of different Python packages and out of them, I have found only a select few resorting to the use of NPM to do the heavy lifting at the end of the day. This means, as a requirement for your project, your developers may need to have NPM installed on their machine or even on their server depending on how you want to use Node.js. For the examples in this book, I will gravitate toward Python packages as much as possible and you are free to integrate these into your project as you see fit. I'll try to avoid going into code examples pertaining to NPM packages, but I encourage you to use the packages in your development environments.

> **Tip**
> The latest and most stable version of Node.js and NPM can be found here: `https://nodejs.org/en/download/`. For Windows users, there is an easy-to-use installer file that will install both Node.js and NPM for you.
>
> You can find the Gulp installation guide here: `https://gulpjs.com/docs/en/getting-started/quick-start/`. Gulp requires that the Gulp **Command-Line Utility** (**CLI**) is installed first, then install Gulp itself. Gulp is considered a task runner and helps to automate a vast majority of development tasks, such as SCSS transpiling, CSS linting, vendor prefixing, minification, and bundling; ECMAScript compiling; and other code linting.

Designing doesn't mean how the project should look; the process should also focus on how it will work or rather the nuts and bolts of the engine. When it comes to designing a project, use as many diagrams as possible to visualize each process. Visualization can be broken down into two main categories: **Behavioral Diagraming** and **Structural Diagraming**. Once you have created a set of diagrams, those can be used for collaboration with your stakeholders to ensure that you have everything needed. Your developers will also use these as blueprints for what they will be building.

There are many different diagram types in the **Unified Modeling Language** (**UML**), as listed here:

- Activity diagram
- Class diagram

- Communication diagram
- Component diagram
- Composite diagram
- Deployment diagram
- Entity relationship diagram
- Flowchart
- Interaction diagram
- Object diagram
- Package diagram
- Profile diagram
- Sequence diagram
- State diagram
- Timing diagram
- Use case diagram

Discussing each of these diagrams in depth can be rather lengthy. In the following subsections, we will discuss only six of the most commonly used diagrams today and how they can help you build a project of any size and type.

Class diagrams

A class diagram is used to illustrate the different classes or components of a system and how they relate to each other. A class is best known as a group of objects with shared or similar roles within your system. Similar to an **Entity Relationship Diagram** (**ERD**), class diagrams depict the objects that would be tables in a database, the interactions that could take place, and any other main elements of your system. This diagram is usually structured in a way where the top compartment is the class name, the middle compartment contains all the attributes, also known as the fields, and the bottom compartment shows any functions or actions that could take place.

The following figure shows the relationship between a user, team, and award. The class diagram shows how a team can have a collection of users and a team may also have a collection of awards issued to them. In this example, awards are given to teams and not individual users themselves. A `Team` model object can have a function called `getAwards()`, where it will get a collection of all the awards that the team has earned:

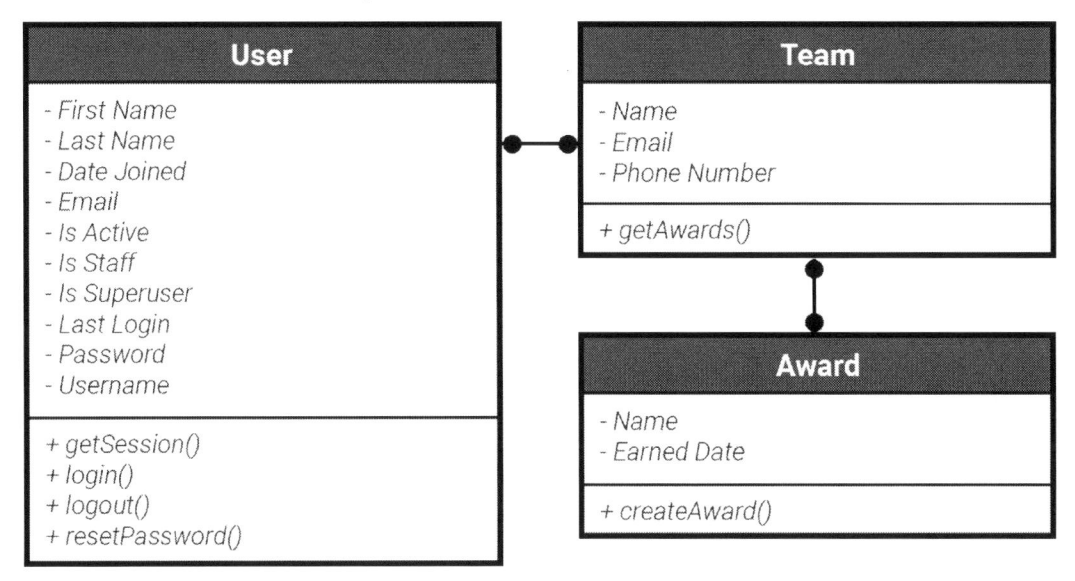

User
- First Name - Last Name - Date Joined - Email - Is Active - Is Staff - Is Superuser - Last Login - Password - Username
+ getSession() + login() + logout() + resetPassword()

Team
- Name - Email - Phone Number
+ getAwards()

Award
- Name - Earned Date
+ createAward()

Figure 1.2 – Class diagram

Deployment diagrams

A deployment diagram is used for high-level planning. This is how developers will collaborate and code will be updated between different environments. Network engineers will use the diagram to map out physical nodes that will be used within their configuration. Developers will use it to have a better understanding of how code will update between different environments and where they may need to push or pull that code to and from when updates need to be made. The primary components of a deployment diagram include artifacts, devices, and nodes:

- An artifact is a digital asset, such as a file or an executable script of some kind.
- A device is a node that represents a computational resource, such as the application server or the domain server.
- A node is a physical entity that executes a component, subsystem, or process. Nodes can comprise a physical hardware component or a virtual, cloud-based component.

Entity relationship diagrams

An ERD visualizes the relationships between objects within your system. It's best used for mapping how different tables are linked within a database and is sometimes called an entity relationship model after modeling relationships in a database. These are used by your backend to help create the structure of the database and what fields should be included. On the other hand, these can be created by accessing existing databases to help map the current structure of a system and help you to see how best to rebuild it. It's like accessing blueprints of an existing building. Auto-generating these can mean they are so accurate that they even tell you about renovations done to that building after those initial blueprints were first drafted.

There are many ways to automatically generate an ERD. I'll share with you two of my favorite ways to go about doing that, assuming you already have a Django project up and running when reading and following along with this chapter. If not, I explain how to start a Django project from scratch as well as how to install the pgAdmin tool in the next chapter, *Chapter 2, Project Configuration*. The first way is with pgAdmin, which is a popular database tool used by Django developers today for working with PostgreSQL databases. This is very easy if you are using the most recent version of pgAdmin; older versions do not have this feature. The current version of pgAdmin, as of the time of writing this book, is v5.6. Just right-click on the database for which you want to generate a diagram and click **Generate ERD**.

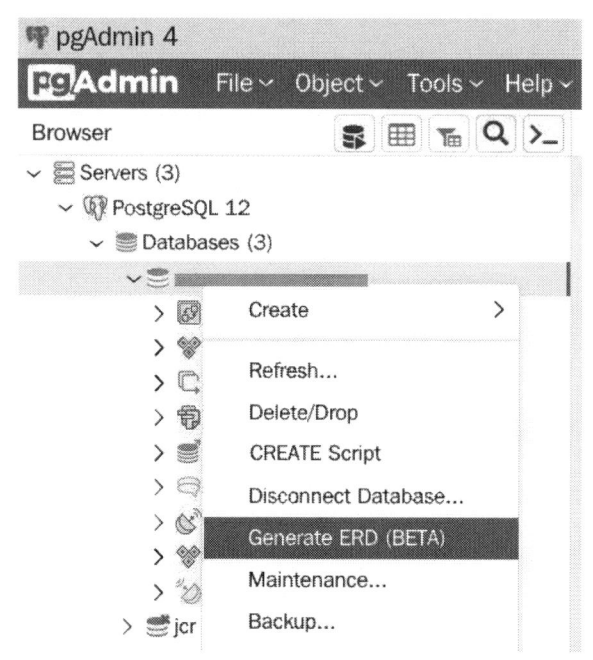

Figure 1.3 – Generate ERD with pgAdmin

The second way is using a popular command-line tool called **Graph Models**. You can find this in a pip package called `django-extensions`. This is the example where I have provided a Django app called `chapter_1` with the code provided with this book for people who are already familiar with Django. You can run these examples in your existing project. For people new to Django, it is recommended to skip to the next subsection of this chapter, titled *Flowcharts*, and then come back and practice using this package after you have worked through the examples provided in *Chapter 2, Project Configuration*, to configure your project for the very first time.

To install the `django-extensions` package on an existing Django project, follow these steps:

1. Run the following command:

   ```
   PS C:\Your_Project_Folder> pip install django-extensions
   ```

2. In your `settings.py` file, add this app to your `INSTALLED_APPS` variable:

   ```python
   # /becoming_a_django_entdev/settings.py
   INSTALLED_APPS = (
       ...
       'django_extensions',
       ...
   )
   ```

3. You will also need to install a diagram generator that will draw the diagram for you. This is done using the `pydotplus` pip package:

   ```
   PS C:\Your_Project_Folder> pip install pydotplus
   ```

4. Now, you can run the following command to generate all of the tables:

   ```
   PS C:\Your_Project_Folder> python manage.py graph_models -a -o diagrams/chapter_1/all_models.png
   ```

   Specific models can be targeted, or a set of models can be targeted, separated by a comma with no spaces. In the following example, we are targeting the `User`, `Team`, and `Award` models:

   ```
   PS C:\Your_Project_Folder> python manage.py graph_models -a -I User,Team,Award -o diagrams/chapter_1/team_models.png
   ```

24   Undertaking a Colossal Project

The following diagram was auto-generated by running the last command, generating the `User`, `Team`, and `Award` models and their relationships with one another:

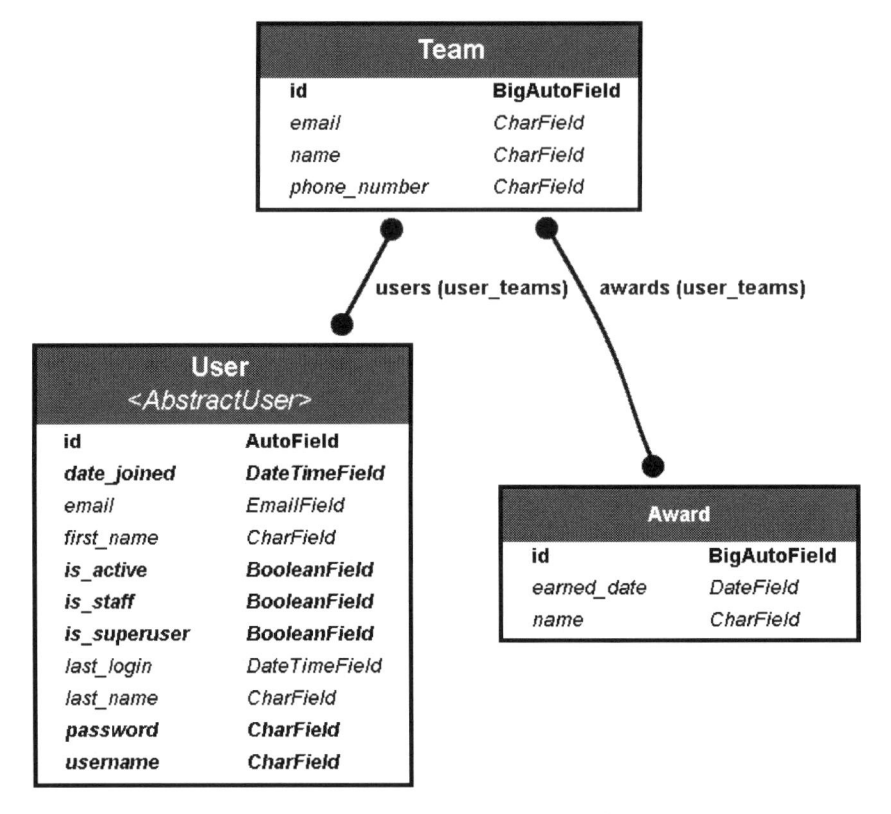

Figure 1.4 – ERD from Graph Models

For a complete breakdown of how to use the Graph Models plugin, go to https://django-extensions.readthedocs.io/en/latest/graph_models.html.

> **Note**
>
> For Windows users, you will also need to install the GraphViz application on your computer for the `graph_models` command to work. Also, select **Add Graphviz to the system PATH** for all or current users when performing the install: https://graphviz.org/download/.
>
> There is also an installer for Linux, Mac, and Solaris operating systems. GraphViz may also be required to generate these diagrams on those operating systems. If you are experiencing errors running the preceding commands on Linux, Mac, or Solaris, try installing GraphViz on your system.

Next, let's discuss flowcharts and what they are used for.

Flowcharts

Flowcharts represent the flow of data within the system. They provide a step-by-step approach to solving a particular problem or task. These diagrams are used by developers to gain an understanding of what rules apply when writing code. Rules can include logic such as data validation scenarios before proceeding to the next step. Flowcharts can be simple to fairly complex, and often provide decisions the user can make along the way. This diagram type depicts a user's possible interactions within a particular flow or set of flows.

If you have a single page that has a form broken down into many parts that the user must complete before navigating to a new page, a flowchart can be a handy tool for your frontend developer or even your designer to understand how a user will proceed from one step to another within the form and one page to another within the larger flow of the site. The diagrams can be broken down into smaller, more granular or defined flows as needed.

The following diagram is a small example to show the flow of a user as they log into a system. Does a page require a user to be logged in? If so, a decision must be made: is the user logged in? If no, prompt the login screen; if yes, a new decision must be made: does the user have permission to view the page?

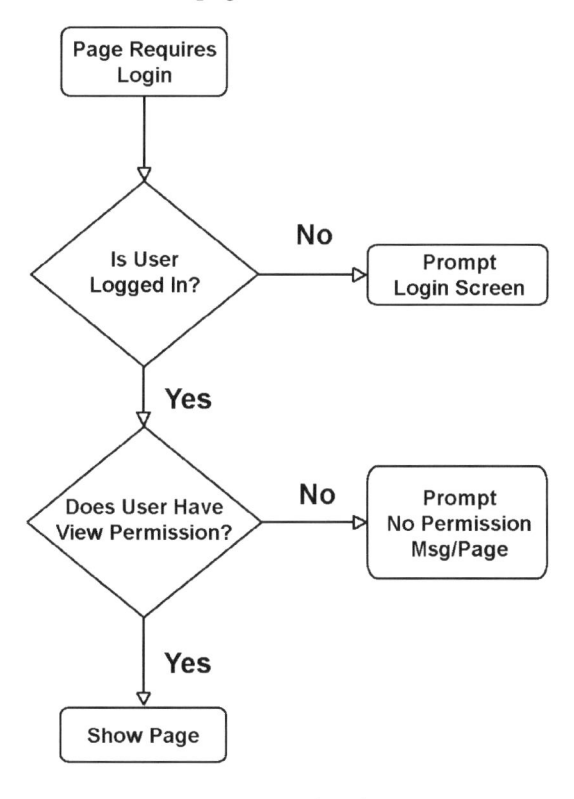

Figure 1.5 – Flowchart

State diagrams

A state diagram shows the behavior of objects within a system. The diagram shows possible conditions or states that something can be in at any given time, such as depicting whether a user is either logged in or logged out; an order is either received, processing, or out for delivery, or an order is fulfilled or returned. These are great for showing a particular shift in behavior versus decisions that can be made. They may even depict certain triggers that cause a state to change as an operation moves through its life cycle toward completion.

Use case diagrams

A use case diagram represents the behavior of a user and the system. These are fairly similar to a flowchart but often focus on the bigger picture. These are used by teams such as the creative department, stakeholders, project managers, and directors, to help understand the concept of what this particular flow or use case will do.

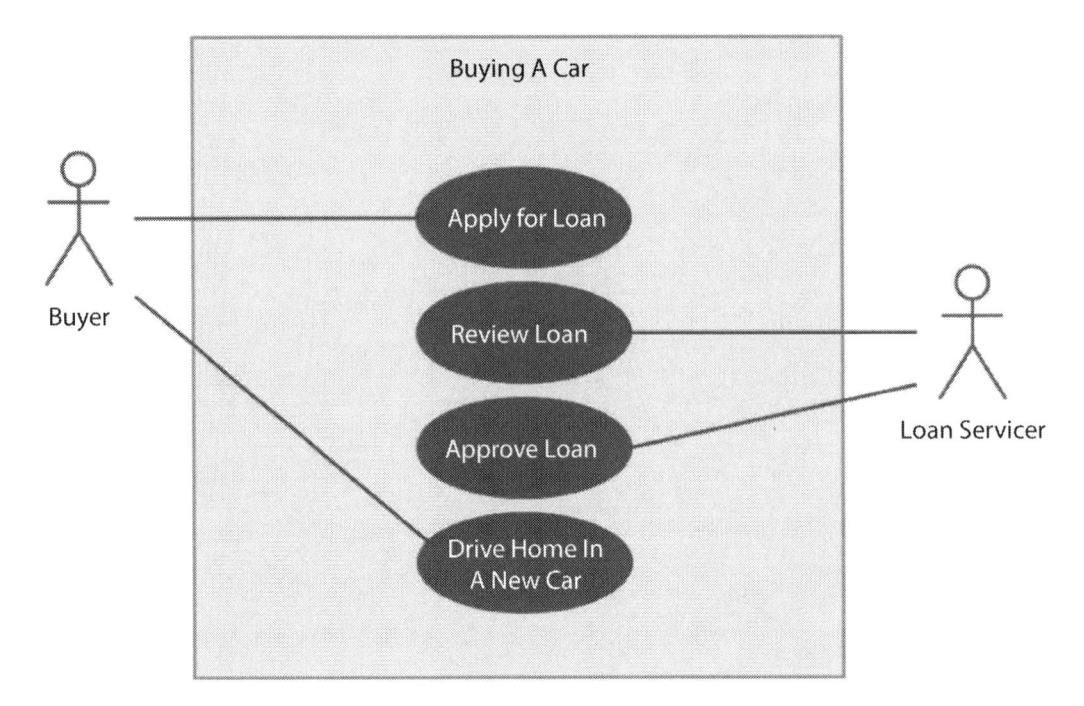

Figure 1.6 – Use case diagram

At this point, we have gone over common ways people plan for and design web applications today. Use these concepts to plan for your project the best that you can. In the next section, we'll discuss hosting your application as well as different deployment methodologies.

Hosting and deployment

All websites and apps need a physical location for all of their files to live in; this is also known as web hosting. Web hosting is a service that provides the physical hardware for files to live in and where information is processed. A hosting plan provides a solution consisting of an operating system, such as Linux, and includes the actual hardware of the networking system. Servers will come with a web server of some kind installed for you, such as NGINX or the Apache web server.

A web server, otherwise known as a **Hypertext Transfer Protocol** (**HTTP**) server, is software that will send and receive HTTP requests, which are basically messages sent over the internet. Web servers can be thought of as software that runs on the operating system using HTTP, which is a standard network protocol used to distribute your website or application over the internet. With the HTTP that all browsers use today, a user can access your site when they navigate to your domain through the browser's address bar. Web servers help you with load balancing and caching and serve as your reverse proxy server, which makes your files available to the rest of the world via the internet. Hosting services will often provide you with options to scale up when your site experiences an increase in user traffic and data access, where you need more processing power or storage space.

Huge projects tend to gravitate toward services such as **Amazon Web Services** (**AWS**) or Microsoft Azure and even Heroku. These are cloud-based hosting services, meaning your sites' files will live on physical hardware that is likely shared with other clients. However, options to have a dedicated and far more secure server space are available for a price from any of these providers. Hosting plans also provide advanced options that give you the ability to install and configure your own operating system and/or your own web server. NGINX is the preferred choice when working with Django projects because the web server has a reputation for performing far better than an Apache installation and can handle far more HTTP requests per second. When thinking of performance, it is of no surprise that many Django projects use NGINX for their web server. If you do need to configure your very own web server, you can start with the official NGINX installation manual, found here: https://www.nginx.com/resources/wiki/start/topics/tutorials/install/. The Apache web server will also work with Django and is desirable because it is far easier to install than an NGINX installation. If Apache is the route you need to go down, start by reading the official Django documentation on working with the Apache web server here: https://docs.djangoproject.com/en/4.0/howto/deployment/wsgi/modwsgi/.

Creating and configuring a Heroku plan

For the examples provided in this book, I will be using the free plans that Heroku offers because of the service's ease of use, zero-cost features, and growing popularity. Heroku is known as a **Platform as a Service** (**PaaS**), meaning that it enables developers to build, run, and deploy websites and apps entirely in the cloud. You can be up and running in a matter of minutes with this option, which can cut down the cost of hiring teams of network engineers to run a system for you. To follow along with this exercise, go to the Heroku website and sign up for a free account at `https://www.heroku.com/`. Then, once you have verified your email address and logged into your account, navigate to your dashboard at `https://dashboard.heroku.com/apps` and click on **New** | **Create New App**, then fill in the page, as depicted here:

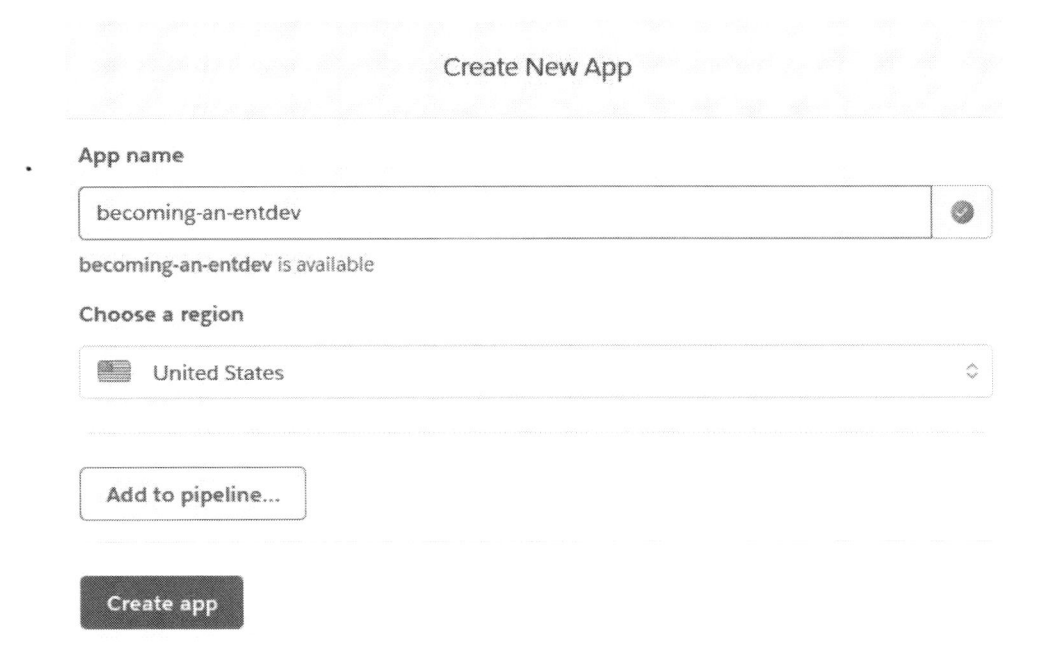

Figure 1.7 – Creating a new Heroku app

Enter a name for this app. The name is for internal use only and does not need to be exact. Keep in mind that since the app name must be unique within all Heroku apps, you will need to choose a different name from the name provided in this demonstration, `becoming-an-entdev`. Also, don't worry about pipelines just yet. We can always add them later if we need or want to. We will go over pipelines later, in the *Advanced deployment* subsection of this chapter. You may want to change your region to one closer to you if the United States is not your closest region.

Since we are building a Django project, we will need to select the Python buildpack. A **buildpack** is Heroku's way of using scripts to automatically build and compile various kinds of apps on Heroku. From the dashboard of your Heroku app that you just created, scroll down to the **Buildpacks** section and select **Add Buildpack**. The following screenshot depicts the popup that should appear next:

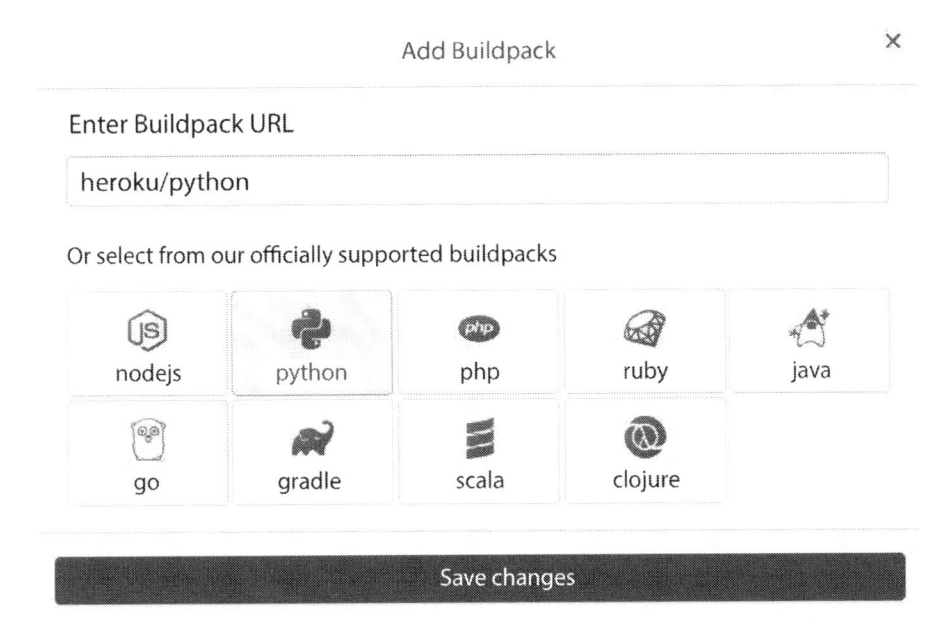

Figure 1.8 – Heroku buildpack choices

You may add any buildpack that is relevant to the needs of your project, but for anything related to this book, **python** is the only buildpack needed. If you choose any other buildpack, additional configuration steps may be required that have not been provided in this book, so use with caution.

Next, we'll discuss environments, which in this context refers to the testing and development stages, where we will present code running in action at different stages of development. Environments can be used in other contexts, such as a web server or operating system. *Environment* can have many meanings in the world of programming and generally refers to a configuration, setup, or structure of something that you are working with, on, or in.

Configuring Heroku environments

A Heroku app, in its most basic form, will consist of at least two environments, the first being a production environment, where your site or app will be accessed by the public and its users, and the second being your local machine, which is the computer where you and your development team will do all of your coding and where you will run the site locally. Heroku will default to using **Heroku Git** when an app is created, where it uses the Heroku CLI to commit changes from your local machine to your production environment. On your Heroku accounts dashboard at `https://dashboard.heroku.com/apps`, click the **Deploy** tab to see the choices shown in the following screenshot:

Figure 1.9 – Heroku deployment methods

Using the Heroku CLI

You will need to install the Heroku CLI on Mac, Windows, or Linux, by downloading the appropriate installer found here: `https://devcenter.heroku.com/articles/heroku-cli#download-and-install`.

For Windows users, remember to select the checkbox labeled **Set PATH to heroku** when you are prompted to do so during your install.

Next, navigate to the folder where you want your project to live on your local machine, and then open a new terminal or command-line window within that directory. You will need to log into Heroku using the following command:

```
PS C:\Projects\Packt\Repo> heroku login
```

Remember, you will need to log in any time you open a new terminal or command-line window and perform tasks. It will prompt you to open a new browser tab to log in. Once you have done so, you should see a message such as the following:

```
heroku: Press any key to open up the browser to login or q to exit:
Opening browser to https://cli-auth.heroku.com/auth/cli/browser/03be4a46-28f4-479a-bc10-8bd1bdcdd12b?requestor={{ ... }}
Logging in... done
Logged in as {{ youremail@yourdomain.com }}
PS C:\Projects\Packt\Repo>
```

If you see the preceding message, then you have successfully logged into your account and may begin using the Heroku commands.

> **Tip**
>
> In Windows, an easy way to run PowerShell as an administrator is to navigate to the folder that you wish to run commands from within the File Explorer window and then click **File | Open Windows PowerShell | Open Windows PowerShell as administrator**. This will start the command line in that directory, reducing the steps needed to navigate to it by typing a series of change directory commands.
>
> Clicking the options in *Figure 1.10* will open the command line in the following directory:
>
> `PS C:\Projects\Packt\Repo>`

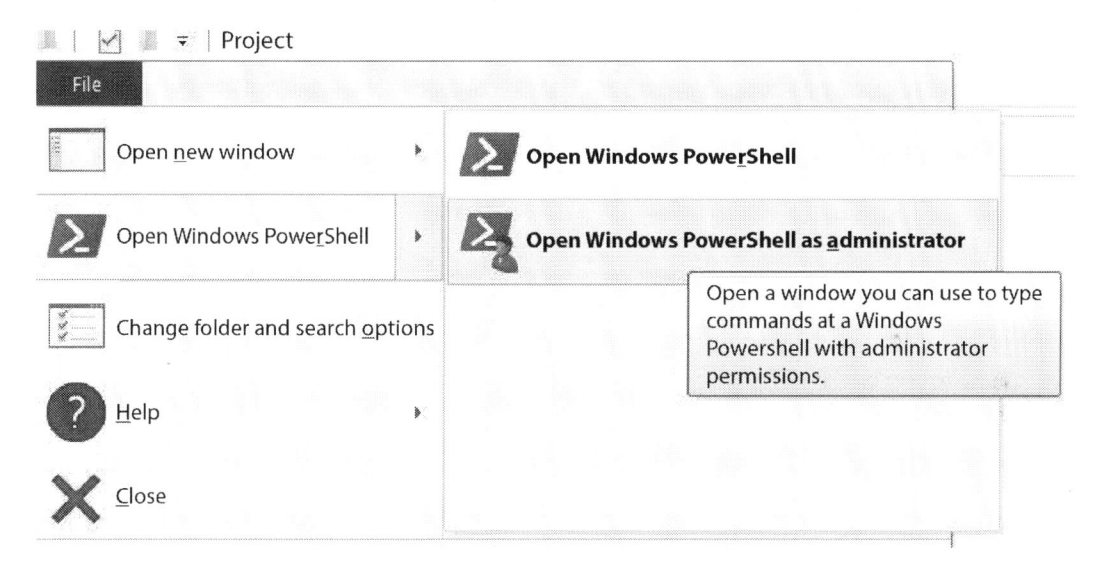

Figure 1.10 – Open Windows PowerShell as administrator

Next, let's initialize our local Git repository for the first time.

Initializing a Git repository and commiting changes

To say you are initializing a Git repository on your local machine means that you are generating a `.git` folder in the directory of your choice. The configuration files found in the `.git` folder are responsible for establishing a line of communication between your local repository and the remote repository. The remote repository we are going to link to is the location of the Heroku app.

Follow these steps to configure your Git settings:

1. Execute the following commands to first log into your Heroku account and then initialize a local Git repository linking your local repository with your Heroku app:

    ```
    PS C:\Projects\Packt\Repo> heroku login
    PS C:\Projects\Packt\Repo> git init
    PS C:\Projects\Packt\Repo> heroku git:remote -a {{ your_project_name }}
    ```

    This directory is where your Django project's source code files will live. In *Chapter 2, Project Configuration*, we will explain how to create your first Django project. For now, we just need to perform our first commit in order to establish a proper line of communication with each remote environment. In order for Heroku to accept a commit, the Heroku system needs to detect that it is a valid app that is being committed. Certain files must exist in order to pass this test. The first file is not necessarily required but I am suggesting you include it anyway; this is a **README file**. A `README.md` file uses **Markdown language**, which is a lightweight **markup language** used to store information such as your build processes or instructions for how a developer can get up and running for the first time. It's commonly used on the web to allow for the quick and easy formatting of plain text to keep important notes that can be viewed with many different web-based text editors today. When this file is viewed in the web browser, it is viewed, formatted, and styled in an easy-to-read format.

2. To do this, create a file by running the following `touch` command from the root of your local repository:

    ```
    PS C:\Projects\Packt\Repo> touch README.md
    ```

    For a complete guide on how to use Markdown language to style your README documents, visit https://guides.github.com/features/mastering-markdown/.

> **Tip**
>
> Windows users will likely have to install touch-cli via NPM, if you haven't already done so. You need to do this before you can use the preceding `touch` command. Alternatively, you can right-click and select **New | Text Document** within your File Explorer, using your mouse instead.
>
> To install touch-cli, run the following command using the `-g` attribute to denote that this is a global package for your development machine and not local to this project only:
>
> ```
> PS C:\Projects\Packt\Repo> npm install touch-cli -g
> ```

3. Go ahead and add what you like to your README file and get ready to make your first commit to your Heroku Git repository.

   We will also need to create one more file in order to perform a successful commit on Heroku, that being a `requirements.txt` file. Otherwise, Heroku will give you an error when it sees that this file does not exist. The error message will read **App not compatible with buildpack**. This error suggests that you did not include the Python buildpack for your Heroku app as noted at the beginning of this section, but it also means that the `requirements.txt` file does not exist in the root of your repository. These files can both remain blank for now if you desire, but the `requirements.txt` file must at least exist.

4. Run the following command to create your `requirements.txt` file from the root of your local repository:

   ```
   PS C:\Projects\Packt\Repo> touch requirements.txt
   ```

5. To perform your commit, just run these commands:

   ```
   PS C:\Projects\Packt\Repo> git add .
   PS C:\Projects\Packt\Repo> git commit -am "Created Blank README and Requirements Files"
   PS C:\Projects\Packt\Repo> git push heroku main
   ```

   The `-am` option performs the action of staging all modified files that are being tracked and allows us to add a personal commit message at the same time.

Next, we will clone an existing Heroku repository.

Cloning an existing Heroku Git repository

If you have already performed the steps in the previous subsection, where you have an existing repository for your project, you now need another developer to clone a copy of it to begin working. The next two commands will be needed. Don't forget to log in first if you have not already done so:

```
PS C:\Projects\Packt\Repo> heroku login
PS C:\Projects\Packt\Repo> git init
PS C:\Projects\Packt\Repo> heroku git:remote -a {{ your_project_name }}
```

Then, run this command to clone the repository:

```
PS C:\Projects\Packt\Repo> heroku git:clone -a {{ your_project_name }}
```

To run any standard Git command, such as `push` or `pull`, use the following command, changing `pull` to `push` as needed:

```
PS C:\Projects\Packt\Repo> git pull heroku main
```

Managing environments in Heroku

It's generally unwise to manage large projects with only two basic environments: standard production and local environments. The purpose of having many environments in your **Software Development Life Cycle (SDLC)** is to provide an application to your client with as few bugs as possible at the time of delivery. Use those environments to filter out as many bugs as possible in the process. Each environment or team that tests the application from beginning to end acts as a filter, weeding out different problems along the way.

You can implement as many or as few environments in your deployment strategies as you see fit. Most projects include at least a development and staging environment in addition to the first two baseline environments: production and local. Development would be used by your developers as a way to do their own testing, just for the sake of running their project on something other than their own computer for the first time to see what the project does. Common build problems are spotted here that would otherwise just waste the time of a team testing for data and flow bugs. Then, when the developer is happy with how the code runs in the development environment, it can be pushed to a staging environment. Here, a different testing team can review the app, going through the flow and searching for ways to intentionally break the system. Then, when they are happy, the code can get pushed to your production environment. Theoretically, no bugs should exist in this environment; however, this is not a perfect world and so we just want our primary goal to be having as few bugs as possible when the project gets to production.

Open your terminal or command-line window and navigate to the directory of your repository on your local machine. You can run the two commands shown in the following code block to create a development and staging environment for your app. If you haven't already done so, make sure you are logged into your Heroku account:

```
PS C:\Projects\Packt\Repo> heroku login
PS C:\Projects\Packt\Repo> heroku create --remote development
PS C:\Projects\Packt\Repo> heroku create --remote staging
```

You should see the following message, indicating the operation was a success:

```
Creating app... done,  pure-atoll-19670
https://pure-atoll-19670.herokuapp.com/ | https://git.heroku.com/pure-atoll-19670.git
```

Basically, what you are doing in this process is creating a new Heroku app that this environment lives in. That is done automatically for you.

Now, we can take the same two files we created earlier, README.md and requirements.txt, which should still be in your folder, and push them to development and staging. We can rest assured at this point of the SDLC that all three environments are exactly the same. We ensure this by executing the following two commands, pushing our code to those environments:

```
PS C:\Projects\Packt\Repo> git push development main
PS C:\Projects\Packt\Repo> git push staging main
```

Let's discuss using custom third-party repositories, such as GitHub, next.

Custom repositories

You are not limited to using just Heroku to store your files; you are welcome to use a cloud-based repository hosting service, such as GitHub or Bitbucket, to store them. There are a lot of reasons to decide on using a custom repository in addition to the repository location Heroku offers you. Many people just like to keep things organized and since they already have an account with another repository, they may want to keep all of their projects together. If you do make the decision to use something such as GitHub to store your project files, you would choose the **GitHub | Connect to GitHub** button, as shown in *Figure 1.9*, found earlier under the *Configuring Heroku environments* subsection of this chapter. Keep in mind that if you want to create additional environments, you should still have performed all of the steps prior to this section first. Each environment will be linked to a Git remote of that repository within your GitHub account.

When you choose to connect through GitHub, you will be prompted with a pop-up window in your browser that will ask you to log into your GitHub account. In this example, from within my GitHub account, I created a private repository named `becoming-an-entdev`. In your Heroku account, link your GitHub repository to this Heroku app by searching for the name of the repository that you created. Click **Connect** and if everything was a success, you should see this section change, containing a message reading **Connected to Your Repo Location**.

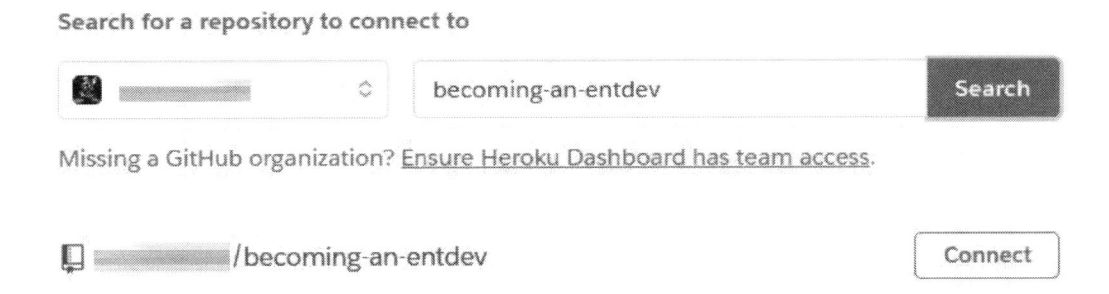

Figure 1.11 – Linking an external GitHub repository to Heroku

Automatic deployment

Next, you can choose to enable automatic deployment every time a change has been detected to a specific branch of the repository you linked to your Heroku app. In the following section, on the same page in your Heroku dashboard, select the branch from the following dropdown and click **Enable Automatic Deploys**:

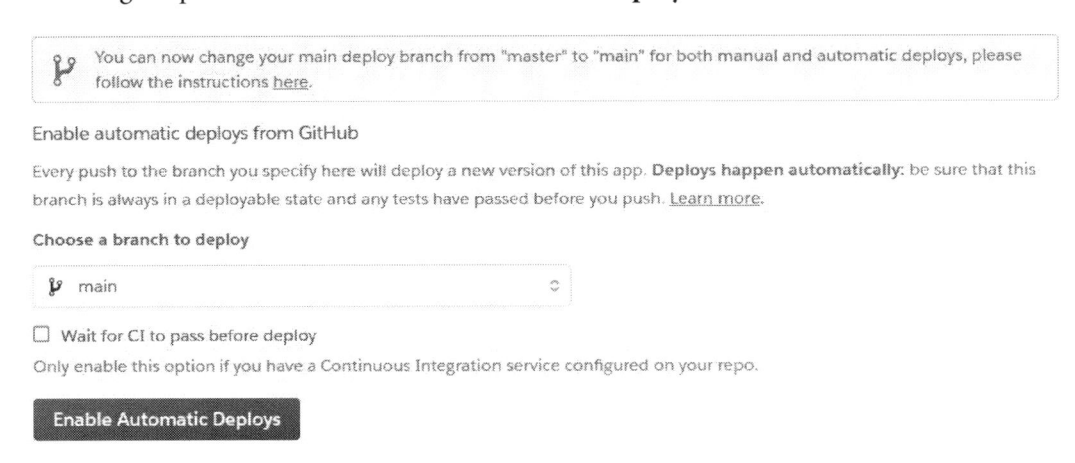

Figure 1.12 – Automatic deployment

There is an option to work with **Continuous Integration** (**CI**) tools, which are also helpful for large-scale projects. Simply enable the checkbox labeled **Wait for CI to pass before deploy** if you need your CI tools to pass their tests before allowing deployment. CI and delivery can get inherently complex to talk about, but they are used to automate the integration of all contributors' work, such as running test scripts or build processes. Heroku's CI does this in regular intervals, sometimes multiple times a day.

If your automatic deployment was successfully linked to your GitHub repository, you will see a new **webhook** for that repo. A webhook is a fancy term in web development used to describe a signal that is sent to a listener on another system when some kind of event or trigger occurs. For example, when you push changes to your GitHub repository, a signal is sent to Heroku triggering a script to grab all the latest changes and merge them into the Heroku app automatically. Webhooks are sometimes referred to as **reverse APIs** because they just send a signal; there is no request to send the signal followed by a response, as is the default behavior of any standard API request. You can find webhooks in your settings for your repository within your GitHub account. If you are using a different service, just look for something similar to a webhook or reverse API.

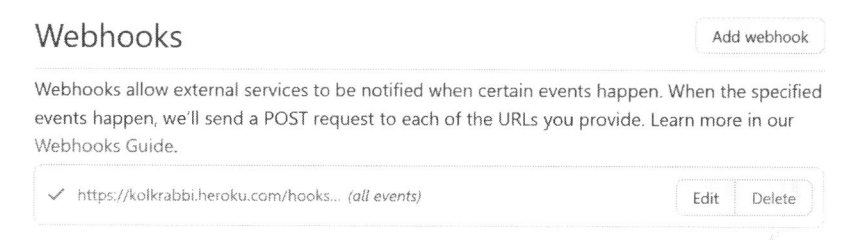

Figure 1.13 – GitHub Heroku webhook

Configuring remotes

Now that you have a GitHub repository that is created and linked to your production Heroku app and you have also wired up automatic deployments, you will need to specify in your local Git repository your remotes for linking your local repository to the production environment. Start by creating a `git-production` remote linked to your GitHub repository by using the Git URL provided in your account. You may name this anything you want.

Follow these steps to configure your remotes:

1. Run this command to create your remotes:

    ```
    PS C:\Projects\Packt\Repo> git remote add git-production
    https://github.com/{{ your_username }}/becoming-an-
    entdev.git
    ```

The preceding command is run only if you have already run the `git init` command to create your local repository first.

2. Next, create a `main` branch for this remote:

   ```
   PS C:\Projects\Packt\Repo> git branch -M main
   ```

   I am naming the branch `main` to remain consistent with the branches on the Heroku apps.

3. Now, you can push your first two files to this remote branch by running the following command. If you have made new changes to these files, remember to stage and commit them before the push:

   ```
   PS C:\Projects\Packt\Repo> git push -u git-production main
   ```

4. Now that we have the main repository to work with in production, we need to include the other environments, called development and staging. While Heroku separates environments into completely separate apps, you can either create new branches on `git-production` and call them development and staging or go into your GitHub account and create completely new repositories to link these to. For this book, we will separate them into completely new repositories for demonstration and practice. I went ahead and created two new repositories in my personal GitHub account called `becoming-an-entdev-dev` and `becoming-an-entdev-staging`.

5. We will link them using the following example commands:

   - For the development environment, use the following:

     ```
     PS C:\Projects\Packt\Repo> git remote add git-development https://github.com/{{ your_username }}/becoming-an-entdev-dev.git
     PS C:\Projects\Packt\Repo> git branch -M main
     PS C:\Projects\Packt\Repo> git push -u git-development main
     ```

   - For the staging environment, use the following:

     ```
     PS C:\Projects\Packt\Repo> git remote add git-staging https://github.com/{{ your_username }}/becoming-an-entdev-staging.git
     PS C:\Projects\Packt\Repo> git branch -M main
     PS C:\Projects\Packt\Repo> git push -u git-staging main
     ```

Next, we will configure our Git branches.

Configuring branches

All of the remotes in the examples provided have a branch named `main` that serves as the parent to all of the children branches and forks created when moving forward; some people also call this `master`. For working locally, you'll want to create local branches that are set up to track one of your remote branches. **Tracking**, in Git terminology, simply means a local branch is mapped to a remote repository or branch located somewhere else.

Similar to how we ran the `git branch -M main` command previously, which we did for the sake of creating the `main` branch to be used for the remote version only, locally, we will run the following command to add a new local branch to our Git config file that helps track or map it to the environment we set:

```
PS C:\Projects\Packt\Repo> git branch production
git-production/main
PS C:\Projects\Packt\Repo> git branch development
git-development/main
PS C:\Projects\Packt\Repo> git branch staging git-staging/main
```

If you are using something such as Sourcetree as a GUI for interacting with Git repositories, you should see something as in the following screenshot on the left sidebar of the app:

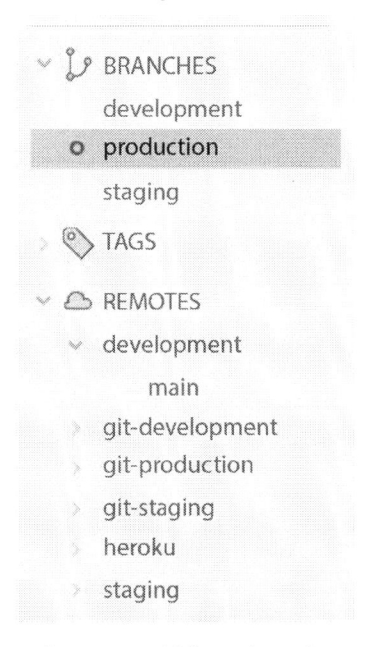

Figure 1.14 – Sourcetree sidebar – branches and remotes

The default name given by Heroku to reference the production environment of the app that you are working with is `heroku`. If you were to expand all of the remote repositories in the list, you would see that they all have a `main` branch, as depicted in the preceding screenshot under the repository named `development`. Now, from one single folder on your hard drive, you can navigate to and from all of these environments, also known as versions of your app, to work as needed.

Some simple and helpful commands are provided here:

- Switch branches with the following:

    ```
    PS C:\Projects\Packt\Repo> git checkout development
    ```

    This command switches to the `development` remote.

- Stage everything and include a message to commit changes with the following:

    ```
    PS C:\Projects\Packt\Repo> git commit -am "Added notes to README File"
    ```

- Push code specifying a **HEAD** location with the following:

    ```
    PS C:\Projects\Packt\Repo> git push development main
    ```

    If you run into an error stating **error: src refspec main does not match any** when you try to run the preceding command, try the following command instead:

    ```
    PS C:\Projects\Packt\Repo> git push development HEAD:main
    ```

Up to now, each remote repository we created only consisted of one branch. Your team will need other branches, which for the most part will branch off of the `main` branch when they are created. Other times, you may want to branch off a child branch for a number of reasons. Many people may even prefer one repository where each environment is a different branch. I won't go into all the different methodologies for organizing and using a specific Git workflow because this subject is so complex. You would have to adopt something that best fits your needs, but a good start would be to review this guide or anything on the subject of Git workflows: `https://backlog.com/git-tutorial/branching-workflows/`.

You may need to separate branches by feature. My favorite approach is to give each developer their own branch named after themselves, which they can use to commit all of their daily work to at the end of each day. Later, a designated person can then merge all `pull` requests into the `main` branch at designated intervals throughout the SDLC. One option can be to store all these branches in your development environment and then, in your staging and production environments, you can leave just one branch, called the `main` branch. Then, when it comes time to push or pull something from development into staging, just push those changes into the `main` branch on staging. The choices are nearly infinite and there is no definitive right or wrong way to go about this.

You could create branches on your other environments if you wanted to. Just keep an eye on versions of your app getting out of sync with one another. The idea is that as long as it makes sense and it doesn't create a lot of wasted time and headaches when merging, you are on the right path. In any strategy, it's usually wise to pull the `main` branch into a current working branch as often as possible while a developer works, in order to keep code in sync with other developers who have already merged their code into `main`. That developer could work out conflicts they know are specific to them on their machine, saving time later when working on other merge conflicts that could arise when it comes time to push this working branch into `main`. It's very easy to fall behind the changes that other developers are contributing, and merging your code into `main` later could prove to be difficult with the number of code conflicts that can result.

Advanced deployment

Of course, not everything has to be fully automated. A much smaller team or project can get by when they dedicate a single person to merge branches manually, edit code conflicts, and perform a final build of all the asset files before pushing to a test or production environment. If your team is building enterprise-level software, then you most certainly have the need to automate this step of production as much as possible. Since there are so many ways this can be done, the rest of this lies beyond the scope of this book. You may even hire a dedicated person or team of people whose only job is to build and manage deployment strategies, write build scripts, process pull requests, work through code conflicts, and test for bugs.

Build scripts can be used to compile ES6 to JavaScript or even transpile SCSS to CSS, where a smaller team may do this manually when merging branches. Test scripts can help you run test cases. You can test every method or class and even get to a granular level by testing specific data that is inputted into the system. Look into writing and running Node.js and Python build scripts on deployment based on your project's own needs.

Two more things for you to explore are **pipelines** and **containers**, which add additional layers of enhancements to a project. We will discuss them next.

Pipelines

A pipeline in software development is commonly known as a series of objects that are linked together where the output of one functions as the input of the other. This is best described as linking your development environment to your staging environment and then linking your staging environment to your production environment. There are a lot of tools that can be inserted here that can help with reviewing your code every step of the way. Services such as Heroku and GitHub offer ways to allow your developers to create **pull requests**, which comprise a method of submitting your code to a shared development project. The method even provides ways to create **tickets**, which are used to track and manage bugs or issues found in your application. They can be assigned to one or many people, and a status can be assigned to them providing team leaders or project managers with a method of knowing what is done and what is being worked on.

If you did decide to follow along with this chapter and use Heroku, their service offers many different ways to work with and configure pipelines. They can get very complex if you need them to be. One really cool feature of how Heroku manages pipelines is that a brand-new review app will automatically be created when a developer creates a **pull request**. A pull request is a way of submitting a request to merge code into a shared project. The request is sent to a reviewer who will merge the code and approve or deny the changes. If the reviewer has trouble resolving conflicts found in the merging of the code, they may reject the code and send it back to the developer to revise. This gives the reviewer a very easy way to launch the app with the code contained in the pull request to see whether it works or not.

In other words, you can run whatever version, or whatever state the app is in, with that pull request without affecting your current development, staging, or production environments in any way. When a new app is created via a Pull request, that new app does not show up on your main dashboard, but instead is considered a *review app* of the environment or Heroku app that you are reviewing. Heroku will also automatically deploy changes to the `main` branch of the environment that is next in line in your pipeline queue, whenever a reviewer has approved changes included in a particular pull request.

Containers

A virtual environment in Python is best described as a way to encapsulate all of the packages or dependencies that your project relies on. What is known as a container, or **containerization**, is a step above, in that it encapsulates the entire operating system, your Django project, its own virtual environment, and all of its packages and dependencies. **Docker containers** are used to create images that are exact replicas of their production environments and are used by developers in every stage of development during the app's development life cycle. The benefit of doing this is that no matter what operating system your developers are working on, they will all virtually be running the same setup and should face little to no issues.

In my experience, the phrase "*it works on my computer*" is often used among developers. This isn't a genuine issue often, but it does happen where a project on a Windows machine will act differently from the same project running on a Mac or Linux machine and vice versa. Containers let your developers continue to use the operating systems that they have become the most comfortable and familiar with during their careers. They ensure consistency among every moving part in development.

Another benefit of using containers is that they can help to get a brand-new developer or new hire to the team to get their project to run locally for the first time in as little time as possible. A container repository is similar to a traditional repository but is used to store a collection of container images. These can be completely different projects or a collection of different versions or environments of the same app. Either way, a container repository is used to store and distribute these images to developers who need them. If you predict many developers will come and go throughout the life cycle of your project, I highly recommend taking the time to build a container image for your team.

If you are using Heroku along with this book, choose the **Container Registry | Use Heroku CLI** button, as shown in *Figure 1.9*, found earlier in the *Configuring Heroku environments* section of this chapter. From here, you can integrate your container image into your deployment. The image can include any add-ons and app variables and even work with your pipelines and review apps. Heroku and Docker also work together with third-party CI services, such as Codefresh, CodeShip, and CircleCI. There is quite a bit more configuration that will need to be done to use these third-party services, but you can review their documentation to help you get started.

Domain Name System

When an environment or a review app is created, Heroku will generate a new URL based on the name of the app that you created. Since Heroku's system is set up to use the name of your app as a subdomain of its URL structure, the name of your app must be unique. For example, the main project on Heroku for this book is named `becoming-an-entdev` and generates the URL `https://becoming-an-entdev.herokuapp.com/`. The development app created for this book automatically generates the URL `https://mighty-sea-09431.herokuapp.com/`, and the staging environment generates the URL `https://pure-atoll-19670.herokuapp.com/`. `mighty-sea-09431` and `pure-atoll-19670` are the names of the apps that were automatically created by Heroku when those environments were created.

The final step in the app configuration is to link the Heroku URL to a **Domain Name System** (**DNS**), which is best described as a public phone book of websites that links the URL names to individual IP addresses like names to phone numbers. While Heroku may generate a URL for your app that looks like `https://pure-atoll-19670.herokuapp.com/`, it still produces a numeric IP address that you can use to register to your site when someone goes to `www.your-domain.com`. You will have to link your app to this phone book registry so that the public can get to your website or API using your domain name and not the URL provided by Heroku.

Popular registrars, such as Domain.com, Bluehost, GoDaddy, and Namecheap, allow you to register a domain name, which will look like `www.your-domain.com` or `http://www.your-domain.custom.tld/`, where `.tld` refers to any of the over 1,500 **Top-Level Domains** (**TLD**) that are available to choose from today, such as `.edu`, `.gov`, or `.food`, to name a few. Some TLDs are restricted to certain entities and may not be available to everyone. There are two ways you can link your Heroku app to a DNS. The first way is to use **domain forwarding**. You'll need to work with your domain registrar to set up forwarding in your app. Domain forwarding will point `www.your-domain.com` to your Heroku app location where the user will no longer see your domain in the browser's address bar. Instead, they will see `becoming-an-entdev.herokuapp.com` in the address bar. If you want the user to continue to see `www.your-domain.com` in their browser's address bar, along with your site as the body content, you'll need to set up forwarding with **masking** as an option instead. Masking will keep your domain in the address bar but will also mask **Search Engine Optimization** (**SEO**), such as your title, description, and keywords, embedded in the `<head>` of your document.

Forwarding with masking is generally considered bad in terms of SEO, which is ways to improve the visibility of your site in search results on search engines such as Google, Bing, and Yahoo. It's usually difficult or more complex for a search engine to link information from one site via an IP address and map it to your physical domain, and generally, you will get a lower search rating because of that. It may be that search engines are working to improve upon this in the future or at least working to not penalize websites for using forwards and redirects. For now, you should not consider this if SEO is a big requirement for your project.

The alternative to using domain forwarding would be to map your domain to the system's nameservers that deliver your app. Whichever you are using, you need to first make your Heroku app available to the domain of your choice if it is anything other than the standard Heroku domain. Start by adding your domain to your app in Heroku by running the following command. Make sure to log in first if you haven't already done so:

```
PS C:\Projects\Packt\Repo> heroku login
PS C:\Projects\Packt\Repo> heroku domains:add www.your-domain.com --app becoming-an-entdev
```

To use subdomains to act as your different environments, run the next two commands:

```
PS C:\Projects\Packt\Repo> heroku domains:add dev.your-domain.com --app mighty-sea-09431
PS C:\Projects\Packt\Repo> heroku domains:add staging.your-domain.com --app pure-atoll-19670
```

Here, we append the `--app` attribute setting and specify the app we want to link to. Since we created different environments, we need to include this specification or we will get an error. The `dev` and `staging` subdomains are used in the preceding commands as the environment-specific domains of our site. If the command is successful, it will print out your DNS target, but you can always run this command to list all of the domains, and it will also print out your DNS target for you:

```
PS C:\Projects\Packt\Repo> heroku domains --app {{ your_project_name }}
=== {{ your_project_name }} Heroku Domain
{{ your_project_name }}.herokuapp.com
=== {{ your_project_name }} Custom Domains
Domain Name            DNS Record Type DNS Target            SNI Endpoint
www.your-domain.com CNAME              {{ randomly_generated_name }}.herokudns.com undefined
```

You will then need to use the DNS target that was provided to configure your DNS records within your registrar's account for your domain. If you're using domain forwarding, many registrars have an option to create a forward and will ask you a few questions. For manually mapping your domain to your nameserver, this is usually done by editing `A-Record` in your DNS settings by providing a name of @ and giving it a value of the DNS target that was provided previously.

You can even set up a custom subdomain for different projects, departments, and versions of your app or environments, such as `dev.your-domain.com` or `staging.your-domain.com`. Subdomains can be linked by creating a new `CNAME-Record` with the names `dev` or `staging` and giving the records the value of the DNS target that was provided in the examples previously for their respective apps. For registrars that won't accept a value that is not a numeric IP address, you will have to use something such as Cloudflare, which is a web infrastructure and security company, to sit in the middle and act as your nameserver. It acts as a content delivery network and your nameserver, which you can then configure in your registrar using the nameserver settings provided by Cloudflare. Nameserver records are known as `NS-Record` within the DNS settings of your registrar.

Summary

It can be very easy for someone to get caught up in how to do something versus actually doing something. Overthinking is a very common thing among programmers. Sometimes, it's wise to just accept a certain level of work is needed for your workflow and then scale up and extend as much as needed later on as the need arises. While gathering requirements is important to obtain a clear understanding of what it is you are trying to achieve, many of the steps and concepts discussed in this chapter can be thought of as just another tool in your toolbox, or in other words, the right tool for the right job.

Things such as containerizing your project with Docker can be easily added to your workflow and deployment routines later on. The same can be said if you need to add additional environments to your workflow later on. New developers could easily be given a new branch as the need also arises. Teams who dedicate one person to manually run, build, and test tasks can always automate their tasks later on when work begins to pile up. Pipelines can be created even after you have been developing a project for a while. However, other decisions, such as choosing what framework to use on your frontend, can prove to be disastrous if you decide to change the technology halfway through the development life cycle.

What is known as **agile development** is the process of an ever-changing and always fluid development environment. This is where many different collaborators share ideas and those ideas often change over time, meaning that the scope of the project will also change. A lot of projects today are built in an agile setting. Use your initial requirements gathering to probe for possible changes in the future and then align yourself with as many open doors as possible. Remember that a strong home always needs a strong foundation to rest upon; a weak foundation will result in your home crumbling to the ground.

This chapter focused on pouring the foundation of a home. In the next chapter, *Chapter 2, Project Configuration*, we will be building what can be considered the frame of the house that sits upon that foundation. The frame of that house will consist of building a project, virtual environment and database needed for development.

2
Project Configuration

Source code is considered the meat and bones, or the framing of a home, in any software. In this chapter, we will build a project that contains the files where the source code lives. We will discuss several tools that will come in handy when developers are working directly with their source code. When working with Django, while any tool can be used to edit the source code, some tools are more productive than others. In this chapter, we will explore some of the countless tools that exist and discuss why an **Integrated Development Environment** (**IDE**) might also be used.

We'll also learn about the importance of working with the Django `settings.py` file(s) of a project. Of course, software also requires a database to store and retrieve data entered and created by its users, and we will install a local and remote database for each environment of a project. We will go over the various database types that are available and then focus on the most popular type to use for the examples throughout this book. It is not required to use the same database type that we will be using, but you might encounter slight variations if you use a different one; proceed with caution. Reading this chapter is crucial before going through the rest of the book.

In this chapter, we will cover how to do the following:

- Choosing developmental tools
- Starting a project
- Creating a virtual environment
- Project configuration
- Using basic database settings
- Preparing PostgreSQL for Heroku

Technical requirements

To work with the code in this chapter, the following tools will need to be installed on your local machine:

- Python version 3.9 – used as the underlying programming language for the project
- Django version 4.0 – used as the backend framework of the project
- pip package manager – used to manage third-party Python/Django packages

Next, you will need a way to edit the code that we will be writing in this chapter and throughout the rest of this book. The first section of this chapter will provide you with several development tool choices from text editors to IDEs. The same IDE will be used to demonstrate a few actions but it is not necessary to use the same tool. You are welcome to use any IDE you like or use no IDE at all, using the terminal or command-line window instead. A database will also be required, and the third section of this chapter will provide several options to choose from. Any database type will work with your project and configuration examples will be provided, but only PostgreSQL will be used to work with our project and Heroku.

This book will focus on the concepts of Django and enterprise development, instead of guiding you through how to use Git operations. For a crash course on how to use Git operations, you can watch the video found here: `https://www.packtpub.com/product/git-and-github-the-complete-git-and-github-course-video/9781800204003`.

All of the code created in this chapter can be found in the GitHub repository for this book: `https://github.com/PacktPublishing/Becoming-an-Enterprise-Django-Developer`. The code used throughout this chapter will relate to every file in the core of the project. In every chapter, starting from *Chapter 3*, *Models, Relations, and Inheritance*, code related to a particular chapter will reside in its own Django app folder. Refer to the subsection of this chapter titled *Creating a Django app* to learn more about what that means.

Check out the following video to see the *Code in Action*: `https://bit.ly/3NqNuFG`

Choosing development tools

Configuring our project refers to how we will structure and arrange the files that make up an application. This also refers to how we share those files within a collaborative team. Some tools create files that can be shared among your team members, such as preconfigured settings related to development and debugging features. These files are sometimes referred to as configuration or solution files. This means you can preconfigure a set of development tools to help get your team up to speed quickly. Making sure that all members use similar tools makes debugging and looking at code that is not written by you much easier. This consistency also makes verbal and written communication among members of your team more efficient when synchronizing workflows.

While there are benefits to sharing project configuration files, it is also not necessary for everyone on your team to be using the same tools. In fact, it's even possible to create many different configuration files for a variety of development tools all included in the same repository, giving your developers a multitude of preconfigured project files to choose from. Even if we provide configuration files in a repository, a developer can still use a basic text editor with the terminal or command-line window to make edits and run the project locally. Let's compare several of these text editor tools and discuss some of the benefits that they provide. Then, we will discuss what IDEs are and how they differ from text editors.

Text editors

A **text editor** is quite simply exactly what it sounds like, a means to edit text, or in our case, source code. Text editors are sometimes referred to as lightweight IDEs, given the number of features that some of these popular editors come packed with.

Likely, what are considered the three most popular text editors today are the following:

- **Atom**
- **Notepad++**
- **Sublime Text**

Atom

Atom is intended to be a fully editable and customizable text editor. The tool's official website uses the term *hackable* when describing their software. This editor allows you to install packages that help enhance your code-writing abilities. It has smart code auto-completion and code styling to let you type less and see more. This tool has a built-in file browser that allows you to find and replace code in the folders and files that you choose to search through. Atom also works on all three major operating systems, Windows, Mac, and Linux. It is free to use and also open source, allowing you to modify the editor's source code itself. To download Atom and start using it today, visit `https://atom.io/`.

Notepad++

Notepad++ is another free and open source editor that comes with a stylish code syntax highlighter and provides code auto-completion suggestions. It was built to work with and run a vast number of different programming languages. It even lets you write macros and run custom scripts directly from the editor. Like Atom, it also has the capability of installing plugins. It's really lightweight and can be a nice editor to set as the default for your operating system. To download Notepad++, visit `https://notepad-plus-plus.org/downloads/`.

Sublime Text

Sublime Text is another popular choice. This editor allows you to create project files and includes features to build a wide variety of programming languages. One cool feature is how it will use your **Graphical Processing Unit** (**GPU**) to improve the performance of the editor's UI while you work. It uses what they call context-aware auto-completion, meaning the editor will intelligently offer code completion suggestions based on what code exists on the page, regardless of whether you are in a file that is of another language. For example, you can edit code contained in a `<script type="text/javascript"></script>` that lives inside of a `.html` document to be styled and displayed differently from the HTML found in that same file.

Another application in the Sublime family is called Sublime Merge, which is a simple way to merge code and perform Git operations. My favorite feature is using it to view history states and commit logs. Sublime Text is free to evaluate for a certain amount of time but eventually, it will prompt you to purchase a license after the trial period is over. To get started with Sublime Text, visit `https://www.sublimetext.com/`.

There are dozens, if not hundreds, of other text editors to choose from that were not mentioned in this chapter. Don't limit yourself to only the popular choices provided and feel free to explore many other tools. The number of features and capabilities that some text editors provide can sometimes be referred to as a lightweight IDE; let's discuss what an IDE is next.

Integrated development environments

An IDE is what we call software that combines many different programming tools into one single desktop application that a developer can use to build other applications. It is a development tool that your team can use and benefit from to stay productive. IDEs primarily consist of a way to view and edit source code, automate local build processes, and provide ways to help you debug and analyze your code. The tool contains ways to style and format code, show you errors as you type, and provide code completion suggestions to reduce keystrokes as you work. These environments also provide ways to search other code files contained in your project and push or deploy your code to external repositories. For example, the Sourcetree app that was mentioned in *Chapter 1*, *Undertaking a Colossal Project*, would no longer be needed if you are using an IDE that has Git features built into it.

The same applies to a text editor choice that also has Git features included. Similar to some of the text editors with fancy features, IDEs will create common configuration files that can be shared with your team. Some of these files we don't want to share, such as files that store breakpoints and other local debugging settings specific to that developer and local instance only. However, sharing configuration settings with your team allows members to get their IDEs up and running on their machines much easier and quicker, with all of the tools ready or almost ready to use.

A simple text editor is really all you need. A project could start out this way and then your team could introduce the use of an IDE later on. Sometimes, when using an IDE, you can structure your project files in subdirectories that would otherwise not exist. If you already know your team will need the productivity tools from the get-go, you can start out with an IDE and create a project through the IDE itself, letting the IDE structure your files in a way that is natural to that IDE. It's sometimes easier this way because some IDEs may configure your file structures slightly differently than what would otherwise be created by using just the Django `startproject` command from a terminal or command-line window.

Let's discuss some of the popular IDE choices that developers use with Django today and then settle upon one of these choices to demonstrate the concept of using an IDE. This chapter will demonstrate working with Django management commands both in the IDE and the terminal to showcase the benefits of using one versus the other. For every action demonstrated using the IDE in this chapter, the command-line-driven command equivalent of that action will also be provided. This will also allow you to bypass the IDE altogether if you wish to do so. Moving forward, all future chapters will only provide the standard command-line-driven Django management commands and continuing to use the IDE will be optional.

PyDev with Eclipse

PyDev is actually a plugin for the **Eclipse IDE** but it can also be used as a standalone IDE. PyDev can be downloaded and installed directly by itself because it will come preinstalled with **LiClipse**, a lightweight version of the Eclipse IDE. The Eclipse IDE is a fully integrated development experience. It allows the debugging of code in a variety of ways. Profiling is just one of those ways, which is a tool that helps the developer understand the timing of events, memory usage, disk usage, or any other diagnostics. The term CPU Profiler is often used to discuss tools that can help you find out what specific process is bogging down your system. It will tell you things such as how long it was hanging for and give you an idea as to how to fix it. All of the bells and whistles that come with all of the text editors I mentioned previously also come with Eclipse. PyDev has a vast library of packages to choose from for many different languages that exist today. Eclipse and PyDev both work on all standard operating systems today, such as Windows, Mac, and Linux. To download Eclipse, visit `https://www.eclipseclp.org/download.html`.

Eclipse and PyDev are both free to use and are both open source licenses, allowing you to modify the IDE software itself. The Eclipse IDE is a bit more difficult to install than other desktop applications today. Its installers require a good deal of reading before you know how to get started with installing it. Eclipse also requires **Java** to be installed and running on your machine. Java is a high-level programming language and a computing platform that is usually not required to work with Django and Python unless you are working with Eclipse. For this reason, we will not be using this IDE in this chapter. To download PyDev, visit `https://www.pydev.org/download.html`.

PyCharm

PyCharm is likely the most popular choice among Python and Django developers today. It is easy to use and much easier to install than PyDev by using a simple executable file available for Windows, Mac, or Linux machines. It comes with a free community version as well as a paid professional version. The paid version offers many more features and provides more specialized scientific and web development tools, such as advanced database integration and database development, directly from within the IDE, as well as other debugging and profiling tools. The free community version is enough for most Django developers to get by on. This version allows developers to work with Django project integrations and run virtual environments while connecting to remote Git repositories. To download and install PyCharm, visit `https://www.jetbrains.com/pycharm/download/`.

While this is likely the most popular IDE among Django developers, Visual Studio is likely the most popular IDE among developers of any language or framework. For this reason, we will use Visual Studio to demonstrate the examples throughout this chapter.

Visual Studio

Visual Studio has been a very popular tool of choice among many .NET, C#, C++, and other developers for over 20 years now. It's a very robust IDE that comes packed with all of the tools that you can think of and then more. It comes in many different varieties and flavors, and for years it was only available for a price. Then, around 2013, Microsoft started offering the Visual Studio Community Edition for free to the public. A drawback for some was that Visual Studio was only available on Windows platforms until the year 2017, when it became available on Mac platforms. Currently, Linux is not supported. However, Visual Studio Code, a lightweight IDE, is available on all three platforms, Windows, Mac, and Linux.

Visual Studio Code has likely become the most popular tool of all time among any type of developer. Both Visual Studio and Visual Studio Code support using Python and Django. Upon installing either of these tools, you will need to select related Python/Django packages that will be included in your installation or install them separately. For those of you working on a Linux machine, or if you just don't want to use an IDE, refer to the management commands provided after the IDE demonstration of each action involved in creating a project. If you are on a Windows or Mac system and wish to follow along using an IDE, download the **Visual Studio 2019 – Community Edition** installer found here: `https://visualstudio.microsoft.com/downloads/`. Make sure, during your installation, that you select any Python development extensions that it offers, as shown in the following screenshot:

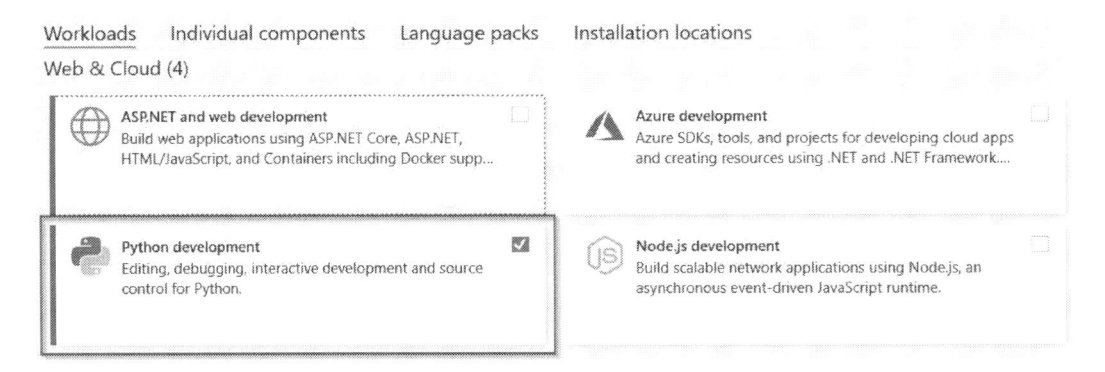

Figure 2.1 – Visual Studio – Python development extension

You might find other useful tools under the **Individual components** tab of this interface. Include any other tools that you would like to include before proceeding with your installation. Now that we have **Visual Studio 2019 – Community Edition** installed, let's build a solution file for a project that can be shared with other developers in a repository.

> **Note**
> While Visual Studio 2019 is the latest product available from Microsoft, Visual Studio 2022 will be released about the same time this book will be published. If you are using the newer version of Visual Studio, you should be able to perform all of the same actions as depicted in this chapter. The screenshots of the Visual Studio IDE may not appear exactly the same and some code adjustments might also be necessary.

Starting a project

There are two ways to start a project and this chapter will allow you to choose which method you want to follow. We encourage you to use the IDE as becoming proficient with using this tool in your team will be beneficial in the long run. However, if your team is using an IDE other than Visual Studio or you are only using a text editor to work with your code, the command-line equivalent of performing each step is also provided to allow anyone to work through this chapter. All other chapters in this book will focus on code only, which can be used with or without an IDE.

Using the IDE

Open the Visual Studio IDE and select **Create New Project**. When you are directed to the next screen, search for the `django` keyword and in the list of results, select **Blank Django Web Project**, as depicted here:

Figure 2.2 – Visual Studio – Create a new project

On the next screen, enter `becoming_a_django_entdev` for **Project Name**. This will auto-populate your **Solution Name** field as you type. For the **Location** option, select the folder on your drive where you placed your local Git repository from *Chapter 1, Undertaking a Colossal Project*, as your location. At the bottom, make sure the checkbox labeled **Place solution and project in the same directory** is checked as is done in the following screenshot. Enabling this checkbox will place a solution file in the same folder as the `manage.py` file, known as the root of a project. It will make using things such as the terminal that is provided within the IDE just a little easier:

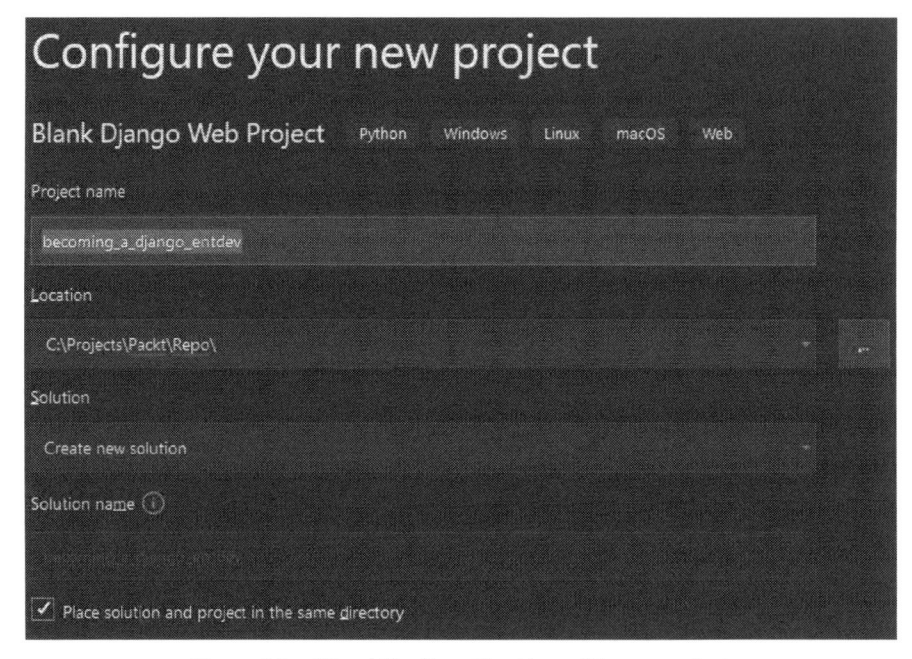

Figure 2.3 – Visual Studio – Creating a Django project

> **Note**
> When using the Visual Studio IDE to create a project, the files found in the `/becoming_a_django_entdev/becoming_a_django_entdev/` folder, such as the `settings.py` and `urls.py` files, are automatically generated using Django 2.1.2. These files will still work when used with later versions of Django. Additionally, when we get to the *Creating a virtual environment* section of this chapter, we will actually be installing the Django 4.0 package, which is the version used throughout this book. Even though version 2.1.2 was used to initially create some of the project files, the project will always use version 4.0 and run successfully. When using the terminal or command-line window to create a project, this scenario will not occur. Later, in *Chapter 9, Django Testing*, you will learn how to verify what version is actually installed and being used.

Using the command line

The Django terminal or command-line window equivalent of starting a Django project is the `startproject` command. There are two ways to create a project using this command. The first method is to create your project using the version of Django that was installed on your machine globally and then build your virtual environment next.

The other way is to create your virtual environment first and then activate your environment, install the version of Django that you desire, and then build your project using the version of Django that was installed in your virtual environment. What the IDE did for us was create a project first using a version of Django that the IDE provides, and then when we created the virtual environment, the version of Django was updated to the version specified in the `requirements.txt` file.

When a package gets updated in the virtual environment, the old version gets uninstalled and the new version gets installed fresh. For this exercise, we will uninstall any version of Django that may exist globally, then install the latest version available when this book was written. Then, we will create the virtual environment using the command line in the next section, following along as close as we can to the examples provided using the IDE.

Follow these steps to create your project files:

1. Open your terminal or command-line window and navigate to your local repository folder created in *Chapter 1, Undertaking a Colossal Project*. Make sure you are not in a virtual environment at this time. Then, execute the following commands to uninstall any existing versions of Django and then install the proper version of Django that we will be using globally on your machine:

   ```
   PS C:\Projects\Packt\Repo> pip uninstall django
   PS C:\Projects\Packt\Repo> pip install django==4.0
   ```

2. Execute the Django command that will create a project and all of the core files necessary to work with Django, based on Django version 4.0. We will name this project the same as in the IDE example: `becoming_a_django_entdev`. The `startproject` command creates a `manage.py`, `wsgi.py`, and `asgi.py` file and several other boilerplate files that serve as the foundation of all Django projects. The `becoming_a_django_entdev` option is the name of the project and the folder that a project will be placed in. Execute the following command to create the project:

   ```
   PS C:\Projects\Packt\Repo> python -m django startproject becoming_a_django_entdev
   ```

The preceding is a friendly command that has been tested and proven to work on a Windows machine. Traditionally, developers would use the following command to start a project; however, this command does not work on a Windows operating system:

```
PS C:\Projects\Packt\Repo> django-admin startproject becoming_a_django_entdev
```

Next, let's create and configure a virtual environment, which is needed to work with any third-party packages included in a project.

Creating a virtual environment

We should not have a virtual environment for our project at this time. If you do have one, go ahead and disregard it and create a new one for this next exercise. Whether you created a project using the Visual Studio IDE or by using the Django commands from a terminal or command-line window in the previous exercises, the file structure in your repository should look like the following tree structure:

```
├── .git
├── readme.md
├── requirements.txt
├── becoming_a_django_entdev
│   ├── .vs
│   ├── becoming_a_django_entdev.sln
│   ├── db.sqlite3
│   ├── manage.py
│   ├── obj
│   ├── requirements.txt
│   ├── staticfiles
│   └── becoming_a_django_entdev
│       ├── __init__.py
│       ├── asgi.py
│       ├── settings.py
```

```
|           ├── urls.py
|           └── wsgi.py
```

We now have two `requirements.txt` files and two folders called `/becoming_a_django_entdev/becoming_a_django_entdev/`, where various files reside. We will leave the folder structure the way it is now and configure additional settings later to allow Heroku to work with this folder structure. We are doing this because creating a project through the IDE will only produce this result, and note that other IDEs or even lightweight IDE text editors may create folder structures that even vary from the preceding tree. If you decide to use the Django commands to create a new project, you do have the option to specify an additional option to prevent creating your project in a subdirectory. This would put the `manage.py` file in the same directory as the root of a repository and result in only one `requirements.txt` file. Doing that would require using the following command example:

```
PS C:\Projects\Packt\Repo> python -m django startproject
 becoming_a_django_entdev ./
```

Here, we add the additional `./` option at the end of the preceding command, which states to put the project in the folder that we are located in now. Without this option, an additional subfolder would have been created by default, naming that folder the same as the name provided for the project name. However, doing this would result in no solution file and now no way to run the project through the Visual Studio IDE. Since the objective of this chapter is to demonstrate the use of an IDE, this is the reason we are keeping the preceding tree structure. There are alternative options to doing this, which would lead you down the path in Visual Studio of creating a new project using the **from existing code** option. This would allow you to create a project using the terminal or command-line window, structuring the folders how you desire and then creating your IDE solution files afterward. Due to the complexity involved in doing that, we will not discuss how to do that. Instead, we can write one line of code in the first `requirements.txt` file in the root of our repository to work with this configuration.

We will discuss doing that next.

Configuring the requirements.txt file(s)

In the same folder that the `manage.py` file is located in, Visual Studio created for us a `requirements.txt` file. In *Chapter 1*, *Undertaking a Colossal Project*, we already created a blank `requirements.txt` file just so that we can satisfy the needs of Heroku during deployment to each environment that we created. If the `requirements.txt` file in the root of the repository does not exist, Heroku will fail to deploy. Heroku needs that copy in order to identify a project as a Python project; that's just how their test scripts have been written to work. This is why we now have two `requirements.txt` files to work with. The other file, nested one folder down in `/becoming_a_django_entdev/`, is needed to enable all of the features and services that the Visual Studio IDE offers us. This `requirements.txt` file is where we will write all of our required dependencies.

In the `requirements.txt` file found in the root of your local repository, which is the same folder that your `.git` folder is located in, add the following code:

```
# ././requirements.txt in Root Directory
# Path to Visual Studio requirements.txt below
-r becoming_a_django_entdev/requirements.txt
```

The preceding code declares the path to the `requirements.txt` file nested in what we will call the root of our project from now on, `/becoming_a_django_entdev/`. Open the `requirements.txt` file in the root of your project, which is also the same folder that the `manage.py` file resides in, and then add the following items:

```
# requirements.txt
django~=4.0
django-extensions
django-heroku
dj-database-url
gunicorn
python-dotenv
pydotplus
psycopg2
psycopg2-binary==2.8.6
whitenoise
secret-key-generator
```

Make sure each item is located on its own line. Any packages that are required for your project will always be put in this file. You can get even more modular and add other imports to these files, for what is called **cascading requirements files**. This is done the same way, using `-r becoming_a_django_entdev/requirements.txt` to specify the path of the file.

In the preceding example, the `~=` operator is used and indicates greater than or equal to the version number specified. For example, it will provide Django in the version 4.0 range, meaning it will go to 4.0.9 if that exists but it will not provide 4.1 or higher. It will only provide the highest version of the 4.0.X range. The `==` operator would mean to include the package that matches the exact version number specified. Not denoting any version at all means it will grab the latest version that exists for that package at the time of installation, re-installation, or when an upgrade is performed. Anything you would find in the PyPI package library can be placed in this file, requiring that it be installed in your virtual environment.

The `django` package is the most important as it is the basis of the framework we are using. The `django-heroku` package is a package created by Heroku that includes a series of other packages that Heroku itself depends on. Those Heroku dependencies will be automatically installed for you when the parent package is installed. The other packages listed previously will be used in the next sections to help us configure a project properly for how we will be using Django throughout the rest of this book.

Now that we have defined a number of packages to install into a virtual environment, let's create our virtual environment using the Visual Studio IDE.

Using the IDE

For those of you who wish to use the command line instead, skip ahead to the subsection titled *Using the command line*.

Within your Visual Studio IDE, navigate to the **Solution Explorer** section of your IDE, right-click where it says **Python Environments**, and then select **Add Environment**. The window that opens is shown here:

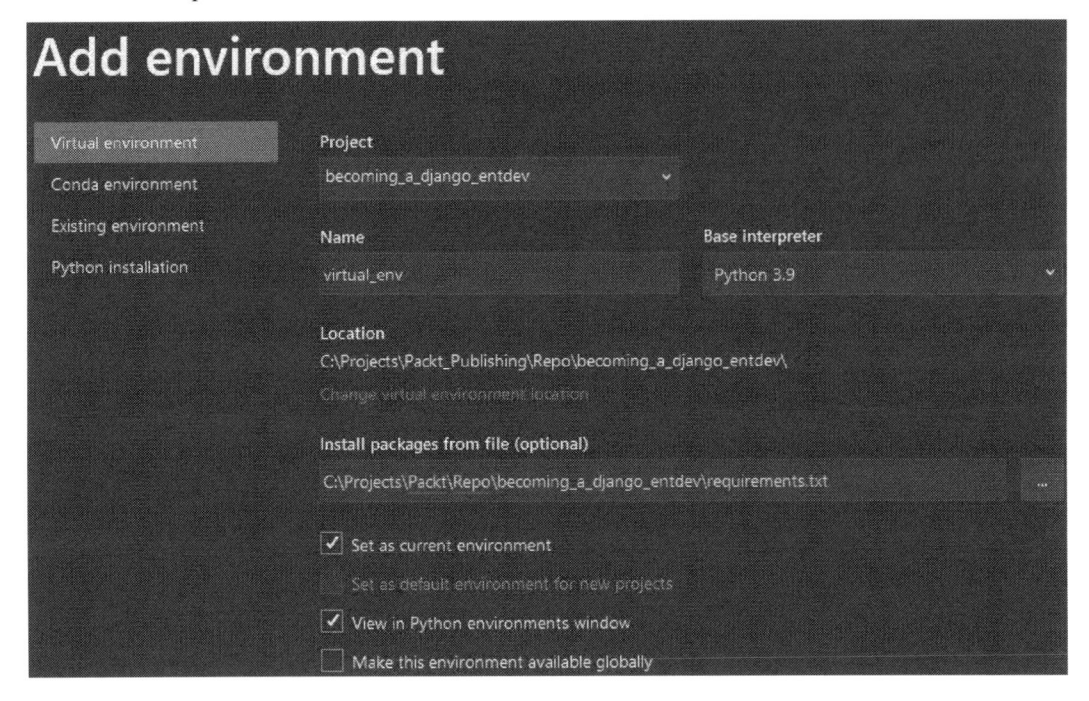

Figure 2.4 – Visual Studio – Add environment

When the window pops up, enter `virtual_env` as the name of your virtual environment and choose your base interpreter. This name can be anything you choose but name it `virtual_env` to be consistent with the examples throughout this book. Python version 3.9 was chosen as the base interpreter at the time of creating this exercise. The location is very important, where it asks whether you want to **Install packages from a file (optional)**; this option refers to the location of your `requirements.txt` file that lives in the same folder as your `manage.py` file. Changing this location may break some of the features of using your IDE, such as operations that work with your virtual environment, and lead you to experience unresolved import issues. Unresolved imports may allow your project to still run, but code highlighting and formatting will often break. You should now see your virtual environment in your **Solution Explorer** and your **Python Environments** window within your IDE, as depicted here:

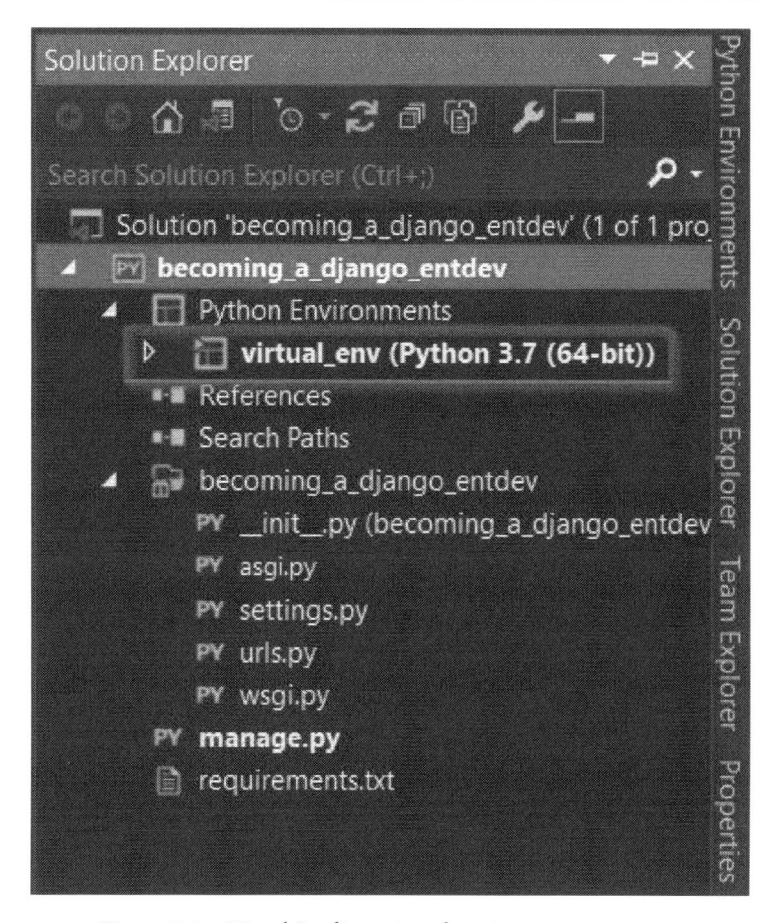

Figure 2.5 – Visual Studio – virtual environment a success

If you did want to install packages later, for instance, if someone added a package to the `requirements.txt` file 2 months from now, a developer could right-click on the virtual environment in the **Solution Explorer** and then select **Install from requirements.txt**. Visual Studio will then update any versions and install any missing packages. Visual Studio and pip do not usually remove unused packages; you may have to manually uninstall a package if you are experiencing conflicts.

Running/activating the project

By now, everything we did should allow us to run a project locally because Visual Studio did a lot of the heavy lifting for us. If you decided not to use the IDE, you cannot currently run your project and would have to work through most of this chapter before achieving this result. In either scenario, you will not currently be able to run your project on Heroku. Using the **Play/Run Web Server** button found at the top of the IDE, select your desired browser, if it provides a dropdown of choices, and then press play, as depicted in the following screenshot:

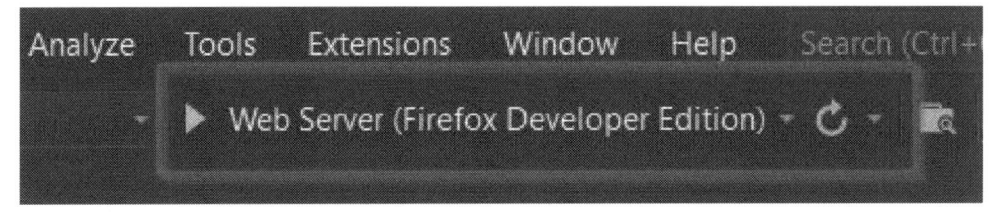

Figure 2.6 – Visual Studio – run project

When play is pressed, a command window will open where you can watch any console messages being printed to the screen and a new tab in the browser chosen will also open. The address in the address bar will point to `http://localhost:#####/` and your project should now be running successfully. The port number will usually be a random number. Visual Studio uses a port that it determines is currently unused on your machine and that is also not a default or reserved port, such as `8000`. This is a built-in feature of Visual Studio for people who run multiple projects side by side, as I often find myself doing.

If you do not see this button, you can add it to your toolbar by right-clicking a blank space in the toolbar area of Visual Studio. In the dropdown that appears, select **Standard** from the list of choices. If you select **Python** from this list, you can include tools that work with your virtual environment directly from your toolbar.

Along with the command-line window that opens up, the browser you selected will also open with a new tab pointing to `http://127.0.0.1:#####/`, where ##### is the random port that Visual Studio used. Here, you will see the iconic landing page for a successful Django installation, as depicted in the following screenshot:

The install worked successfully! Congratulations!

You are seeing this page because DEBUG=True is in your settings file and you have not configured any URLs.

Figure 2.7 – Django installation success

To use the standard port `8000` with the play button in Visual Studio, pointing to `http://localhost:8000/`, follow the steps in the next subsection.

Manually setting a port

We can specify the port number very easily in Visual Studio to control which port each project is using. On the **Project** tab at the top of your IDE, select **becoming_a_django_entdev Properties** from the dropdown that appears. On the tab that opens in your editor, click on the **Debug** tab inside and specify the port number in the field titled **Port Number**.

Next, we'll see how to create a virtual environment using the command line.

Using the command line

For many of you who prefer the terminal or command-line window, a popular module used to create virtual environments that is available for Windows, Mac, and Linux is called `venv`.

Follow these steps to create your virtual environment:

1. Open up your terminal or command-line window and navigate to the local Git repository that we created in *Chapter 1*, *Undertaking a Colossal Project*.
2. Navigate into your first folder called `becoming_a_django_entdev`. This folder should already exist and be populated with files created when using the command line or IDE to start a project earlier in this chapter:

   ```
   PS C:\Projects\Packt\Repo> cd becoming_a_django_entdev
   ```
3. In this directory, the same directory that the `manage.py` file lives in, run the following command to create a virtual environment called `virtual_env`:

   ```
   PS C:\Projects\Packt\Repo\becoming_a_django_entdev>
   python -m venv virtual_env
   ```

   The `venv` module should come standard with all Python installations, but if you have problems running this command on any of the three major platforms, visit the documentation found here to help you debug the issue: https://docs.python.org/3/library/venv.html.
4. For Windows, activate your virtual environment:

   ```
   PS C:\Projects\Packt\Repo\becoming_a_django_entdev>
   virtual_env/Scripts/activate
   ```

   Mac and Linux users should jump to the *Activating the virtual environment* subsection to learn how to activate a virtual environment on those platforms.
5. Next, install the packages defined in the `requirements.txt` file found in the root of a project, where the `manage.py` file lives, by running the following command:

   ```
   PS C:\Projects\Packt\Repo\becoming_a_django_entdev> pip
   install -r requirements.txt
   ```

   An alternative method to creating a virtual environment on Windows, Mac, and Linux is using `virtualenv`, as shown:

   ```
   PS C:\Projects\Packt\Repo\becoming_a_django_entdev> pip
   install virtualenv
   PS C:\Projects\Packt\Repo\becoming_a_django_entdev>
   virtualenv virtual_env
   ```

Now that we have created a virtual environment for our project, let's activate that virtual environment and run the project next.

Activating the virtual environment

Instead of using the IDE, we can activate a virtual environment and run a project directly from the command line. If you already activated your virtual environment in the previous subsection, you can skip this subsection. The following are examples that show how to activate your virtual environment for each major platform (Windows, Mac, and Linux).

Follow these steps to activate your virtual environment:

1. For Windows users, navigate into the root of your project, where the `manage.py` file is located, and then activate your virtual environment by using the following command:

    ```
    PS C:\Projects\Packt\Repo\becoming_a_django_entdev>
    virtual_env/Scripts/activate
    ```

2. Mac and Linux users will need to run the following command instead:

    ```
    PS C:\Projects\Packt\Repo\becoming_a_django_entdev>
    source virtual_env/bin/activate
    ```

If successful, you will now see the following prompt in your terminal, waiting for the next command to be executed from within your virtual environment:

```
(virtual_env) PS C:\Projects\Packt\Repo\becoming_a_django_
entdev>
```

You can only execute standard Django management commands when your virtual environment is activated.

> **Note**
> From now on, the preceding example will be depicted as the following in order to save space, remove clutter, and prevent confusion when providing terminal or command-line examples from within an active virtual environment:
>
> ```
> (virtual_env) PS >
> ```

Now that the virtual environment is activated, let's run our project.

Running the project

If you decided to create your project using the command line and not the Visual Studio IDE, you will not currently be able to run your project. This is because Visual Studio created a local SQLite database, made any necessary migrations, and migrated them automatically for every package that we included in the `requirements.txt` file. For reference, the command to run your project is shown in the following code snippet. You will have to work through the exercises found in the *PostgreSQL* section of this chapter to configure your database before successfully executing the following command. You can come back to this section after having done that.

Making sure you are still in the same folder as the `manage.py` file and that your virtual environment is active, execute the `runserver` command shown here:

```
(virtual_env) PS > python manage.py runserver
```

If this was successful, you will then see the following information printed in your terminal. Whenever you load a page and your project is running, you will see all messages that get printed to the screen in this terminal:

```
Watching for file changes with StatReloader
Performing system checks...

System check identified no issues (0 silenced).
Django version 2.2.24, using settings 'becoming_a_django_entdev.settings'
Starting development server at http://127.0.0.1:8000/
Quit the server with CTRL-BREAK.
```

Manually setting a port

Manually specifying a port number is easy using the terminal or command-line window. However, this must be done every time we run the project, unlike in the IDE where we set it in the configuration of the project within the IDE. The following example adds a port number option to the same `runserver` command used in the previous section, stating to use port 8000 to run the project:

```
(virtual_env) PS > python manage.py runserver 8000
```

Project configuration

All projects need configuring in some way to work with all of the packages and hosts that are involved. We will take the project that we just created and configure files such as `settings.py`, `.env`, `procfile`, and `.gitignore`. Take the `settings.py` file—this file or files will store all of the global constants that are used throughout the code of your project. When packages are used, they usually provide a way to customize the behavior of that package from within the main settings file. Other files, such as `.env` and `procfile`, will be used to prevent deployment issues when working with Heroku as the host. Currently, we would not be able to deploy successfully to the Heroku environment as we have created the project files. Work through the following configuration sections before attempting a successful deployment.

Django settings.py file

In the `settings.py` file that was automatically generated for us when we created a project, we need to add settings specific to our project.

Follow these steps to configure your project settings:

1. At the top of the `settings.py` file, add `import django_heroku` just below the first two imports that exist. Also, add `import dotenv` and `dj_database_url`. These two packages will be used to establish a database connection. The top of your `settings.py` file should look as in the following example:

    ```
    # /becoming_a_django_entdev/settings.py
    import os
    import posixpath
    import django_heroku
    import dj_database_url
    import dotenv
    ```

    Note, that some systems may display `from pathlib import Path` at the top of their files instead of `import os` and `import posixpath`.

    At the bottom of the `settings.py` file, add the following code:

    ```
    # /becoming_a_django_entdev/settings.py
    ...
    django_heroku.settings(locals())
    ```

    This statement will import Heroku-specific settings from the `django_heroku` package.

2. In order for your DNS to work properly, you will need to tell Django that you are allowing a host to gain access to this site. This is a built-in security feature of Django that is intended to block common **HTTP Host Header Attacks**. We also need to add the URLs of each of the Heroku apps to make sure those databases will function properly. Your `ALLOWED_HOSTS` should look similar to the following example:

```
# /becoming_a_django_entdev/settings.py
...
ALLOWED_HOSTS = [
    'your-domain.com',
    'www.your-domain.com',
    'dev.your-domain.com',
    'staging.your-domain.com',
    'becoming-an-entdev.herokuapp.com',
    'mighty-sea-09431.herokuapp.com',
    'pure-atoll-19670.herokuapp.com',
]
```

Some options that are available include a wildcard such as the asterisk character (*), which will allow anything. However, this is not considered a best practice and is extremely insecure. If a domain starts with a single period, like the second entry of the following example, it will also act as a wildcard, allowing all subdomains of the corresponding parent domain. Use these wildcard options with caution if you decide to use them at all:

```
# /becoming_a_django_entdev/settings.py
...
ALLOWED_HOSTS = [
    '*',
    '.your-domain.com',
]
```

3. Starting with Django 3.2, we have to add a variable to the settings file named DEFAULT_AUTO_FIELD. Prior to this version of Django, this was not necessary. This setting tells Django how to process and handle all primary keys of objects. Without this setting, we would otherwise have to add a field called id = models.AutoField(primary_key=True) to every model class that we created. Since this is a daunting task, we can avoid it altogether by using the following example, placed anywhere in our settings.py file:

```
# /becoming_a_django_entdev/settings.py
...
DEFAULT_AUTO_FIELD = 'django.db.models.AutoField'
```

For now, let's just leave the default DATABASES = {...} setting as it is. In the *Preparing PostgreSQL for Heroku* section of this chapter, we will discuss changing this setting for our particular use case. Other examples will be provided for all the supported database types, providing a quick reference when working on a project that does not follow along with every example in this book.

Let's create our environment files next.

Creating an environment file

Heroku will use an environment file called .env to store environment-related variables that are used when running a project in each environment. We use this to tell Heroku things such as what database is being used for each environment or if debug should be turned on/off. Heroku recommends that we use SQLite locally for a Django/PostgreSQL setup but not in their environment apps. It can be configured to use PostgreSQL locally, which we will demonstrate near the end of this chapter. Even if you are using SQLite3 locally, you still need to install the PostgreSQL software suite on your machine in order for the drivers to work with all of your remote connections. We will need to walk through the rest of configuring a project before we can discuss setting up PostgreSQL for use locally.

Local variables

To create your local variables, follow these steps:

1. Run the following command from your project's root directory, where your manage.py file exists:

    ```
    (virtual_env) PS > echo 'DATABASE_URL=sqlite:///
    db.sqlite3' > .env
    ```

    The echo statement is used to create a new file called .env with a single line of content, that content being DATABASE_URL=sqlite:///db.sqlite3.

    Windows users might experience an error message such as UnicodeDecodeError: 'utf-8' codec can't decode byte 0xff in position 0: invalid start byte when trying to run the preceding command. There is an encoding issue that often arises on Windows machines that triggers this kind of error. To overcome this, open your .env file in Notepad++, go to the **Encoding** dropdown, select **UTF-8** from the list of choices, and then save. If that fails, which is possible, just delete the file and recreate it from scratch using Notepad++ to create the file, using the proper encoding.

2. Whichever way this file was created, make sure the following line of code is in your local .env file:

    ```
    # /becoming_a_django_entdev/.env
    DATABASE_URL = sqlite:///db.sqlite3
    ```

    The code we placed in this file points to the location of your SQLite3 database file called db.spqlite3. If you didn't use the Visual Studio IDE to create your project, this file will not exist yet and your project will not currently run.

3. We can also add other variables to this file, and then access those variables using the python-dotenv package in the settings.py file. To access these variables, we have to load the .env file in the settings.py file using the following example:

    ```
    # /becoming_a_django_entdev/settings.py
    ...
    import dotenv
    BASE_DIR = os.path.dirname(
        os.path.dirname(os.path.abspath(__file__))
    )
    dotenv_file = os.path.join(BASE_DIR, ".env")
    if os.path.isfile(dotenv_file):
    ```

```
        dotenv.load_dotenv(dotenv_file)
SECRET_KEY = os.getenv('SECRET_KEY')
```

Place the highlighted code somewhere near the top of the settings.py file, just below the existing BASE_DIR variable. In this example, we also replaced the string value of the SECRET_KEY variable with os.getenv('SECRET_KEY'), with os.getenv() we can access any variable found in the .env file.

4. We need to add the string value of the SECRET_KEY variable that was in the settings.py file to the .env file in order for our project to work locally. Write your variable using the following example, without quotation marks for any string values found in this file:

```
# /becoming_a_django_entdev/.env
...
SECRET_KEY = my_randomly_generated_key
```

That's it, our local variables are now configured. Let's configure our remote variables next.

Remote variables

Remote variables are the same local .env variables that we created, now with values that pertain to each remote environment. Since we will be ignoring the .env file in our repository, which we will discuss in the subsection titled *Creating a .gitignore file*, we need to manually create the SECRET_KEY variable inside of the .env file for each Heroku environment that exists. Since Heroku already created these .env files for us, we will just use this as an opportunity to add the variables that are needed. These steps can also be used at any time during the SDLC to add variables as they are needed.

To add your remote variables, use the Heroku **Command-Line Interface** (**CLI**) to log into your Heroku account and replace the app name provided in the following code block with your Heroku app name:

```
(virtual_env) PS > heroku login
(virtual_env) PS > heroku config:add SECRET_KEY=my_randomly_generated_key --app becoming-an-entdev
(virtual_env) PS > heroku config:add SECRET_KEY=my_randomly_generated_key --app mighty-sea-09431
(virtual_env) PS > heroku config:add SECRET_KEY=my_randomly_generated_key --app pure-atoll-19670
```

In the preceding code, one example is provided for each of the three environments that exist. Execute them one at a time for each of your environments.

It is best to provide a different `SECRET_KEY` value for each environment. In *Chapter 3, Models, Relations, and Inheritance*, after we discuss working with the Django shell in the subsection titled *Generating a SECRET_KEY variable*, we will explore how to generate a `SECRET_KEY` variable in a safer way. Adding that `SECRET_KEY` variable to each Heroku environment will still be done as in this section.

Next, let's create a **Procfile**, short for **process file**.

Creating a Procfile

A **Procfile** is used to store additional project-related settings. Heroku uses the concept of containerization to host all of their apps for all of their clients. This is why we need to create a file with no file extension named `procfile` located in the root of a repository, where the `.git` folder is located. This file tells Heroku where the rest of your project's files live, specifically, the location of the `wsgi.py` or `asgi.py` file inside of the `procfile` file, using standard Python path syntax. The `wsgi.py` file is commonly found in the `project_name` folder of any Django project, upon creation; that folder is found in the same folder that the `manage.py` file resides in. If you wanted to use an asynchronous server gateway interface, you would specify the location of the `asgi.py` file instead.

Hypothetically speaking, if the `manage.py` file and the Django project folder lived in the same folder as the root of a repository, we would include the following path inside of that procfile:

```
# ./Procfile in Root of Repository
web: gunicorn becoming_a_django_entdev.wsgi
```

Our project files are nested one level deep in the `/becoming_a_django_entdev/` folder, as was done using the IDE or when using the `startproject` command to create a project earlier in this chapter. If we tried to add this directory using standard Python path syntax, we would have problems during deployment to Heroku. Instead, in one line of code, tell Heroku to change directory first and then execute the preceding command, using the following code example:

```
# ./Procfile in Root of Repository
web: sh -c 'cd ./becoming_a_django_entdev/ && exec gunicorn becoming_a_django_entdev.wsgi --log-file -'
```

Please use the second example. Only use the first example if you have structured your project to live in the root of your repository and are likely not using Heroku as your host. Heroku will also fail to deploy without the `--log-file -` parameter shown previously. With the `log` parameter, you may read deployment errors from within your Heroku dashboard for each app.

Next, we need to control how the static files are managed when Django is used with Heroku.

Django static files

Traditionally, we do not need to modify the settings files to allow Django to work with static files in a project. In our case, we will need to add to the settings that exist in order for Heroku to work with them. Heroku uses a package called `whitenoise`, installed in the `requirements.txt` file, to work with your static files. These are files such as a `.css`, `.js`, image, or font files that are found in any Django app's `static` folder.

Follow these steps to configure your project to work with the `whitenoise` package:

1. Add the following line to the `MIDDLEWARE` setting found in your `settings.py` file. Add it below any item that already exists in that list:

    ```
    # /becoming_a_django_entdev/settings.py
    ...
    MIDDLEWARE = [
        ...,
        'whitenoise.middleware.WhiteNoiseMiddleware',
    ]
    ```

2. Heroku will also need us to add a variable called `STATICFILES_STORAGE`. Add this variable to your `settings.py` file just above your `STATIC_URL` and `STATIC_ROOT` variables, as shown:

    ```
    # /becoming_a_django_entdev/settings.py
    ...
    STATICFILES_STORAGE = 'whitenoise.storage.CompressedManifestStaticFilesStorage'
    STATIC_URL = '/staticfiles/'
    STATIC_ROOT = posixpath.join(
        *(BASE_DIR.split(os.path.sep) + ['staticfiles'])
    )
    ```

3. Change the value of your `STATIC_URL` and `STATIC_ROOT` variables to equal what is shown in the preceding code, if your value has not already changed.

Our static files should now be wired up properly. At this point in time, we have configured everything locally in order to successfully deploy to any of our remote Heroku environments.

> **Note**
>
> In Django, when a project is run locally, with `DEBUG = False`, static files will fail to load even if they appear in your remote environments. The reason why this happens is that the server is usually configured to handle how it serves up your static files versus Django controlling that, similar to how Heroku uses the `whitenoise` package to serve up its static files. The `whitenoise` package is also used to serve up static files locally when `DEBUG` is set to `False`.

Let's wire up our media files next.

Django media files

Similar to the static files, media file paths need to be configured in order to work with the `whitenoise` package and Heroku. Media files are considered anything that the user uploads to your system, such as an image, audio file, or another document. The two variables, `MEDIA_URL` and `MEDIA_ROOT`, are defined in Django by default as empty strings; we just need to set their values to point to the media folder that we want to place them in. In addition to these settings, additional steps may also be necessary to work with Heroku and media files. Please refer to the detailed Python guide found here to learn more: https://devcenter.heroku.com/articles/s3-upload-python.

To define your media-related variables, in your `settings.py` file, just below your `STATIC_URL` and `STATIC_ROOT` variables, include the following two variables:

```python
# /becoming_a_django_entdev/settings.py
...
MEDIA_URL = '/media/'
MEDIA_ROOT = posixpath.join(
    *(BASE_DIR.split(os.path.sep) + ['media'])
)
```

That's it, this is all that we need to configure in our `settings.py` file to wire up static and media files. In *Chapter 4, URLs, Views, and Templates*, in the subsection titled *Function – static()*, we will need to configure additional URL patterns before these are considered fully integrated into our project.

Before we attempt to deploy, we need to create the `.gitignore` file, which was mentioned earlier, as well as working through the *Preparing PostgreSQL for Heroku* section of this chapter.

Creating a .gitignore file

The last file that we want to create before we deploy is a `.gitignore` file so that we can share only what we want and leave out things like all of those bulky files that are now seen in the `virtual_env` and `.vs` folders. This file will be used to ensure we don't accidentally push any unwanted code to our remote repositories. Once a file has been pushed to a repository, it will always be tracked until it has been deleted; so, we want to make sure we do this first. It's a good idea to also ignore the `.suo` files created by Visual Studio. These files contain user-specific information, such as breakpoint and debugger watches. You will also want to ignore any `build`, `bin`, and `log` files that do not need to be shared with other developers. This is also where we will define a pattern to ignore the `.env` file, which defines the environment-specific variables. We will be creating the `.env` files in development, staging, and production soon when we get to the *PostgreSQL* subsection of this chapter, which will be needed to successfully deploy.

Create a file called `.gitignore` in the root of your repository, where your `.git` folder resides. Then, add the items shown here. They will serve as your ignore patterns:

```
# ./.gitignore in Root of Repository
# Keep Rule
!gitkeep.txt

# Django #
db.sqlite3
*.log
*.pyc
__pycache__

# Media - User Generated Content #
media/
```

```
# Environments #
.env
virtual_env/

# Visual Studio and Visual Studio Code #
*.suo
*.pyproj
*.pyproj.user
*.history
.vs/
obj/

# Heroku
staticfiles/
```

These are just a few examples that relate to our specific Heroku/Django and Visual Studio configuration. Your `.gitignore` file can contain many more ignore patterns. In the source code provided with this book, many other ignore patterns have been provided as examples, broken down into categories that you are welcome to use if you need to.

Ignore patterns accept wildcards such as the asterisk (*) that is used in the preceding examples. They also accept an exclude operator denoted by the exclamation mark (!) symbol. The `!gitkeep.txt` pattern is commonly used in situations where an empty folder is needed to live in a repository, such as the media folder. Git will automatically ignore a folder if nothing exists inside of it; if we place a `gitkeep.txt` file inside that media folder, we can get around this dilemma when ignoring everything within that folder. The media folder is used for user-generated content but we do not want to track files that get placed inside of it. Some of these empty folders are actually needed to prevent errors during runtime, such as when uploading an image to the system and the media folder does not exist yet. Sometimes, this can prevent a fresh clone of a repository from running properly for the first time altogether, depending on the existence of that folder.

You may now push your code to development, staging, or production as you see fit. Just be aware of what remote environment and branch you are pushing to or pulling from, when you perform your Git operations. When this is done, you can visit your Heroku dashboard as was discussed in *Chapter 1, Undertaking a Colossal Project*, to see whether a deployment was successful, and if not, read the logs to see why it failed.

Creating a Django app

In Django, the entire set of files from the folder where your `manage.py` file is located is considered your project. Your project can contain many apps, where an **app** in Django is considered a process that does something within your project, such as logging, trivia, or record keeping, to name a few processes. They can also be something simple, such as a special form field or an event listener that comes from a PyPI package, where that particular package is essentially considered a Django app that we are installing.

Apps are where we write models, views, test cases, forms, admin classes, HTML templates, and static files pertinent to that app. Apps are also where the bulk of the code in a project will exist. They are also designed to be modular where an app can be shared in many projects if we want to. Next, we will create an app for ourselves and call it `chapter_2`. Every upcoming chapter will follow the same app naming convention. We will attempt to organize apps by the content of each chapter in this book. Some chapters may involve every file of the project, which is the case for this chapter of this book. This is because, in this chapter, we are working with the global files of a project. Choose the route you would like to use to create your app, whether that is using the IDE or the command-line-driven approach.

Using the IDE

To create an app easily, right-click the name of your project in the **Solution Explorer**, called **becoming_a_django_entdev**, and then click **Add | Django App...**. When prompted to do so, enter the name `chapter_2`, as shown here:

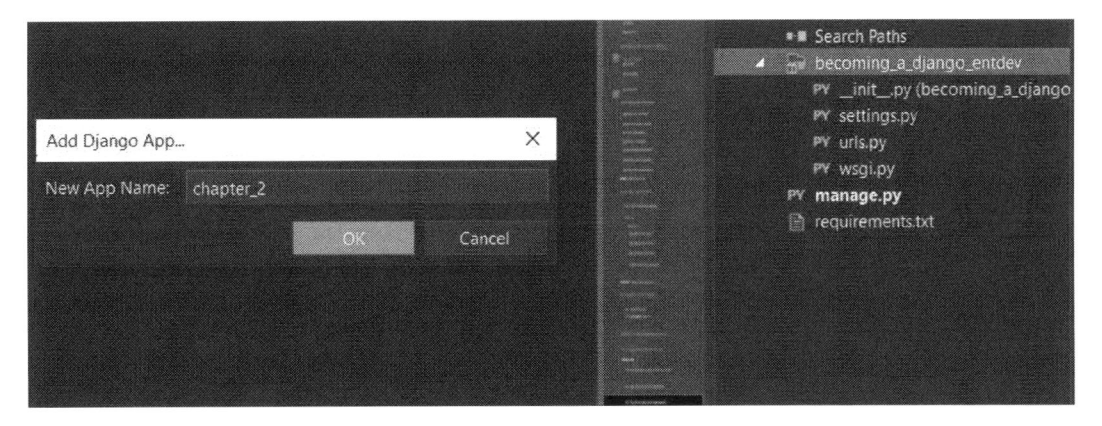

Figure 2.8 – Visual Studio – adding app

In Visual Studio, you can select any folder or subfolder within your project to create a Django app in. Just right-click the folder you want to create that app in instead of the one described previously if you wish to structure your project in a different way.

> **Note**
> Visual Studio will install apps using the version of Django that was installed or updated in the virtual environment. There is no special version 2.1.2 use case like before when we created a project through the IDE; the version of the app files to be installed will be Django 4.0. Also note that you can create an app using the IDE in any directory found in your project root. You are not limited to installing them in the directory used in this exercise.

Let's create a Django app using the command line next.

Using the command line

To create a Django app using the command line, you first need to create the folder structure for that new app. Here, we want it to mimic exactly how the IDE created its folder structure in the previous exercise, to make sure each approach produces the same results and works with the rest of the book. From the same folder that the `manage.py` file lives in, make sure your virtual environment is activated and run the following create folder command. Then, execute the traditional `startapp` command shown after, to create the app called `chapter_2`:

```
(virtual_env) PS > mkdir becoming_a_django_entdev/chapter_2
(virtual_env) PS > python manage.py startapp chapter_2 becoming_a_django_entdev/chapter_2
```

In the preceding examples, we first created the `chapter_2` folder with the `mkdir` command and then executed the `startapp` command. We also provided a parameter that designates the folder that the app will be installed into, the same folder that Visual Studio placed it in for us. Again, you are not limited to installing apps in this directory—adjust where needed throughout this book if you created your folder structure in a different way.

Activating a new Django app

Once a Django app has been created, it will not automatically work in your project until you actually include it as an installed application within Django.

To activate your app, follow these steps:

1. All Django apps must be included in the `INSTALLED_APPS` list. Add your chapter app, as shown:

```
# /becoming_a_django_entdev/settings.py
...
```

```
INSTALLED_APPS = [
    ...
    'django_extensions',
    'becoming_a_django_entdev.chapter_2',
]
DEFAULT_AUTO_FIELD'= 'django.db.models.AutoField'
```

2. Sometimes, it is necessary to tell Django where to look for your app in your directory tree. In the apps.py file of the app you just created, you can specify the location of your app using standard Python path syntax. Modify the value of the name = variable in the following example:

```
# /becoming_a_django_entdev/chapter_2/apps.py
from django.apps import AppConfig

class chapter_2Config(AppConfig):
    name= 'becoming_a_django_entdev.chapter_2'
```

Note that you will have to do this for all future chapter apps that you create.

The project's file structure should now look like the following tree, with the highlighted items being the additions that we have made since we began configuring the virtual environment:

```
├── .git
├── .gitignore
├── procfile
├── requirements.txt
├── readme.md
├── becoming_a_django_entdev
│   ├── .vs
│   ├── becoming_a_django_entdev.sln
│   ├── db.sqlite3
│   ├── manage.py
│   ├── media
│   ├── obj
```

```
|       ├── requirements.txt
|       ├── virtual_env
|       ├── staticfiles
|       └── becoming_a_django_entdev
|            ├── chapter_2
|            ├── __init__.py
|            ├── asgi.py
|            ├── settings.py
|            ├── urls.py
|            └── wsgi.py
```

Next, let's discuss the different types of databases supported by Django.

Using basic database settings

A website by itself is far from useful without a database to talk to; this is why the Visual Studio IDE comes with a lightweight and portable SQLite3 database. Visual Studio will create a file called `db.sqlite3` in the same folder as your `manage.py` file whenever the `startproject` command is executed. If you created your project using the terminal or command-line window, then you will not have a SQLite database that is used in the following configuration examples, and if you attempt to run your project without this database, it will fail. This is one of the five standard database types that Django directly supports. Database types other than the five types that Django directly supports can also be used. We will also provide an example of how to configure other types of databases, such as the Microsoft SQL Server database. Types that are not any of the five standard types will require using a different engine than the engines that Django provides, which means you will need to find a PyPI package to install or write your own for the database type that you are supporting.

The five standard Django database types are as follows:

- **SQLite**
- **MySQL**
- **MariaDB**
- **Oracle**
- **PostgreSQL**

The following examples will help you to configure an existing database of your choice. The last example, PostgreSQL, will be the type used when moving forward with the examples of this chapter. You may use any type for the remaining chapters of this book. There is more to using a database, such as creating tables and performing queries, that will be discussed in the chapters to come. These examples relate to settings written just to establish a working connection to your database, whether that connection is local or remote.

SQLite

SQLite is a **Relational Database Management System (RDBMS)** based on the C language. It is extremely lightweight and portable and is sometimes referred to as the *on-disk* method of choice when it comes to database management. This is the method of choice to get a *proof-of-concept* project up and running in a very short amount of time. This database type can even be shared on drives and repositories for quick transportation and portability of the project and its data. This is not recommended if security is as important to you as it should be.

There are a lot of problems with using this database type in real-world applications and in combination with Heroku like we are doing to host the app. You may find that you can get it to work in a remote Heroku environment momentarily. However, each deployment of your app throughout its life cycle will result in the complete loss of data. For this reason, we will have to deviate from the standard database that comes with Django and rely on a more robust database system for our environment instead.

A standard SQLite3 database configuration will look like the following example:

```python
# /becoming_a_django_entdev/settings.py
...
DATABASES = {
    'default': {
        'ENGINE': 'django.db.backends.sqlite3',
        'NAME': os.path.join(BASE_DIR, 'db.sqlite3'),
    }
}
```

Add additional `default` parameters as needed.

MySQL

MySQL is a more robust SQL RDBMS. It is open source and, just like SQLite, it is compatible with Windows, Mac, and Linux systems. It is made to work as a client-server model, meaning the software is installed on the client's machine in order to perform request operations that the server side will listen to and respond to. MySQL has become one of the most popular and most used database types of all time, especially if you consider all the other database choices that were built using a fork of MySQL.

Follow these steps to configure your MySQL database connection:

1. A standard connection to a MySQL database would look like the following example:

```python
# /becoming_a_django_entdev/settings.py
...
DATABASES = {
    'default': {
        'ENGINE': 'django.db.backends.mysql',
        'NAME': 'database_name',
        'USER': 'database_user',
        'PASSWORD': 'database_password',
        'HOST': 'localhost',
        'PORT': '3306',
    }
}
```

2. In order for this database type to work, you also need to install the following package and include it in your `requirements.txt` file:

```
# requirements.txt
...
Mysqlclient
```

Adjust your default parameters as needed for your project.

MariaDB

MariaDB is actually a fork of MySQL; it is a community-developed version that evolved over time into what it is today. Technical support is available for both the MariaDB and MySQL database types. With both being open source, there is also a lot of information and resources available online for free. MariaDB is not used as much as MySQL but it is still very popular. Since MariaDB is essentially just another MySQL installation, the `ENGINE` in the `DATABASES` configuration of your `settings.py` file will be the same as the example in the previous subsection, titled *MySQL*. Both will also require that you install the same `mysqlclient` package and include it in your `requirements.txt` file.

Oracle

Oracle Database is a multimodel, object-relational database management system created by Oracle. It's primarily used for **Online Transaction Processing (OLTP)** and **data warehousing**. This database is a bit more complicated in terms of its use and capabilities compared to other web development databases. It is intended for enterprise grid computing, which is a method of grouping a series of network computers to act as one larger virtual super-computer. Oracle has developed a database specifically to be used in network cluster configurations such as these. It's considered one of the most complex and robust database systems that exist today and is beyond the scope of this book. Much of the code in this book can still be used with this database type but some alterations may be necessary.

Follow these steps to configure your Oracle database connection:

1. A typical Oracle database connection can be established using the following example:

   ```python
   # /becoming_a_django_entdev/settings.py
   ...
   DATABASES = {
       'default': {
           'ENGINE': 'django.db.backends.oracle',
           'NAME': 'xe',
           'USER': 'database_user',
           'PASSWORD': 'database_password,
           'HOST': 'database_host',
           'PORT': 'database_port_#',
       }
   }
   ```

2. The Oracle database type also requires installing the following package and including it in the `requirements.txt` file:

```
# requirements.txt
...
cx_Oracle
```

Oracle also requires following additional setup and configuration steps and they provide directions on their website here: https://cx-oracle.readthedocs.io/en/latest/user_guide/installation.html.

SQL Server

This is the one database type that is not one of the five standard types supported by Django that we will provide an example of. Developed by Microsoft, the Microsoft SQL Server database type is also a fork of MySQL and is widely used in Microsoft enterprise database systems today. Many systems today rely on this database type, which is often used in combination with Azure-hosted apps.

Follow these steps to configure your Microsoft SQL Server database connection:

1. A Microsoft SQL Server database type can be established using the following connection settings:

```python
# /becoming_a_django_entdev/settings.py
...
DATABASES = {
    'default': {
        'ENGINE': 'sql_server.pyodbc',
        'NAME': 'database_name',
        'USER': 'database_user',
        'PASSWORD': 'database_password',
        'HOST': 'database_host',
        'PORT': '1433',
        'OPTIONS': {
            'driver': 'ODBC Driver 17 for SQL Server',
        },
    }
}
```

2. This database type also requires installing the following packages and including them in your `requirements.txt` file. Depending on your setup, you may only need one or two of the following three packages; however, adding all three will not hurt either:

```
# requirements.txt
...
pyodbc
django-pyodbc
django-pyodbc-azure
```

Next, we will be installing the type used throughout the rest of this book, PostgreSQL.

PostgreSQL

PostgreSQL has become the go-to database of choice for most Django developers when there is no specific reason to use any of the other choices. It is considered an RDBMS, which is a common tool for storing object-oriented data in tables that relate to other tables, known as objects. Its primary features includes **ANSI SQL Compliance** and extensibility, meaning it is a database type built with the idea of people being able to build onto it. It will run on every major operating system, such as Windows, Mac, and Linux, making it versatile.

Standard PostgreSQL settings.py

If you are working with a normal Django project outside of Heroku, configure your PostgreSQL database connection.

Add the following settings to your `settings.py` file:

```
# /becoming_a_django_entdev/settings.py
...
DATABASES = {
    'default': {
        'ENGINE': 'django.db.backends.postgresql',
        'NAME': 'database_name',
        'HOST': 'localhost',
        'USER': 'database_user',
        'PASSWORD': 'database_password',
```

```
        'P'RT': '5'32',
    }
}
```

Since we are working with Heroku, we cannot use the preceding settings even though we are still using PostgreSQL for each remote Heroku environment. The next section will provide us with the settings and tools specific to a Heroku environment, as well as providing the rest of the instructions on how to use PostgreSQL locally.

Preparing PostgreSQL for Heroku

This section is dedicated to actually configuring each of your environments, whether using an IDE or command-line window or terminal. To install and use PostgreSQL, we will need to install it locally and then again in each of our remote environments.

Installing PostgreSQL

This section will guide you through installing the PostgreSQL software needed on your local and remote machines.

Local installation

To use PostgreSQL, we will need to install a suite of software and drivers on each of our machines. In the Heroku dashboards, we will need to include add-ons to get PostgreSQL installed in those environments. To install it on your development machine, you can choose to download the installer for your platform directly from the publisher's website, found here: https://www.postgresql.org/download/. During installation, make note of the port that you set, the password that you create, and whether it asks you to add anything to your environment PATH variables, do so! It is always easier to check/enable these options during installation versus manually configuring them later.

During installation, the installer will ask whether you want to install any development tools, such as database command-line tools or a database management tool. Select **PgAdmin** during the installation of your PostgreSQL drivers; we will be using this tool to demonstrate several examples in this chapter. The PgAdmin management tool is used to access and view the database table structures and the data within them. PgAdmin is also compatible with every major operating system, and it can be downloaded and installed separately from the PostgreSQL installation; it can be found on their website here: https://www.pgadmin.org/download/.

In the .env file found in the local repository that we created earlier, replace DATABASE_URL=sqlite:///db.sqlite3 with the following value:

```
# .env
DATABASE_URL=postgres://postgres:your_password@localhost:5432/local_postgresql
```

Replace the your_password placeholder with the password that you entered during your installation of PostgreSQL and PgAdmin. Replace any other placeholders as needed. The username is usually postgres by default, but this can be changed to something else during installation. We will need to work with a database management tool, PgAdmin, to create a local database before we can actually run the project now. Even if you used the Visual Studio IDE earlier to create your project, it will now be broken.

There is a file called example.env provided with the code of this book that you can use as a reference to make sure your file consists of the proper settings for our software stack.

Remote installation – Heroku dashboard

In Heroku, we have to add PostgreSQL one at a time to all three of our remote environments. There are two ways to do this: through the Heroku dashboard or the Heroku CLI. We will demonstrate both ways. Navigate to the Heroku dashboard, found here: https://dashboard.heroku.com/apps. We should see all three environments, also known as Heroku apps. Click on each app and navigate to the **Resources** tab, scroll down that page, and under **Add-ons**, type Heroku Postgres into the search field provided. Next, it will ask you what plan to choose; you can use the free plan called **Hobby-Dev**, which is what will be used for the demonstrations in this book. Later, you can decide whether upgrading and paying for a new plan is what you need. For more technical needs, these plans include support for increased traffic, the number of connections at one time, the amount of RAM, encryption measures, added security, and so much more. Visit their plans page found here to learn more about what they offer: https://elements.heroku.com/addons/heroku-postgresql.

If successful, you will see that Heroku automatically created a **DATABASE_URL** configuration variable for us. This variable can be found in your Heroku dashboard by going to the **Settings** tab, then scrolling down on the page, under **Config Vars**, and it can be found after clicking **Reveal Config Vars**. The following screenshot also shows us that the same **SECRET_KEY** variable that we created using the CLI earlier in this chapter can also be found here. Any other sensitive environment variables can be created the same way and found here. Clicking the **Add** button eliminates the need to use the CLI to create an environment variable operation:

Figure 2.9 – Heroku – DATABASE_URL

Let's walk through installing PostgreSQL with the Heroku CLI instead of the Heroku dashboard next.

Remote installation – Heroku CLI

Using the Heroku CLI, we first need to log into our account in the terminal or command-line window. The following examples show how to install PostgreSQL on each of our remote environments, starting with production:

```
(virtual_env) PS > heroku login
(virtual_env) PS > heroku addons:create heroku-postgresql:hobby-dev
(virtual_env) PS > heroku addons:create heroku-postgresql:hobby-dev --app mighty-sea-09431
(virtual_env) PS > heroku addons:create heroku-postgresql:hobby-dev --app pure-atoll-19670
```

We have to specify the randomly generated app name that Heroku gave us when we created these environments. If we need to specify the version of PostgreSQL that we want to use, we can do that with the following example. Without specifying a version number, the latest version available will be used:

```
(virtual_env) PS > heroku addons:create heroku-postgresql:hobby-dev --version=10
```

Instead of going to your Heroku dashboard to view these variables, executing the following commands will also display a list of the variables that exist for each environment. Replace the app name for each of the following examples with your Heroku app name:

```
(virtual_env) PS > heroku config --app becoming_an_entdev
(virtual_env) PS > heroku config --app mighty-sea-09431
(virtual_env) PS > heroku config --app pure-atoll-19670
```

Using the PgAdmin tool

PgAdmin is the database management tool that we are going to use to manage all local and remote databases, as well as creating the local database that we need to connect to. This tool should have been installed earlier in the *Installing PostgreSQL* subsection. If it has not been installed, please revisit that subsection for more information.

Creating a local database

Within the **Browser** tab, you should see an existing server connection, such as **PostgreSQL 13**. Other version numbers may be depicted if you installed another version and it's also possible that your system's installation did not create anything in this list. If so, follow the steps to establish a remote database connection in order to create your local server. For those of you for whom this already exists, right-click where it says **Databases** and select **Create | Database....** When the next window opens, give it a database name of your choice and ensure the encoding is set to **UTF-8**, and the owner/user should be set to postgres. The database name I have given to my local database is local_postgresql when referenced in code examples later.

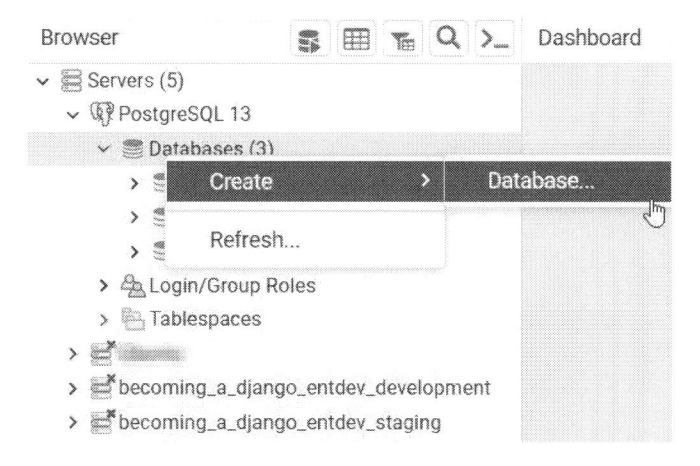

Figure 2.10 – PgAdmin – creating a local database

Next, we will connect to a remote database.

Connecting to a remote database

For each remote database, we need to add a new server connection inside of the PgAdmin tool.

Follow these steps to connect to a remote database:

1. Start by gathering some information from your Heroku account first. In your Heroku dashboard, under each Heroku app, navigate to the **Resources** tab and, under **Add-ons**, click on the **opens in a new tab** icon, as depicted in the following screenshot:

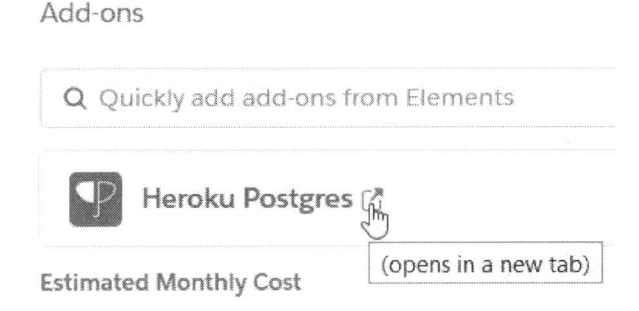

Figure 2.11 – Heroku – opening a database in a new tab

2. In the new browser tab that opens, navigate to the **Settings** tab and make note of the information that is provided. The highlighted fields in the following screenshot are the important pieces that we will need to establish a connection inside the PgAdmin tool. Make note of them:

Please note that **these credentials are not permanent**.

Heroku rotates credentials periodically and updates applications where this database is attached.

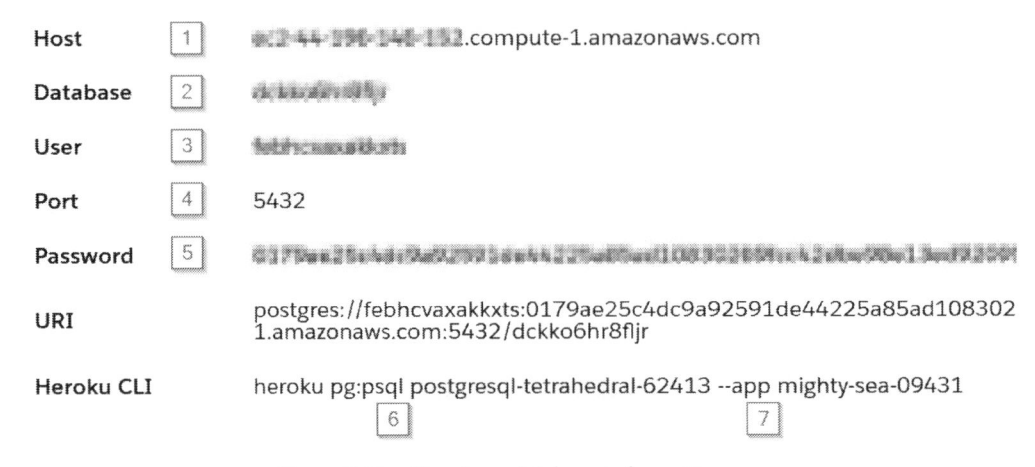

Host	1	●●●●●●●●●●●●.compute-1.amazonaws.com
Database	2	●●●●●●●●●
User	3	●●●●●●●●●
Port	4	5432
Password	5	●●●●●●●●●●●●●●●●●●●●●●●●●●●●●●●●●●●●
URI		postgres://febhcvaxakkxts:0179ae25c4dc9a92591de44225a85ad108302 1.amazonaws.com:5432/dckko6hr8fljr
Heroku CLI		heroku pg:psql postgresql-tetrahedral-62413 --app mighty-sea-09431

Figure 2.12 – Heroku – database information

3. Open PgAdmin and from the top navigation bar of this app, under the **Object** tab, select **Create | Server**. In the window that opens, under the **General** tab, enter any name of your choice. This is to name your server connections for local reference only. Name them so that you know which environment is which, as shown in the following screenshot:

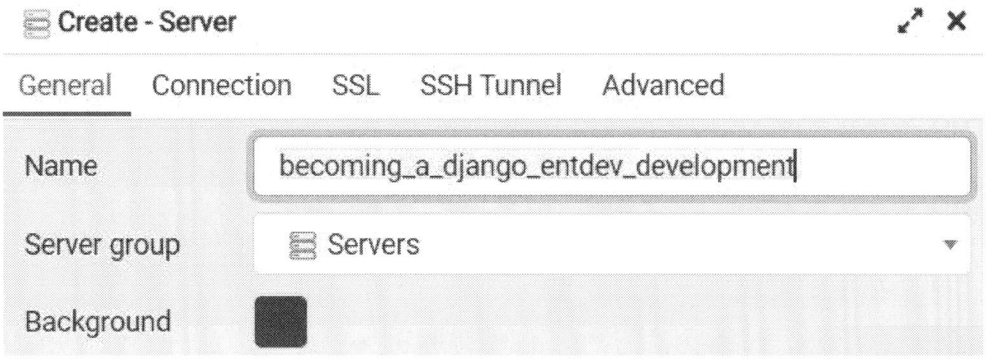

Figure 2.13 – PgAdmin – Create - Server

4. This task only creates your server connection inside the PgAdmin tool; it is not creating the database server itself. Using the information that was found previously in *Figure 2.12*, under the **Connection** tab, fill in the corresponding fields, as highlighted in the following screenshot:

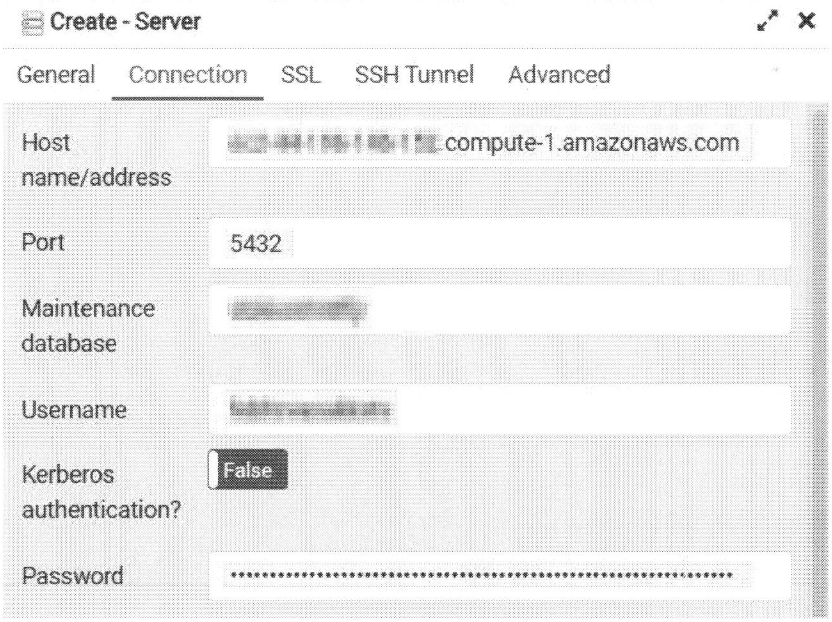

Figure 2.14 – PgAdmin – creating a server connection

5. Replace the value in the field labeled **Maintenance database** with the database name provided by Heroku; do the same for **Username**.
6. If successful, you will now see your new server connection in the **Browser** panel of the **PgAdmin** app. The **Browser** panel is often found on the left-hand side of the PgAdmin program. Since we are using the free plan called **Hobby-Dev**, we will see dozens and dozens of other databases in this list. All but one will be grayed out, just like in the following screenshot:

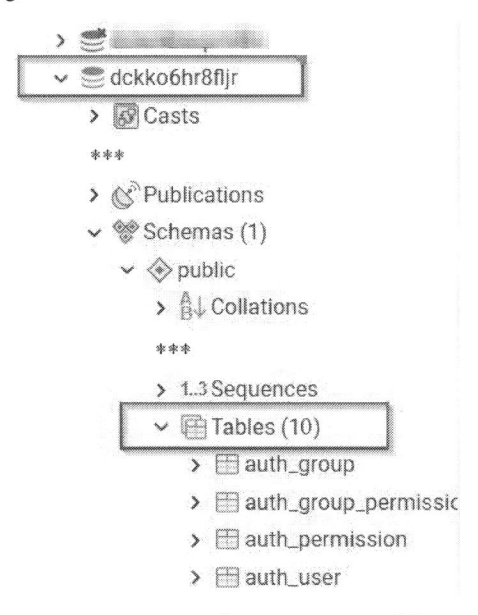

Figure 2.15 – PgAdmin – viewing tables

The one database that is colored is your database name, displayed in *Figure 2.12*. Expand your database and you should be able to gain access; attempting to open any other database will result in **permission denied**. You can avoid a shared plan like this by purchasing a dedicated database hosting plan that Heroku does offer, which is much more secure.

Now, push your file changes to your Git development repository and you should see a successful deployment to your Heroku app.

Next, we will adjust our environment connection settings for use with PostgreSQL locally.

Environment connection settings

For our Heroku configuration, we need to define a default database using the following example, in your `settings.py` file, instead of using a standard PostgreSQL connection setting.

To configure PostgreSQL for use with Heroku and local use, follow these steps:

1. Change your DATABASES variable to use the code shown here:

    ```
    # /becoming_a_django_entdev/settings.py
    ...
    DATABASES = {
        'default': dj_database_url.config(
            conn_max_age=600
        )
    }
    ```

    You can also increase the length of time allowed for established database connections to exist by adjusting the value of conn_max_age. The default value is 600 seconds, which equates to 10 minutes. Since the dj_database_url module will try to log into Heroku using a **Secure Sockets Layer (SSL)** connection, we will have issues running the project locally when connected to a remote database. To avoid those issues, we will have to add the following code to the bottom of the settings.py file.

2. Place the following code under the django_heroku.settings(locals()) line that we placed at the bottom of this file earlier; it should look like the following example:

    ```
    # /becoming_a_django_entdev/settings.py
    ...
    django_heroku.settings(locals())
    options = DATABASES['default'].get('OPTIONS', {})
    options.pop('sslmode', None)
    ```

That's it. Let's build our initial table structures locally next.

Building initial table structures

Next, we need to create the table structures that relate to the models within a project and any third-party packages that we installed. These operations can be performed using the Visual Studio IDE or through a terminal or command-line window. Choose your method from the following.

Using the IDE

In your IDE, you need to perform three actions: make migrations, migrate, and create a superuser, in that order. Within the Visual Studio IDE, go to your **Solution Explorer** and right-click on your project name. In the menu that pops up, under **Python**, select **Django Make Migrations** and then **Django Migrate…**, as shown in the following screenshot. Then, select the **Django Create Superuser** operation:

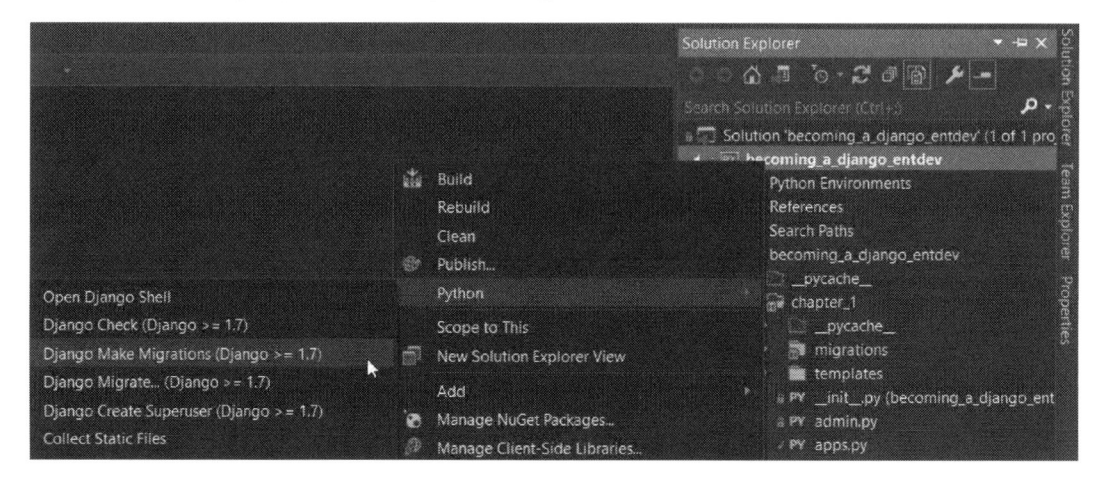

Figure 2.16 – Visual Studio – manage.py commands

Next, we will use the command-line-driven approach.

Commands – makemigrations and migrate

If you are not using an IDE or decide to run your project outside of the IDE, these commands are for you. Make sure you have activated your virtual environment and you are in the same directory as your `manage.py` file. Using the terminal or command-line window, create your table structures in your local database by using the following two examples:

```
(virtual_env) PS > python manage.py makemigrations
(virtual_env) PS > python manage.py migrate
```

Since we have not created any models yet, these two commands will only create the default `User Auth` and other Django management models that come as standard with all Django installations.

Command – createsuperuser

The first time we create database tables, we are required to create a superuser so that we can access the admin panel successfully. Additional users can be created from within the Django admin panel itself or by executing the command again, as shown in the following code snippet. Run this command now to create a superuser:

```
(virtual_env) PS > python manage.py createsuperuser
```

Next, when you are prompted to do so, enter the username, email address, and password that it will ask you to provide. Remember this information as you will need it to access the Django admin site, introduced in *Chapter 6, Exploring the Django Admin Site*.

Remote data migrations

Performing **remote data migrations** means running the same migration commands that we executed for a local database except on each remote database.

To run the migration commands manually for each of the remote environments that we created, we need to activate the **Bash shell** for each one first. Follow these steps to do that:

1. Log into your Heroku account and then execute each of the following commands, one at a time, for each environment that exists. Note that after each shell that is started, you should follow these steps before starting the next shell:

    ```
    (virtual_env) PS > heroku login
    (virtual_env) PS > heroku run bash --app becoming-an-entdev
    (virtual_env) PS > heroku run bash --app mighty-sea-09431
    (virtual_env) PS > heroku run bash --app pure-atoll-19670
    ```

2. For each environment that you activated a Bash shell for, once it has finished loading, you will see your command line now starts with the dollar sign character ($). You will also notice that no matter what directory you were in before, it will put you in the same directory that your .git folder lives in now. Navigate to where your manage.py file is located using the cd command and then run the following migration commands just like we did for a local database:

    ```
    $ cd becoming_a_django_entdev
    $ python manage.py makemigrations
    $ python manage.py migrate
    ```

3. Type exit and wait for it to escape each shell and proceed to the next environment.

Keep in mind that all these commands do is migrate your table structures; they don't actually migrate data found within those tables.

Next, we will practice using the push/pull operations provided by Heroku to migrate data and table structures for us, eliminating the need to run these commands from within the Bash shell.

Heroku database push/pull operations

Heroku has built-in functionality to push and pull data to and from the database indicated. These commands will allow us to merge data and table structures. With this, we can run the `makemigrations` and `migrate` commands locally, populate our database with sample data, and then push it to our other environments, eliminating the need to run these commands individually on each remote environment. You should be very cautious of performing these tasks as it is entirely possible to override or experience a complete loss of data when the wrong operation is executed. The good news is that whenever any of these commands are executed, Heroku will automatically generate a data backup of the current state of your database before any action is performed, allowing you to reverse any action that has been done.

Follow these steps to perform your operations:

1. To visibly see the changes that are happening, navigate to the **Overview** tab of your database dashboard in Heroku. Here, we can see a numeric count of the tables that exist for the remote database we are viewing. We can watch this number to see how a database changes as we execute each `push` or `pull` operation that includes adding or removing tables.

2. Using the information that we gathered from the page in *Figure 2.12*, execute the following command to push your database, including a parameter to indicate which environment we are pushing to:

```
(virtual_env) PS > heroku login
(virtual_env) PS > PGUSER=postgres PGPASSWORD=password heroku pg:push local_postgresql postgresql-tetrahedral-62413 --app mighty-sea-09431
```

Make sure you use the username and password that were specified when creating your local PostgreSQL database. Replace `postgresql-tetrahedral-62413` with the contents of label number **6** in *Figure 2.12*. This is the database name that Heroku generated when we created our database in that environment. The database name can also be found at the top of your database dashboard. Number **7** of that same image is your app name, which is declared using the `--app` parameter. `local_postgresql` is the name I used for my local database.

You should now be able to see a total of 10 tables in the **Overview** tab of your database dashboard. These 10 tables are the standard `Auth` and Django management tables that were created when we first ran the migration commands locally.

Note for Windows users

Windows users might have difficulty executing the preceding command. Make sure the path to your `bin` folder is included in your Windows environment variables settings. That folder is usually found at `C:\Program Files\PostgreSQL\##\bin` on a Windows 10 installation, where ## is the numeric version number of PostgreSQL that is installed on your machine. This will get the `heroku pg:` command and the `psql` command to work from within your CLI. A restart of your CLI or operating system is usually recommended after making changes to your environment variables. The following commands will set variables that are used during the time that your CLI terminal window is open. Running them together on one line in Windows will usually give you errors. When these variables are set and your window remains open, you will be able to run your `push` or `pull` commands as you need them:

```
(virtual_env) PS > heroku login
(virtual_env) PS > set PGHOST=localhost
(virtual_env) PS > set PGUSER=postgres
(virtual_env) PS > set PGPASSWORD=password
(virtual_env) PS > set PGPORT=5432
(virtual_env) PS > heroku pg:push local_postgresql postgresql-tetrahedral-62413 --app mighty-sea-09431
```

If we wanted to pull data instead of push data, that command is just as simple as changing `push` to `pull`, as depicted in the following example:

```
(virtual_env) PS > heroku pg:pull local_postgresql postgresql-tetrahedral-62413 --app mighty-sea-09431
```

For a complete guide on how to use Heroku command-line operations pertaining to PostgreSQL, view their knowledge base article here: `https://devcenter.heroku.com/articles/heroku-postgresql`.

Summary

By now, we have done a lot of work but we still haven't really begun building any Django apps for a project yet. All of the work done up until now can be thought of as the preliminary work necessary before handing over a project to the development team. Two methods of creating a project have been provided: one method using a tool to help streamline production, called an IDE, and another method using commands in a terminal or command-line window. We are tracking a solution file in the repository so that we can share it within a team but we are not tracking personal settings and debug files that are automatically created when running a project. Developers who are not using an IDE can still work with the code base even when sharing project configuration files with those who are using an IDE. After we did that, we configured Django to work with the host provider Heroku on both the project level and the database level. Finally, we activated tools that allow developers to view and edit data inside of a local or remote database.

You can now hand this solution over to your team and begin delegating tasks to each member within that team. In the next chapter, we will start creating models that build tables inside a database. These models can be thought of as the elements that construct the rest of the chapters after *Chapter 3, Models, Relations, and Inheritance*, in this book.

3
Models, Relations, and Inheritance

Models represent tables, also known as objects, within a database. Django provides a simple way to map objects to a project's underlying database(s). We will use this mapping system to work with other components of Django in later chapters of this book, such as a template, view, or form, to name a few. Anything that relies on accessing data from within a database will rely on the models that we create. If a project connects to an external database system or the project uses an API to interact with data, then there is no need to create any models in that situation.

In this chapter, we will cover the following:

- Writing model classes to create database tables
- Using standard field types and third-party field types
- Configuring field validators
- Linking tables through field relationships
- Working with model meta classes and options
- Using model methods and method decorators
- Practicing extending models

- Introducing using the Django shell as a tool to perform queries and add data
- Creating a model manager to format and control data

Technical requirements

To work with the code in this chapter, the following tools will need to be installed on your local machine:

- Python version 3.9 – used as the underlying programming language for the project
- Django version 4.0 – used as the backend framework of the project
- pip package manager – used to manage third-party Python/Django packages

We will continue to work with the solution created in *Chapter 2, Project Configuration*. However, it is not necessary to use the Visual Studio IDE. The main project itself can be run using another IDE or independently using a terminal or command-line window from within the project root folder. This is where the `manage.py` file resides. Whatever editor or IDE you are using, a virtual environment will also be needed to work with the Django project. Instructions for how to create a project and virtual environment can be found in *Chapter 2, Project Configuration*. You will need a database to store the data contained in your project. PostgreSQL was chosen for the examples in the previous chapter; however, any database type that you choose for your project can be used to work with the examples in this chapter.

All of the code created in this chapter can be found in the GitHub repository for this book: `https://github.com/PacktPublishing/Becoming-an-Enterprise-Django-Developer`. The bulk of the code depicted in this chapter can be found in the `/becoming_a_django_entdev/becoming_a_django_entdev/chapter_3/` directory.

Check out the following video to see the *Code in Action*: `https://bit.ly/3zZ68RS`

Preparing for this chapter

Start by creating a new app in your project called `chapter_3` by following the steps discussed in *Chapter 2, Project Configuration*, under the subsection titled *Creating a Django app*. As discussed in that section, don't forget to change the value of the `name =` variable for your app class found in the `/becoming_a_django_entdev/becoming_a_django_entdev/chapter_3/apps.py` file to now point to the path where you installed your app. Be sure to also include this app in your `INSTALLED_APPS` variable found in the `settings.py` file as well.

Writing model classes

Each model in your project represents a table within your database. The fields that are created in those models all relate to columns within that table. Django provides a technique called **Object-Relational Mapping** (**ORM**) to map models to the underlying database(s) that are configured in the settings.py file of a project. The ORM technique is a process used to convert data between two systems of incompatible data types. This means that Django takes the headache out of working directly with **Structured Query Language** (**SQL**) to perform queries. The Django ORM irons out odd differences between the various database types when interpreting SQL, making it a universal tool for working with all data structures. Now, you and your developers can focus more on developing and less on the headaches involved. Django does not require the use of SQL as a standard writing practice. However, if you want or need to, Django does provide a way to use basic SQL when performing query operations.

Next, imagine we are building a site that allows a user to view a page providing details about a specific car, commonly referred to as a detail page/view. Let's say we are building a basic site just to store and look up details about cars that are listed for sale. A user could do this for a number of reasons; perhaps they are renting, buying, leasing, or selling a car. In any scenario, we would need a table that represents a vehicle object, another table for the model of the vehicle (not to be confused with a Django model), and another table for the engine type. In a real-world scenario, your project may consist of many other tables and the structure of these tables may also differ in many ways. In this particular exercise, we won't create a model for the manufacturer, also known as the make of a vehicle. The manufacturer will be created as a set in order to demonstrate certain concepts for educational purposes:

1. Inside the models.py file of the chapter_3 directory that was just created, write three empty classes, one for each of the tables related to our vehicle exercise, following this example:

    ```
    # /becoming_a_django_entdev/chapter_3/models.py
    from django.db import models

    class Vehicle(models.Model):
        pass
    ```

2. Create one class each for Vehicle, VehicleModel, and Engine. We will name the class pertaining to a model of a vehicle as VehicleModel instead of Model in order to prevent confusion as we work through each exercise.

> **Tip**
> In the preceding example, three classes were created that do absolutely nothing at this time by writing the `pass` statement directly in them. This is a tool to add to your toolbox for writing skeleton code and allowing other components to continue to function while you write. Python will give you errors if nothing is placed in a class and when you are ready to write code for that class, remove the `pass` statement and replace it with your actual code.

The names given to model classes can be almost anything you would like, but they cannot be any of the reserved Python keywords, such as `True`, `False`, `class`, `pass`, and `import`. Name your classes anything that makes sense when you are using them elsewhere in your code. You can use uppercase or lowercase letters, but when Django creates your tables, the names will always be lowercase. This is why it is unacceptable to name two different classes the same name with different letter casings. For example, if we named two classes `class Vehicle` and `class vehicle`, Django would then tell us we have the following `RuntimeError` when attempting to make migrations:

```
RuntimeError: Conflicting 'vehicle' models in application 'chapter_3':
```

This is why it is better to adopt a writing style that uses one or the other letter casing and stick with that pattern throughout your project.

Let's discuss the various field types that exist and see which ones we can use for our vehicle exercises.

Standard field types

Right out of the box, Django offers numerous **Standard Field Types** to choose from. The following tables can be used as cheat sheets when writing your models:

AutoField	EmailField	PositiveIntegerField
BigAutoField	FileField	PositiveSmallIntegerField
BigIntegerField	FilePathField	SlugField
BinaryField	FloatField	SmallAutoField
BooleanField	ImageField	SmallIntegerField
CharField	IntegerField	TextField
DateField	GenericIPAddressField	TimeField
DateTimeField	JSONField	URLField
DecimalField	NullBooleanField	UUIDField
DurationField	PositiveBigIntegerField	

Relationship Fields
`ForeignKey`
`ManyToManyField`
`OneToOneField`

For a complete breakdown of all of the field types to choose from, you can visit the official Django documentation on field types here: `https://docs.djangoproject.com/en/4.0/ref/models/fields/`.

Field arguments

Every field class will accept **arguments**, also known as **field options**. They customize the behavior, or rather the field constraints, that are being created. **Field constraints** are the rules enforced on the data within your tables. In the code we will soon write, we will be using the `verbose_name`, `blank`, and `null` arguments on our fields quite often. `verbose_name` will specify the human-readable name for a field. We should specify a `max_length` argument for any `CharField` instances that we use, to limit the character length of that field. Without setting a `max_length` argument, the character length limit is theoretically unlimited. However, you are limited by the physical restrictions of the database that you are using; the limit would then be several thousand or hundreds of thousands of characters instead of the literal infinite limit. The `null` and `blank` arguments are almost considered the same thing, except that the `null` argument says that the database can store a null value for any empty records. The `blank` argument is related to validation performed on that field, at the database level, to check whether a user attempted to enter a null value when saving or creating that record in the database.

A `default` argument will be used to assign a value to a field by default, should a value not be provided at the time an object is created or updated. Default values are used in circumstances where, say, data is being migrated into your database from an outside source, with data that isn't in synchronization with the constraints set on your tables. For example, if you had a field argument set to `null=False` and you imported data that contained a null value, errors would likely result. Say you had a `BooleanField` with the `default=True/False` argument, and then performed the same data import; then, all those null values would be converted to `True/False` automatically during your import. A `default` argument can be applied to virtually every field type.

The `choices` argument allows us to pass in a predefined set of choices that contain a value and a human-readable interpretation of that value. Choices can be used on `CharField` and `BooleanField` instances, as well as a handful of other field types. They can be made into a drop-down select box or be used in a collection of checkboxes or radio buttons. The `choices` argument accepts a list of tuples, where each tuple consists of the first element being the value of the field and the second element being the human-readable string representation of that value. For this exercise, we will be converting the human-interpreted *yes/no* choices into a computer-interpreted *true/false* value on a `BooleanField`. We will also apply this technique to the manufacturer/make field later in this chapter, in order to store an integer value.

Another argument that can be useful is the `editable=False` attribute. This attribute would render a field hidden in any form object within a template. This field would not be visible or editable by the user in any way. The `unique=True` argument can also be useful. This argument states that two rows/records in your table cannot have the same value for that particular field. This would be useful if, say, an email field is used as a unique identifier for a model, preventing duplicates from existing. We would get conflicting results with errors telling us that the email address already exists when saving or creating a new record.

Model field arguments differ from form field arguments in that the model arguments will apply rules to your columns on the database level. Your form field arguments, which we will cover in *Chapter 5*, *Django Forms*, are rules that only apply to a field as it is used within a particular form. This means you can set `blank=True` on a model field, making it not required on the database level but in a `required=True` form field set, making it required for that particular form. Alternatively, we could make that field required in all forms by setting the constraint at the database level using `blank=False`. Keep that in mind when writing your model classes.

Next, let's begin writing the different fields that are needed for our vehicle scenario.

Adding a standard field type

From the Django fields list provided earlier, we will use `CharField` for each of the models. `CharField` will be used to provide a name for each item as we add them to the database, except for the `Vehicle` model class. For the `Vehicle` model, we will use `CharField` as the **Vehicle Identification Number** (**VIN**), because a VIN accepts a combination of both letters and numbers. We also need a `BooleanField` on the `Vehicle` model, to store a value indicating whether or not this vehicle has been sold. This is the field where we will create a list of *yes/no* choices to use instead of the *true/false* values.

Follow these steps to create the fields for each of your model classes. Remember to remove the `pass` statement:

1. In your `/chapter_3/models.py` file, create the set of *yes/no* choices above your model classes and below your `import` statements, as depicted:

   ```
   # /becoming_a_django_entdev/chapter_3/models.py
   from django.db import models

   YESNO_CHOICES = (
       (True, 'Yes'),
       (False, 'No')
   )
   ...
   ```

2. Add the following field to your `VehicleModel` class:

   ```
   # /becoming_a_django_entdev/chapter_3/models.py
   ...
   class VehicleModel(models.Model):
       name = models.CharField(
           verbose_name = 'Model',
           max_length = 75,
           unique = True,
           blank = True,
           null = True,
       )
   ```

3. Add the following field to your `Engine` class:

   ```
   # /becoming_a_django_entdev/chapter_3/models.py
   ...
   class Engine(models.Model):
       name = models.CharField(
           verbose_name = 'Engine',
           max_length = 75,
           blank = True,
           null = True,
       )
   ```

4. Add the following fields to your `Vehicle` class:

```python
# /becoming_a_django_entdev/chapter_3/models.py
...
class Vehicle(models.Model):
    vin = models.CharField(
        verbose_name = 'VIN',
        max_length = 17,
        unique = True,
        blank = True,
        null = True,
    )
    sold = models.BooleanField(
        verbose_name = 'Sold?',
        choices = YESNO_CHOICES,
        default = False,
        blank = True,
        null = True,
    )
```

The `name` field on the `VehicleModel` class shown previously will use the `unique` argument, allowing only names that do not already exist in that table. The `name` field on the `Engine` class will not use the `unique` argument, so we can allow engines of the same name but assign them to different vehicle models. The `YESNO_CHOICES` variable is used as a global variable placed outside of any model class so that it can be used in many fields if needed. If a variable or set of choices is extremely unique, then it is best practice to place it above your field declarations, within the model class that is it being used in. You could also store these variables in an entirely separate file as well, as long as the code remains clean and simple.

> **Note**
>
> The preceding code is a relaxed style of the PEP-8 style guide where we are placing each argument on its own line, separated by a comma while also following basic Python indentation rules. Most of the code throughout this book will be written in this way.

5. Run the Django `makemigration` and `migrate` commands, as shown:

```
(virtual_env) PS > python3 manage.py makemigrations
Migrations for 'chapter_3':
  becoming_a_django_entdev\chapter_3\migrations\0001_initial.py
    - Create model Engine
    - Create model Vehicle
    - Create model VehicleModel
(virtual_env) PS > python3 manage.py migrate
Operations to perform:
  Apply all migrations: admin, auth, chapter_1, chapter_3, contenttypes, sessions
Running migrations:
  Applying chapter_3.0001_initial... OK
```

Every time a model is changed, created, or deleted, these Django migration commands will need to be executed in order to prevent runtime errors. They can be executed from either your IDE or within a command line or terminal window, executed from within your project's root directory, where your `manage.py` file lives. Refer to *Chapter 2, Project Configuration*, in the subsection titled *Building initial table structures* to learn more about the different ways to execute these commands.

If those two Django migration commands were successful, three more tables will have been created in your database. When viewed from within your PgAdmin tool or any other database management tool that you decided to use, those tables will look similar to as in the following screenshot:

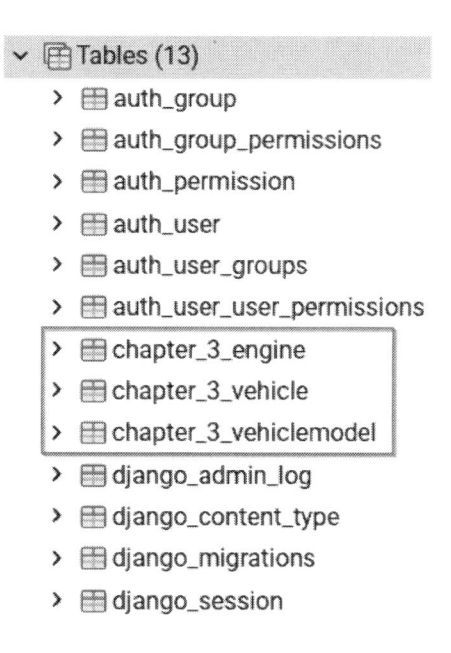

```
∨ ⊞ Tables (13)
    > ⊞ auth_group
    > ⊞ auth_group_permissions
    > ⊞ auth_permission
    > ⊞ auth_user
    > ⊞ auth_user_groups
    > ⊞ auth_user_user_permissions
    > ⊞ chapter_3_engine
    > ⊞ chapter_3_vehicle
    > ⊞ chapter_3_vehiclemodel
    > ⊞ django_admin_log
    > ⊞ django_content_type
    > ⊞ django_migrations
    > ⊞ django_session
```

Figure 3.1 – PgAdmin – created vehicle, model, and engine tables

If we needed to use fields that don't come standard in Django, such as `AddressField`, `MoneyField`, or `PhoneField`, we would have to install packages and also configure settings before we can use them. Let's prepare our project next to let us do just that, by integrating `MoneyField` into these examples.

Third-party field types

A **third-party field type** is a custom field created by a third-party provider. There are many other PyPI packages that can add field types to your arsenal: dozens and dozens more. For example, some of my favorite and most used include an address field, phone field, rich text field, money field, and even an image cropping tool. The `django-address` package uses the Google Maps API to suggest addresses related to what the user has typed as the user is typing into a single text field. This means that the package provides the model class as well as the form field class it creates and any other related tools. Related tools such as, all of the JavaScript and CSS libraries that help a form work. The `django-image-cropping` tool is also very powerful: it allows a user to upload an image and let the user crop the image however they desire.

There is a package specifically made to handle currency called `django-money`. This package takes `DecimalField` from the list of standard field types and provides many different actions that involve working with money in a financial industry-accepted way. The `django-money` package provides definitions for all currencies that exist today and includes their corresponding currency sign. In addition to performing arithmetic operations, such as addition and subtraction, currencies can also be converted from one sign to another using current exchange rates. This means that this package will communicate with an API to retrieve that information.

The `django-phone-field` package will accept a phone number that is rather versatile. The phone field allows for country codes and accepts special characters so that it can be masked to any format you need. The `django-ckeditor` package is a tool used for adding rich text editors to your pages, allowing users to enter HTML into one of your form fields. If you're using django CMS, they also make a version of the django-ckeditor package specifically for use with the django CMS package.

Here is a short list of third-party field types to add to your field type cheat sheet from before:

- `AddressField` – https://pypi.org/project/django-address/
- `ImageCropField` – https://pypi.org/project/django-image-cropping/
- `MoneyField` – https://pypi.org/project/django-money/
- `PhoneField` – https://pypi.org/project/django-phone-field/
- `RichTextField` – https://pypi.org/project/django-ckeditor/
- (*django CMS*) `RichTextField` – https://pypi.org/project/djangocms-text-ckeditor/

Next, we will add `MoneyField` to our `Vehicle` model class.

Adding a third-party field type

Since some of the fields, such as `AddressField`, require obtaining a personal Google API key directly from Google, we will not be using that field type. We will only demonstrate using one of these third-party field types and then move on to the next topic.

To include `MoneyField` in a project, follow these steps:

1. Add `django-money` to your `requirements.txt` file and install it in your virtual environment or run the following command to manually install this package. Make sure your virtual environment is already activated:

   ```
   (virtual_env) PS > pip install django-money
   ```

2. In your `settings.py` file, add the following app to your `INSTALLED_APPS` list:

   ```
   # /becoming_a_django_entdev/settings.py
   ...
   INSTALLED_APPS = [
       ...,
       'djmoney',
       'becoming_a_django_entdev.chapter_3',
   ]
   ```

   Make sure it is located above your local apps and below all of your `django.contrib` apps, as shown previously, where it is placed before the `chapter_3` app.

3. Using `MoneyField`, you can specify the different currencies available in your project within the `settings.py` file. In the following example, we specify the US dollar and European euro as the two currencies available in this project:

   ```
   # /becoming_a_django_entdev/settings.py
   ...
   CURRENCIES = ('USD', 'EUR')
   CURRENCY_CHOICES = [
       ('USD', 'USD $'),
       ('EUR', 'EUR €')
   ]
   ```

4. Add the following highlighted `import` statement to the top of your `/chapter_3/models.py` file:

   ```
   # /becoming_a_django_entdev/chapter_3/models.py
   from django.db import models
   from djmoney.models.fields import MoneyField
   ```

5. In your `Vehicle` class, add the price field shown here:

```
# /becoming_a_django_entdev/chapter_3/models.py
...
class Vehicle(models.Model):
    ...
    price = MoneyField(
        max_digits = 19,
        decimal_places = 2,
        default_currency = 'USD',
        null = True,
    )
```

You will also need to use the field arguments depicted in the preceding example (adjust the values as needed).

Let's explore what validation we can apply to the field types that we are using.

Model field validators

Field validators are database-level rules that can be set on model fields. They are useful in situations where instead of `DecimalField`, using a `max_length` argument to control the character length, we are defining a minimum or maximum numeric value. A Django **model field validator** is a callable that allows us to take in a value and then perform an operation to see whether it meets certain criteria, raising `ValidationError` if that criterion is not met. Since this is a callable, you can write your own function to suit your needs or use one of the many different callable functions that come included with Django. For instance, we could use the `MinValueValidator` and `MaxValueValidator` functions when specifying a constraint for a minimum or maximum numeric value. You can view a complete list of validator functions provided by Django here: https://docs.djangoproject.com/en/4.0/ref/validators/.

Setting a field validator

`MoneyField` offers a few of its own field validators that add constraints on currency values of whatever type is defined in your project. The money validators take the leg work out of using a Django `DecimalValidator` or writing your own callable method.

Follow these steps to set your validator on the existing `Vehicle` model:

1. At the top of your `/chapter_3/models.py` file, and just below your existing `import` statements, add the following `import` statement:

   ```
   # /becoming_a_django_entdev/chapter_3/models.py
   ...
   from djmoney.models.validators import MaxMoneyValidator, MinMoneyValidator
   ```

2. Whether it is a standard Django field validator or another one provided by a third-party package, it will go in the validator argument of a field, as shown on the `price` field of the `Vehicle` model here:

   ```
   # /becoming_a_django_entdev/chapter_3/models.py
   ...
   class Vehicle(models.Model):
       ...
       price = MoneyField(
           max_digits = 19,
           decimal_places = 2,
           default_currency = 'USD',
           null = True,
           validators = [
               MinMoneyValidator(
                   {'EUR': 500, 'USD': 400}
               ),
               MaxMoneyValidator(
                   {'EUR': 500000, 'USD': 400000}
               ),
           ])
   ```

These functions usually take in one or more arguments themselves. In this example, we are specifying the parameters for the minimum and maximum currency values. The preceding example states that all Euro (`EUR`) values should be between 500 and 500,000 Euros and the American dollar values (`USD`) should be between 400 and 400,000 dollars. These are rough estimates used for demonstration only and are not exact conversion rates.

Currently, our three model classes exist independently from one another. This means they are not linked to each other in any way just yet. We will need them to be related to one another before we are done. Next, we will be linking those tables by working with model field relationships.

Working with model field relationships

Django provides three relationship types for linking tables:

- **Many-to-one**
- **Many-to-many**
- **One-to-one**

A *many-to-one* relationship is defined by using a `ForeignKey` field, and the other two relationship types are defined using the self-explanatory `ManyToManyField` and `OneToOneField`. These fields are named appropriately after the relationship type that they represent.

Next, we will discuss the key components of working with model field relationships.

Field arguments

The three field types, `ForeignKey`, `ManyToManyField`, and `OneToOneField`, all accept the standard `default`, `blank`, and `verbose_name` field arguments that other field types accept. The `null` argument will have no effect on a `ManyToManyField` and will only apply to the `ForeignKey` and `OneToOneField` types. Two of these field types—`ForeignKey` and `OneToOneField`—require at least two positional arguments, the first being the model class that the field relates to and the second being the `on_delete` argument. Positional means they need to be in that order and required means they must be specified. The `on_delete` argument specifies what the database will do with records from related tables if a parent or child object is deleted.

The `on_delete` choices include the following:

- `models.CASCADE` – used to automatically delete any related objects when an object is deleted from that table.
- `models.PROTECT` – used to prevent deletion of any of the objects.
- `models.RESTRICT` – used to prevent deletion in certain scenarios.
- `models.SET_DEFAULT` – used to set the field of related objects to a default value.

- `models.SET_NULL` – used to set the field of related objects to a null value.
- `models.SET()` – accepts a callable to write your own function for setting a value.
- `models.DO_NOTHING` – will take no action; using this option could cause **IntegrityError** and should be used with caution.

We will set the value for the `on_delete` argument to `models.CASCADE`, ensuring that if a `Vehicle` is deleted from the database, nothing will happen to the related `VehicleModel` and `Engine` objects. But if we deleted a `VehicleModel` or `Engine` object from the database, the related `Vehicle` that depends on that soon-to-be-deleted object will also be deleted. If we want to preserve `Vehicle` in the scenario of when either of those two is deleted, we should use the `models.SET_DEFAULT` value instead.

The three field types—`ForeignKey`, `ManyToManyField`, and `OneToOneField`—all allow for us to follow relationships forward and backward when performing queries, which means if you query a parent object, you can follow that lookup forward to get all of its child objects. A reverse lookup would mean you query a child object and follow its lookup backward to get its parent object. These forward and reverse relationships are defined on fields by using the `related_name` and `related_query_name` arguments, which will soon be demonstrated.

A `ForeignKey` field and `ManyToManyField` can accept a `limit_choices_to` argument, which applies a filter to the related queries. The `limit_choices_to` argument will accept a dictionary or Q object. It will also accept a callable function that returns either a dictionary or Q object.

> **Note**
>
> A **Q object** will encapsulate a SQL expression in a Python object used in database-related operations. Q objects add advanced-level query operations that sometimes a `filter()`, `all()`, or `order_by()` statement cannot provide. To learn more about complex lookups with Q objects, visit the official Django documentation here: `https://docs.djangoproject.com/en/4.0/topics/db/queries/#complex-lookups-with-q-objects`. To learn more about performing queries in general, jump ahead to the section titled *Performing queries* later in this chapter.

Continuing on with our vehicle classes, we can apply some of these model relations and arguments to the classes we already wrote. They will help us link a hypothetical `Seller` to a `Vehicle`, a `Vehicle` to a `VehicleModel`, and that `VehicleModel` to an `Engine`.

Field type – ForeignKey

We will be using a `ForeignKey` field to represent a *many-to-one* relationship between the `Vehicle` class and the `VehicleModel` and `Engine` classes.

Follow these steps to create your `ForeignKey` field:

1. In your `/chapter_3/models.py` file, add the following two fields to your existing `Vehicle` model class, as shown:

    ```python
    # /becoming_a_django_entdev/chapter_3/models.py
    ...
    class Vehicle(models.Model):
        ...
        vehicle_model = models.ForeignKey(
            VehicleModel,
            on_delete = models.CASCADE,
            verbose_name = 'Model',
            related_name = 'model_vehicle',
            blank = True,
            null = True,
        )
        engine = models.ForeignKey(
            Engine,
            on_delete = models.CASCADE,
            verbose_name = 'Engine',
            related_name = 'engine_vehicle',
            blank = True,
            null = True,
        )
    ```

2. In your `/chapter_3/models.py` file, add the following field to your existing `Engine` model class, as shown:

    ```python
    # /becoming_a_django_entdev/chapter_3/models.py
    ...
    class Engine(models.Model):
        ...
        vehicle_model = models.ForeignKey(
            VehicleModel,
    ```

```
            on_delete = models.CASCADE,
            verbose_name = 'Model',
            related_name = 'model_engine',
            blank = True,
            null = True,
        )
```

3. Now, run your Django migration commands one more time, as discussed in the subsection titled *Building initial table structures* in *Chapter 2, Project Configuration*. You can see the two fields that we created, `vehicle_model` and `engine`, are now in the list of columns shown in our database management tool:

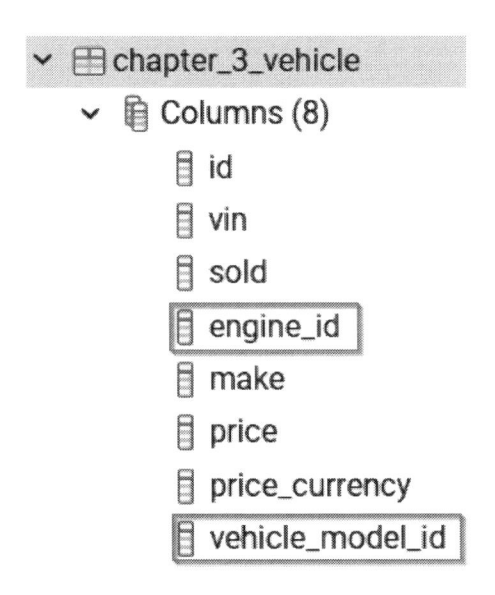

Figure 3.2 – PgAdmin – ForeignKey field

In the preceding screenshot, these fields are shown as `vehicle_model_id` and `engine_id`. The `_id` suffix automatically gets added to the column name in your database.

Field type – ManyToManyField

Here, we will represent a *many-to-many* field relationship between a seller and the vehicles they are selling with a `ManyToManyField` type. `ManyToManyField` will not accept the `on_delete` argument. Instead, when a child or parent is deleted, the other will always remain in your database since many other objects could relate to it as well.

Follow these steps to create `ManyToManyField`:

1. In your `/chapter_3/models.py` file, create a new `Seller` model class with a `name` field and a `vehicle` field to use as your *many-to-many* relationship. Your code should now resemble the following example:

   ```
   # /becoming_a_django_entdev/chapter_3/models.py
   ...
   class Seller(models.Model):
       name = models.CharField(
           verbose_name = 'Seller Name',
           max_length = 150,
           blank = True,
           null = True,
       )
       vehicle = models.ManyToManyField(
           Vehicle,
           verbose_name = 'Vehicles',
           related_name = 'vehicle_sellers',
           related_query_name = 'vehicle_seller',
           blank = True,
       )
   ```

   We will link `ManyToManyField` to the `Vehicle` model class in the first positional argument. It's given a `related_name` argument with a value of `vehicle_sellers` and a `related_query_name` argument with a value of `vehicle_seller`. These two arguments are used for linking and mapping to this field later on in *Chapter 10, Database Management*.

2. Go ahead and run your Django migration commands one more time. You should see the columns that were created for this table in your database management tool, similar to the following screenshot:

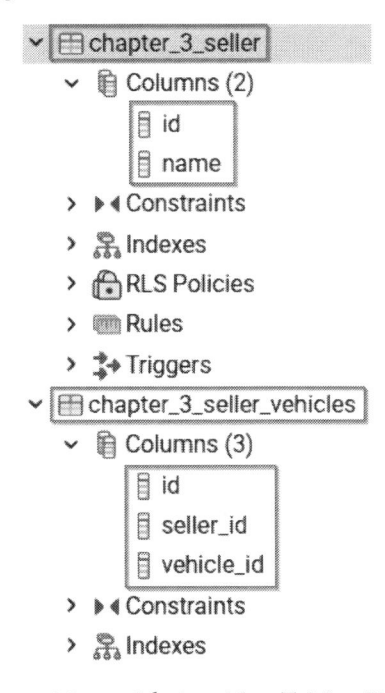

Figure 3.3 – pgAdmin – ManyToManyField

We should also see any additional tables that automatically get created, which are used to manage the relationships between `Seller` and `Vehicle`. That table is shown in the preceding screenshot as **chapter_3_seller_vehicle**.

Mutable versus immutable objects

Mutability is a fundamental concept of the Python language and is broken down into mutable and immutable objects. An object is said to be **mutable** if its values can change over time. If an object's value will not change, then that object is said to be **immutable**. In Python, an object's mutability is also defined by the data type that it is. For example, mutable objects are represented using a *list*, *dictionary*, *set*, or *QuerySet*. Immutable objects are defined by using the *bool*, *decimal*, *float*, *int*, *range*, *string*, and *tuple* data types. Queries will perform better if the object being searched is immutable rather than mutable. Most of the time, the difference is miniscule, literally in nano-or milliseconds. When your project goes live and your database starts to collect thousands, if not millions, of records, the time it takes to query something will then be noticed when it takes seconds, if not minutes or tens of minutes, to complete a single query.

For example, we could represent a set of choices as a `PositiveIntegerField` using a tuple object to associate a human-readable string representation to a numeric integer value. Take the make/manufacturer of a vehicle that was mentioned earlier in this chapter. We don't really need a table to store this information unless we have other related information that needs to be stored or have a project requirement stating that the user should have the ability to add/edit these choices.

Hardcoding these values as an immutable data type can be done by following these steps:

1. In the `/chapter_3/models.py` file, add the following set above your model classes and below your `import` statements:

    ```
    # /becoming_a_django_entdev/chapter_3/models.py
    ...
    MAKE_CHOICES = (
        (1, 'Buick'),
        (2, 'Cadillac'),
        (3, 'Chevrolet'),
        ...
    )
    ```

2. Use that set as the value of the `choices` argument of your `make` field within your `Vehicle` class, as shown:

    ```
    # /becoming_a_django_entdev/chapter_3/models.py
    ...
    class Vehicle(models.Model):
        ...
        make = models.PositiveIntegerField(
            choices = MAKE_CHOICES,
            verbose_name = 'Vehicle Make/Brand',
            blank = True,
            null = True,
        )
    ```

Next, let's discuss what the `Meta` subclass is and how it is used to control the behavior of models even more than what we have already done.

Using the Meta subclass

Model metadata is an inner class of a model called `Meta`. It is not required and completely optional but it does make using Django much more useful when it is included in your models. Metadata provides all of the "other" information that is not defined in model field arguments. The settings that are defined inside this class are called **meta options,** and there are quite a lot to choose from. We will go over only some of the most commonly used options in the following sections and how they can be helpful. A complete breakdown of all of the options is available here: `https://docs.djangoproject.com/en/4.0/ref/models/options/`.

Meta options – verbose_name and verbose_name_plural

We can use the `verbose_name` and `verbose_name_plural` options to specify what human-readable text is used in areas of the Django admin site or if we look it up later in the code that we write. We will introduce the Django admin site in *Chapter 6, Exploring the Django Admin Site*.

To add these options to your model classes, using the class named `VehicleModel`, set these two verbose options to read as `Vehicle Model` and `Vehicle Models`, as depicted:

```
# /becoming_a_django_entdev/chapter_3/models.py
...
class VehicleModel(models.Model):
    ...
    class Meta:
        verbose_name = 'Vehicle Model'
        verbose_name_plural = 'Vehicle Models'
```

Now, throughout your code and the Django admin site, these values will be used as the singular and plural representations of your object(s).

Meta option – ordering

The `ordering` option is used when obtaining a list of objects. This setting will accept one or many fields as a parameter to order by default if no other ordering rules have been specified when the query is performed. It will order in ascending order unless a dash (–) character has been placed before the value; if a dash is used, then the results will appear in descending order instead.

To add this option to your model classes, we can order the `VehicleModel` class by name in ascending order, and then again in descending order, as shown in the following code:

```
# /becoming_a_django_entdev/chapter_3/models.py
...
class VehicleModel(models.Model):
    ...
    class Meta:
        ...
        #ordering = ['name', 'secondary_field',]
        ordering = ['-name']
```

The first example, commented out in the previous code block, shows us that we can order by additional fields, separated by a comma as well as in ascending order. The last example in the preceding code block depicts ordering the results in descending order alphabetically, from Z to A.

Meta option – indexes

The `indexes` option relates to a standard data architecture concept called **database indexing**, which helps to improve the time it takes to perform database queries. Indexes look up data without having to search through every record or row that exists in your tables. They essentially do the work to search tables prior to actually being searched by a user. Django makes it really easy to implement database indexing on tables by using the `indexes` meta option.

Follow these steps to add this option to your model classes:

1. To index the name field on the `VehicleModel` class, it would be written as shown here:

    ```
    # /becoming_a_django_entdev/chapter_3/models.py
    ...
    from django.db.models.functions import Lower
    ...
    class VehicleModel(models.Model):
        ...
        class Meta:
            ...
            indexes = [
    ```

```
                models.Index(fields=['name']),
                models.Index(
                    fields = ['-name'],
                    name = 'desc_name_idx'
                ),
                models.Index(
                    Lower('name').desc(),
                    name = 'lower_name_idx'
                )
            ]
```

The preceding example creates three separate indexes, one for the name in ascending order, one in descending order, and another for lowercase-only names in ascending order.

2. Next, run your Django migration commands one more time. In your command-line or terminal window, the following messages should appear:

```
    - Create index chapter_3_v_name_055414_idx on
field(s) name of model vehiclemodel
    - Create index desc_name_idx on field(s) -name of
model vehiclemodel
    - Create index lower_name_idx on
OrderBy(Lower(F(name)), descending=True) on model
vehiclemodel
```

If we don't specify a `name=` attribute, as was not done in the first index of the preceding example, Django will name it using its default naming convention instead. This is what resulted in the name `chapter_3_v_name_055414_idx` for the first index message in the preceding example. The preceding example imports a class from the `django.db.models.functions` library, called `Lower`. The `Lower` class allows us to create an index on all of the lowercase character representations for the `name` field in the last index in the previous code block. There are numerous database functions that Django provides, and a complete breakdown of these functions can be found in the official Django documentation here: `https://docs.djangoproject.com/en/4.0/ref/models/database-functions/`.

The indexes for each table are usually shown within a database management tool. For example, in PgAdmin, navigate the data tree from within the **Browser** tab to find the **chapter_3_vehiclemodel** indexes. It is a very deep navigation: go to **PostgreSQL 13** | **Databases** | **local_postgresql** | **Schemas** | **public** | **Tables** | **chapter_3_vehiclemodel** | **Indexes** and you should see your indexes, as shown in the following screenshot:

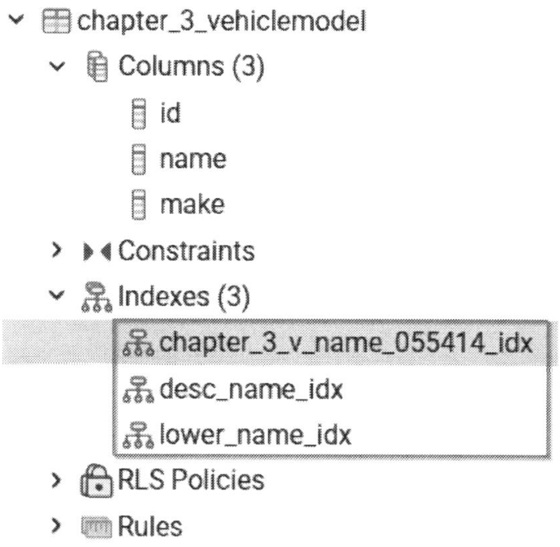

Figure 3.4 – PgAdmin – model indexes

Meta option – db_table

Sometimes, a project might have so many models that they start to conflict with each other or it just becomes too confusing to manage. The `db_table` option is used to specify the name of the table in a database. If this option is not set, by default Django will name your tables using the `{{ app_name }}_{{ model_name }}` naming convention. We can use this option to specify a unique table name on a case-by-case basis that differs from the default naming convention.

For example, let's create a new class named `engine2`, in lowercase this time. This way, we know that the lowercase classes are meant for side practice, separate from the main classes, which will be named with the first letter capitalized. Here, we will add the number **2** to avoid `RuntimeError`, which was mentioned earlier in this chapter, in the *Writing model classes* section.

Follow these steps to add this option to your model classes:

1. In the `/chapter_3/models.py` file, create the `engine2` class and copy the name field from the `Engine` class into it, as shown:

    ```
    # /becoming_a_django_entdev/chapter_3/models.py
    ...
    class engine2(models.Model):
    ```

```
    name = models.CharField(
        verbose_name = 'Engine',
        max_length = 75,
        blank = True,
        null = True,
    )
```

2. Create the `Meta` subclass and set the `db_table` option as depicted here. Do not use this option on the `Engine` class:

```
# /becoming_a_django_entdev/chapter_3/models.py
...
class engine2(models.Model):
    ...
    class Meta:
        db_table = 'chapter_3_practice_engine'
```

Set the value of `db_table` to `'chapter_3_practice_engine'`, as shown.

3. Next, run your Django migration commands one more time. In your database management tool, such as PgAdmin, the `chapter_3` tables should look similar to the following:

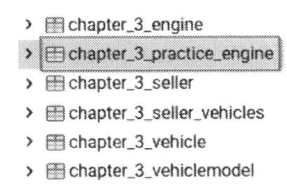

Figure 3.5 – PgAdmin – db_table option

We can see the **chapter_3_engine** and **chapter_3_practice_engine** tables in the preceding screenshot. The **chapter_3_practice_engine** table is used instead of what would have been named **chapter_3_engine2** for the `engine2` model class. Another valuable meta option that you may find yourself using a lot is the abstract option. This is primarily used for extending model classes and is best explained later in the section titled *Extending models* of this chapter.

Before we extend model classes, let's explore using model methods and method decorators.

Customizing models

Model methods are custom functions written within a model class that provide added functionality related to a single record within a table. They let us create our own business logic and format field data as we need to. Django provides us with several default methods and we can also write our own custom methods. Custom methods can combine fields and return data derived from those two or more fields. Decorators are sometimes used in combination with model methods to provide even more functionality.

Some methods can let us perform special operations when an object is saved and/or deleted at the database level. Other methods are used when queries are performed or when rendering an object within a template. We will discuss some of the methods that Django provides and then demonstrate their uses. For a complete breakdown of the full capabilities of using Django's model methods, visit their documentation, found here: `https://docs.djangoproject.com/en/4.0/topics/db/models/#model-methods`.

Writing methods

Writing a model method is similar to writing a `Meta` subclass, except instead of writing a class, we are now writing a function inside that class using the `def` keyword.

The four most helpful and most used methods are defined here:

- `def save(self, *args, **kwargs)` – used to override the save action of this model at the database level. You can inject your own logic either before or after the save has occurred by tapping into this method.

- `def delete(self, *args, **kwargs)` – this is similar to the `save` method, except that you can add your own logic before or after an object has been deleted at the database level.

- `def get_absolute_url(self)` – used by Django to formulate a canonical URL for that object. This is used to redefine the default behavior of how Django creates a URL structure for these objects. This is also the URL used within the Django admin site to access this object.

- `def __str__(self)` – used to redefine the default manner that Django will use to create a string representation of a single record within that table.

We will use the `__str__()` method to demonstrate how to override a Django-provided method and access methods throughout the code of your project.

Model method – __str__

Using the same `MAKE_CHOICES` tuple that was created earlier, we will override the `__str__()` method to formulate a custom name for all `Vehicle` objects. The default string representation of a `Vehicle` object that we will define will use the following naming convention, `{{ vehicle make }} {{ vehicle model }}`, with a space in between.

To configure this method in your `Vehicle` class, in your `/chapter_3/models.py` file, write the `__str__()` method, as depicted in the following code block, in your existing `Vehicle` model class:

```python
# /becoming_a_django_entdev/chapter_3/models.py
...
class Vehicle(models.Model):
    ...
    def __str__(self):
        MAKE_CHOICES_DICT = dict(MAKE_CHOICES)
        return MAKE_CHOICES_DICT[self.make] + ' ' + self.model.name
```

It's easy to see that model methods are just functions that take in an instance of itself, perform an operation of some kind on itself, and then return the transformed value. The value in the preceding example is a string, and for the `__str__()` method, it should always return a string, whereas other methods, including custom methods that you create, can return any other data type, such as an *integer*, *dictionary*, *QuerySet*, or *date/time* object, to name a few.

Next, let's discuss writing our own custom model methods, one that Django does not provide for us.

Custom model method

A custom method would come in handy if say we want to display a more in-depth name than what the `__str__()` method already does for a model class. For example, let's include the engine type in addition to the information returned from the `__str__()` method. The naming convention will be `{{ vehicle make }} {{ vehicle model }} - {{ vehicle engine }}`, with the space and dash in between.

To create your own model method on the `Vehicle` class, in your `/chapter_3/models.py` file, create a new method within your `Vehicle` model and call it `full_vehicle_name()`, as shown:

```
# /becoming_a_django_entdev/chapter_3/models.py
...
class Vehicle(models.Model):
    ...
    def full_vehicle_name(self):
        return self.__str__() + ' - ' + self.engine.name
```

The preceding example uses the same logic found in the `__str__()` method. We are just calling that method from within the custom method using the `self.__str__()` expression, instead of writing the same code in two different places.

Next, we will apply a decorator around the newly created custom method, changing how we interact with this data.

Decorators

A decorator is a standard Python design pattern that allows developers to extend the functionality of an object without permanently changing the behavior of that object. The concept of decorators can be applied to virtually any class or method that exists in a project. We will be applying this concept to the `full_vehicle_name()` method that we just created, to change it from a callable to now a meta property of that model.

Decorator – @property

A `@property` decorator allows us to write a method to act as a regular property of a model instance, rather than act as a function. Using this decorator, we can access `full_vehicle_name` just like we would any other field found in that table. The only thing we cannot do is save data as we would for any other field, because that property is not technically its own column in that table to store data in.

With no `@property` decorator present, data would be accessed similar to the following demonstration:

```
>>> print(my_object.my_custom_method())
```

With the `@property` decorator present, the `print` statement would be written similar to the following demonstration:

```
>>> print(my_object.my_custom_method)
```

To wrap your method in a @property decorator, in your /chapter_3/models.py file, within the Vehicle model class, create a new method called fullname(), as depicted here:

```
# /becoming_a_django_entdev/chapter_3/models.py
...
class Vehicle(models.Model):
    ...
    @property
    def fullname(self):
        return self.__str__() + ' - ' + self.engine.name
```

The preceding example will perform the same task as the full_vehicle_name() method except with the @property decorator applied. When we perform query operations later, in the section titled *Performing queries*, we will compare the difference between the two methods to see how that data is returned and used.

Now that we have discussed most of the core concepts of what makes up a Django model, let's practice extending these models in an effort to keep to a **Don't Repeat Yourself** (**DRY**) style of writing.

Extending models

Extending a model is a way to write a set of fields and methods that can be shared in many different classes. This is also known as **inheritance**, which is a fundamental principle of the Python language, letting us write code once and reuse it over and over again. It is also a way to reuse or modify a class provided by Django itself, such as the built-in User model, which is a very common model to extend.

Next, we will practice extending our practice model called engine2 and then extend the Django User model, turning it into the Seller model. This would make the Seller object related to a Vehicle and also act as a User, provided with permission-based roles and permission group capabilities.

Extending basic model classes

Extending regular model classes is pretty easy to do. Follow these steps to extend the `engine2` practice class:

1. In your `/chapter_3/models.py` file, in the class named `engine2`, keep the name field as is and then add a new field called `vehicle_model`, with the `related_name` attribute value that is depicted in the following code block:

   ```
   # /becoming_a_django_entdev/chapter_3/models.py
   ...
   class engine2(models.Model):
       name = models.CharField(...)
       vehicle_model = models.ForeignKey(
           VehicleModel,
           on_delete = models.CASCADE,
           verbose_name = 'Model',
           related_name = 'model_engine2',
           blank = True,
           null = True,
       )
   ```

2. Make sure your `engine2` class has the following `Meta` class options:

   ```
   # /becoming_a_django_entdev/chapter_3/models.py
   ...
   class engine2(models.Model):
       class Meta:
           abstract = True
           db_table = 'chapter_3_practice_engine'
           ordering = ['name',]
           verbose_name = 'Practice Engine'
           verbose_name_plural = 'Practice Engines'
   ```

We basically want `engine2` to resemble the `Engine` class exactly, except that we want to keep the original class untouched and write a new class called `engine3` constructed from `engine2`. We also have to give the `vehicle_model` field in the `engine2` class a new and unique value for the `related_name` argument. Otherwise, when we run the Django migration commands, we will experience conflicting errors with the `Engine` class. In the `engine2` class, specify the `abstract = True` option as we did in the preceding example. That option allows us to use that class as a parent class.

3. Now, create a new class called `engine3` below your `engine2` class, as depicted in the following code block:

```
# /becoming_a_django_entdev/chapter_3/models.py
...
class engine3(engine2):
    other_name = models.CharField(
        verbose_name = 'Other Engine Name',
        max_length = 75,
        blank = True,
        null = True,
    )
```

In the `engine3` class shown here, we are not creating a `Meta` subclass and we will only give it one field. We also replaced `models.Model` with `engine2`. That is where we pass in the name of the class that we want to construct the new class from, otherwise known as extending or inheriting from that parent class.

Running your Django migration commands now will result in an error, telling us that the `chapter_3_practice_engine` table already exists. To prevent this, we can do one of two things. We could rename the `Meta` class option `db_table` of the `engine2` class or we can drop all of the tables in the database and start fresh.

Dropping database tables

Since, currently, we do not have any real data to worry about and because we are so early in the development life cycle, it's okay to drop our tables. It is acceptable because we are still getting started with building the skeleton code of our project. We are also working with a local database, meaning we won't disrupt other developers' workflows by performing this task. Dropping your tables can be done using any database management tool.

Follow these steps to drop your tables using PgAdmin:

1. In PgAdmin, navigate to **Tools | Query Tool**.
2. In the tab that opens, enter the following two commands:

   ```
   # In the Query Tool of the PgAdmin App
   DROP SCHEMA public CASCADE;
   CREATE SCHEMA public;
   ```

3. Execute these commands by hitting the **Execute/Refresh** button or pressing *F5* on your keyboard.
4. You will also need to delete all migration files found in any migrations folder, such as the `/chapter_3/migrations/` and `/chapter_3/migrations/__pycache__/` folders.

> **Note**
> Every time tables are dropped, data is lost. The next time the Django migration commands are executed, the `createsuperuser` command should be executed and/or data fixtures loaded.

5. Execute your Django migration commands one more time. The following screenshot shows that all of the fields and `Meta` class options that existed before in the `engine2` class now exist in the `engine3` class even though we did not write them for the `engine3` class:

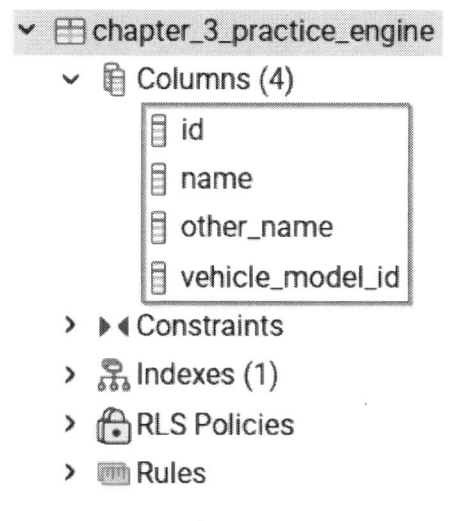

Figure 3.6 – PgAdmin – extended engine

We can see this because the Meta class `db_table = 'chapter_3_practice_engine'` option is placed in the `engine2` class and is what the `engine3` table is named. No table was created for the `engine2` class because it is configured as an abstract class. We also see that the two fields, `name` and `vehicle_model`, from the `engine2` class also get applied to the `engine3` class.

Let's extend the built-in Django `User` class next.

Extending the Django User model

Extending the Django `User` model will transform the `Seller` model, making it act as a `User` in the system. This means you can create a user profile that will have fields that do not come standard with Django; it will have fields that we create. This is done by constructing the `Seller` class using the `AbstractUser` or `AbstractBaseUser` class as the parent class.

Follow these steps to extend your `User` class:

1. In your `/chapter_3/models.py` file, in the `Seller` class, replace `models.Model` with the `AbstractUser` parent class and include the `import` statement shown here:

    ```
    # /becoming_a_django_entdev/chapter_3/models.py
    ...
    from django.contrib.auth.models import AbstractUser
    ...
    class Seller(AbstractUser):
        ...
    ```

    An `AbstractUser` class will allow us to keep all of the original fields that exist in the `User` model. If we want to create a brand-new `User` model from scratch, use the `AbstractBaseUser` parent class instead.

2. We also need to adjust the value of the `AUTH_USER_MODEL` variable in the `settings.py` file, as shown:

    ```
    # /becoming_a_django_entdev/settings.py
    ...
    AUTH_USER_MODEL = 'chapter_3.Seller'
    ```

Use the `app_name.model_name` naming convention, paying attention to model class letter casing. Without adjusting this value, we will get a **Reverse accessor error for 'auth.User.groups'** error when we try to run the Django migration commands. This also means that Django will not use the standard `User` model for this project; instead, the `Seller` model will be used.

3. If we try to run the Django migration commands now, Django will ask us to assign a default value to the username and password fields. Since a username field needs to be unique, we can't just set a default value for this object easily because that will result in duplicate usernames. The reason this will happen is that we destroyed the previous `auth_user` tables in the database and created an entirely new set of relations for a `User`. Go ahead and drop your tables just like you did in the previous subsection, titled *Dropping database tables*. Now run the Django migrations commands. The following screenshot shows the `chapter_3_seller` table now has many other fields that we did not write:

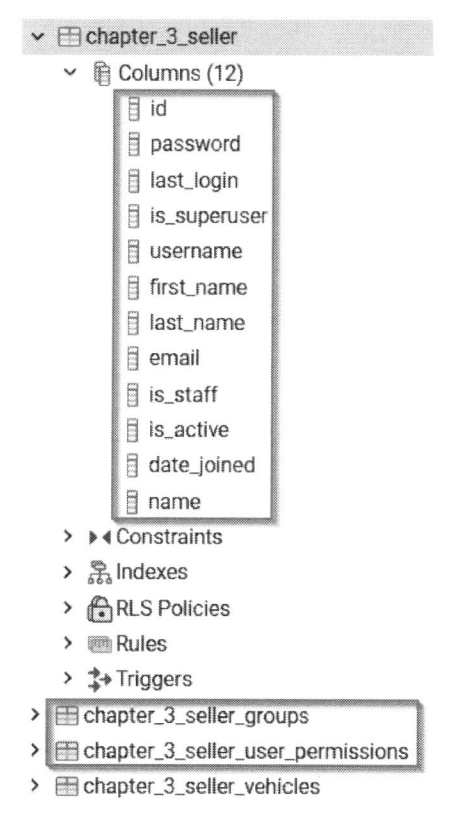

Figure 3.7 – PgAdmin – user model extension

Now that we have covered the basics of writing and extending models, let's use the Django shell to perform queries. We can use the Django shell to see the results of queries without having to learn about rendering templates first, which is what all of *Chapter 4, URLs, Views, and Templates*, will cover.

Using the Django shell

The **Django shell** is a powerful tool to add to any toolbox. It will activate the Python interactive interpreter and uses the Django database abstraction API to let us connect directly to the database(s) configured in a project. With this, we can write Python and perform queries directly from a terminal or command-line window.

To activate the Django shell, follow these steps:

1. Open your terminal or command-line window and navigate to the root of your project. Make sure your virtual environment has been activated and then execute the following command:

    ```
    (virtual_env) PS > python3 manage.py shell
    ```

2. You should see it print out the following information about the `InteractiveConsole` that was launched:

    ```
    Python 3.7.8 (tags/v3.7.8:4b47a5b6ba, Jun 28 2020,
    08:53:46) [MSC v.1916 64 bit (AMD64)] on win32
    Type "help", "copyright", "credits" or "license" for more
    information.
    (InteractiveConsole)
    >>>
    ```

3. Your console will now display three right-angle brackets, where you can begin writing and executing Python code one line at a time. Theoretically, you could input an entire script this way, but it will not be saved anywhere, and your code will be lost when the window is closed or the `InteractiveConsole` is terminated.

Now that this shell is activated, let's add sample data and perform a few queries to observe how it behaves.

Running basic Python scripts

Earlier in this chapter, in the subsection titled *Mutable versus immutable objects*, it was mentioned that a Python string is one of the immutable data types that exist. An immutable string is one that cannot be reassigned a character at a particular index of that string after it has been created. This means that what is allowed is reassigning the value to that string altogether, and what is not allowed is changing the value of a character at a particular index. This is a basic fundamental of Python, and those who are new to Python can find this to be confusing. In this next example, we will demonstrate how to use the Django shell and at the same time demonstrate what makes a string immutable:

1. Launch the Python interactive interpreter by running the following Django shell command:

   ```
   (virtual_env) PS > python3 manage.py shell
   ```

2. Assign a new variable called `myvar` and give it an initial value of `my_string`, as shown:

   ```
   >>> myvar = 'my_string'
   >>> myvar[2] = ''
   Traceback (most recent call last):
     File "<console>", line 1, in <module>
   TypeError: 'str' object does not support item assignment
   >>>
   ```

   By executing the second statement shown in the previous code block, where we try to remove the underscore from the string at index 2, we are receiving an error stating `TypeError: 'str' object does not support item assignment`.

3. If we just reassign the value of the `myvar` variable, as is done in the following code block, we will be able to remove the underscore this way:

   ```
   >>> myvar = 'my_string'
   >>> print(myvar)
   my_string
   >>> myvar = 'mystring'
   >>> print(myvar)
   mystring
   >>>
   ```

In the preceding example, the first `print` statement returns `my_string` and then, after we change the value of `myvar`, the next `print` statement returns `mystring`.

4. We could use string indexes to look up characters and combine them but we cannot reassign a character at an index. The following example would remove the underscore by looking up characters at specified index ranges:

```
>>> myvar = 'my_string'
>>> print(myvar[0:2] + myvar[3:9])
mystring
>>>
```

5. Type `exit()` to quit using the interactive interpreter and return to using your `manage.py` commands:

```
>>> exit()
```

Now that we know how to execute basic Python scripts in the interactive interpreter, let's use this tool to generate a custom `SECRET_KEY` and set a project's `.env` file.

Generating a SECRET_KEY variable

A `SECRET_KEY` variable in Django is used as a hash to secure things, such as your sessions, cookie storage, password tokenization, and all other methods of cryptographic signing that act to secure your site. Instead of using an online tool to generate this key, where the transmission either to or from that source could be compromised, you could generate your own using the Django shell. All we are doing is generating a random string. There is nothing special about this operation; you could technically use any combination of letters and numbers that you enter on a keyboard too. While this is not necessary since Django already generates a unique key for us when we create a new Django project, it is a useful step to allow us to create different keys to use on each of our Heroku environments. This way, we don't share the same `SECRET_KEY`.

To generate your own `SECRET_KEY`, follow these steps:

1. Activate the Django shell in your terminal or command-line window and then import the method shown in the following code block:

```
(virtual_env) PS > python3 manage.py shell
>>> from secret_key_generator import secret_key_generator
```

The method shown here comes from the package called `secret_key_generator`, which we installed in *Chapter 2, Project Configuration*.

2. Next, execute the following `print` statement:

    ```
    >>> print(secret_key_generator.generate())
    your_randomly_generated_key_printed_here
    ```

3. Take the key that gets printed onscreen and use it to set or reset your environment variables. To reset your variables, just follow the same steps as were discussed in *Chapter 2, Project Configuration*, under the subsection titled *Remote variables* and it will update your value with the new value.

The preceding shell command also created for us a text file called `.secret.txt`, found in the root of your project, where your `manage.py` file is located. You can delete the `.sectret.txt` file as it is not needed.

Now, let's use the Django shell to add data to our tables next, allowing us to use the Django shell to perform queries after that.

Saving data

Creating and saving objects to your database using the Django shell is easy. After we have activated the Django shell, we need to import the models that we want to work with into memory just like when we import something at the top of any `.py` file.

Follow these steps to create and save data using the Django shell:

1. Import your vehicle class objects using the `InteractiveConsole` window by executing the following commands:

    ```
    (virtual_env) PS > python3 manage.py shell
    >>> from becoming_a_django_entdev.chapter_3.models import Engine, Seller, Vehicle, VehicleModel
    ```

    These objects will be available for you to use until that window is closed or the `exit()` command is executed.

2. While these objects are loaded, it only takes the two lines of code shown in the following code block to create a new object and then save it:

    ```
    >>> vehicle_model = VehicleModel(name = 'Enclave Avenir', make = 1)
    >>> vehicle_model.save()
    ```

The preceding lines will create and then save a `VehicleModel` object with the name of `Enclave Avenir` into the `chapter_3_vehiclemodel` table. In the creation of the `vehicle_model` object previously, we provided values to all of the fields that exist for that class. The value of the `make` field uses the numeric value of the tuple that we created earlier, called `MAKE_CHOICES`.

3. However, if we try to create an `Engine` object using a numeric value for the `vehicle_model` field, then we will be given a `ValueError`, as shown:

```
>>> engine = Engine(name = '3.6L DI DOHC 6cyl', vehicle_
model = 1)
Traceback (most recent call last):
  ...
ValueError: Cannot assign "1": "Engine.model" must be a
"VehicleModel" instance.
```

4. In order to successfully create an `Engine` object, we first have to create a `VehicleModel` object as we did for the `vehicle_model` temporary object in *step 2*. Then, use that variable to set as the value of the `model` field instead of using a numeric integer, as shown:

```
>>> vehicle_model = VehicleModel(name = 'Enclave Avenir',
make = 1)
>>> vehicle_model.save()
>>> engine = Engine(name = '3.6L DI DOHC 6cyl', vehicle_
model = vehicle_model)
>>> engine.save()
```

Step 4 of the preceding example will likely result in an error due to us adding the `unique = True` argument to the `name` field of the `VehicleModel` class. This is also because we just created an object using the same name in *step 2*. You can get around that by providing a unique name or disregarding it and moving forward. This error was made intentionally for learning purposes. The error you receive should look like the one shown in the following code block, indicating that you have duplicate entries:

```
Traceback (most recent call last):
  File "C:\Projects\Packt_Publishing\Repo\becoming_a_django_
entdev\virtual_env\lib\site-packages\django\db\backends\utils.
py", line 84, in _execute
    return self.cursor.execute(sql, params)
psycopg2.errors.UniqueViolation: duplicate key value violates
unique constraint "chapter_3_vehiclemodel_name_a94a4619_uniq"
```

```
DETAIL:  Key (name)=(Enclave Avenir) already exists.
...
The above exception was the direct cause of the following
exception:
django.db.utils.IntegrityError: duplicate key value violates
unique constraint "chapter_3_vehiclemodel_name_a94a4619_uniq"
DETAIL:  Key (name)=(Enclave Avenir) already exists.
```

To get around this, we need to use the `update_or_create()` method instead of the `save()` method.

If we try to create and then save an engine with a `vehicle_model` field that has not been already saved to the database, we will get a `ValueError` informing us that there is an unsaved related object present. If you wish to see this, create the `vehicle_model` object using the following values. Then, use that object to assign as the value of the `vehicle_model` field on the `engine` object and try to save:

```
>>> vehicle_model = VehicleModel(name = 'Blazer LT', make = 3)
>>> engine = Engine(name = '4 Cylinders 4 2.0L DI Turbo DOHC
122 CID', vehicle_model = vehicle_model)
>>> engine.save()
Traceback (most recent call last):
   ...
ValueError: save() prohibited to prevent data loss due to
unsaved related object 'model'.
```

Once you try to save that `engine`, the error shown in the preceding code block would print to your screen, which is the reason why we need to save each related object before creating an object that they rely on.

Let's discuss using the `update_or_create()` method next.

Model method – update_or_create()

We use the `update_or_create()` method instead of the `save()` method to create or modify an existing object.

Follow these steps to use this method:

1. Make sure the Django shell is activated and then execute the following command:

   ```
   (virtual_env) PS > python3 manage.py shell
   >>> vehicle_model, created = VehicleModel.objects.update_or_create(name = 'Enclave Avenir', make = 1, defaults={'name': 'Enclave Avenir', 'make': 1},)
   ```

   The preceding example should have been successful. If it was, then you received no errors, and you'll see the three right-angle brackets waiting for your next input command.

2. Using a database management tool such as PgAdmin, check to see that you have a `VehicleModel` record in your table with the name `Enclave Avenir`. The `defaults` argument in the preceding example is an optional argument that defines the values that you want to set if this operation creates a new record. Without it, the system will default to values set on your model fields instead.

3. In this step, we will add a `Vehicle` to the database. It requires the use of a `Money` class to create a `Money` object. To use the `Money` class, execute the following `import` statement:

   ```
   >>> from djmoney.money import Money
   ```

4. Now, execute the following three `update_or_create()` commands:

   ```
   >>> vehicle_model, model_created = VehicleModel.objects.update_or_create(name = 'Blazer LT', make = 3,)
   >>> engine, engine_created = Engine.objects.update_or_create(name = '3.9L DI DOHC 6cyl', vehicle_model = vehicle_model,)
   >>> vehicle, vehicle_created = Vehicle.objects.update_or_create(vin = 'aa123456789012345', sold = True, price = Money(10000, 'USD'), make = 3, vehicle_model = vehicle_model, engine = engine,)
   ```

The commands in this subsection should have all resulted in success without errors.

> **Note**
> If a vehicle with the same VIN as the one shown previously is already created for you by importing the data found in the `chapter_3` data fixture, then you can just change the `vin` value in the preceding example to a new and unique `vin` value. This allows you to witness a new record being added to your table when viewed in a database management tool such as PgAdmin.

Let's discuss loading the `chapter_3` data fixture next.

Loading the chapter_3 data fixture

Instead of providing steps on how to create all of the data that will be needed to demonstrate the exercises throughout the rest of this chapter and this book, we will be adding data from a data fixture. Adding data can be done in a much simpler way than how it was done from within the Django shell. We will discuss this concept in more depth and create our own fixtures later in *Chapter 10, Database Management*. For now, make sure the `/becoming_a_django_entdev/becoming_a_django_entdev/chapter_3/fixtures/` folder and all of the files found in this folder from the code of this book are copied into your `/chapter_3/` app folder. The `chapter_3` fixture will provide enough data for us to work with the remaining examples of this chapter.

To load your data fixture make sure you have exited your Django shell and that your virtual environment is active and then execute the following command:

```
(virtual_env) PS > python3 manage.py loaddata chapter_3
```

If you have issues with importing this fixture, double-check that your table structures match the structures of the models provided with the code of this book in the `chapter_3` app.

The alternative would be to follow the steps in the *Saving data* subsection of this chapter to add your own sample data one painstaking item at a time. Create and save as many objects as you would like using those examples. If you were to create a `Vehicle` object, it would be done in the same way as creating an `Engine` objcct, except now you are defining the values of two related objects instead of one in order to save successfully. We just need to have a few objects to play around with in the next exercises of this chapter.

Performing queries

Performing queries using the Django shell will give us some insight into how queries work. In the following subsections, we will discuss some common methods that are used.

Model method – all()

The `all()` method returns all records found in the table for that model object. This method will return a QuerySet in the following format, representing all entries that it finds:

```
(virtual_env) PS > python3 manage.py shell
>>> from becoming_a_django_entdev.chapter_3.models import Engine, Seller, Vehicle, VehicleModel
>>> VehicleModel.objects.all()
<QuerySet [<VehicleModel: Blazer LT>, <VehicleModel: Enclave Avenir>, <VehicleModel: Envision Avenir>]>
```

The `chapter_3` data fixture only provides three VehicleModel and that is why a collection of only three objects is returned to us. Your results may vary. One of the reasons why we created a `__str__()` method, as was done earlier in this chapter, in the subsection titled *Model method – __str__*, is so that it could be represented in a logical way in code usage such as this, where the object name that gets printed out is a name that makes sense to us and not something that won't make sense. Without the `__str__()` method defined in the `VehicleModel` class, the QuerySet would have been returned to us in a manner that looks like the following example:

```
<QuerySet [<VehicleModel: VehicleModel object (3)>, <VehicleModel: VehicleModel object (2)>, <VehicleModel: VehicleModel object (1)>]>
```

We would have no way to distinguish which object is which and what order they are in just by looking at the collection printed in this code block.

Model method – get()

The `get()` method is used to target a specific database record.

Follow these steps to see this method in action:

1. Use `get()` to target the `vin` value of a vehicle when performing a query, as is done here:

   ```
   >>> vehicle = Vehicle.objects.get(vin =
   'aa123456789012345')
   >>> print(vehicle)
   Chevrolet Blazer LT
   ```

2. Using the single object that was returned to us, run the `print` statement again using the `full_vehicle_name()` method that we created earlier, to see the difference in the results that are generated:

   ```
   >>> print(vehicle.full_vehicle_name())
   Chevrolet Blazer LT - 3.6L DI DOHC 6cyl
   ```

3. Next, use the other `fullname` method with the `@property` decorator to return the exact same results:

   ```
   >>> print(vehicle.fullname)
   Chevrolet Blazer LT - 3.6L DI DOHC 6cyl
   ```

Django is using the format that we defined earlier in the `__str__` method to generate a string that gets printed to the screen in *step 1*. We already know that the `vin` field is set to `unique = True`, meaning there will never be two objects with the same `vin` value in the database, so we know that it is safe to use the `get()` method in all the preceding steps. If there are numerous items with the same value and a `get()` method is used, then you will need to use a `filter()` method instead.

Model method – filter()

The `filter()` method is used to look up records in a database that may have the same field values. This method will return a collection of results instead of a single result. The collection will be returned to us as a `QuerySet`. For example, we can filter the `VehicleModel` table, which we already know contains three rows.

The following example will filter the `make` field by the value of `Buick`, to return a collection of only two objects instead of three:

```
>>> print(VehicleModel.objects.filter(make = 1))
<QuerySet [<VehicleModel: Enclave Avenir>, <VehicleModel: Envision Avenir>]>
```

Queries can get much more complex than using a simple `all()`, `get()`, or `filter()` method. Q objects provide more complicated queries as well. For a complete breakdown of how to use Q objects in Django, visit the documentation here: https://docs.djangoproject.com/en/4.0/ref/models/querysets/#q-objects.

We can even obtain a summary of objects using arithmetic functions, which brings us to our next subsection, discussing aggregates.

Aggregates

Django provides an easy way to generate a summary of a collection of objects, known as **aggregates**. What this means is that we can perform a query and use any one of the many **aggregation functions** that Django provides. This can be used to generate an average price for all the vehicles, generate an average price of just the sold vehicles, or generate a total count of vehicles for a particular seller. While there is a lot of information regarding the topic of aggregates and annotates, we will discuss some basic usages. A complete guide to generating aggregates in Django can be found here: https://docs.djangoproject.com/en/4.0/ref/models/querysets/#aggregation-functions.

Model method – aggregate()

Aggregates are used to generate a summary of every object in a QuerySet. To get an average price of every vehicle that exists in that table, we can use the `Avg` aggregate function. The argument that we pass into the `Avg` function is the field that we want to perform this operation on.

Follow these steps to practice using aggregates:

1. Import your `Vehicle` model and the `Avg` class objects, as shown:

    ```
    (virtual_env) PS > python3 manage.py shell
    >>> from becoming_a_django_entdev.chapter_3.models import Vehicle
    >>> from django.db.models import Avg
    ```

2. Perform a query lookup using the `all()` method combined with the `aggregate()` method, as shown:

   ```
   >>> vehicles = Vehicle.objects.all().aggregate(Avg('price'))
   ```

3. Print your `vehicles` object:

   ```
   >>> print(vehicles)
   {'price__avg': Decimal('16335.428571428571')}
   ```

   The summary is returned as a dictionary object.

4. You can get the value of the `price__avg` key by executing the following `print` statement:

   ```
   >>> print(vehicles['price__avg'])
   16335.428571428571
   ```

   The result of the average is, of course, not actually formatted in any particular currency type yet.

5. We can format it in US dollars by applying the same `Money()` conversion that we did before when we created and then saved our first vehicle in the database, by executing the following commands:

   ```
   >>> from djmoney.money import Money
   >>> print(Money(vehicles['price__avg'], 'USD'))
   $16,335.43
   ```

Where we wrote `Vehicle.objects.all().aggregate()` in *step 2* previously, the `all()` method is redundant. The `aggregate()` method basically does the same thing as the `all()` method, meaning we could write our statement as follows and produce the same results:

```
>>> vehicles = Vehicle.objects.aggregate(Avg('price'))
```

We can also replace the `all()` method with any of the standard query methods, such as `get()` or `filter()`, as depicted in the following example:

```
>>> vehicles = Vehicle.objects.filter(sold=False).aggregate(Avg('price'))
>>> print(Money(vehicles['price__avg'], 'USD'))
$18,419.60
```

Let's discuss annotations next.

Model method – annotate()

Annotations are used when we have objects that relate to other objects in a QuerySet and we want to generate a summary of every related object in that QuerySet.

Follow these steps to practice using annotations:

1. Execute the following commands to provide a query of all sellers that exist in a table and then generate a count of only the sold vehicles that it finds:

    ```
    (virtual_env) PS > python3 manage.py shell
    >>> from becoming_a_django_entdev.chapter_3.models import Seller, Vehicle
    >>> from django.db.models import Avg, Count
    >>> sellers = Seller.objects.filter(vehicles__sold=True).annotate(Count('vehicles'))
    >>> print(sellers[0].vehicles__count)
    2
    ```

2. Alter the preceding `filter` statement to count only the unsold vehicles, as shown:

    ```
    >>> sellers = Seller.objects.filter(vehicles__sold=False).annotate(Count('vehicles'))
    >>> print(sellers[0].vehicles__count)
    5
    ```

    We need to specify the index at `sellers[0]` because a `filter()` method will always return a collection of objects, even if the query only results in one object.

3. Print the `sellers` collection to the screen, as shown:

    ```
    >>> print(sellers)
    <QuerySet [<Seller: admin>]>
    ```

    We can see that there is only one `Seller` in the database at this time. We got the numbers 2 and then 5 as the results, for a total of seven vehicles that relate to that seller.

Next, we will discuss model managers and how they can be used to perform advanced queries.

Writing model managers

We now know that when we want to apply logic that pertains to a single object within a table, we will look into writing a model method. An advanced Django concept can allow us to add logic that would relate to the entire table of objects instead. That would be written using a **model manager** instead of a model method. By default, Django automatically creates a model manager for every model that you write. That manager is called the `objects` manager, as in when we write a query statement such as `MyModel.objects.all()`. Since the `objects` manager is already created for us, there is technically no need for us to create a model manager at all. However, custom model managers can be used in a project to provide additional methods that the entire table uses. We will discuss a simple use of this concept that adds filters to a table. To learn more about how model managers can be used in more depth, visit the official Django documentation, found here: https://docs.djangoproject.com/en/4.0/topics/db/managers/.

Take the following steps to apply a filter, separating the vehicle objects by make/manufacturer. Here, we will write a manager for the `Buick` vehicles and another manager for the `Chevy` vehicles. In a large project, it would also be wise to place your managers in a separate `managers.py` file and import them into `models.py` before using them. Let's just add them all to the `models.py` file for now:

1. In the `/chapter_3/models.py` file, add the following two model manager classes above your model classes and below any existing `import` statements, as shown:

    ```python
    # /becoming_a_django_entdev/chapter_3/models.py
    ...
    class BuickVehicleManager(models.Manager):
        def get_queryset(self):
            return super().get_queryset().filter(make=1)


    class ChevyVehicleManager(models.Manager):
        def get_queryset(self):
            return super().get_queryset().filter(make=3)
    ...
    ```

2. In the /chapter_3/models.py file, add the following three model manager statements to your existing Vehicle class, below the model fields found in that class and above the Meta subclass, as shown:

```python
# /becoming_a_django_entdev/chapter_3/models.py
...
class Vehicle(models.Model):
    # Place Model Fields Here

    # The Default Model Manager
    objects = models.Manager()
    # The Buick Specific Manager
    buick_objects = BuickVehicleManager()
    # The Chevy Specific Manager
    chevy_objects = ChevyVehicleManager()

    # Place Meta Class and Model Methods Here
```

3. Next, open your terminal or command-line window and activate your virtual environment and the Django shell. Then, import the Vehicle model into InteractiveConsole, as is done here:

```
(virtual_env) PS > python3 manage.py shell
>>> from becoming_a_django_entdev.chapter_3.models import Vehicle
```

4. Execute the following objects manager count() method:

```
>>> Vehicle.objects.all().count()
7
```

5. Execute the following buick_objects manager count() method:

```
>>> Vehicle.buick_objects.all().count()
2
```

6. Execute the following chevy_objects manager count() method:

```
>>> Vehicle.chevy_objects.all().count()
5
```

What we get in return are the vehicles that relate to each manager that we created, starting with the `objects` manager, then `buick_objects` and `chevy_objects`. This counts the filtered objects instead of providing us with a total count of all objects in that table. Even though we are still using the `all()` method, we only get all of the objects related to that filter. We also apply the `count()` method to print a numeric count of what gets returned in a QuerySet versus printing the names of each object, as was depicted in previous query examples.

Summary

In this chapter, we learned that models are building blocks of everything else we build that accesses data in a database. They provide the containers where all of a project's data will exist as a data storage device for this application. We now have a toolbox with tools related to the structure of the tables, such as the columns that exist or rules/constraints that we apply to them. Other tools help us to link these tables together that build the relationships between those tables. We also know how to transform the data that we have to provide other data not kept in those tables, but rather derived from it. Some of the concepts add performance power by doing work in the background, indexing data, and reducing the time that it takes to look up information. Querying objects is also a complex subject and there is a lot of material regarding it; use the concepts in this chapter to help guide you through researching more advanced ways of querying data, to help with complex real-world scenarios. Later, in *Chapter 10, Database Management*, we will discuss other tricks that help to enhance database performance when performing database queries.

Next, let's take the models that we created in this chapter and render that data onto an actual web page, finally viewing something within a browser. These will be the URLs, views, and templates that we create in the next chapter.

Part 2 – Django Components

In this part, you will be introduced to major components of the Django framework and how they can be used in a project. You will learn about Django templates, email templates, PDF templates, URL patterns, views, forms, and the Django admin site. These are the fundamental components of the Django framework necessary for almost any project.

This part comprises the following chapters:

- *Chapter 4, URLs, Views, and Templates*
- *Chapter 5, Django Forms*
- *Chapter 6, Exploring the Django Admin Site*
- *Chapter 7, Working with Messages, Email Notifications, and PDF Reports*

4
URLs, Views, and Templates

In this chapter, we will build the **URL** patterns that route to different **views**, processing a request sent to the server. One of the jobs of a view is to send processed information in the form of **context** to a **template** that will be used to render static or dynamically changing content. By the end of this chapter, we will have created several URL patterns for the user to visit and view data. Some examples will trigger errors or not-found exceptions on purpose to help demonstrate the concepts provided in this chapter.

Django is based on what is called the **Model-Template-View** (**MTV**) architectural design pattern, which is similar to the well-known **Model-View-Controller** (**MVC**) design pattern used for a variety of popular web-based software systems today. The view in both of these architectural design patterns is what sometimes confuses people who are starting to learn Django and come from an MVC background. In both patterns, the model is the same, and both correspond to the tables within a database. In Django, the view is best compared to the controller used in the MVC design pattern, while the template in Django's MTV pattern is best compared to the view in an MVC design pattern.

We will begin this chapter by discussing URL patterns that let us tell Django what paths we want available on a website, within our project. A **path** is considered anything found after the suffix of a web address, where a **suffix** is the .com, .org, or .edu part of a URL. The path in www.example.com/my-url-pattern/ would be /my-url-pattern/. We can tell Django to map different URL patterns to different views and we can point different URL patterns to the same view. Views are what process a request and return a response. Usually, a response is returned in the form of an HTML template, but a response can also be in the form of JSON, XML, or any other data type. Templates take context provided by a view and/or a context processor and then use that context data to render dynamic HTML in a client's browser. **Context** is actually a dictionary of dynamic variables that change as conditions and states change within your app. Data that lives in the database is also provided to the template through that same context. Views perform queries and/or communicate with caching systems and APIs to fetch data from a data storage device, used when rendering templates.

In this chapter, we will cover the following:

- Configuring URL patterns
- Mapping URL patterns
- Resolving URLs
- Resolving absolute URLs
- Working with complex views
- Working with templates

Technical requirements

To work with the code in this chapter, the following tools will need to be installed on your local machine:

- Python version 3.9 – used as the underlying programming language for the project
- Django version 4.0 – used as the backend framework of the project
- pip package manager – used to manage third-party Python/Django packages

We will continue to work with the solution created in *Chapter 2, Project Configuration*. However, it is not necessary to use the Visual Studio IDE. The main project itself can be run using another IDE or run independently using a terminal or command-line window from within the project root folder. This is where the `manage.py` file resides. Whatever editor or IDE you are using, a virtual environment will also be needed to work with the Django project. Instructions for how to create a project and virtual environment can be found in *Chapter 2, Project Configuration*. You will need a database to store the data contained in your project. PostgreSQL was chosen for the examples in the previous chapter; however, any database type that you choose for your project can be used to work with the examples in this chapter.

We will also be using data that is in the form of a Django fixture, provided previously in *Chapter 3, Models, Relations, and Inheritance*, in the subsection titled *Loading the Chapter_3 data fixture*. Make sure the `chapter_3` fixture is loaded into your database. If this has already been done, then you may skip the next command. If you have already created the tables found in *Chapter 3, Models, Relations, and Inheritance*, and have not loaded that fixture yet, then run the following command, after activating your virtual environment:

```
(virtual_env) PS > python manage.py loaddata chapter_3
```

All of the code created in this chapter can be found in the GitHub repository for this book: https://github.com/PacktPublishing/Becoming-an-Enterprise-Django-Developer. The bulk of the code used in this chapter can be found in the /becoming_a_django_entdev/becoming_a_django_entdev/chapter_4/ directory.

Check out the following video to see the *Code in Action*: https://bit.ly/3A6AxNU.

Preparing for this chapter

Start by creating a new app in your project called `chapter_4` by following the steps discussed in *Chapter 2, Project Configuration*, in the subsection titled *Creating a Django app*. As discussed in that section, don't forget to change the value of your `name` = variable for your app class found in the `/becoming_a_django_entdev/becoming_a_django_entdev/chapter_4/apps.py` file to now point to the path where you installed your app. Be sure to also include this app in your `INSTALLED_APPS` variable found in the `settings.py` file as well.

Configuring URL patterns

Django controls and processes URL patterns in what it calls a **URL dispatcher**. Django starts with the `urls.py` file, which is specified as the `ROOT_URLCONF` variable, found in the `settings.py` file. Visual Studio automatically created the `ROOT_URLCONF` variable for us when we created a project and it should have also done so when executing the Django `startproject` command.

If your project did not create this variable, add the following setting to your `settings.py` file:

```
# /becoming_a_django_entdev/settings.py
...
ROOT_URLCONF = 'becoming_a_django_entdev.urls'
```

The `urls.py` file defined in the `ROOT_URLCONF` variable is what Django considers the **root URLconf** of any project, short for **URL configuration**. Other `url.py` files can be linked together by importing them using an `import()` function. Django looks for only one thing in these `urls.py` files, a single variable named `urlpatterns`, which contains a set of URL patterns that have been defined for a project or reusable app. This file can contain many methods, classes, and other utilities that help you formulate those patterns.

Basic path functions

Django provides us with a variety of path functions to build URL patterns. These functions create and return elements that will be included within any `urlpatterns` variable. The `path()` and `re_path()` functions can accept up to four positional arguments in the following order: `route`, `view`, `kwargs`, and `name`. The first two of these arguments are required and must be defined. The first argument, `route`, expects a string; this can be a simple string or a fairly complex string when combining path converters and using regular expressions. If you are using a method to perform logic of some kind for this argument, it just needs to return a string. The `route` argument is the path that Django is listening for and then mapping to the second argument, `view`. The `view` argument is used to tell Django how to process the GET request of a URL pattern. `view` can perform any kind of logic. The third argument is the **Keyword Arguments** (**kwargs**), and this is a dictionary of additional keywords to pass into `view`. The last argument, `name`, is a way to map URL patterns when using other functions, such as a reverse lookup.

Let's go over some examples of using basic functions before we dive into more complicated URL patterns, using path converters.

Function – static()

The `static()` function is provided by Django to help serve up static files when running a project locally and with debug mode turned on. These are files such as images, CSS, and JavaScript files that are placed in the `static` folder of a Django app. This function will enable access to those static folders, allowing you to run your project and add, delete, and edit those files all without having to run the `python manage.py collectstatic` command to reflect those changes in your browser. Of course, in the browser, you still have to hit refresh unless you have other tools/plugins installed in your browser to update a page when it detects changes to files that it is using.

Static files

To activate static files in your local environment, in your main `urls.py` file, add the following `import` statements and append the following function to the `urlpatterns` variable:

```
# /becoming_a_django_entdev/urls.py
from django.conf import settings
from django.conf.urls.static import static

urlpatterns = [...] + static(
    settings.STATIC_URL,
    document_root = settings.STATIC_ROOT
)
```

In the preceding example, we imported the `settings.py` file to gain access to the values of the `STATIC_URL` and `STATIC_ROOT` variables. Since we installed the `pip whiteNoise` package, to work with Heroku as our host, we actually do not need to write the `static()` function depicted previously. This means we can skip writing the preceding code if we want to, but adding it will not hurt either and will allow your project to work on other hosts.

This can also be written using a conditional that checks whether `DEBUG` is enabled.

The alternative would be written as follows:

```
# /becoming_a_django_entdev/urls.py
...
urlpatterns = [...]

if settings.DEBUG:
    urlpatterns += static(
        settings.STATIC_URL,
        document_root = settings.STATIC_ROOT
    )
```

Please use only one of the examples depicted in this subsection and not both of them at the same time. You can comment out the unused one.

Let's configure media files next.

Media files

Even with the `whitenoise` package, we still need to use the `static()` function to serve up media files. **Media files** are just like static files except they are considered what a user would upload through `FileField`, `ImageField`, or several other methods of uploading files to a media storage device. These files are also known as **User-Generated Content** (**UGC**) and they can range from anything such as an image to a PDF document, Excel document, Word document, audio file, or even movie file. The file that gets uploaded is placed in the media folder that we created and configured in *Chapter 2, Project Configuration*.

To access these images when running a project locally, follow these steps:

1. In your main `urls.py` file, insert the following highlighted code:

   ```
   # /becoming_a_django_entdev/urls.py
   ...
   from django.conf import settings
   from django.conf.urls.static import static

   urlpatterns = [...] + static(
       settings.STATIC_URL,
       document_root = settings.STATIC_ROOT
   ) + static(
   ```

```
        settings.MEDIA_URL,
        document_root = settings.MEDIA_ROOT
)
```

2. This can also be added to the debug conditional statement shown in the previous subsection, titled *Static files*.

3. If you downloaded the code that came along with this book, a sample image has been included in the directory called /media and is used to test whether accessing media files is actually working. If the /media folder is not created at this time in your project, go ahead and create that in your IDE or file browser or by running the following command:

```
(virtual_env) PS > mkdir media
```

4. Copy the /becoming_a_django_entdev/media/media.jpg file into your project in the same directory.

5. Run your project and attempt to navigate to the URL http://localhost:8000/media/media.jpg without the preceding code and you should get a 404 response. Then try it with the preceding code and you should see the media image shown here:

MEDIA

Figure 4.1 – Media sample image

Let's take these functions a step further and build our first path next.

Function – path()

A `path()` function takes in the `route`, `view`, `kwargs`, and `name` attributes and returns a single element to be included in the `urlpatterns` list. A `path()` function can be thought of as handling static paths as well as dynamic paths using path converters. If you want to use regular expressions to register a dynamic path converter, you will want to use the `re_path()` function instead.

Follow these steps to work with the `path()` function in your project:

1. First, run your project and navigate to the base URL of the project at `http://localhost:8000/`. You might be wondering why we are seeing a `Page not found (404)` message, as shown here:

   > **Page not found** (404)
   >
   > Directory indexes are not allowed here.
   >
   > **Request Method:** GET
   > **Request URL:** http://localhost:8000/
   > **Raised by:** django.views.static.serve
   >
   > Using the URLconf defined in `becoming_a_django_entdev.urls`,
   >
   >   1. admin/
   >   2. ^static/(?P<path>.*)$
   >   3. ^(?P<path>.*)$
   >
   > The empty path matched the last one.
   >
   > You're seeing this error because you have `DEBUG = True` in your

   Figure 4.2 – 404 with debug turned on

   When we activated the `static` and `media` URL patterns, we caused this error message to happen. This is the reason we are not seeing the famous Django success rocket ship that we are used to seeing. It's nothing to be alarmed about; it just means that we haven't created a URL pattern to handle the home page yet. This error message can be thought of as a reminder to create that home page, which we will do next.

   Using the `path()` function, we will define a single static URL pattern that will listen for the home page URL. Before we do that, let's create the HTML file that it will serve up. When we used Visual Studio to create the `chapter_4` app, a file named `index.html` was automatically created for us in the `/becoming_a_django_entdev/chapter_4/templates/chapter_4/` directory.

2. If you do not have the `/chapter_4/templates/chapter_4/index.html` file in that directory, go ahead and create this file now, or copy the one provided with this book. Sometimes this file is not automatically created for us.

   The `index.html` file will be used as a custom home page and we will focus on just the URL pattern at this time; we will have dived into templates in more depth by the end of this chapter.

Writing a URL pattern to listen for the home page is pretty easy compared to how complex other URL patterns can be to write. Django will try to match a URL to a pattern by starting from first to last in the order that they are placed within the `urlpatterns` list. It's usually best to include static URL patterns at the top and then place your dynamic patterns below them. If a static pattern is similar to a dynamic pattern, the static URL pattern will be matched first, which is likely what you want to happen.

3. In your main `/becoming_a_django_entdev/urls.py` file, add the following code:

```python
# /becoming_a_django_entdev/urls.py
...
from django.urls
import path
from django.views.generic
import TemplateView
urlpatterns = [
    path(
        '',
        TemplateView.as_view(
            template_name = 'chapter_4/index.html'
        )
    ),
]
```

The preceding `path()` function is used to listen for a route/path defined as nothing (`''`), and then we are using the built-in `TemplateView` class, provided by the `django.views.generic` library, to serve up the home page in template form. Since this is a static page and a static URL, meaning no content on the page will change and the URL itself will not change either, we do not need to write a view class to handle how the context of the page will change. Instead, we can skip creating the view in this example by using the `TemplateView` class. With a `TemplateView` class, we could still pass in keyword arguments and define the `name` argument if we wanted to. If we did want to pass in `kwargs`, that would be done using the following step.

4. Add `kwargs` to your home page:

```python
# /becoming_a_django_entdev/urls.py
...
urlpatterns = [
    path(
        '',
        TemplateView.as_view(
            template_name = 'chapter_4/index.html'
        ),
        kwargs = {
            'sub_title': 'I am the sub title.'
        }
    ),
]
```

5. In the /chapter_4/index.html file that is provided with this book, a conditional will check whether `sub_title` has a value and then displays that value in your template. Copy that conditional into your file, as highlighted here:

```html
# /becoming_a_django_entdev/chapter_4/templates/chapter_4/index.html
{% load static %}

<html>
    <head><title></title></head>
    <body style="text-align:center">
        <p>Home Page</p>
        <img src="{% static 'chapter_4/home_page.jpg' %}" role="img" alt="Home Page Image" width="400" style="margin: 0 auto" />
        {% if sub_title %}
        <p>{{ sub_title }}</p>
        {% endif %}
    </body>
</html>
```

We will explain more about building templates before the end of this chapter, in the *Working with templates* section.

One of the reasons we configured our project to handle static files in *Chapter 2, Project Configuration*, and in this chapter, under the subsection titled *Static files*, was to access those files within a template, as is done in the example shown previously. The `{% load static %}` tag statement allows us to begin using the `static` template tag, such as `{% static 'chapter_4/home_page.jpg' %}`. The `{% static %}` tag returns a working URL, pointing to the image file at `http://localhost:8000/chapter_4/home_page.jpg`.

6. Create the `/static/chapter_4/` folder in your project using the IDE, file browser, or the following command:

   ```
   (virtual_env) PS > mkdir becoming_a_django_entdev/
   chapter_4/static/chapter_4
   ```

7. Copy the `/chapter_4/home_page.jpg` file provided with the code of this book into your project.

   Django automatically searches the `static` folder found in each app of a project. It is common practice to override static files, such as images, CSS, and JavaScript files, of packages that are installed in your virtual environment by including the same path and filename in the static folder of any app in your project. The same principle also applies when working with template files.

   In *step 5*, the highlighted `{{ sub_title }}` variable tag is the keyword argument that was passed into that URL pattern in *step 4*. A custom function/callable can also be used instead of hardcoding a value here. Any context variable can be recalled in a template using the bracket syntax, `{{ }}`. Objects such as a dictionary, list, set, and query set can all be accessed using a period for each key and subkey, as in `{{ context_variable.key.subkey }}`.

8. Now, run your project and you should no longer see a 404 debug message. Instead, you should see the following screenshot:

Home Page

Chapter 4

HOME PAGE

I am the sub title.

Figure 4.3 – Project home page

Next, let's work with the `include()` function to import URL patterns from other apps/packages.

Function – include()

The `include()` function is used to import additional `urls.py` files that contain their own `urlpatterns` variable. This is how we can write URL patterns for reusable apps, and then include them for use in a project within `ROOT_URLCONF` of a site.

Let's use this to better organize our chapter-specific URL patterns by following these steps:

1. If this file was not already created for you, go ahead and create a `urls.py` file inside of your `/becoming_a_django_entdev/chapter_4/` folder, and then add the following URL pattern to that file:

```python
# /becoming_a_django_entdev/chapter_4/urls.py
from django.urls import path
from django.views.generic import TemplateView
urlpatterns = [
    path(
        'chapter-4/',
        TemplateView.as_view(
            template_name='chapter_4/chapter_4.html'
        )
    ),
]
```

2. In the main /becoming_a_django_entdev/urls.py file that we have been using, comment out the previous patterns that we created in this chapter and add the following path statement:

```
# /becoming_a_django_entdev/urls.py
...
from django.urls
import include, path

urlpatterns = [
    path(
        '',
        include(
            'becoming_a_django_entdev.chapter_4.urls'
        )
    ),
]
```

3. Copy the chapter_4.html template file that is provided with the code of this book into your project, found in the /becoming_a_django_entdev/chapter_4/templates/chapter_4/ directory.

4. Navigate to the URL http://localhost:8000/chapter-4/, and you should see a white page that only says **This is Chapter 4**, as shown in the following screenshot:

This is Chapter 4

Figure 4.4 – URL pattern – include()

Now that we have the `include()` example working, we will put all new URL patterns in the `/chapter_4/urls.py` file and organize all future chapters in a similar manner.

Now, let's practice redirecting URLs.

Redirecting patterns

Instead of using the `TemplateView` class as we have been, we can write URL patterns to handle redirects from within the project, without having to configure them directly in a web server. This is convenient because in traditional web development, redirects are handled by the web server and it is much easier to manage in a project than it is in a web server. Redirects can be handled using the `RedirectView` class provided by Django.

We are going to specify a redirect rule on the `http://localhost:8000/my_path/my_unwanted_url/` path to take us to `http://localhost:8000/my_wanted_url/` instead. Follow these steps to configure your redirect:

1. Add the following pattern to your existing `/chapter_4/urls.py` file:

    ```
    # /becoming_a_django_entdev/chapter_4/urls.py
    ...
    from django.urls
    import include, path
    from django.views.generic
    import (
        TemplateView,
        RedirectView
    )
    urlpatterns = [
        ...,
        path(
            'my_path/my_unwanted_url/',
            RedirectView.as_view(
                url = 'http://localhost:8000/my_wanted_url/'
            )
        ),
    ]
    ```

2. Run your project and navigate to the URL http://localhost:8000/my_path/my_unwanted_url/. You should now be redirected to, and also see in the address bar of the browser, http://localhost:8000/my_wanted_url/. In the body of the page, you should see a 404 response because we have not yet defined a URL pattern for the my_wanted_url path. This is to be expected when performing this step.

3. Additional arguments can be included, such as stating that we want this to be a permanent or temporary redirect, by writing the path using the following example:

```
# /becoming_a_django_entdev/chapter_4/urls.py
...
urlpatterns = [
    ...,
    path(
        'my_path/my_unwanted_url/',
        RedirectView.as_view(
            url = 'http://localhost:8000/my_wanted_url/',
            permanent = True
        )
    ),
]
```

Django also allows us to define `pattern_name` and `query_string` as additional arguments of the `RedirectView` class.

> **Note**
> The preceding path has a hardcoded value of http://localhost:8000/, which can become a problem in a remote environment that is not your local machine. To overcome this, you will need to adopt the concept of global context variables discussed later in this chapter in the subsection titled *Creating a context processor*.

Next, let's discuss using path converters to listen for dynamic path routes.

Using path converters

A **path converter** in Django is a URL pattern that is designed to listen to a dynamic path, where that path can change. There are five standard path converters built into Django and available to use: `str`, `int`, `slug`, `uuid`, and `path`. These are preformatted converters that allow a variety of choices and permit strings and integers within a pattern. For example, the path converter called `path` is used in the following code to search for any variety of characters, numbers, and certain symbols that a URL can possess.

To practice using path converters, follow these steps:

1. Add the following URL pattern to your `/chapter_4/urls.py` file:

    ```python
    # /becoming_a_django_entdev/chapter_4/urls.py
    ...
    from django.urls import include, path
    from django.views.generic import ..., TemplateView

    urlpatterns = [
        ...,
        path(
            'my_path/<path:my_pattern>/',
            TemplateView.as_view(
                template_name = 'chapter_4/index.html'
            )
        ),
    ]
    ```

2. Now, navigate to the URL `http://localhost:8000/my_path/testing/`, and you should see the same home page that we saw before. We are seeing the same page because we are pointing to the same `index.html` file, just to see that it is working. Additionally, if we navigate to the URL `http://localhost:8000/my_path/2022/`, we will also see the same home page. This is to be expected. The one thing we won't see is the value of the `sub_title` keyword argument on this page because we did not pass that into this URL pattern. The conditional `{% if sub_title %}` statement found in that template is used to prevent breakage if no `sub_title` is provided.

3. Change the existing `my_path` path converter shown in *step 1* from path to int and change `my_path` to `my_year_path`, as shown in the following code, allowing for the URL `http://localhost:8000/my_year_path/2022/` to work:

   ```
   # /becoming_a_django_entdev/chapter_4/urls.py
   ...
   from django.urls
   import include, path
   from django.views.generic
   import ..., TemplateView

   urlpatterns = [
       ...,
       path(
           'my_year_path/<int:my_year>/',
           TemplateView.as_view(
               template_name = 'chapter_4/index.html'
           )
       )
   ]
   ```

4. Next, run your project again. With the `int` path converter, the URL `http://localhost:8000/my_year_path/testing/` should no longer work when we try to navigate to it. Instead, we should see the same 404 debug message that we saw earlier. It will only allow a numeric value of any length now. This means we should see the home page image when we visit the URL `http://localhost:8000/my_year_path/2/`, or any numeric value.

When we wrote `int:my_year`, the `my_year` in this argument can be named anything we want. The same applies to the `my_pattern` in the `path:my_pattern` argument and in any other converter type. The second parameter is what is used to access that key word argument in a view class or method.

Let's write a custom path converter next.

Custom path converters

A custom path converter is a way for us to write a class that uses a regular expression to define the path that Django listens for. The converter class is structured in a way to return the data type that is intended to be used in the view, such as an `int` data type used in the example of the previous subsection. This class also returns another string representation of the data type sent to the view that is intended to be used in the URL. For example, if we do not want `http://localhost:8000/my_year_path/2/` to be a valid URL and we only want to allow four-digit numbers, a custom path converter can be used to accomplish this.

Follow these steps to create your custom path converter:

1. In your `/chapter_4/` app directory, create a new file called `converters.py`.
2. Inside the file, add the following class, with the two methods provided:

   ```python
   # /becoming_a_django_entdev/chapter_4/converters.py
   class YearConverter:
       regex = '[0-9]{4}'

       def to_python(self, value):
           return int(value)

       def to_url(self, value):
           return '%04d' % value
   ```

3. In your `/chapter_4/urls.py` file, add the following code, which registers the newly created converter class for use where it is highlighted in `<year:year>` in the following code block:

   ```python
   # /becoming_a_django_entdev/chapter_4/urls.py
   ...
   from django.urls
   import path, register_converter
   from .converters
   import YearConverter

   register_converter(YearConverter, 'year')
   urlpatterns = [
       ...,
   ```

```
        path(
            'my_year_path/<year:year>/',
            TemplateView.as_view(
                template_name = 'chapter_4/index.html'
            )
        ),
    ]
```

4. Now, run your project and navigate to the URL `http://localhost:8000/my_year_path/2/`; you should see a 404 debug message. This occurs because the preceding pattern will only accept a four-digit integer now, including `0001` and `1111`, which is to be expected.

We can get even more in-depth by writing a method-based or class-based view and in that view compare whether a year is greater than, say, the year 1900, and if it is not, return a 404 response. We will discuss doing that soon in the section titled *Working with conditional responses* of this chapter.

Next, let's practice working with regular expression paths.

Function – re_path()

A `re_path()` function, better known as a regular expression path function, is similar to a `path()` function but allows us to pass in a formatted regular expression string as the route parameter without the need to create a custom path converter.

For example, we could write the same year example as previously without the converter class. In your `/chapter_4/urls.py` file, add the path shown as follows, and comment out the previous `my_year_path`:

```
# /becoming_a_django_entdev/chapter_4/urls.py
...
from django.urls
import path, re_path
...
urlpatterns = [
    ...,
    re_path(
        'my_year_path/(?P<year>[0-9]{4})/$',
        TemplateView.as_view(
            template_name = 'chapter_4/index.html'
```

```
            )
        ),
    ]
```

There is actually a difference between using a `re_path()` function and writing your own converter class. The difference is in the data type of the value of the pattern recognized when we use that value within a view class or method. With the `re_path()` function, the data type of this value when used in a view will always be a string, whereas the data type of the value when using a converter class will always be the data type defined by the `def to_python()` method of that class, meaning you can transform the data type to anything you want, if you need to.

Before we illustrate the difference in data types between using a converter class and using the `re_path()` function, let's map a URL pattern to a simple view.

Mapping URL patterns

Writing custom views is a way for us to perform all of the tasks and services needed to render a page that includes all of the content that we want. Within a view, we can validate against business logic rules to determine how to handle a request.

In this exercise, we will use the year pattern that we wrote earlier in this chapter, to only allow a year greater than 1900. Anything less than that, we will tell Django to serve up a 404 response.

Using simple views

A **simple view** is also known as a method-based view, which is a callable function in Python.

Follow these steps to map to a simple view in your project:

1. In your `/chapter_4/urls.py` file, revert to using the same converter class that we wrote in the *Using path converters* subsection of this chapter. Reference a view that we will write next in a different file called `practice_view()`, as highlighted here:

   ```
   # /becoming_a_django_entdev/chapter_4/urls.py
   ...
   from django.urls
   import ..., register_converter
   from .converters
   ```

```
import YearConverter
from .views import practice_view

register_converter(YearConverter, 'year')
urlpatterns = [
    ...,
    path(
        'my_year_path/<year:year>/',
        practice_view
    ),
]
```

The thing we did differently from before is that we replaced the `TemplateView` class with a custom simple view class, called `practice_view`.

2. Create the view method called `practice_view()` in a `views.py` file in your `/becoming_a_django_entdev/chapter_4/` directory. Then, add the code shown here:

```
# /becoming_a_django_entdev/chapter_4/views.py
from django.template.response import (
    TemplateResponse
)

def practice_view(request, year):
    return TemplateResponse(
        request,
        'chapter_4/my_practice_page.html',
        {
            'year': year
        }
    )
```

3. Copy the template file provided with the code of this book into your project, located at `/becoming_a_django_entdev/chapter_4/templates/chapter_4/my_practice_page.html`.

4. Navigate to the URL http://localhost:8000/my_year_path/1066/ and you should see the practice page shown in the following screenshot:

My Practice Page

1066

Figure 4.5 – Out-of-bounds year returns valid response

We are almost there. The success message we see here is to be expected. What we actually want is to return a 404 response instead of a valid path, in order to comply with the business logic discussed earlier, to only allow a year greater than or equal to 1900. Therefore, we need to use keyword arguments and conditional statements to perform custom validation when a request is processed, which we will do next.

Using kwargs in views

To access keyword arguments inside of a view method, we need to pass it in as a positional argument of that method. In the example, `def practice_view(request, year):`, `year` would be the positional keyword argument. Since we defined a path converter in the `urls.py` file with the name of `year`, we are required to include `year` as a positional argument when accessing a view with that same name. Without this argument, Django would give us an error during runtime.

Follow these steps to configure your `view` method:

1. In your `/chapter_4/urls.py` file, use the following URL pattern along with the same path converter class that we created earlier. Comment out the other `my_year_path` patterns:

```
# /becoming_a_django_entdev/chapter_4/urls.py
...
from django.urls
import ..., register_converter
from .converters
import YearConverter
from .views
import ..., practice_year_view

register_converter(YearConverter, 'year')
urlpatterns = [
```

```
    ...,
    path(
        'my_year_path/<year:year>/',
        practice_year_view
    ),
]
```

2. In your /chapter_4/views.py file, write the new method provided here:

```
# /becoming_a_django_entdev/chapter_4/views.py
from django.template.response import (
    TemplateResponse
)
...
def practice_year_view(request, year):
    print(type(year))
    print(year)

    return TemplateResponse(
        request,
        'chapter_4/my_year.html',
        {'year': year}
    )
```

3. Copy the template file provided with the code of this book, found in /becoming_a_django_entdev/chapter_4/templates/chapter_4/my_year.html.

4. Now, navigate to the URL `http://localhost:8000/my_year_path/2022/` and you should see a successful response. When we look at the terminal or command window, we will see that it is telling us the value of `year` is `2022` and that it is of an integer, `<class 'int'>`, data type, as depicted in the following screenshot:

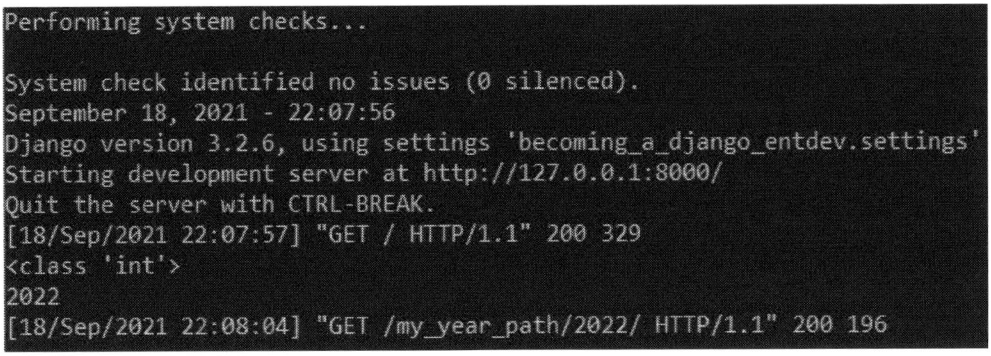

```
Performing system checks...

System check identified no issues (0 silenced).
September 18, 2021 - 22:07:56
Django version 3.2.6, using settings 'becoming_a_django_entdev.settings'
Starting development server at http://127.0.0.1:8000/
Quit the server with CTRL-BREAK.
[18/Sep/2021 22:07:57] "GET / HTTP/1.1" 200 329
<class 'int'>
2022
[18/Sep/2021 22:08:04] "GET /my_year_path/2022/ HTTP/1.1" 200 196
```

Figure 4.6 – Converter class – integer data type

5. Change the URL pattern in your `/chapter_4/urls.py` file back to using the `re_path()` function instead of the custom `YearConverter` example, as shown:

```python
# /becoming_a_django_entdev/chapter_4/urls.py
...
from .views
import ..., practice_year_view

#register_converter(YearConverter, 'year')
urlpatterns = [
    ...,
    re_path(
        'my_year_path/(?P<year>[0-9]{4})/$',
        practice_year_view
    ),
]
```

You can comment out the `register_converter` that we previously used.

6. Visit the URL `http://localhost:8000/my_year_path/2022/` one more time. You should see how the output will change from `<class 'int'>` to `<class 'str'>` in your terminal or command-line window, as depicted here:

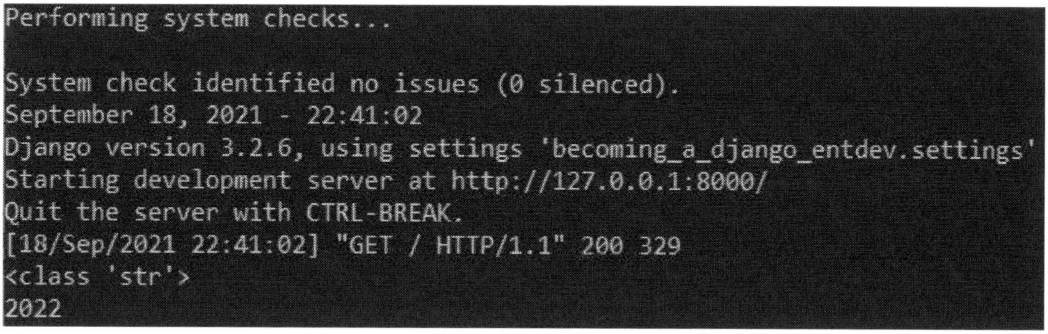

```
Performing system checks...

System check identified no issues (0 silenced).
September 18, 2021 - 22:41:02
Django version 3.2.6, using settings 'becoming_a_django_entdev.settings'
Starting development server at http://127.0.0.1:8000/
Quit the server with CTRL-BREAK.
[18/Sep/2021 22:41:02] "GET / HTTP/1.1" 200 329
<class 'str'>
2022
```

Figure 4.7 – Converter class – string data type

Now, we can actually see the differences between writing a pattern using `re_path()` and the alternative, going through the steps to create a custom converter class. With the `re_path()` function, we now have to take additional steps in a view to convert a keyword argument into an integer before we can even check whether the `year` value is greater than a certain year. If we do not do that conversion, we would wind up with an error telling us `'>='` **not supported between instances of 'str' and 'int'**. If the same regular expression pattern is used over and over again, it would mean converting a string into an integer many times, one time for each view that is being used by that pattern. This is what is known as the **Write Everything Twice** (**WET**) design principle and is usually frowned upon. Writing a converter class will solve that problem and allow you to write it just once according to the **Don't Repeat Yourself** (**DRY**) design principle.

Let's work with conditional responses next.

Working with conditional responses

Instead of returning a valid `TemplateResponse()` like we have been doing in previous exercises, we will finally check if the value of the `year` kwarg is greater than or equal to `1900`. If the `year` value is less than `1900`, we are going to raise a `Http404()` response. Using the URL pattern that uses the custom path converter `YearConverter` class that we wrote earlier, we will serve up an integer instead of a string as the data type of the keyword argument `year`, allowing us to perform mathematical operations using that value.

Follow these steps to configure your conditional statements:

1. In your `/chapter_4/urls.py` file, add the following code, making sure to comment out or delete the other `my_year_path` patterns:

    ```
    # /becoming_a_django_entdev/chapter_4/urls.py
    ...
    from django.urls
    import ..., register_converter
    from .converters
    import YearConverter
    from .views
    import ..., practice_year_view

    register_converter(YearConverter, 'year')
    urlpatterns = [
        ...,
        path(
            'my_year_path/<year:year>/',
            practice_year_view
        ),
    ]
    ```

2. In your `/chapter_4/views.py` file, modify `practice_year_view()` to look like the following highlighted code:

    ```
    # /becoming_a_django_entdev/chapter_4/views.py
    from django.http
    import Http404
    from django.template.response
    import (
    ```

```
        TemplateResponse
    )

    def practice_year_view(request, year):
        if year >= 1900:
            return TemplateResponse(
                request,
                'chapter_4/my_year.html',
                {'year': year}
            )
        else:
            raise Http404(f'Year Not Found: {year}')
```

3. Now, visit the URL `http://localhost:8000/my_year_path/1066/`, and you should see the following 404 message, which is intentional:

Page not found (404)

Year Not Found: 1066

Request Method: GET
Request URL: http://localhost:8000/my_year_path/1066/
Raised by: becoming_a_django_entdev.chapter_4.views.practice_year_view

Using the URLconf defined in `becoming_a_django_entdev.urls`, Django tried these URL patterns, i
1.
2. admin/
3. my_year_path/<year:year>/

The current path, `my_year_path/1066/`, matched the last one.

You're seeing this error because you have DEBUG = True in your Django settings file. Change that to

Figure 4.8 – Out-of-bounds year returns invalid response

4. Next, visit a path with a year greater than 1900, such as `http://localhost:8000/my_year_path/2022/`, and you should see a successful response, as on the year page depicted here:

Year Page

2022

Figure 4.9 – In-bounds year returns valid response

Let's link models to our views and templates next.

Linking models to views and templates

Using the same models that we created in *Chapter 3, Models, Relations, and Inheritance*, we can provide information about those objects within a template. We will write a URL pattern that will point to a new simple view method and display information about a vehicle.

Follow these steps to display model information in your templates:

1. In your `/chapter_4/urls.py` file, include the following URL pattern:

    ```
    # /becoming_a_django_entdev/chapter_4/urls.py
    ...
    from .views
    import ..., vehicle_view

    urlpatterns = [
        ...,
        path(
            'vehicle/<int:id>/',
            vehicle_view,
            name = 'vehicle-detail'
        ),
    ]
    ```

    Our new view will listen for the primary key, also known as the ID, that is passed in to us as a keyword argument of that path converter. The ID is used to look up that object in the database, and if not found, it will serve up a 404 response instead. Instead of writing `<int:id>`, we could target the path converter to listen for a string, such as the VIN using `<str:vin>`. Then, in the view where we perform the database query, search for a record matching the VIN instead of the ID of a vehicle. You are welcome to practice both options.

2. In your `/chapter_4/views.py` file, add the following `import` statement and `view` method:

    ```
    # /becoming_a_django_entdev/chapter_4/views.py
    ...
    from django.http
    import Http404
    from ..chapter_3.models
    import Vehicle
    ```

```python
def vehicle_view(request, id):
    try:
        vehicle = Vehicle.objects.get(id=id)
    except Vehicle.DoesNotExist:
        raise Http404(f'Vehicle ID Not Found: {id}')

    return TemplateResponse(
        request,
        'chapter_4/my_vehicle.html',
        {'vehicle': vehicle}
    )
```

The preceding `import` statement uses two periods (..), which is Python path syntax, to navigate up one directory level and enter the sibling `chapter_3` folder, to access the models that are written in the `chapter_3` app. When you are working with many different apps in your project, this is common practice. The `try/except` block shown previously checks to see whether the requested object exists and if it does exist, a 404 response is raised.

3. Copy the template file that has been provided along with the code of this book, located at `/becoming_a_django_entdev/chapter_4/templates/chapter_4/my_vehicle.html`.

We can access any field in a model object from within the template by using the name of the context variable that we passed into `TemplateResponse`. For example, when used in a template file, the `vehicle` context variable would be written as `{{ vehicle.vin }}`. This is already done in the template file you just copied into your project.

4. Run your project and navigate to `http://localhost:8000/vehicle/4/`. You should see vehicle detail information on this page, as shown in the following screenshot:

Vehicle Page

aa456789012345678

False

$32,600.00

3

Blazer LT

3.6L DI DOHC 6cyl

Figure 4.10 – Vehicle ID = 4

If you change the ID in your URL, the vehicle will change. If you activated the VIN as the path converter, then you would navigate to `http://localhost:8000/vehicle/aa456789012345678/` in order to see the same results, using the data provided in the `chapter_3` data fixture.

Now that we have views to work with, we can practice getting the reverse URL when providing only the `kwarg` of a path converter and the `name` attribute value.

Resolving URLs

Resolving a URL is the process of taking a relative path or object and obtaining the URL that relates to a unique field such as a primary key. Django's reverse resolution of URL patterns is a method of generating a URL structure using argument values that we provide instead of hardcoding URL paths in places, which can break over time. We can use template tags and statements throughout the project to use the `name` argument of a URL pattern. This is encouraged as best practice and follows a DRY design principle, which is less prone to breakage as your project evolves.

Let's discuss how to use the `name` attribute to get a reverse resolution pattern.

Naming URL patterns

Using the same custom `YearConverter` class and the same `my_year_path` URL pattern that we created earlier in this chapter, do the following to configure your URL pattern.

In your `/chapter_4/urls.py` file, you should have the path shown in the following code block, using the highlighted `name` attribute:

```python
# /becoming_a_django_entdev/chapter_4/urls.py
...
from django.urls
import ..., register_converter
from .converters
import YearConverter
from .views
import ..., practice_year_view

register_converter(YearConverter, 'year')
urlpatterns = [
    ...,
    path(
        'my_year_path/<year:year>/',
        practice_year_view,
        name = 'year_url'
    ),
]
```

Now we can use a `reverse()` function, which we will do next.

Using the reverse() function

The `reverse()` function provides us with the relative URL of an object, providing the `name` attribute value. In our view, we will write several `print` statements to tell us the relative path of objects when provided with different input arguments.

Follow these steps to configure your `view` method:

1. In your `/chapter_4/views.py` file, add the following `import` statement, below the existing `import` statements:

    ```python
    # /becoming_a_django_entdev/chapter_4/views.py
    ...
    from django.urls import reverse
    ```

2. In your /chapter_4/views.py file, and in the same practice_year_view() method, go ahead and include the following print statements. Make sure these are placed before your conditional statement that executes the return/raise calls:

```python
# /becoming_a_django_entdev/chapter_4/views.py
...
def practice_year_view(request, year):
    ...
    print(reverse('year_url', args=(2023,)))
    print(reverse('year_url', args=(2024,)))
    ...( Repeat as desired )...
```

3. Run your project and navigate to any URL using this pattern, such as http://localhost:8000/my_year_path/2022/. What will be printed in your terminal or command-line window is the formatted relative path for each of the URLs, as shown in the following screenshot:

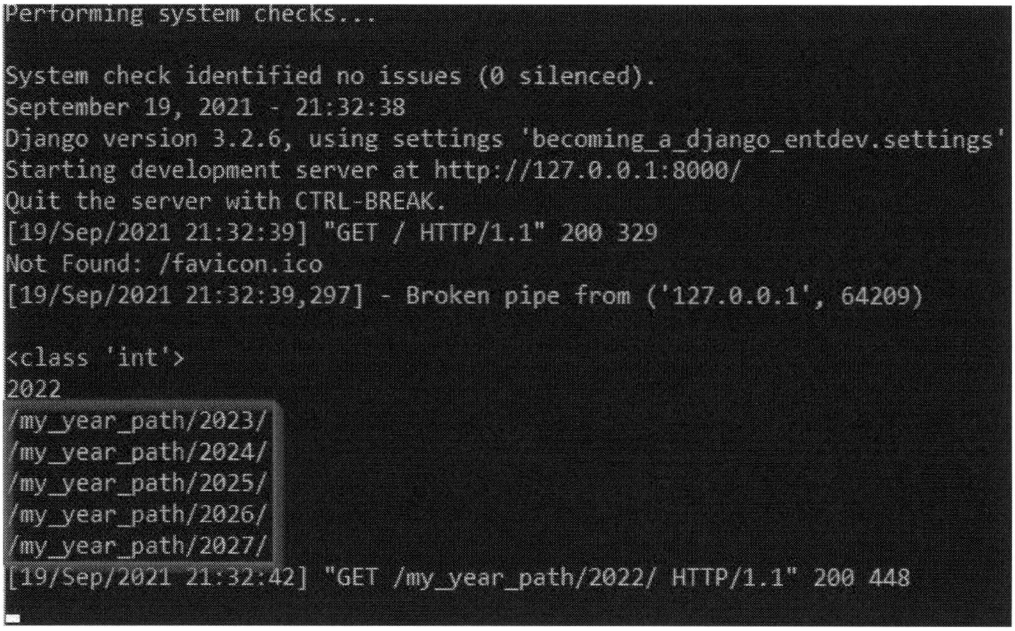

```
Performing system checks...

System check identified no issues (0 silenced).
September 19, 2021 - 21:32:38
Django version 3.2.6, using settings 'becoming_a_django_entdev.settings'
Starting development server at http://127.0.0.1:8000/
Quit the server with CTRL-BREAK.
[19/Sep/2021 21:32:39] "GET / HTTP/1.1" 200 329
Not Found: /favicon.ico
[19/Sep/2021 21:32:39,297] - Broken pipe from ('127.0.0.1', 64209)

<class 'int'>
2022
/my_year_path/2023/
/my_year_path/2024/
/my_year_path/2025/
/my_year_path/2026/
/my_year_path/2027/
[19/Sep/2021 21:32:42] "GET /my_year_path/2022/ HTTP/1.1" 200 448
```

Figure 4.11 – Naming URL – view usage

The `reverse()` method is how we can look up a URL, using the arguments that are passed into that function. The `reverse()` method can be imported and used anywhere within a project, not just within a view class or method. This method takes in two positional arguments, the first being the name of a URL pattern, such as `year_url` highlighted in the preceding example, and is required. The second positional argument is the keyword arguments that get passed into the `reverse()` method, which is sometimes required. If there is more than one path converter defined for a URL pattern, they would be included in the `reverse()` method in the order in which they were created for that pattern and separated by a comma. Remember that the position of the keyword arguments pertaining to each path converter is important and follows the order in which keyword arguments were created for that URL pattern.

Using the {% url %} template tag

The `{% url arg1 arg2 %}` template tag works just like the `reverse()` method, except used directly in a template. This tag also takes in two positional arguments, just like the `reverse()` method does. The first argument listens for the name of the URL pattern and the second is the arguments list. These arguments are separated with a space when using this template tag. Additional arguments are provided in the order the path converters were created for that URL pattern. When using the `{% url %}` tag, it is acceptable to include arguments written with and without keyword syntax. For example, both of the following tags and how they are used are valid:

```
# Dummy Code
{% url 'year_url' 2023 5 25 %}
{% url 'year_url' year=2023 month=5 day=25 %}
```

The second example in the preceding code block would be used if we had actually created three path converters for the URL pattern, being `year`, `month`, and `day`.

They can also be replaced by using context variables, if we created the three context variables called `year`, `month`, and `day` to be used in a template, as shown in the following code block:

```
# Dummy Code
{% url 'year_url' year month day %}
```

The code shown previously was for illustrative purposes only and will break if you try to use it without building the related URL patterns and views.

Follow these steps to configure your project for this exercise:

1. In your existing /chapter_4/my_year.html file, uncomment the following hyperlinks that have been provided with the code of the book when you copied this file into your project or add them manually as shown. They are formatted using the Django {% url %} template tag:

    ```
    # /becoming_a_django_entdev/chapter_4/templates/
    chapter_4/my_year.html
    ...
    <html>
        ...
        <body style="text-align:center">
            ...
            <br /> <br />
            <a href="{% url 'year_url' 2023 %}">2023</a>
            <a href="{% url 'year_url' 2024 %}">2024</a>
            ...( Repeat as desired )...
        </body>
    </html>
    ```

2. Run your project and navigate to the same URL, http://localhost:8000/my_year_path/2022/, and you should now see what is depicted in the following screenshot, with the hyperlinks rendered to the page:

Year Page

2022

2023 2024 2025 2026 2027

Figure 4.12 – Naming URL – template usage

Each hyperlink that is rendered points to the correlating relative path at href="/my_year_path/####/". We can continue modifying these two examples to format absolute URLs instead of relative URLs. This means we will include the www.example.com part of the URL. We will discuss that in the section titled *Resolving absolute URLs* later in this chapter. Let's process trailing slashes next.

Processing trailing slashes

In Django, we can use the `re_path()` function in combination with the custom `YearConverter` class to write one URL pattern accepting a path with and without a trailing slash, /. What this means is that we can write a URL to listen for www.example.com/my_path/ and will also allow www.example.com/my_path to render a success, essentially combining two paths into one statement.

To process your trailing slashes, in your /chapter_4/urls.py file, add the following path and comment out all other my_year_path examples:

```python
# /becoming_a_django_entdev/chapter_4/urls.py
...
from django.urls import (
    ...,
    re_path,
    register_converter
)
from .converters import YearConverter
from .views import ..., practice_view

register_converter(YearConverter, 'year')
urlpatterns = [
    ...,
    re_path(
        r'^my_year_path/(?P<year>[0-9]+)/?$',
        practice_view
    ),
]
```

route is defined in the `re_path()` function as `r'^my_year_path/(?P<year>[0-9]+)/?$'`, which constructs the path in a way that will listen for an optional forward slash. `year` is also written using just the tag name. If we were to write the statement using `<year:year>` as we did in previous exercises, then we would receive the following error message in the terminal or command-line window:

```
django.core.exceptions.ImproperlyConfigured: "^my_year_path/
(?P<year:year>[0-9]+)/?$" is not a valid regular expression:
bad character in group name 'year:year' at position 18
```

Since we are listening for a trailing slash via the use of regular expression operations, there is no need to modify values in the `settings.py` file, such as `APPEND_SLASH`. In order to actually use the `APPEND_SLASH` variable, Django requires the `common` middleware to be installed. You can learn more about using this approach instead of the regular expression approach here: https://docs.djangoproject.com/en/4.0/ref/settings/#append-slash. Using the regular expression basic structure shown previously, we don't need to worry about middleware.

Now that we have resolved relative URLs, let's resolve absolute URLs next.

Resolving absolute URLs

An absolute URL includes the scheme, host, and port of a URL, as in the following format, `scheme://host:port/path?query`. This is an example of an absolute URL: `https://www.example.com:8000/my_path?query=my_query_value`.

Next, we will resolve an absolute URL while introducing the practice of using custom context processors.

Creating a context processor

Context processors are useful in many ways: they provide context that is shared globally among all templates and views within a project. Alternatively, the context being created in a view can only be used by the template that the view is using and no other templates. In the next example, we will create and then activate a custom global context processor where we will add the base URL of the site. We will call the context variable `base_url`, referring to `scheme://host:port` of the URL found throughout this project's site.

Follow these steps to create your context processor:

1. In the same folder as your `settings.py` file, create a new file called `context_processors.py`.
2. Inside this file, place the code provided as follows, which will construct the `http://localhost:8000` portion of the site based on the environment we are running the project on:

   ```
   # /becoming_a_django_entdev/context_processors.py
   def global_context(request):
       return {
           'base_url': request.build_absolute_uri(
               '/'
           )[:-1].strip('/'),
       }
   ```

   Context is returned as a dictionary of key-value pairs, where we can pack as many keys as we would like to.

3. To register this context processor for inclusion during runtime, we need to add it to the `settings.py` file, under the `TEMPLATES` variable. Include the path to your `global_context()` method, as shown:

   ```
   # /becoming_a_django_entdev/settings.py
   TEMPLATES = [
   {
       ...
       'OPTIONS':
       {
           'context_processors': [
               ...,
               'becoming_a_django_entdev.context_processors.global_context',
           ],
       },
   },]
   ```

   Place your custom context processor below any existing `context_processors` in the preceding list.

Context processors can be broken down into individual apps within a project as well. Include each additional context processor that you create inside the preceding list and in the order desired. Additional global context processor variables have been included with the code of this book for extra practice as well.

Let's use our newly created `base_url` context in a template next.

Using context processor data in a template

Using a `{% url %}` template tag, we can modify hyperlinks to use the context that we just made available in the previous example as a context processor called `global_context()`.

Follow these steps to configure your template:

1. In your `/chapter_4/urls.py` file, add the following path and comment out all other `my_year_path` examples:

   ```
   # /becoming_a_django_entdev/chapter_4/urls.py
   ...
   from django.urls
   import ..., register_converter
   from .converters
   import YearConverter
   from .views
   import ..., practice_year_view

   register_converter(YearConverter, 'year')
   urlpatterns = [
       ...,
       path(
           'my_year_path/<year:year>/',
           practice_year_view,
           name = 'year_url'
       ),
   ]
   ```

2. In your `my_year.html` file, write/uncomment the following hyperlink examples:

```
# /becoming_a_django_entdev/chapter_4/templates/
chapter_4/my_year.html
...
<html>
    ...
    <body style="text-align:center">
        ...
        <br /> <br />
        <a href="{{ base_url }}{% url 'year_url' 2023 %}">2023</a>
        <a href="{{ base_url }}{% url 'year_url' 2024 %}">2024</a>
            ...( Repeat as desired )...
    </body>
</html>
```

3. Navigate to `http://localhost:8000/my_year_path/2022/` one more time. Your `href` attribute on each hyperlink will now look like `href="http://localhost:8000/my_year_path/####/"` instead of what it was rendering before, as `href="/my_year_path/####/"`.

When we added the `{{ base_url }}` template variable, we referenced the dictionary key of the context that was provided.

From the request object

In this exercise, we will resolve the absolute URL using a `request` object. Follow these steps to do that in your project:

1. In your `/chapter_4/views.py` file, in your existing `practice_year_view()` method, include the following `print` statements. These statements will use the `build_absolute_uri()` method provided in your `request` object, as part of the Django framework. This will return to us the absolute URL of the reverse lookup:

```
# /becoming_a_django_entdev/chapter_4/views.py
...
from django.urls import reverse
```

```python
def practice_year_view(request, year):
    ...
    print(
        request.build_absolute_uri(
            reverse('year_url', args=(2023,))
        )
    )
    print(
        request.build_absolute_uri(
            reverse('year_url', args=(2024,))
        )
    )
    ...( Repeat as desired )...
```

The preceding `print` statements also utilize the `reverse()` method found in the `django.urls` library.

2. Run your project and navigate to `http://localhost:8000/my_year_path/2022/`. You should see the following paths printed in your terminal or command-line window:

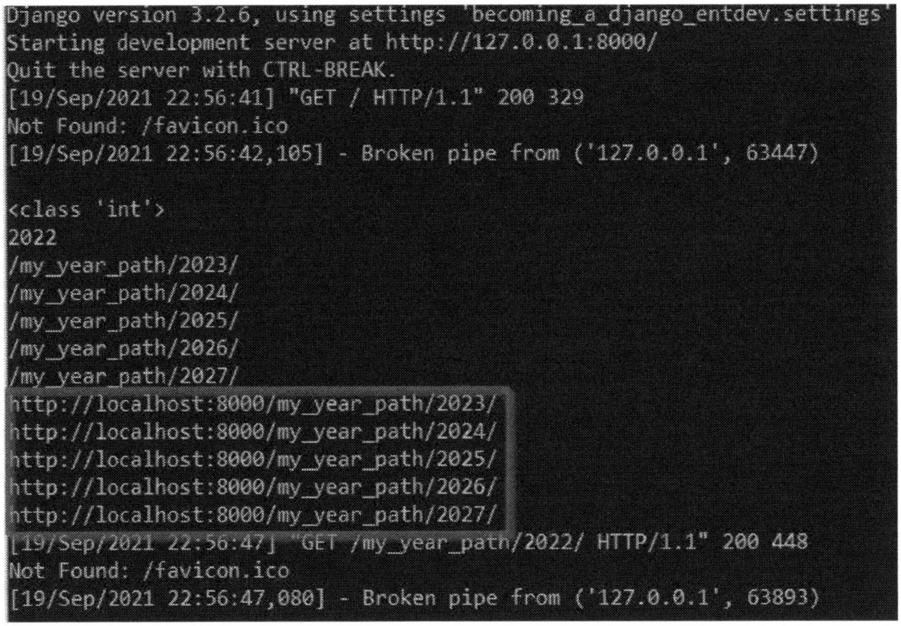

Figure 4.13 – Naming URL – view usage – absolute URL

> **Note**
>
> The relative path of the current page can be retrieved from the `request` object using `print(request.path)`. On this page, it would return `/my_year_path/2022/`. Using `print(request.build_absolute_uri())` without the `reverse()` lookup function will return the absolute path of that particular request.

Let's practice looking up absolute URLs from within a model class next.

From within a model class

We will be expanding on the same `vehicle_view()` method for this next example, to get a formatted URL from an existing object. We are going to work in the same `/chapter_3/models.py` file that we worked on in *Chapter 3, Models, Relations, and Inheritance.*

Follow these steps to configure your model class:

1. In your `/chapter_3/models.py` file, add the following two methods (`get_url()` and `get_absolute_url()`) to your existing `Vehicle` model class:

    ```python
    # /becoming_a_django_entdev/chapter_3/models.py
    class Vehicle(models.Model):
        ...
        def get_url(self):
            from django.urls import reverse
            return reverse(
                'vehicle-detail',
                kwargs = {'id': self.pk}
            )

        def get_absolute_url(self, request):
            from django.urls import reverse
            base_url = request.build_absolute_uri(
                '/'
            )[:-1].strip('/')
            return base_url + reverse(
                'vehicle-detail',
                kwargs = {'id': self.pk}
            )
    ```

These methods import the `reverse()` function that was introduced earlier in this section to get the URL of the object in reference. The `import` statements are added to the methods themselves instead of at the top of this document to allow for better performance handling when using these model class methods. The first method, `get_url()`, is used to return a relative URL path to that object, while the other method, `get_absolute_url()`, is intended to return the absolute path to that object.

2. In your /chapter_4/views.py file, in the existing `vehicle_view()` method, add the following `print` statements as part of the `else` catch, just after the `except` catch:

```python
# /becoming_a_django_entdev/chapter_4/views.py
...
from django.http import Http404
from ..chapter_3.models import Vehicle
...
def vehicle_view(request, id):
    try:
        vehicle = Vehicle.objects.get(id=id)
    except Vehicle.DoesNotExist:
        raise Http404(f'Vehicle ID Not Found: {id}')
    else:
        print(vehicle.get_url())
        print(vehicle.get_absolute_url(request))
...
```

The `else` catch means the `Vehicle` object that it was searching for was found without errors. Remember to leave the same `return` statement that we previously wrote at the end of this `vehicle_view()` method.

3. Run your project and navigate to `http://localhost:8000/vehicle/4/`. In your terminal or command-line window, you should see the two different relative and absolute paths to the object that we looked up in the `vehicle_view()` method, as shown:

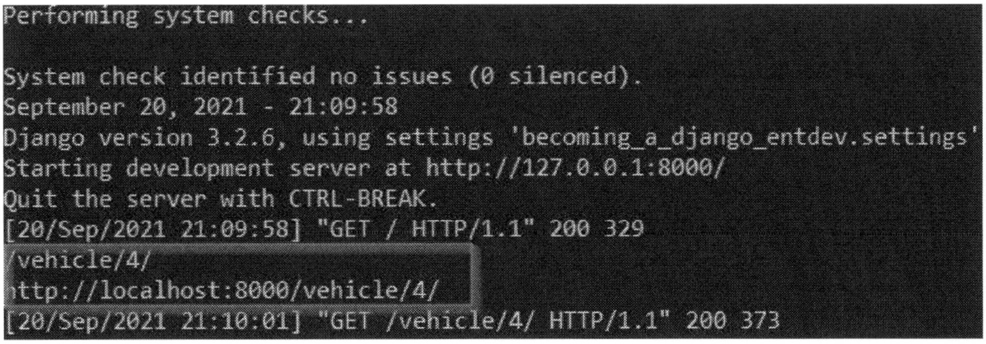

```
Performing system checks...

System check identified no issues (0 silenced).
September 20, 2021 - 21:09:58
Django version 3.2.6, using settings 'becoming_a_django_entdev.settings'
Starting development server at http://127.0.0.1:8000/
Quit the server with CTRL-BREAK.
[20/Sep/2021 21:09:58] "GET / HTTP/1.1" 200 329
/vehicle/4/
http://localhost:8000/vehicle/4/
[20/Sep/2021 21:10:01] "GET /vehicle/4/ HTTP/1.1" 200 373
```

Figure 4.14 – Model URLs

We have been practicing with simple views, otherwise known as method-based views. Many projects need views to provide a bit more power and usability, which can be achieved with class-based views, which we will create next.

Working with complex views

A view method will suffice for a lot of different situations. For more robust and large-scale projects, we can apply a few tricks to make these views more adaptable in complicated use cases. Class-based views are used when writing adaptable and reusable applications.

Class-based views

With class-based views, we can write code that can be reused and extended easily. Just like when we extended models in *Chapter 3, Models, Relations, and Inheritance*, we can extend view classes in the exact same way, whereas function-based view methods cannot provide this ability. Two templates have been provided with the source code of this book to be used in the next exercise. These two files are the exact same file as the `my_vehicle.html` file, except that the title of the `<h1>` tag in each has been changed to **VehicleView Class 1** and **VehicleView Class 2** so that when we run the following examples, we can see the differences between them.

Follow these steps to configure your class-based views:

1. Copy the files called my_vehicle_class_1.html and my_vehicle_class_2.html in the /becoming_a_django_entdev/chapter_4/templates/chapter_4/ directory of the code provided with this book into your project at the same directory.

2. In your /chapter_4/urls.py file, add the following import statement and URL pattern:

   ```
   # /becoming_a_django_entdev/chapter_4/urls.py
   ...
   from .views
   import ..., VehicleView

   urlpatterns = [
       ...,
       path(
           'vehicle/<int:id>/',
           VehicleView.as_view(),
           name = 'vehicle-detail'
       ),
   ]
   ```

   Don't forget to comment out the old /vehicle/ URL patterns that were written before experimenting with this one.

3. In your /chapter_4/views.py file, create the class-based view called VehicleView and add the import statements, as shown:

   ```
   # /becoming_a_django_entdev/chapter_4/views.py
   ...
   from django.http
   import Http404
   from django.template.response
   import (
       TemplateResponse
   )
   from django.views.generic
   import View
   from ..chapter_3.models
   ```

```
import Vehicle
...
class VehicleView(View):
    template_name = 'chapter_4/my_vehicle_class_1.html'
```

4. Add the following get() method to your VehicleView class:

```
# /becoming_a_django_entdev/chapter_4/views.py
...
class VehicleView(View):
    ...
    def get(self, request, id, *args, **kwargs):
        try:
            vehicle = Vehicle.objects.get(id=id)
        except Vehicle.DoesNotExist:
            raise Http404(
                f'Vehicle ID Not Found: {id}'
            )
        return TemplateResponse(
            request,
            self.template_name,
            {'vehicle': vehicle}
        )
```

5. Add the following post() method and import to your VehicleView class:

```
# /becoming_a_django_entdev/chapter_4/views.py
...
from django.http
import ..., HttpResponseRedirect
...
class VehicleView(View):
    ...
    def post(self, request, *args, **kwargs):
        return HttpResponseRedirect(
            '/success/'
        )
```

202　URLs, Views, and Templates

6. Run your project and navigate to `http://localhost:8000/vehicle/4/`. You should see the main title is displayed as **VehicleView Class 1** now.

7. Next, modify the URL pattern to overload `template_name`, using the following example:

```
# /becoming_a_django_entdev/chapter_4/urls.py
...
from .views
import ..., VehicleView
urlpatterns = [
    ...,
    path(
        'vehicle/<int:id>/',
        VehicleView.as_view(
            template_name = 'chapter_4/my_vehicle_class_2.html'
        ),
        name = 'vehicle-detail'
    ),
]
```

8. Now, rerun your project and navigate to the URL at `http://localhost:8000/vehicle/4/`. You should see the title on the page displayed as **VehicleView Class 2** this time.

The `def get()` submethod depicted in *step 4* is where all of the code in the method-based view is moved to. It's also the only required method. Other optional methods, such as `def post()`, are used when working with form objects, when a postback response is executed. It can also be used to redirect the user to a success page, which is illustrated in the code of *step 5*, but you will never get Django to trigger this redirect with how we are using this class now, which is to be expected. We will discuss this in more depth later in *Chapter 5*, *Django Forms*. When we are working with positional keyword arguments of a URL, they are passed into the view class, where the `id` attribute is written in the preceding `get()` method. If you have more than one keyword argument, they would be added after `id` in the order that they exist in that URL pattern.

We performed *step 7* and *step 8* just to check that this is working and to see how we can still override default settings just like we did earlier in this chapter. Let's extend our class-based views next, also known as inheritance.

Extending class-based views

Extending class-based views, also known as inheritance, is done in the exact same way as when we extended model classes in *Chapter 3, Models, Relations, and Inheritance*. We can display the same title on the page by extending the first class into a second class, eliminating the need to define `template_name` in the URL pattern itself, among many other benefits.

Follow these steps to extend your class:

1. In your `/chapter_4/urls.py` file, comment out the previous URL patterns and write a new one using the code provided, where we are using `VehicleView2` as the view class now:

    ```
    # /becoming_a_django_entdev/chapter_4/urls.py
    ...
    from .views
    import ..., VehicleView2
    urlpatterns = [
        ...,
        path(
            'vehicle/<int:id>/',
            VehicleView2.as_view(),
            name = 'vehicle-detail'
        ),
    ]
    ```

2. Next, in your `/chapter_4/views.py` file, add the following `VehicleView2` class constructed from the `VehicleView` class:

    ```
    # /becoming_a_django_entdev/chapter_4/views.py
    ...
    class VehicleView2(VehicleView):
        template_name = 'chapter_4/my_vehicle_class_2.html'
    ```

3. Run your project and navigate to the URL `http://localhost:8000/vehicle/4/`. You should see the same title, **VehicleView Class 2**, displayed on the page.

The preceding example is just a very simple extension of the existing `VehicleView` class that demonstrates how to extend a view class. The only thing we are changing/overriding in this exercise is the `template_name` variable in order to demonstrate this concept.

Next, let's learn what asynchronous views are used for.

Asynchronous views

Django also offers support of asynchronous views, a feature first introduced in Django 3.1. Asynchronous views are views that can be processed in individual processing threads and run together at the same time. These are used to build better multithreaded apps. Traditional Django projects use the **Web Server Gateway Interface** (**WSGI**) by default. To actually use asynchronous function- and class-based views, we need to configure a project and the server to use the **Asynchronous Server Gateway Interface** (**ASGI**) instead of WSGI. Since this requires quite a bit more work to configure the server and potentially the hosting provider, we will skip providing any examples for this section, but if this is something you want or need in your project, you can get started here: `https://docs.djangoproject.com/en/4.0/topics/async/`.

Up to now, we have been using templates that have been pre-built and provided with the code of this book in order to demonstrate core programming concepts. Next, let's explore what it takes to actually build those templates on our own.

Working with templates

The Django template language provides us with a set of template tags and template filters that are used to perform simple actions directly within a template. It makes it easy to perform simple logic operations, such as Python operations. Tags and filters are actually two different things that closely resemble each other. The Django template language can be closely compared to Shopify's Liquid syntax and is similar to the Razor syntax used in ASP.NET frameworks, but the Django template language is a bit easier to use and read. Django also allows us to create custom tags and filters for use within a project. Custom filters are most commonly used to transform a single context variable. Custom tags provide for more robust and complex use cases. For a complete breakdown of all of the template tags and template filters that exist, read the official Django documentation about them here: `https://docs.djangoproject.com/en/4.0/ref/templates/builtins/`.

Next, we will touch briefly on the features and capabilities of the most commonly used template tags and filters that are available.

Template tags

We can structure a template to feel more like an app by breaking it down into smaller components. Those components can then be used interchangeably within other templates. For example, we can write a base template that contains the `<head>` and `<body>` elements of a page and then break apart subtemplates that structure the body content of each of those templates. Areas can be created in the `<head>` and `<body>` of a document where we can pass dynamic text and HTML into them, such as the `<title>` tag.

For the next example, let's use the `{% block %}`, `{% extend %}`, and `{% include %}` template tags to create two template files, demonstrating how to break templates down into manageable pieces.

Follow these steps to configure your template tags:

1. In your `/chapter_4/urls.py` file, comment out the other paths and include the following path:

    ```
    # /becoming_a_django_entdev/chapter_4/urls.py
    ...
    from .views
    import ..., TestPageView
    urlpatterns = [
        ...,
        path(
            'test_page_1/',
            TestPageView.as_view(),
            name = 'test-page'
        ),
    ]
    ```

2. In your `/chapter_4/views.py` file, create the following class-based view called `TestPageView`, using the code provided here:

    ```
    # /becoming_a_django_entdev/chapter_4/views.py
    ...
    from django.template.response
    import (
        TemplateResponse
    )
    from django.views.generic
    ```

```python
import View
...
class TestPageView(View):
    template_name = 'chapter_4/pages/test_page_1.html'

    def get(self, request, *args, **kwargs):
        return TemplateResponse(
            request,
            self.template_name,
            {
                'title': 'My Test Page 1',
                'page_id': 'test-id-1',
                'page_class': 'test-page-1',
                'h1_tag': 'This is Test Page 1'
            }
        )
```

In the `TestPageView` class, we are defining a default `template_name` as `'chapter_4/pages/test_page_1.html'`. In the `get()` method, we pass in hardcoded context variables to be used in this demonstration. In a real-world scenario, this information would be generated after performing logic that is written to generate those values.

3. Create the /becoming_a_django_entdev/chapter_4/templates/chapter_4/pages/test_page_1.html file and add the following code:

```
# /becoming_a_django_entdev/chapter_4/templates/
chapter_4/pages/test_page_1.html
{% extends 'chapter_4/base/base_template_1.html' %}
{% load static %}

{% block page_title %}{{ title }}{% endblock %}
{% block head_stylesheets %}{% endblock %}
{% block js_scripts %}{% endblock %}
{% block page_id %}{{ page_id }}{% endblock %}
{% block page_class %}{{ block.super }} {{ page_class }}
{% endblock %}

{% block body_content %}
```

```
        {% if h1_tag %}
            <h1>{{ h1_tag }}</h1>
        {% else %}
            <h1>Title Not Found</h1>
        {% endif %}
    {% endblock %}
```

This template starts with the {% extends %} template tag, which states that we want to actually start with the /chapter_4/base/base_template_1.html file, even though we specified the test_page_1.html file in our view class. Then, everywhere there is a {% block %} tag found in this file, we override or append to that same {% block %} found in the base_template_1.html file that we are extending. We are passing the value of {{ title }}, which was defined in the view, into the {% block page_title %} tag of the /chapter_4/pages/test_page_1.html file. The {{ block.super }} tag can be used to keep what is found in that same block of the base_template_1.html file. Without this tag, all code inside the parent block will be overwritten. HTML can be written inside of any block; the {% block body_content %} block, shown in *step 5* that follows, is where the bulk of the page content will be found.

4. Create the /chapter_4/base/base_template_1.html file and add the code shown here:

```
# /becoming_a_django_entdev/chapter_4/templates/
chapter_4/base/base_template_1.html
{% load static %}
<!DOCTYPE html>
<html lang="en" xmlns="http://www.w3.org/1999/xhtml">
    <head>
        <meta charset="utf-8" />
        <title>{% block page_title %}My Page Title{% endblock %}</title>
        <link rel="stylesheet" href="{{ base_url }}{% static 'chapter_8/css/site.css' %}">
        {% block head_stylesheets %}{% endblock %}
        <script defer type="text/javascript" src="{{ base_url }}{% static 'chapter_8/js/site-js.js' %}"></script>
    </head>
</html>
```

5. In the same /chapter_4/base/base_template_1.html file that you just created, insert the body code provided next, just below your existing closing </head> tag:

```
# /becoming_a_django_entdev/chapter_4/templates/
chapter_4/base/base_template_1.html
...
    </head>
    <body id="{% block page_id %}{% endblock %}" class="{% block page_class %}base-template-class{% endblock %}" style="text-align: center;">
        {% block header %}
            {% include 'chapter_4/headers/header_1.html' %}
        {% endblock %}
        {% block site_container %}
            <div class="site-container">
                <div class="body-content">
                    {% block body_content %}
                    {% endblock %}
                </div>
                {% block footer %}
                    {% include 'chapter_4/footers/footer_1.html' with message='Footer of Document' %}
                {% endblock %}
            </div>
        {% endblock %}
        {% block js_scripts %}{% endblock %}
    </body>
</html>
```

6. Copy the /chapter_4/headers/header_1.html and /chapter_4/footers/footer_1.html files provided with the code of this book into your project in the same directory.

7. Copy the /chapter_4/static/chapter_4/css/site.css and /chapter_4/static/chapter_4/js/site-js.js files provided with the code of this book into your project at the same directory.

8. Run your project and navigate to `http://localhost:8000/test_page_1/`. You should see the following information in your browser window:

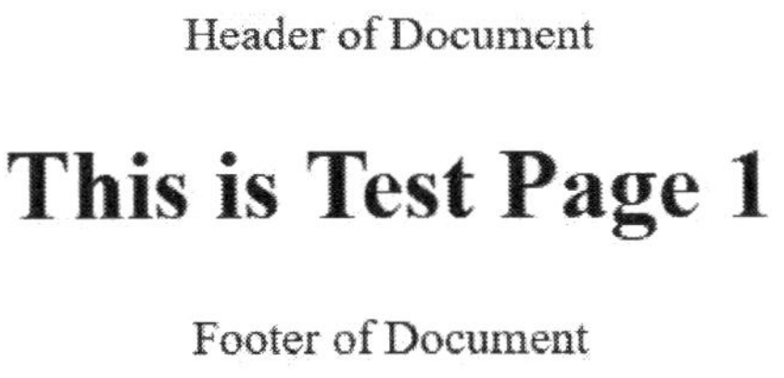

Header of Document

This is Test Page 1

Footer of Document

Figure 4.15 – Extending templates

In the preceding steps, the main HTML of the page is broken down into a header, body content, and footer format. The `{% include %}` tags used previously demonstrate different ways of working with those files. Adding a `with` attribute to any `{% include %}` tag is how we can pass context into that file from the parent template. That is what is done to the preceding footer file. This means making context available without the need for a context processor or by writing code twice. The preceding HTML is structured in a way that allows us to get fancy by modifying everything within the `{% block site_container %}` tag, if we wanted or needed to. In order to do that, we would write the `{% block site_container %}` block again in the file that extends this template file and write the modified code there. That is essentially what *step 3* did for us, with the `{% block body_content %}` tag.

Let's work with template filters next.

Template filters

Template filters are a way to transform the value of a context variable. They can do things such as make a string upper or lowercase using the `{{ context_variable|upper }}` or `{{ context_variable|lower }}` filters. They can be used to find the number of items in a list using the `{{ my_list|length }}` filter or even format time with a `{{ my_time|time:"n/j/Y" }}` filter. When using a `time` filter, it is not necessary to specify the `:"n/j/Y"` argument of that filter. Even without these specifications, Django will default to the setting specified in your `settings.py` file as the `TIME_FORMAT` variable. To learn about all of the filters that are available, visit the official Django documentation found here: `https://docs.djangoproject.com/en/4.0/ref/templates/builtins/#built-in-filter-reference`.

Let's check out custom tags and filters next.

Custom tags and filters

Earlier, in *Figure 4.10*, we saw that the value of the make of the vehicle was displayed as the number **3**. This is a perfect example of how we can write a custom filter that takes in a numeric value and returns the string representation of that value.

Follow these steps to create your custom filter:

1. Create a new folder in the /becoming_a_django_entdev/chapter_4/ directory called templatetags.
2. Create a new file in this folder called chapter_4.py and inside this file, place the following code:

```python
# /becoming_a_django_entdev/chapter_4/templatetags/
chapter_4.py
from django.template
import Library
register = Library()

@register.filter(name = 'vehicle_make')
def vehicle_make(value):
    from ...chapter_3.models import MAKE_CHOICES
    for i, choice in enumerate(MAKE_CHOICES):
        if i == value:
            try:
                return choice[1]
            except ValueError:
                pass
    return ''
```

Here, we are writing a very simple method called vehicle_make() that takes in the numeric value of 3 and returns to us the string representation of Chevrolet, when used in a template. In this method, we are using Python path syntax to import the MAKE_CHOICES variable, which we created in *Chapter 3, Models, Relations, and Inheritance*, in the subsection titled *Mutable versus immutable objects*.

3. Make sure you have uncommented previous URL patterns and use the one shown in the following code block:

```
# /becoming_a_django_entdev/chapter_4/urls.py
...
from .views import ..., vehicle_view
urlpatterns = [
    ...,
    path(
        'vehicle/<int:id>/',
        vehicle_view,
        name = 'vehicle-detail'
    ),
]
```

4. In your existing /chapter_4/my_vehicle.html file, change {{ vehicle.make }} to the statement we can see highlighted in the following code block, and add the chapter_4 template tag library to your {% load %} tag:

```
# /becoming_a_django_entdev/chapter_4/templates/
chapter_4/my_vehicle.html
{% load static chapter_4 %}
...
    {% if vehicle %}
        ...
        <p>{{ vehicle.make }}</p>
        <p>{{ vehicle.make|vehicle_make }}</p>
        ...
    {% endif %}
...
```

In order to use the template filter that we registered, we import it into the HTML file using the {% load chapter_4 %} tag, where the name of the template tag set that we are loading is the name of the Python file that we created in any templatetags folder of an app.

5. Now, making sure your project is running, you can navigate to the URL at http://localhost:8000/vehicle/4/ to see that our vehicle now says **Chevrolet**.

Creating custom template tags instead of custom filters can be done by changing `@register.filter(name = 'my_filter')` to `@register.tag(name = 'my_tag')`. In this scenario, the tag can be used in a template similar to `{% my_tag %}`. To learn more about the complexities of writing your own template tags and how they can be useful in your project, visit the official documentation on that subject found here: https://docs.djangoproject.com/en/4.0/howto/custom-template-tags/#writing-custom-template-tags.

Next, let's add some custom error pages.

Error page templates

Django provides a very easy way to create your own custom error page templates for errors such as 400, 403, 404, and 500. Other errors, such as a **502 Bad Gateway** error, will not work since the error implies there is a problem with your web server and not with Django itself. For the four error types that we can manipulate, we can create four files in any of the `templates` directories, `400.html`, `403.html`, `404.html`, and `500.html`, as long as they are not placed in a subfolder. These four template files have been provided with the code of this book and follow the same design pattern as depicted in the subsection titled *Template tags* of this chapter. In order to see a custom debug template, we must turn off `DEBUG` in the `settings.py` file.

Follow these steps to configure your error pages:

1. Copy the four error page template files found in the `/becoming_a_django_entdev/chapter_4/templates/` directory provided with the code of this book into the same directory of your project. Those four files are `400.html`, `403.html`, `404.html`, and `500.html`, and also copy the `base_error.html` file found in the same directory.

2. In your `settings.py` file, change the following value to `False`:

   ```
   # /becoming_a_django_entdev/settings.py
   ...
   DEBUG = False
   ```

3. Make sure your virtual environment is activated and run the `collectstatic` command shown here, in order to have access to the static files that have been created up to this point in time:

   ```
   (virtual_env) PS > python manage.py collectstatic
   ```

4. With DEBUG turned off, we have to run the `collectstatic` command in order to see changes reflect in the browser every time a static file is changed.

5. Now, run your project and navigate to any non-existent URL on the site, a URL that we have not created a URL pattern for yet, such as `http://localhost:8000/asdfasdf`. You should see the following message in your browser window instead of the debug error message we are used to seeing, such as in *Figure 4.2*:

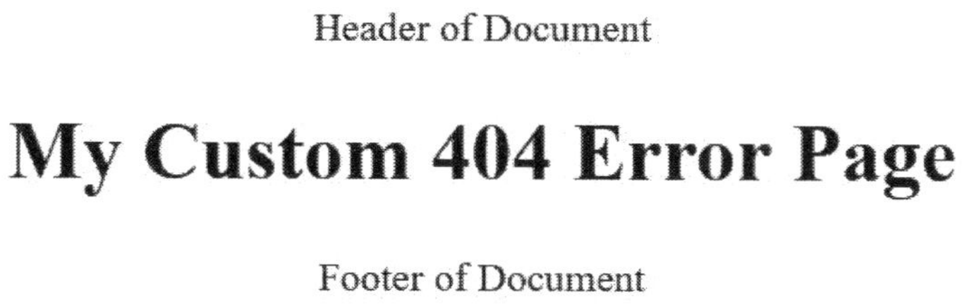

Header of Document

My Custom 404 Error Page

Footer of Document

Figure 4.16 – Custom error page

Summary

By now, we have constructed what might feel like an entire project, but in reality, an application will consist of so much more than what was covered in this chapter. What we do have is a way to route URL paths to views and render different contexts in each template used. We learned how we can query the database in a view to get the data that we want to render in a template. We even covered the different ways we can handle and process an error page or simply redirect a URL to another path. We even used class-based views to write reusable class structures, making a project more adaptable to change in the long run.

In the next chapter, we will discuss how we can use form objects in combination with the function-based and class-based views and templates we learned how to create in this chapter.

5
Django Forms

In programming, a **form** is an object that contains input fields, drop-down boxes, radio buttons, checkboxes, and a submit button. The duty of the form is to capture information from the user; what is done after that can be anything including storing that information in a database, sending an email, or generating a reporting document using that data. In this chapter, we discuss as much as we can about how forms are used in Django. Form objects are a very complex subject to discuss; we only have enough room in this chapter to cover the essentials and some advanced topics. Some of the topics in this chapter can be combined with other topics covered later in *Chapter 8, Working with the Django REST Framework*, to create form objects on SPA-like pages.

In our first form, we will create a class called `ContactForm` and build an email field in three different ways. Later, when we render that form in the browser, we will observe how its behavior changes using those three different mechanisms. We want to watch how validation is performed on each email field and watch how the behavior differs among them. This will give us a better understanding of which mechanism is needed for the intended behavior that we wish to achieve as the outcome. We will even look into writing custom field classes and learn how they can benefit us in the long run.

Depending on your project's needs, validation of your form may require a lot of custom JavaScript in order to accomplish your goals. The focus of this book is not on JavaScript but rather on the concepts of Django. However, by the end of this chapter, we will have provided an example that demonstrates how JavaScript can be blended into your project when working with dynamic inline formsets on a form object. You can expand upon this to build your own custom JavaScript functions that suit your project's needs.

In this chapter, we will cover the following:

- Types of forms
- Using form fields
- Cleaning forms
- Creating custom form fields
- Working with form views
- Rendering forms in templates
- Linking models to a form
- Adding inline formsets

Technical requirements

To work with the code in this chapter, the following tools will need to be installed on your local machine:

- Python version 3.9 – used as the underlying programming language for the project
- Django version 4.0 – used as the backend framework of the project
- pip package manager – used to manage third-party Python/Django packages

We will continue to work with the solution created in *Chapter 2, Project Configuration*. However, it is not necessary to use the Visual Studio IDE. The main project itself can be run using another IDE or run independently using a terminal or command-line window from within the project root folder. This is where the `manage.py` file resides. Whatever editor or IDE you are using, a virtual environment will also be needed to work with the Django project. Instructions for how to create a project and virtual environment can be found in *Chapter 2, Project Configuration*. You will need a database to store the data contained in your project. PostgreSQL was chosen for the examples in the previous chapter; however, any database type that you choose for your project can be used to work with the examples in this chapter.

We will also be using data that is in the form of a Django fixture, provided in *Chapter 3, Models, Relations, and Inheritance*, in the subsection titled *Loading the Chapter_3 data fixture*. Make sure the `chapter_3` fixture is loaded into your database; if this has already been done, then you may skip the next command. If you have already created the tables found in *Chapter 3, Models, Relations, and Inheritance*, and have not loaded that fixture yet, then run the following command, after activating your virtual environment:

```
(virtual_env) PS > python manage.py loaddata chapter_3
```

All of the code created in this chapter can be found in the GitHub repository for this book: https://github.com/PacktPublishing/Becoming-an-Enterprise-Django-Developer. The bulk of the code depicted in this chapter can be found in the /becoming_a_django_entdev/becoming_a_django_entdev/chapter_5/ directory.

Check out the following video to see the *Code in Action*: https://bit.ly/3xQQ2H3.

Preparing for this chapter

Start by creating a new app in your project called `chapter_5` by following the steps discussed in *Chapter 2, Project Configuration*, in the subsection titled *Creating a Django app*. As discussed in that section, don't forget to change the value of the `name =` variable for your app class found in the /becoming_a_django_entdev/becoming_a_django_entdev/chapter_5/apps.py file to now point to the path where you installed your app. Be sure to also include this app in your `INSTALLED_APPS` variable found in the `settings.py` file. At the end of *Chapter 4, URLs, Views, and Templates*, we set `DEBUG = False` as part of an exercise. Be sure to set this back to `DEBUG = True` for the remainder of this book.

In the main `urls.py` file of the site, add the following path, which points to the URL patterns of this chapter that we will be creating:

```
# /becoming_a_django_entdev/urls.py
...
urlpatterns = [
    path(
        '',
        include(
            'becoming_a_django_entdev.chapter_5.urls'
        )
    ),
]
```

Now that we've created the app for this chapter, let's begin using the Django admin site to manage the models created in *Chapter 3, Models, Relations, and Inheritance*.

Types of forms

Django is designed to simplify a great deal of work involved when handling forms. It does this by providing ways to render your form object as HTML and process data on form submission. There are a lot of different ways to use and work with form objects but they all start with a form class. Django provides two different classes for us to use, `ModelForm` and `Form`. The differences between the two are that one links directly to the tables in a database and the other does not. The `ModelForm` class, the one that links to a database, will automatically create fields and perform field validation based on the field constraints set within that model class, from the database level.

Form classes also use a `Meta` subclass, as was used on a model class in *Chapter 3, Models, Relations, and Inheritance*. There are other form classes that Django provides, such as `BaseForm` and `BaseModelForm`, which are used to write abstract base form classes, but these form classes are beyond the scope of this book. Other classes relate to inline formsets, which are basically forms within a form. By the end of this chapter, we will have inserted an inline formset onto the page when the form gets rendered and used JavaScript to add more of them when the user clicks a button.

Let's discuss importing and using the `Form` and `ModelForm` classes when creating a form class first.

Form class – Form

The `Form` class is used to create fields that don't link to a database. This is used when a form is sending an email or generating a PDF report, just to name a few examples.

Follow these steps to create your `Form` class:

1. Create a file called `forms.py` in your `/becoming_a_django_entdev/chapter_5/` directory.
2. Inside this file, include the following code:

   ```
   # /becoming_a_django_entdev/chapter_5/forms.py
   from django.forms
   import Form

   class ContactForm(Form):
       pass
   ```

We will discuss working with fields in a moment, but let's discuss importing the `ModelForm` class next.

Form class – ModelForm

The `ModelForm` class is used when we want to create or modify data directly in a database. Each field is linked to a column of the table it represents. Additional fields can be created and used in ways that are not linked to your database. For instance, you could fire off an email that contains the data from an added field. This field could also be a comment, timestamp, or another type of hidden data field.

To create your `ModelForm` class, inside your existing `/chapter_5/forms.py` file, include the following class:

```
# /becoming_a_django_entdev/chapter_5/forms.py
from django.forms
import Form, ModelForm
class VehicleForm(ModelForm):
    pass
```

Later in this chapter, we will link this class to the `Vehicle` model, created in *Chapter 3, Models, Relations, and Inheritance*.

Next, let's remove these `pass` statements and begin working with field arguments.

Using form fields

Similar to the standard model field classes introduced in *Chapter 3, Models, Relations, and Inheritance*, Django also provides a number of form field classes that are available to use. The difference is that a model field class works with the columns of a database and a form field class is used only as an input field within an HTML `<form></form>` object in a template.

The following table can be used as a cheat sheet to reference what fields are available when writing your `Form` and/or `ModelForm` classes:

BooleanField	FilePathField	NullBooleanField
CharField	FloatField	RegexField
ChoiceField	ImageField	SlugField
ComboField	IntegerField	SplitDateTimeField
DateField	JSONField	TimeField
DateTimeField	GenericIPAddressField	TypedChoiceField
DecimalField	ModelChoiceField	TypedMultipleChoiceField
DurationField	ModelMultipleChoiceField	URLField
EmailField	MultipleChoiceField	UUIDField
FileField	MultiValueField	

Form fields also accept a variety of different field arguments that customize the behavior of each field. In the next section, we will use some of the field types in the preceding list to write fields on our form classes, discussing the different arguments that can be used.

For a complete breakdown of each of these field types, visit the official Django documentation on field classes and arguments, found here: https://docs.djangoproject.com/en/4.0/ref/forms/fields/.

Common field arguments

We will begin adding fields to a form class and introduce field arguments in this exercise. Field arguments are a way for us to set properties on a field.

To create your field, in your `/chapter_5/forms.py` file, add the `import` statement highlighted in the following code block, and in the same `ContactForm` class, add a field called `full_name`:

```
# /becoming_a_django_entdev/chapter_5/forms.py
from django
import forms
from django.forms
import Form, ModelForm

class ContactForm(Form):
    full_name = forms.CharField(
        label = 'Full Name',
        help_text = 'Enter your full name, first and last name please',
```

```
        min_length = 2,
        max_length = 300,
        required = True,
        error_messages = {
            'required': 'Please provide us with a name to address you as',
            'min_length': 'Please lengthen your name, min 2 characters',
            'max_length': 'Please shorten your name, max 300 characters'
        }
    )
```

In the preceding example, we defined an HTML `<input type="text">` object using the `forms.CharField` field class. A `CharField` object's default widget is an input `type="text"` field. The `label` argument lets us define the text that would render as `<label for="my_field_id">My Form Field Label</label>` of this field.

The `help_text` argument will render a `<span class="helptext">{{ your_help_text_message</span>` element, right after your input field in the **Document Object Model** (**DOM**).

> **Document Object Model**
>
> The DOM is an interface found in all browsers that presents HTML in a tree-like structure of nodes. The nodes represent objects in this tree, where the `<span>` or `<input>` nodes comprise a single object.

The `min_length` and `max_length` arguments are used among most field types; they define the minimum and maximum character count, respectively, allowed in the field. The `required` argument will define whether the field must contain a value in order to be valid. These will render as attributes of an `<input type="text" maxlength="300" minlength="2" required="" />` object.

Next, let's discuss form validation a little bit more. In the next two subsections, we will cover the `widget` and `validator` arguments. For a complete breakdown of all the field arguments that are available and not covered, visit https://docs.djangoproject.com/en/4.0/ref/forms/fields/#core-field-arguments.

Field widgets

A field's `widget` argument allows us to define what kind of field to use, such as an input object of the date, email, password, or text type. This can also be a checkbox, radio button, drop-down select, or text area, to name a few examples. We don't have to specify the `widget` argument unless we want to change the default widget or override its initial properties.

Follow the next step to override the `full_name` field to render an input with the `id`, `class`, and `placeholder` attributes. The rendered output we hope to achieve should look like the following dummy code:

```
# Demo Code
<input type="text" name="full_name" id="full-name" class="form-input-class" placeholder="Your Name, Written By...">
```

In your /chapter_5/forms.py file, edit your `full_name` field, as shown:

```python
# /becoming_a_django_entdev/chapter_5/forms.py
from django import forms
from django.forms import Form, ModelForm

class ContactForm(Form):
    full_name = forms.CharField(
        ...,
        widget = forms.TextInput(
            attrs = {
                'id': 'full-name',
                'class': 'form-input-class',
                'placeholder': 'Your Name, Written By...'
            }
        ),
    ),
```

If we changed the default widget of a field from `forms.TextInput` to something else, such as `forms.EmailInput`, that would render as `<input type="email">`. Changing `forms.TextInput` to `forms.DateInput` would render as `<input type="date">`. Using `forms.TextArea` would render as a `<textarea></textarea>` object instead. Of course, these are just some of the many different options that exist. For a complete breakdown of all the widgets available and how they can help you construct your fields, visit https://docs.djangoproject.com/en/4.0/ref/forms/widgets/.

Let's discuss using field validators next.

Field validators

When manually defining widgets, we sometimes have to write specific validation rules. For example, let's take a `forms.EmailInput` class; this would require adding validation rules that determine whether the value of the string the user provided is actually in example@example.com format and not some random string, such as `IAmAString`.

Follow these steps to create and validate an email field:

1. In your /chapter_5/forms.py file, in the existing `ContactForm`, add the email_1 field shown here:

   ```
   # /becoming_a_django_entdev/chapter_5/forms.py
   ...
   from django
   import forms
   from django.forms
   import Form, ModelForm
   from django.core.validators
   import EmailValidator

   class ContactForm(Form):
       ...
       email_1 = forms.CharField(
           label = 'email_1 Field',
           min_length = 5,
           max_length = 254,
           required = False,
           help_text = 'Email address in example@example.com
   ```

```
            format.',
    validators = [
        EmailValidator(
            'Please enter a valid email address'
        ),
    ],
    error_messages = {
        'min_length': 'Please lengthen your name, min 5 characters',
        'max_length': 'Please shorten your name, max 254 characters'
    }
)
```

While fields can be manipulated using validator arguments in this way, Django tries to provide developers with options that minimize or reduce the amount of code that they need to write. For example, instead of writing the preceding example to enforce an email format on `CharField`, we could just use the `EmailField` class instead, which already enforces this rule for us. The `EmailField` class includes all of the logic and validation to handle an email field.

2. To practice using the `EmailField` class, we will create an additional field to compare and contrast both code approaches. In your `/chapter_5/forms.py` file, in the same `ContactForm` class, add the `email_2` field shown here:

```
# /becoming_a_django_entdev/chapter_5/forms.py
from django import forms
from django.forms import Form, ModelForm
...
class ContactForm(Form):
    ...
    email_2 = forms.EmailField(
        label = 'email_2 Field',
        min_length = 5,
        max_length = 254,
        required = True,
        help_text = 'Email address in example@example.com
```

```
            format for contacting you should we have questions about
            your message.',
                    error_messages = {
                            'required': 'Please provide us an email
            address should we need to reach you',
                            'email': 'Please enter a valid email
            address',
                            'min_length': 'Please lengthen your name, min
            5 characters',
                            'max_length': 'Please shorten your name, max
            254 characters'
                    }
            )
```

The difference between the code found in *step 1* and *step 2* is that we do not need to define a widget or validator argument when using an `EmailField` class to produce the same behavior as with a `CharField` class. The error message is now located in the `error_messages` argument using the `email` key, as shown.

For a complete breakdown of all of the validator classes and methods available, visit https://docs.djangoproject.com/en/4.0/ref/validators/. Let's practice cleaning forms next, which is just another way to perform validation.

Cleaning forms

We can perform validation on form fields in other ways as well. Within a form class, we can write methods that validate each field individually by writing them in this format: `def clean_{{ form_field_name }}()`. When doing this, only the value of the field that we are cleaning can be accessed. If we want to access other field values found in that form, we have to write a single `def clean()` method that will allow us to compare two fields against each other. For example, we could use the `def clean()` method to only require a field when another field's value is not empty.

The following two subsections break down these two concepts.

Method – clean_{{ your_field_name }}()

To clean an individual form field, follow these steps:

1. In your /chapter_5/forms.py file, in the same ContactForm class, add a new field called email_3, as shown:

    ```python
    # /becoming_a_django_entdev/chapter_5/forms.py
    from django
    import forms
    from django.forms
    import Form, ModelForm
    ...
    class ContactForm(Form):
        email_3 = forms.CharField(
            label = 'Email Using CharField and Using Clean Method',
            required = False,
            help_text = 'Email address in example@example.com format for contacting you should we have questions about your message.',
        )
    ```

2. In that same ContactForm class, add the clean_email_3 method shown here:

    ```python
    # /becoming_a_django_entdev/chapter_5/forms.py
    ...
    from django.core.exceptions
    import ValidationError
    from django.core.validators
    import (
        EmailValidator,
        validate_email
    )

    class ContactForm(Form):
        ...
        def clean_email_3(self):
            email = self.cleaned_data['email_3']
            if email != '':
    ```

```
                try:
                    validate_email(email)
                except ValidationError:
                    self.add_error(
                        'email_3',
                        f'The following is not a valid email
address: {email}'
                    )
            else:
                self.add_error(
                    'email_3',
                    'This field is required'
                )
            return email
```

In the preceding example, we are importing the `validate_email()` method from the `django.core.validators` library, to determine whether the string is in email format. First, we are using a simple conditional statement to check whether the field has a value or not; if not, we are issuing an error message stating "This field is required". We are performing a validation check even though the email_3 field has a `required` argument set to `False`. This just illustrates another way we can do the same thing. If a value exists, we then wrap the `validate_email()` method in a *Try/Except* statement, and if validation fails, we are adding the "The following is not a valid email address: {{ field_value }}" error message.

The `self.add_error()` method provided in the `Form` and `ModelForm` classes accepts two arguments: the first argument is the name of the field and the second is your custom error message. Instead of using `self.add_error('email_3', 'This field is required')` to add error messages to a form, we can use the `raise ValidationError('This field is required')` class instead. Except, there's one problem: using this class will remove this field from the `cleaned_data` values list. That will work if you only use the `clean_email_3()` method by itself. If you wanted to access that same cleaned data within the `def clean()` method, you'd need to return the value in `def clean_email_3()`, as depicted in the last line of *step 2* previously. Django will fire off the individual clean methods on each field before the `clean()` method is executed, saving that as the last method in the stack of cleaning methods. If your field value is not returned in the clean method specific to that field, we will not be able to access it when we need to later on.

Let's use the `clean()` method next.

Method – clean()

The `clean()` method is used to access all of the field data within a form, upon form submission. It is in this method that you could compare against the values of many fields before allowing a successful form submission. This next example will allow us to compare two fields against each other and raise one or more different field validation messages.

Follow these steps to configure your `clean()` method:

1. In your `/chapter_5/forms.py` file, add another field to your `ContactForm` class called `conditional_required`, as shown:

   ```
   # /becoming_a_django_entdev/chapter_5/forms.py
   from django import forms
   from django.forms import Form, ModelForm
   ...
   class ContactForm(Form):
       conditional_required = forms.CharField(
           label = 'Required only if field labeled "email_3" has a value',
           help_text = 'This field is only required if the field labeled "email_3 Field" has a value',
           required = False,
       )
   ```

2. In that same `ContactForm` class, add the following `clean()` method:

   ```
   # /becoming_a_django_entdev/chapter_5/forms.py
   from django import forms
   from django.forms import Form, ModelForm
   ...
   class ContactForm(Form):
       ...
       def clean(self):
           email = self.cleaned_data['email_3']
           text_field = self.cleaned_data[
   ```

```
                    'conditional_required'
        ]

        if email and not text_field:
            self.add_error(
                'conditional_required',
                'If there is a value in the field labeled
  "email_3" then this field is required'
            )
```

In this `clean()` method, we are assigning the value of the `email_3` field to the variable called `email`. Then, we are assigning the value of the `conditional_required` field to the variable called `text_field`. Using a simple conditional statement, we then check to see whether `email` has a value present, and if so, check whether `text_field` has a value present. If this condition is met, we then add the required error to the `conditional_required` field. Since we set the `conditional_required` field to use the `required = False` argument, if there is no value in the `email_3` field, this field will not be required.

Let's move on to creating our own custom form fields next.

Creating custom form fields

Sometimes, the needs of the project outweigh the options that are provided to us. If a field class is not available by default, we have two options: create our own or use a third-party package where someone else has already written a field class for us.

Continuing with the same `ContactForm` class, we will demonstrate the differences between validation mechanisms by building a `MultipleEmailField`. This will be a single field, accepting a single string of emails, all separated by commas. Each email item will then be checked independently to see whether it is in a valid email string format. We will use the same `validate_email()` function as we did before to enforce this constraint.

Field class – Field

Django provides a class called `Field` found in the `django.forms.fields` library, used to construct custom field classes. Any of the options and methods found in this class can be overwritten as needed. For example, overriding the `def __init__()` method will provide a way to add, change, or remove field arguments, completely transforming how you work with these fields later on. We won't actually be overriding the `__init__()` method for this exercise; instead, we will be working with the `to_python()` and `validate()` methods. These will be the only two methods needed to perform the validation that we need on `MultipleEmailField`.

Follow these steps to write your `Field` class:

1. Create a new file called `fields.py` in your `/becoming_a_django_entdev/chapter_5/` folder.
2. In that file, add the following `MultipleEmailField` class and `import` statements:

```
# /becoming_a_django_entdev/chapter_5/fields.py
from django.core.exceptions import ValidationError
from django.core.validators import validate_email
from django.forms.fields import Field
from django.forms.widgets import TextInput

class MultipleEmailField(Field):
    widget = TextInput
    default_validators = []
    default_error_messages = {
        'required': 'Default Required Error Message',
        'email': 'Please enter a valid email address or addresses separated by a comma with NO spaces'
    }
```

3. If you want to use some of the validators provided by Django, use the `default_validators` option shown in the preceding code. This is where you will define what validator to use. We are using our own logic found in the `validate` method of the `MultipleEmailField` class and will not be using a default validator for what we are trying to achieve. You are welcome to use any of the validators that Django provides for your field classes, found in the `django.core.validators` library.

4. The `default_error_messages` option is used to define the default messages for a field class. In the `default_error_messages` option shown previously, we are specifying two keys: `required` and `email`. These two keys will act as the default message used when a required field has been submitted without a value present and when a value does not meet the email string format. When specifying a default error message in the `default_error_messages` option, we no longer have to use the `error_messages = {}` argument of a field. It is still possible to use the `error_messages` argument on a field-by-field basis if we wanted to.

5. In that same `MultipleEmailField` class, add the following `to_python()` method:

```
# /becoming_a_django_entdev/chapter_5/fields.py
...
class MultipleEmailField(Field):
    ...
    def to_python(self, value):
        if not value:
            return []
        value = value.replace(' ', '')
        return value.split(',')
```

The `to_python()` method is used to transform values into Python objects. This one in particular is written to transform a string into a list of emails, excluding the comma.

6. In that same `MultipleEmailField` class, add the following `validate()` method:

```
# /becoming_a_django_entdev/chapter_5/fields.py
...
class MultipleEmailField(Field):
    ...
    def validate(self, value):
```

```python
            super().validate(value)
            for email in value:
                try:
                    validate_email(email)
                except ValidationError:
                    raise ValidationError(
                        self.error_messages['email'],
                        code = 'email'
                    )
```

The `validate()` method checks each item in the list of emails to make sure it is in email format. We are also overriding the options provided in the `Field` class, such as the `widget` option shown in *step 2*. The default widget is `TextInput`. Since that is already what we need, we don't actually have to include it; it was provided in the preceding example for illustrative purposes. When writing your own custom field, you can replace `TextInput` with any of the Django widgets found in the `django.forms.widgets` library. If you want to take your field one step further, you could even write your own custom widget class, but this is beyond the scope of this book.

Let's work on using our custom field class next.

Using a custom field

To use the `MultipleEmailField` that we created in the previous subsection, in your `/chapter_5/forms.py` file, add the following `import` statement and add the `multiple_emails` field to `ContactForm`, as shown:

```python
# /becoming_a_django_entdev/chapter_5/forms.py
...
from django.forms
import Form, ModelForm
from .fields
import MultipleEmailField

class ContactForm(Form):
    ...
    multiple_emails = MultipleEmailField(
        label = 'Multiple Email Field',
```

```
            help_text = 'Please enter one or more email addresses,
each separated by a comma and no spaces',
            required = True,
    )
    ...
```

In the preceding example, we do not need to include any validation messages because we have already defined the messages we want in the `MultipleEmailField` class.

The arguments that are available are listed here:

disabled	label	show_hidden_initial
error_messages	label_suffix	validators
help_text	localize	widget
Initial	required	

These are the arguments included within the __init__() method of the `Field` class in the Django library. If we needed to use arguments such as `min_length` and `max_length`, as we did for the `full_name` field, we should have constructed the `MultipleEmailField` class using the `CharField` class instead of the `Field` class like we did in *step 2* of the subsection titled *Field class – Field* of this chapter, as depicted here:

```
# Dummy Code
from django.forms.fields
import Field, CharField

class MultipleEmailField(CharField):
```

The reason why we would want to use `CharField` instead of the `Field` class is that it extends the `Field` class and adds logic that includes the `min_length` and `max_length` arguments. Using this notion, you can extend any other field class, making available any of the unique arguments or behaviors of that class when writing your own custom class.

Next, let's take our contact form and use it with a view class to serve up our contact page.

Working with form views

A **form view** is just like any other view class, except that a form view class is designed to process and handle form objects and form submissions.

Django offers four main form view classes, listed here:

- `FormView`
- `CreateView`
- `UpdateView`
- `DeleteView`

These can all be found in the `django.views.generic.edit` library.

If we were to create a view to work with the `ContactForm` class that we created earlier, which does not relate to any models, we would use a simple `FormView` class. The other three classes can be used with forms that relate to models. They each serve a different purpose: to create, update, or delete records in a database. For example, `CreateView` will render a form containing blank or default values intended to create a record that does not exist yet. `UpdateView` uses a form that looks up an existing record, displays the values that exist for that record, and allows changes to be made. `DeleteView` will display to the user a prompt or confirmation page, asking the user whether they actually want to proceed with this task, then delete that record.

Let's use the `FormView` class to begin building a page that displays the `ContactForm` class object. We will be working with `CreateView` and `UpdateView` later in this chapter. For a complete breakdown of how to use all of these form view classes, visit https://docs.djangoproject.com/en/4.0/ref/class-based-views/generic-editing/.

View class – FormView

Let's start by constructing a class called `FormClassView` using Django's `FormView` class. This class will have three options that we will define, the first option being `template_name`, which is used to define the path of the HTML template that we are using. The second option is the `form_class` option, which is used to define the name of the form class that this view is going to process, that being the `ContactForm` class. The third option is `success_url`, which specifies a relative URL path to redirect the user to when the form is successfully submitted.

Follow these steps to configure your `FormClassView` class:

1. Make sure you have a file called `views.py` in your `/becoming_a_django_entdev/chapter_5/` folder. This is usually created automatically for you when a new Django app is created.
2. In that same file, add the code shown here:

    ```python
    # /becoming_a_django_entdev/chapter_5/views.py
    from django.views.generic.edit import FormView
    from .forms import ContactForm

    class FormClassView(FormView):
        template_name = 'chapter_5/form-class.html'
        form_class = ContactForm
        success_url = '/chapter-5/contact-form-success/'
    ```

    Any of these options can use a callable to gain those values, such as the use of the `reverse()` function to specify `success_url`. An example of how this can be done is depicted here, but this is not part of the actual exercise:

    ```python
    # Dummy Code
    from django.urls import reverse
    from django.views.generic.edit import FormView

    class FormClassView(FormView):
        ...
        def get_success_url(self, **kwargs):
            return reverse('pattern_name', args=(value,))
    ```

    We won't actually need the callable shown here to formulate the success URL. All we need is the string representation of `'/chapter_5/contact-form-success/'`.

3. Next, configure the URL pattern for `http://localhost:8000/chapter-5/form-class/`. If this file was not automatically created for you, create the `/chapter_5/urls.py` file and add the following form page pattern and `import` statement:

```python
# /becoming_a_django_entdev/chapter_5/urls.py
from django.urls
import re_path
from django.views.generic
import (
    TemplateView
)
from .views
import FormClassView

urlpatterns = [
    re_path(
        r'^chapter-5/form-class/?$',
        FormClassView.as_view()
    ),
]
```

4. In that same file, add the following success pattern:

```python
# /becoming_a_django_entdev/chapter_5/urls.py
...
urlpatterns = [
    ...,
    re_path(
        r'^chapter-5/contact-form-success/?$',
        TemplateView.as_view(
            template_name = 'chapter_5/contact-success.html'
        ),
        kwargs = {
            'title': 'FormClassView Success Page',
            'page_id': 'form-class-success',
            'page_class': 'form-class-success-page',
```

```
                'h1_tag': 'This is the FormClassView Success
    Page Using ContactForm',
            }
        ),
    ]
```

In this step, we added a second pattern to serve as the success page at `http://localhost:8000/chapter-5/contact-form-success/`. This success page will be used for all exercises in this chapter.

Now that we have a view class to work with and some basic options defined, let's explore what it takes to work with the different request methods.

HTTP request methods

Working with the `FormView` class in Django, there are two HTTP request methods: the `GET` and `POST` methods. The `GET` method is intended to render a form with blank or default values onto a page and wait for the user to fill out the form and submit it. Once the form has been submitted, the `POST` method will be executed.

GET

The `get()` method is just like any other GET method for a view class. It is the go-to method when the page first gets loaded.

Follow these steps to configure your `FormClassView` class's `get()` method:

1. In the `/chapter_5/views.py` file, add the `get()` method to your existing `FormClassView` class using the following code:

   ```
   # /becoming_a_django_entdev/chapter_5/views.py
   ...
   from django.views.generic.edit
   import FormView
   from django.template.response
   import (
       TemplateResponse
   )
   
   class FormClassView(FormView):
       ...
       def get(self, request, *args, **kwargs):
   ```

```python
        return TemplateResponse(
            request,
            self.template_name,
            {
                'title': 'FormClassView Page',
                'page_id': 'form-class-id',
                'page_class': 'form-class-page',
                'h1_tag': 'This is the FormClassView Page Using ContactForm',
                'form': self.form_class,
            }
        )
```

In the preceding `get()` method, we are returning an HTTP response in the form of a `TemplateResponse` class, using the value of `self.template_name` as the path to the template location. We are providing that template with context unique to this page, such as the `title`, `page_id`, `page_class`, `h1_tag`, and `form` variables that are depicted in the preceding code block. The value of `self.form_class` is used to pass the form object into the template. Initial values can be defined on form fields when the page first gets loaded, which is when the form is initialized.

2. Add the following `initial` list to your existing `get()` method of the `FormClassView` class and pass it into your return context, as highlighted in the following code block:

```python
# /becoming_a_django_entdev/chapter_5/views.py
...
class FormClassView(FormView):
    def get(self, request, *args, **kwargs):
        initial = {
            'full_name': 'FirstName LastName',
            'email_1': 'example1@example.com',
            # Add A Value For Every Field...
        }
        return TemplateResponse(
            request, self.template_name, {
                ...
                'form': self.form_class(initial),
```

```
        }
    )
```

In this `get()` method, we added the `initial` variable as a list and then passed that list into the `self.form_class(initial)` object, which lets us set the initial value on fields, defining field names as the keys shown previously with their corresponding values.

POST

A `post()` method is used to render the same page when a form has been submitted. In this method, we can determine whether the form is valid and if so, we want to redirect it to a success URL. If the form is not valid, the page will reload with the values that the user entered into the fields and display any error messages that may exist. We can also alter or add to the context of a page using a `post()` method.

In your `/chapter_5/views.py` file, in the same `FormClassView` class, add the `post()` method shown here:

```python
# /becoming_a_django_entdev/chapter_5/views.py
...
from django.views.generic.edit
    import FormView
from django.http
    import HttpResponseRedirect
from django.template.response
    import (
        TemplateResponse
    )

class FormClassView(FormView):
    ...
    def post(self, request, *args, **kwargs):
        form = self.form_class(request.POST)

        if form.is_valid():
            return HttpResponseRedirect(
                self.success_url
            )
        else:
```

```
                return TemplateResponse(
            request,
            self.template_name,
            {
                'title': 'FormClassView Page - Please
Correct The Errors Below',
                'page_id': 'form-class-id',
                'page_class': 'form-class-page errors-
found',
                'h1_tag': 'This is the FormClassView Page
Using ContactForm<br /><small class="error-msg">Errors Found</
small>',
                'form': form,
            }
        )
```

Inside the `TemplateResponse` return statement, the highlighted text where the context is written represents the context that has changed from the `get()` method to the `post()` method. In order to preserve the data that the user has entered into the form, `request.POST` must be passed into the form class, where `self.form_class(request.POST)` is highlighted in the preceding step. If we didn't pass `request.POST` into `self.form_class()`, then we would have rendered a blank form, as if we were using the `get()` method, upon first visiting this page.

Now that we have our view class written, we can work on the template that will render our form next.

Rendering forms in templates

Django offers five main ways to easily and quickly render a form object onto a page. The first three are to render a form using a paragraph, table, or list structure. The other two include the traditional way of rendering a form, which is based on the template in the `django.forms.templates.django.forms` library called `default.html`, and then a way to render your own template. New to Django 4.0 is the `template_name` option on all form classes. This option allows you to point to a template file where you can structure your own HTML formatting.

Follow these steps to render your form objects:

1. Copy the `base_template_1.html` file that was created in *Chapter 4, URLs, Views, and Templates*, into your `/becoming_a_django_entdev/chapter_5/templates/chapter_5/base/` folder. Copy all related partial template files that are added as `{% include %}` statements into that file as well.
2. That `base_template_1.html` file will be repurposed as the base template for this chapter's exercise. Adjust any paths to point to the new `chapter_5` folder, such as any CSS and JavaScript file paths.
3. Copy all related CSS, JavaScript, and HTML files into your `chapter_5` app as well. These are not required to complete this exercise but will prevent 404 errors in your console logs.
4. Create a new file called `form-class.html` inside your `/becoming_a_django_entdev/chapter_5/templates/chapter_5/` folder and include the tags we can see in the following code block:

    ```
    # /becoming_a_django_entdev/chapter_5/templates/
    chapter_5/form-class.html
    {% extends 'chapter_5/base/base_template_1.html' %}
    {% load static %}

    {% block page_title %}{{ title }}{% endblock %}
    {% block head_stylesheets %}{% endblock %}
    {% block js_scripts %}{% endblock %}
    {% block page_id %}{{ page_id }}{% endblock %}
    {% block page_class %}{{ block.super }} {{ page_class }}
    {% endblock %}
    ```

5. Inside your `/chapter_5/form-class.html` file, add the following code inside the `body_content` block, to render a form in the simplest way possible:

    ```
    # /becoming_a_django_entdev/chapter_5/templates/
    chapter_5/form-class.html
    ...
    {% block body_content %}
        ...
        <form method="post">
            {% csrf_token %}
            {{ form }}
    ```

```
            <input type="submit" value="Send Message">
        </form>
{% endblock %}
```

Here, we need to at least write the `<form>` element and define an attribute of `method="post"` telling the browser how to handle a form submission. The `{{ form }}` tag renders any fields that exist for this form, using the `django.forms.templates.django.forms.default.html` library template. `{% csrf_token %}` is a cross-site request forgery token that is used for security measures and is required on all Django forms. `<input type="submit">` specifies the button that is used to trigger the form's submit action.

Let's dive into the remaining four mechanisms and how they are used.

Render form – as_p

This option will render each field wrapped in a paragraph, `<p></p>`, element. The label will be stacked above the input field with the help text below it. If errors are present, each field will have its own list object rendered above the paragraph objects, listing all the errors relating to that field.

To render your form with `as_p`, in your `/chapter_5/form-class.html` file, change the `{{ form }}` tag to `{{ form.as_p }}`.

This should render each field to look like the demo code depicted here:

```
# Dummy code rendered, for first_name field
<ul class="errorlist">
    <li>Please provide us with a name to address you as</li>
</ul>
<p>
    <label for="full-name">Full Name:</label>
    <input type="text" name="full_name" id="full-name" class="form-input-class field-error" placeholder="Your Name, Written By..." maxlength="300" minlength="2" required="">
    <span class="helptext">Enter your full name, first and last name please</span>
</p>
```

Let's render the form formatted as a table next.

Render form – as_table

This option takes each field and wraps it in a `<tr></tr>` element. The label of this field is wrapped in a `<th></th>` element and the field itself is wrapped in a `<td></td>` element. The label will be stacked to the left with the input object and help text and error message displayed to the right, as shown:

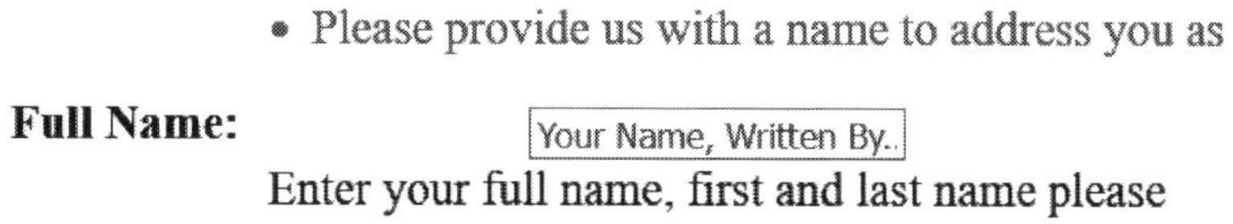

- Please provide us with a name to address you as

Full Name: [Your Name, Written By..]
Enter your full name, first and last name please

Figure 5.1 – Render form – as_table

To use this option, we still have to wrap the form tag in a `<table></table>` element because only the inner contents of a table are rendered.

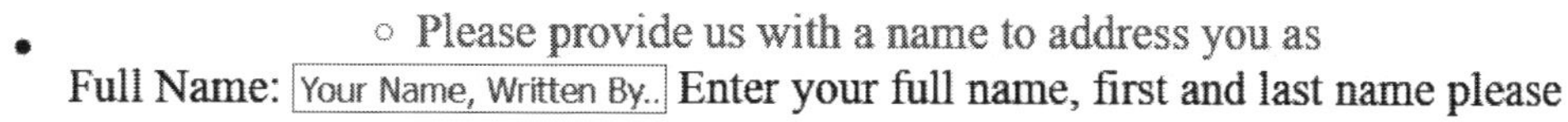

To render your form as a table, in your `/chapter_5/form-class.html` file, change your `{{ form }}` tag to `{{ form.as_table }}` and wrap it in the `<table>` tag, as shown:

```
# /becoming_a_django_entdev/chapter_5/templates/chapter_5/form-class.html
...
        <table>
            {{ form.as_table }}
        </table>
...
```

Let's render the form formatted as a list next.

Render form – as_ul

This option will render your form as a list with each field wrapped in a `<li></li>` element. Inside that element, the label will come first, then the input field, and the help text last. If an error occurs, it gets injected as its own list item above that field, as shown:

- ○ Please provide us with a name to address you as
  Full Name: [Your Name, Written By..] Enter your full name, first and last name please

Figure 5.2 – Render form – As a list

We also have to wrap the form in an element with the `<ul></ul>` list element. To render your form as a list, in your `/chapter_5/form-class.html` file, change the `{{ form }}` tag to `{{ form.as_ul }}` and wrap it in the `<ul>` tag, as shown:

```
# /becoming_a_django_entdev/chapter_5/templates/chapter_5/form-class.html
...
        <ul>
            {{ form.as_ul }}
        </ul>
...
```

Let's use a new approach that was introduced in Django 4.0 next.

Render form – using template_name

New to Django 4.0 is the `template_name` feature. This feature is used to render a form in the style written within a custom template. It gives developers the ability to structure their own HTML when fields are rendered. Developers can create many different template styles and use them as needed. Fields are accessed via the `{{ fields }}` tag inside that custom template.

Follow these steps to configure your custom form template:

1. In your `/chapter_5/forms.py` file, add the `template_name` option to the existing `ContactForm` class, as highlighted:

    ```
    # /becoming_a_django_entdev/chapter_5/forms.py
    ...
    from django.forms
    import Form, ModelForm
    ...
    class ContactForm(Form):
        template_name = 'chapter_5/forms/custom-form.html'
    ```

    > **Note**
    >
    > Make sure that in your `/chapter_5/form-class.html` file, you render your form using only the basic `{{ form }}` tag and not any of the other preconfigured form rendering methods.

2. Next, create the `custom-form.html` file in your `/chapter_5/templates/chapter_5/forms/` folder. We will not be adding an `{% extends %}` tag to this file; instead, we will treat it as if we are using an `{% include %}` tag, where it is just a snippet and not an entire page of HTML.
3. Inside your `/chapter_5/custom-forms.html` file, add the following code:

```
# /becoming_a_django_entdev/chapter_5/templates/
chapter_5/forms/custom-forms.html
{% load static %}

{% for field, errors in fields %}
    <div class="field-box{% if errors %} error{% endif %}">
        <label for="{{ field.id_for_label }}">
            {% if field.field.required %}<span class="required">*</span>{% endif %}{{ field.label|safe }}
        </label>

        <div class="form-group">
            {{ field }}

            {{ errors|safe }}

            {% if field.help_text and field.help_text != '' %}
                <span class="help-text">
                    {{ field.help_text|safe }}
                </span>
            {% endif %}
        </div>
    </div>
{% endfor %}
```

Here, we are looping through all of the fields with the `{% for field, errors in fields %}` tag shown in the preceding code block. We've added our own HTML structure using the `<div>`, `<label>`, and `<span>` elements. The field itself is rendered using the `{{ field }}` tag. Other information, such as the help text, is used in conjunction with the `safe` filter in `{{ field.help_text|safe }}`. The `safe` filter is used to make sure that any HTML contained in the string gets rendered as HTML objects and not printed as the string representation of that object.

Let's demonstrate all of these form renderings in action next.

Render demo

By now, we should have a working form. In your browser, visit the URL `http://localhost:8000/chapter-5/form-class/`, and you should see your form rendered onto the page. Through all of the examples provided using the `ContactForm` class, we should see six fields on this page. Here, we can see how an email field can behave differently as we interact with the form. For example, if we set the required argument in the `email_1` field to equal `False`, we can submit the form with nothing entered into this field and it will succeed. In the field named `email_2`, we specified the `required` argument as equal to `True`. This added the `required` attribute to that input field, preventing the user from submitting that form. This means the user will never see the error message that we provided in the Django code. This route would require the use of JavaScript, such as the jQuery Validate library, to handle the error state and display an error message for us. Doing nothing would result in the browser handling the error state for us, and in Chrome, that would look as in the following screenshot:

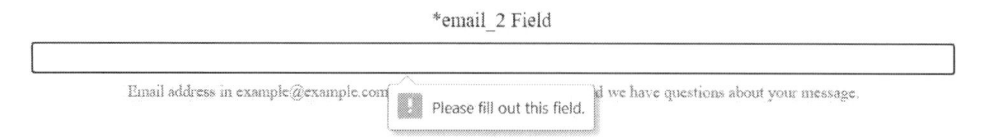

Figure 5.3 – ContactForm email_2 field

However, on the field named `email_3`, we set the required argument to equal `False`, and in the clean method, we are performing the validation that checks whether the field has a value or not. This lets us submit the form and see the error message that was provided on postback, as shown:

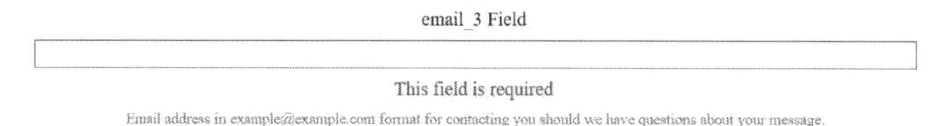

Figure 5.4 – ContactForm email_3 field

Next, let's take Django forms a step further and start working with the models in a form class. We created a placeholder class for this, called `VehicleForm`, in the section titled *Form class – ModelForm*.

Linking a model to a form

Linking a model to a form without needing any special field rendering is fairly easy.

In your `/chapter_5/forms.py` file, add the following code to the existing `VehicleForm` class (remember to remove the `pass` statement that was added to this class earlier):

```python
# /becoming_a_django_entdev/chapter_5/forms.py
...
from django.forms
import Form, ModelForm
from ..chapter_3.models
import Vehicle


class VehicleForm(ModelForm):
    class Meta:
        model = Vehicle
        fields = [
            'vin',
            'sold',
            'price',
            'make',
            'vehicle_model',
            'engine',
        ]
```

In the preceding example, we don't have to create fields for this form. Django will automatically use the form field type associated with the model field type that we wrote for the `Vehicle` model, created in *Chapter 3, Models, Relations, and Inheritance*. If any field behavior needed modifying, we would write form fields the same way we did for `ContactForm` and then customize them as we see fit. The `Meta` subclass used here defines what model class we are using and the `fields` option specifies what fields of that model we want to include and in what order they should be included.

> **Note**
> Using `fields = '__all__'` will include all fields that exist for that model in the order that they were written for that model.

Let's work with the `CreateView` class next.

View class – CreateView

Using the `VehicleForm` class that we now have wired up to the `Vehicle` model, let's create a view that will render a form with no or default field values using the `CreateView` class. It will let us create a new vehicle record in the database when that form is successfully submitted.

Follow these steps to configure your `CreateView` class:

1. In your `/chapter_5/views.py` file, add the following `import` statements and create the `ModelFormClassCreateView` class, as follows:

    ```
    # /becoming_a_django_entdev/chapter_5/views.py
    ...
    from django.http
    import HttpResponseRedirect
    from django.views.generic.edit
    import (
        ...,
        CreateView
    )
    from django.template.response
    import (
        TemplateResponse
    )
    from .forms
    import ContactForm, VehicleForm

    class ModelFormClassCreateView(CreateView):
        template_name = 'chapter_5/model-form-class.html'
        form_class = VehicleForm
        success_url = '/chapter-5/vehicle-form-success/'
    ```

2. In that same `ModelFormClassCreateView` class, add the following `get()` method:

```python
# /becoming_a_django_entdev/chapter_5/views.py
...
class ModelFormClassCreateView(CreateView):
    ...
    def get(self, request, *args, **kwargs):
        return TemplateResponse(
            request,
            self.template_name,
            {
                'title': 'ModelFormClassCreateView Page',
                'page_id': 'model-form-class-id',
                'page_class': 'model-form-class-page',
                'h1_tag': 'This is the ModelFormClassCreateView Class Page Using VehicleForm',
                'form': self.form_class(),
            }
        )
```

3. In that same `ModelFormClassCreateView` class, add the following `post()` method:

```python
# /becoming_a_django_entdev/chapter_5/views.py
...
class ModelFormClassCreateView(CreateView):
    ...
    def post(self, request, *args, **kwargs):
        form = self.form_class(request.POST)

        if form.is_valid():
            vehicle = form.instance
            vehicle.save()
            return HttpResponseRedirect(
                self.success_url
            )
        else:
```

```
                    return TemplateResponse(
                        request,
                        self.template_name,
                        {
                            'title': 'ModelFormClassCreateView
Page - Please Correct The Errors Below',
                            'page_id': 'model-form-class-id',
                            'page_class': 'model-form-class-page
errors-found',
                            'h1_tag': 'This is the
ModelFormClassCreateView Page Using VehicleForm<br
/><small class="error-msg">Errors Found</small>',
                            'form': form,
                        }
                    )
```

In this example, we gave this class the same two methods that we used earlier—get() and post(). These two methods work the same way as when used in a class constructed with the FormView class. In the get() method, we are passing just a blank form into the template as context using self.form_class(). In the post() method, we are once again passing request into the form to get the data that was submitted by the user, using form = self.form_class(request.POST). In that post() method, validation is performed using if form.is_valid(): and it will either redirect to a success page or refresh, serving up the form with the correct error messages. If the form is validated successfully, just before we perform the redirect, we are saving the form using vehicle.save(), the same way we did when we added data using the Django shell in *Chapter 3, Models, Relations, and Inheritance.*

4. Create a URL pattern using the ModelFormClassCreateView class, add the following path to your /chapter_5/urls.py file, and include the following import statements:

```
# /becoming_a_django_entdev/chapter_5/urls.py
from django.urls
import re_path
from django.views.generic
import (
    TemplateView
)
```

Linking a model to a form   251

```python
from .views
import (
    FormClassView,
    ModelFormClassCreateView
)

urlpatterns = [
    ...,
    re_path(
        r'^chapter-5/model-form-class/?$',
        ModelFormClassCreateView.as_view()
    ),
]
```

5. In that same /chapter_5/urls.py file, add the following success URL pattern:

```python
# /becoming_a_django_entdev/chapter_5/urls.py
...
urlpatterns = [
    ...,
    re_path(
        r'^chapter-5/vehicle-form-success/?$',
        TemplateView.as_view(
            template_name = 'chapter_5/vehicle-success.html'
        ),
        kwargs = {
            'title': 'ModelFormClass Success Page',
            'page_id': 'model-form-class-success',
            'page_class': 'model-form-class-success-page',
            'h1_tag': 'This is the ModelFormClass Success Page Using VehicleForm',
        }
    ),
]
```

We added the success URL pattern for a vehicle form at `http://localhost:8000/chapter-5/vehicle-form-success/`.

6. Next, construct your `/chapter_5/model-form-class.html` file the same way that we created the `/chapter_5/form-class.html` file.

7. Now, visit the URL `http://localhost:8000/chapter-5/model-form-class/`, and if you are rendering your form using the standard `{{ form }}` tag, you should see the page looking as in the following screenshot:

This is the ModelFormClassCreateView Class Page Using VehicleForm

VIN: [   ] Sold? [No ▾] Price: [   ] [USD $ ▾] Vehicle Make/Brand: [-------- ▾] Model: [-------- ▾] Engine: [-------- ▾] [Add Another Prospective Buyer] [Save Vehicle]

Figure 5.5 – VehicleForm using ModelFormClassCreateView

Of course, this example is in its simplest form. If you wanted to use another format or a template of your own, you would follow the steps under the *Rendering forms in templates* section of this chapter.

View class – UpdateView

In this example, we need to create a URL pattern using a path converter to capture the ID of the vehicle record that is being looked up.

Follow these steps to configure your `UpdateView` class:

1. In your `/chapter_5/urls.py` file, add the path shown here:

```
# /becoming_a_django_entdev/chapter_5/urls.py
from django.urls
import re_path
from .views
import (
    ...,
    ModelFormClassUpdateView
)
...
urlpatterns = [
    ...,
    re_path(
        'chapter-5/model-form-class/(?P<id>[0-9])/?$',
```

```
            ModelFormClassUpdateView.as_view(),
            name = 'vehicle_detail'
        ),
    ]
```

This pattern will allow us to access a `Vehicle` record by ID, also known as a primary key, in a database. We specify the ID of the `Vehicle` that we want to look up in the URL itself, as in `http://localhost:8000/chapter-5/model-form-class/2/`.

2. In your `/chapter_5/views.py` file, add the `ModelFormClassUpdateView` class and `import` statements shown here:

```
# /becoming_a_django_entdev/chapter_5/views.py
...
from django.http
import HttpResponseRedirect
from django.template.response
import (
    TemplateResponse
)
from django.views.generic.edit
import (
    ...,
    UpdateView
)
from .forms
import VehicleForm
from ..chapter_3.models
import Vehicle

class ModelFormClassUpdateView(UpdateView):
    template_name = 'chapter_5/model-form-class.html'
    form_class = VehicleForm
    success_url = '/chapter-5/vehicle-form-success/'
```

3. In that same `ModelFormClassUpdateView` class, add the `get()` and `post()` methods shown here:

```python
# /becoming_a_django_entdev/chapter_5/views.py
from django.template.response
import (
    TemplateResponse
)
from django.views.generic.edit
import (
    ...,
    UpdateView
)
from ..chapter_3.models
import Vehicle
...
class ModelFormClassUpdateView(UpdateView):
    ...
    def get(self, request, id, *args, **kwargs):
        try:
            vehicle = Vehicle.objects.get(pk=id)
        except Vehicle.DoesNotExist:
            form = self.form_class()
        else:
            form = self.form_class(instance=vehicle)

        return TemplateResponse(
            request,
            self.template_name,
            {
                'title': 'ModelFormClassUpdateView Page',
                'page_id': 'model-form-class-id',
                'page_class': 'model-form-class-page',
                'h1_tag': 'This is the
 ModelFormClassUpdateView Class Page Using VehicleForm',
                'form': form,
            }
```

```
            )

        def post(self, request, id, *args, **kwargs):
            # Use the same code as we did for the
    ModelFormClassCreateView class
```

4. Now, navigate to the URL http://localhost:8000/chapter-5/model-form-class/2/, and you should see the form preloaded with the values found in the database for that Vehicle, as depicted in the following screenshot:

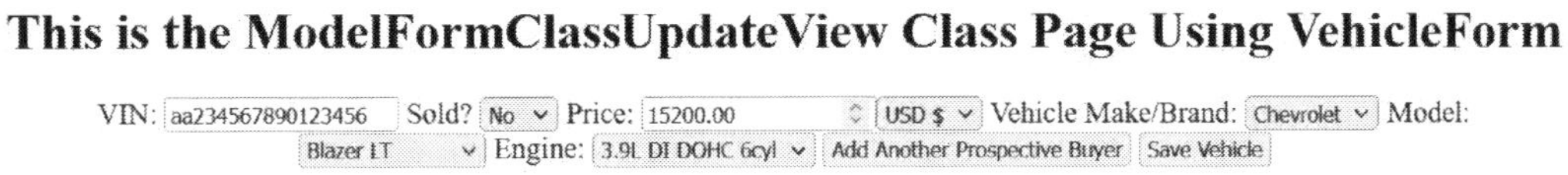

This is the ModelFormClassUpdateView Class Page Using VehicleForm

Figure 5.6 – VehicleForm using ModelFormClassUpdateView

We once again use the same two `get()` and `post()` methods. One minor difference in how we are writing the `get()` method here is that we are performing the `Vehicle` query. We use a `try/except` statement to determine whether the object exists in the database using `vehicle = Vehicle.objects.get(pk=id)`. If it does not exist, we create the form object as a blank form using `form = self.form_class()`. If the `Vehicle` object is found, then we pass that instance into the form that we are initializing, using `form = self.form_class(instance=vehicle)`. The `post()` method is written the same as what we wrote for `ModelFormClassCreateView`, except that we updated the context string variables to reflect this class name.

> **Note**
> When working with fields that have an attribute of `unique = True` and saving that object in a form using the `UpdateView` class, you may get a postback error message telling you that the object already exists. To get around this, try removing the `unique` attribute on your model and implementing your own `clean()` method to enforce that uniqueness. There are also several other approaches to solve this while keeping the `unique` attribute; all are rather difficult to implement and go beyond the scope of this chapter. Practice building a form to update the `Engine` class on your own that does not contain a `unique` field.

Let's add inline formsets next.

Adding inline formsets

An inline formset is a form within a form. It's a way to provide dynamic fields, for example, for additional personnel, comments, or objects. They are commonly used in combination with JavaScript code on the frontend to create or remove sets of fields as desired by the user. In the next exercise, we will expand upon the `ModelFormClassCreateView` class to add our inline formset. This formset will capture prospective buyer information, to capture the first and last name of that lead. We will create an **Add Another** button for the user to add as many prospective buyers as they would like to. JavaScript is used to control creating and/or deleting the new DOM objects. It will also update the Django management form data in the process. You can build upon this concept to make your form more robust with added fields and controls for the user to manipulate inline formsets.

Follow the steps in the following sections to get started with inline formsets.

Formset function – formset_factory

A **formset factory** is a controller that we use to register inline formsets.

Follow these steps to create your formset factory:

1. In the `/chapter_5/forms.py` file, add the following `ProspectiveBuyerForm` class, which will act as the inline form, capturing the first and last name of the prospective buyer:

    ```python
    # /becoming_a_django_entdev/chapter_5/forms.py
    from django import forms
    from django.forms import Form, ModelForm
    ...
    class ProspectiveBuyerForm(Form):
        first_name = forms.CharField(
            label = 'First Name',
            help_text = 'Enter your first name only',
            required = True,
            error_messages = {
                'required': 'Please provide us with a first name',
            }
    ```

```
        )
        last_name = forms.CharField(
            label = 'Last Name',
            help_text = 'Enter your last name only',
            required = True,
            error_messages = {
                'required': 'Please provide us with a last
  name',
            }
        )
```

We are doing nothing different in the `ProspectiveBuyerForm` class in the preceding code compared to what we did in `ContactForm` before. The same concepts and validation measures apply to the fields within an inline formset. Adjust the logic as necessary for your fields.

2. In the same `/chapter_5/forms.py` file, register that form as `formset_factory` using the following example. Make sure to place the `ProspectiveBuyerFormSet` class below the `ProspectiveBuyerForm` class in this file:

```
# /becoming_a_django_entdev/chapter_5/forms.py
...
from django.forms
import (
    ...,
    formset_factory
)
...
ProspectiveBuyerFormSet = formset_factory(
    ProspectiveBuyerForm,
    extra = 1
)
```

In the preceding example, we registered the `ProspectiveBuyerForm` class in a formset factory called `ProspectiveBuyerFormset`, which we will use next in our view class. The `extra = 1` argument is used to include only one instance of this formset when this `formset_factory` is first initialized. There are many other options available, and they are all explained in detail here: https://docs.djangoproject.com/en/4.0/topics/forms/formsets/.

> **Note**
>
> In this example, we are using a standard `formset_factory` for a form with fields that are not linked to a model. Formsets that do link to models would use the `modelformset_factory()` method to link form fields to a model in your database. When using that method, data is saved in the view class the same way as when we saved the `VehicleForm` data.

Let's use this inline formset in a view class next.

Using inline formsets in the view class

Follow these steps to use your newly created inline formset in a view class:

1. In your `/chapter_5/views.py` file, in the existing `ModelFormClassCreateView` class, add a few minor adjustments to the existing `get()` method, as highlighted in the following code:

```python
# /becoming_a_django_entdev/chapter_5/views.py
...
from django.http
import HttpResponseRedirect
from django.template.response
import (
    TemplateResponse
)
from django.views.generic.edit
import (
    ...,
    CreateView
)
from .forms
import ..., ProspectiveBuyerFormSet
from ..chapter_3.models
import Vehicle

class ModelFormClassCreateView(CreateView):
    ...
    def get(self, request, *args, **kwargs):
        buyer_formset = ProspectiveBuyerFormSet()
```

```
        return TemplateResponse(
            request,
            self.template_name,
            {
                ...
                'form': self.form_class(),
                'buyer_formset': buyer_formset,
            }
        )
```

2. In the same `ModelFormClassCreateView` class, add a few minor adjustments to the existing `post()` method, as highlighted in the following code:

```
# /becoming_a_django_entdev/chapter_5/views.py
...
class ModelFormClassCreateView(CreateView):
    ...
    def post(self, request, *args, **kwargs):
        form = self.form_class(request.POST)
        buyer_formset = ProspectiveBuyerFormSet(
            request.POST
        )
        if form.is_valid():
            ...
        else:
            return TemplateResponse(
                request,
                self.template_name,
                {
                    ...
                    'form': form,
                    'buyer_formset': buyer_formset,
                }
            )
```

In the preceding steps, we are passing the inline `ProspectiveBuyerFormset` formset into the template as an additional context variable called `buyer_formset`. This and the form object should always be thought of as entirely separate objects. The form and the formset can also be related if they are using `ForeignKey`, `ManyToMany`, or `OneToOne` model relations.

Let's render these inline formsets into a template next.

Rendering inline formsets in the template

To render your newly created inline formsets into a template file, in your /chapter_5/model-form-class.html file, include all of the nodes, class names, and IDs that exist, as shown in the following code:

```
# /becoming_a_django_entdev/chapter_5/templates/chapter_5/
model-form-class.html
...
{% extends 'chapter_5/base/base_template_1.html' %}
{% load static %}
...
{% block body_content %}
    ...
    <form method="post" id="form">
        {% csrf_token %}
        {{ form }}
        {% if buyer_formset %}
            <h3>Prospective Buyers</h3>
            {{ buyer_formset.non_form_errors }}
            {{ buyer_formset.management_form }}

            {% for form in buyer_formset %}
                <div class="formset-container {{ buyer_formset.prefix }}">
                    <div class="first-name">
                        {{ form.first_name.label }}: {{ form.first_name }}
                    </div>
                    <div class="last-name">
                        {{ form.last_name.label }}: {{ form.
```

```
    last_name }}
                    </div>
                </div>
            {% endfor %}
        {% endif %}

        <button id="add-formset" type="button">Add Another
Prospective Buyer</button>
        <input type="submit" value="Save Vehicle">
    </form>
{% endblock %}
```

The JavaScript we will soon write will depend on this structure, and as your structure changes, be sure to change your JavaScript as well. In the preceding code, the important parts of the form include the ID attribute of the form itself, called `id="form"`. We will use that to target the form as a whole in the JavaScript we are going to write. A conditional is used to check whether the `buyer_formset` variable exists before we do anything with it. For example, if you wanted to serve up an instance of this page that has no formsets at all, then this conditional will prevent breakage.

An important feature to never forget to include is the management form data, which is added using the `{{ buyer_formset.management_form }}` tag. This will include important data that Django needs to process your inline formsets. We then loop through each form in the `buyer_formset` object using `{% for form in buyer_formset %}`. For each form that does exist, we wrap all of the internal HTML in a node called `<div class="formset-container"></div>`. This class is important as it will differentiate between each inline form when we work with JavaScript. Inside, you can structure your fields however you like. Lastly, outside of the loop, just before the submit button, we need to add a new `<button>` of `type="button"` to prevent accidentally submitting the form. Give that button an attribute of `id="add-formset"`.

Now, visit the same URL that we went to before, to add a new vehicle at `http://localhost:8000/chapter-5/model-form-class/`. You should see a form resembling the following:

This is the ModelFormClassCreateView Class Page Using VehicleForm

VIN: [ ] Sold? [No ▾] Price: [ ] [USD $ ▾] Vehicle Make/Brand: [------- ▾] Model: [------- ▾] Engine: [------- ▾]

Prospective Buyers

First Name: [First Name, Prospective] Last Name: [Last Name, Prospective]

[Add Another Prospective Buyer] [Save Vehicle]

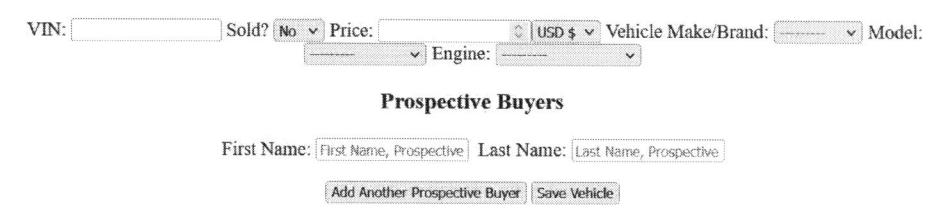

Figure 5.7 – VehicleForm inline formset

There will only be one instance of the prospective buyer for now. Next, we will add the JavaScript controls that let us add more instances to this form.

Dynamic inline formsets

Follow these steps to configure the JavaScript needed to let the user add more instances of an inline formset:

1. In your `/chapter_5/base/base_template_1.html` file, there is already a reference to a JavaScript file in the `<head>` of that document. Make sure the following script is included in your `<head>` of that document:

   ```
   # /becoming_a_django_entdev/chapter_5/templates/
   chapter_5/base/base_template_1.html
   ...
   <html lang="en" xmlns="http://www.w3.org/1999/xhtml">
       <head>
           ...
           <script defer type="text/javascript" src="{{ base_url }}{% static 'chapter_5/js/site-js.js' %}"></script>
       </head>
       ...
   </html>
   ```

   This will load a single JavaScript file that is used to make a form interactive and lets the user add another instance of the inline `ProspectiveBuyerFormset` formset.

2. If you didn't already copy the JavaScript files when copying the `base_template_1.html` file earlier in preparation for a previous exercise, then go ahead and create the `/chapter_5/static/chapter_5/` and `/chapter_5/static/chapter_5/js/` folders and the `site-js.js` file using your IDE, File Explorer, or the following commands:

   ```
   (virtual_env) PS > mkdir becoming_a_django_entdev/chapter_5/static/chapter_5
   (virtual_env) PS > mkdir becoming_a_django_entdev/chapter_5/static/chapter_5/js
   (virtual_env) PS > cd becoming_a_django_entdev/chapter_5/static/chapter_5/js
   (virtual_env) PS > touch site-js.js
   ```

3. Inside your `/chapter_5/js/site-js.js` file, include the following variables:

   ```
   # /becoming_a_django_entdev/chapter_5/static/chapter_5/js/site-js.js
   let formsetContainer = document.querySelectorAll(
           '.formset-container'
       ),
       form = document.querySelector('#form'),
       addFormsetButton = document.querySelector(
           '#add-formset'
       ),
       totalForms = document.querySelector(
           '#id_form-TOTAL_FORMS'
       ),
       formsetNum = formsetContainer.length - 1;
   ```

4. Add the following event listener to that same JavaScript file:

   ```
   # /becoming_a_django_entdev/chapter_5/static/chapter_5/js/site-js.js
   ...
   addFormsetButton.addEventListener(
       'click',
       $addFormset
   );
   ```

5. Add the following function to that same JavaScript file:

```
# /becoming_a_django_entdev/chapter_5/static/chapter_5/
js/site-js.js
...
function $addFormset(e) {
    e.preventDefault();

    let newForm = formsetContainer[0].cloneNode(true),
        formRegex = RegExp(`form-(\\d){1}-`,'g');

    formsetNum++
    newForm.innerHTML = newForm.innerHTML.replace(
        formRegex,
        'form-${formsetNum}-'
    );
    form.insertBefore(newForm, addFormsetButton);

    totalForms.setAttribute(
        'value',
        '${formsetNum + 1}'
    );
}
```

What we are doing is adding an event listener that listens for the click event of the **Add Another Prospective Buyer** button. When clicked, it will clone a single instance of `<div class="formset-container"></div>` and insert that cloned node just before the `<button id="add-formset"></button>` node. Since Django also requires the precise management of form data, we need to be sure that we update the relevant data every time an inline formset is added or removed. This is why we are finding the number of inline formsets that exist before we perform the clone action as the `formsetNum` variable. Then, we increment this number, which starts at index 0, using a regular expression method to search all the inner HTML nodes of the node with the `formset-container` CSS class. That incremented number is used to update all node attributes to the proper index of the new node that we inserted. We also update the value of the form object with `id="id_form-TOTAL_FORMS"` to the new total of inline formsets that exist.

If successful, when we click the **Add Another Prospective Buyer** button, we should see additional inline formsets added, just like the following:

Figure 5.8 – VehicleForm adding another inline formset

Summary

By now, we have completed two major forms, one to act as the contact form and another to handle the vehicle object, created in *Chapter 3*, *Models, Relations, and Inheritance*. We added a variety of fields and discussed the differences between those field types. Using the email example over and over again as we did, we witnessed how validation works in many different ways. Depending on the requirements gathered for a project, we can then decide on several different writing patterns to align with those requirements. For example, if we wanted to completely eliminate the need for JavaScript validation, such as using my favorite library jQuery Validate, we could just write clean methods in form classes to perform all of the validation on the backend. This would use the power of Django to serve up the error messages. However, if we did use JavaScript-based validation on the frontend, we could write fields that create the node attributes for us, such as the `<input>` field attribute of `required=""`, which would prevent a form from submitting if it had no value.

No matter the requirements of a project, we also discovered a really easy way to create our own field classes. Custom field classes let us preformat fields that support a **Don't Repeat Yourself** (**DRY**) style of writing. We explored the differences in view classes, form classes, and field classes, and then discussed ways to render those forms in a template.

In the next chapter, we will explore a user interface specifically tailored for the rapid development of forms that lets users update, create, and delete model objects on their own. This is called the Django admin site, which is basically a glorified way to render forms related to model management.

6
Exploring the Django Admin Site

This chapter will introduce the Django admin site, which is a feature allowing developers to register certain models into a model-centric interface where only permitted users can manage database content. This feature is designed to read the metadata related to models as well as the fields and field constraints set on those models to build a set of pages that search, sort, filter, create, edit, and delete records found in those tables.

The admin site is an optional feature of the Django framework that can be used in projects. It allows us to use user-based roles and permission settings that are built into the Django framework, allowing only permitted users to edit, add, or delete objects. User roles can be modified to only grant permission to edit certain models and can even be set to a granular level, such as only letting a user edit or view data but not add or delete data. This feature can be deactivated if it is not desired or needed in a project.

Models that are not specifically registered in the Django admin site will not be accessible via that interface, giving developers the option to create tables that store data that no users at all can control. By the end of this chapter, we will have registered the models that we created in *Chapter 3, Models, Relations, and Inheritance*. Those models will serve as the foundation for most of the exercises provided throughout this chapter.

In this chapter, we will cover the following topics:

- Using the Django admin site
- Configuring `admin` class options
- Adding `admin` class methods
- Writing custom `admin form classes`
- Using the Django authentication system

Technical requirements

To work with the code in this chapter, the following tools will need to be installed on your local machine:

- Python version 3.9 – used as the underlying programming language for the project
- Django version 4.0 – used as the backend framework of the project
- pip package manager – used to manage third-party Python/Django packages

We will continue to work with the solution created in *Chapter 2*, *Project Configuration*. However, it is not necessary to use the Visual Studio IDE. The main project itself can be run using another IDE or run independently using a terminal or command-line window from within the project root folder, which is where the `manage.py` file resides. Whatever editor or IDE you are using, a virtual environment will also be needed to work with the Django project. Instructions for how to create a project and virtual environment can be found in *Chapter 2*, *Project Configuration*. You will need a database to store the data contained in your project. PostgreSQL was chosen for the examples in the previous chapter; however, any database type that you chose for your project can be used to work with the examples in this chapter.

We will also be using data that is in the form of a Django fixture, provided previously in *Chapter 3*, *Models, Relations, and Inheritance*, in the sub-section titled *Loading the chapter_3 data fixture*. Make sure the `chapter_3` fixture is loaded into your database. If this has already been done, then you may skip the next command. If you have already created the tables found in *Chapter 3*, *Models, Relations, and Inheritance*, and have not loaded that fixture yet, then run the following command, after activating your virtual environment:

```
(virtual_env) PS > python manage.py loaddata chapter_3
```

All of the code created in this chapter can be found in the GitHub repository for this book at `https://github.com/PacktPublishing/Becoming-an-Enterprise-Django-Developer`. The bulk of the code depicted in this chapter can be found in the `/becoming_a_django_entdev/becoming_a_django_entdev/chapter_6/` directory.

Check out the following video to see the *Code in Action*: `https://bit.ly/3ODUaAW`.

Preparing for this chapter

Start by creating a new app in your project called `chapter_6` by following the steps discussed in *Chapter 2*, *Project Configuration*, in the subsection titled *Creating a Django app*. As discussed in that section, don't forget to change the value of your `name =` variable for your app class found in the `/becoming_a_django_entdev/becoming_a_django_entdev/chapter_6/apps.py` file to now point to the path where you installed your app. Be sure to also include this app in your `INSTALLED_APPS` variable found in the `settings.py` file as well.

In the main `urls.py` file of the site, add the following path, which points to the URL patterns of this chapter that we will be creating:

```
# /becoming_a_django_entdev/urls.py
...
urlpatterns = [
    path('', include('becoming_a_django_entdev.chapter_6.urls')),
]
```

Now that we have created the app for this chapter, let's begin using the Django admin site to manage the models created in *Chapter 3*, *Models, Relations, and Inheritance*.

Using the Django admin site

Django makes it easy to use the admin site right out of the box. In order to use this feature, we need to add an app to the `settings.py` file and register a URL pattern to handle any project's admin links. By default, these settings should already exist in the code when a project is created using the `startproject` command or by using the IDE. However, some tools and versions may generate code slightly differently and so it is always good to just double-check that these settings are configured in this way.

Activating the Django admin site

To make sure the Django admin site is activated in your project, follow these steps:

1. In the main `settings.py` file, add the following app to the `INSTALLED_APPS` variable and make sure this is at the top of the list:

    ```
    # /becoming_a_django_entdev/settings.py
    ...
    INSTALLED_APPS = [
        'django.contrib.admin',
        ...
    ]
    ```

2. If the `/chapter_6/urls.py` file does not exist yet, create that file and include the following URL pattern:

    ```
    # /becoming_a_django_entdev/chapter_6/urls.py
    ...
    from django.contrib import admin
    urlpatterns = [
        path('admin/', admin.site.urls),
    ]
    ```

To deactivate the Django admin site, remove the settings described in this section. Template and static files related to the Django admin site can also be overridden to create your own look and feel. You are not restricted to the user interface that is provided right out of the box. Due to the limited space in this book, we will not demonstrate how to override Django admin site templates; however, you can refer to *Chapter 4, URLs, Views, and Templates*, to learn more about overriding third-party templates.

> **Tip**
> Because Django is designed to do all of the heavy lifting, this is the only URL pattern that we need to create in order to activate all URL patterns related to the Django admin site.

Logging into the Django admin site

The Django admin site should now be active and if we navigate to the URL `http://localhost:8000/admin/`, we should see the standard Django admin login screen, as depicted in the following screenshot:

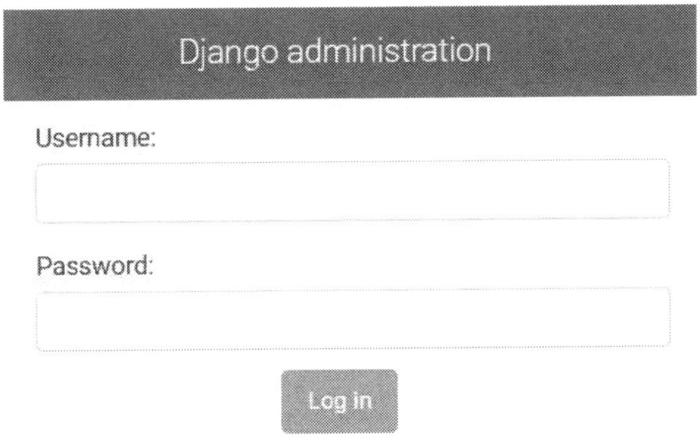

Figure 6.1 – Django admin site login

Use the username and password that were provided when the `createsuperuser` command was executed in *Chapter 2, Project Configuration*. You can log in with those superuser credentials or, if you wish to use the superuser provided with the `chapter_3` data fixture, then use the following credentials instead:

- **Username**: `admin`
- **Password**: `mynewpassword`

Once you are logged in, you should see two main sections, titled **AUTHENTICATION AND AUTHORIZATION** and **CHAPTER_3**, and to the right, a **Recent actions** side-nav section is displayed on your dashboard, as depicted in the following screenshot:

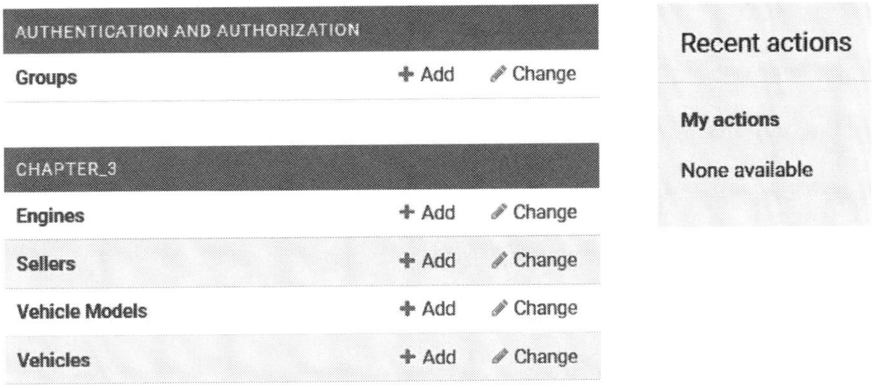

Figure 6.2 – Django admin site dashboard

If you installed the `django-address` package in *Chapter 3, Models, Relations, and Inheritance*, you will see an additional **ADDRESS** section appear stacked on the top. That package did all of the heavy lifting to create those tables and register them in the Django admin site for us. If we did not include this package and the `address` app in the `INSTALLED_APPS` variable of the `settings.py` file, then that section would not appear within the admin dashboard.

The **Recent actions** panel shows us information that tracks when a user created, changed, or deleted a particular object that is registered in the admin site when any of those actions is performed.

In the section titled **AUTHENTICATION AND AUTHORIZATION**, we normally would see two items, **Groups** and **Users**, but here, only the **Groups** item is displayed. Since we defined a custom `User` model in *Chapter 3, Models, Relations, and Inheritance*, using the `AUTH_USER_MODEL` variable in the `settings.py` file to point to the custom `Seller` class that we created, we will have to register the `Seller` model in the admin site in order for it to appear.

Next, let's register that `Seller` model to get it to appear on the dashboard.

Writing admin classes

Here, we will discuss writing a standard `ModelAdmin` class found in the `django.contrib.admin` library. We will also provide an example using the `UserAdmin` class, because we extended the `User` model in *Chapter 3, Models, Relations, and Inheritance*.

Class – ModelAdmin

`ModelAdmin` is the class provided by Django that does all the heavy lifting for us, in regard to models that are not user based. Before a model can be registered, an admin class using the `ModelAdmin` class will need to be created in order to link a model to the admin interface.

In the `/chapter_6/admin.py` file, include the following code:

```
# /becoming_a_django_entdev/chapter_6/admin.py
from django.contrib.admin import ModelAdmin


class SellerAdmin(ModelAdmin):
    pass
```

In the preceding code, the `SellerAdmin` class is constructed using the Django `contrib` class called `ModelAdmin`. Django makes it easy for us by doing a lot of the heavy lifting. Django will automatically configure everything that we do not specify in this class, such as the options we will discuss soon in this chapter. This means if we include the `pass` statement in this class, we will not have to write anything else and Django will create the admin site for that model based on default parameters. Go ahead and write this class another three times for the remaining vehicle model objects, including the `pass` statement for each class as you write them. Name these classes `VehicleAdmin`, `VehicleModelAdmin`, and `EngineAdmin`.

> **Note**
> Each of the class names ends with the word `Admin`. Follow the naming convention of `ModelNameAdmin` when naming future admin classes of your own.

Class – UserAdmin

`UserAdmin` is a special class provided by Django that lets us link a user-based model to the admin interface. The `UserAdmin` class is an extension of the `ModelAdmin` class. Next, we will create the `SellerAdmin` class, which will import all of the functionality available in the Django `UserAdmin` class. We will write the admin class the exact same way as we did in the previous exercise with the `pass` statement. All of the other vehicle-related admin classes will continue to use the standard `ModelAdmin` class.

The following code shows us how the `SellerAdmin` class should look now:

```
# /becoming_a_django_entdev/chapter_6/admin.py
...
from django.contrib.auth.admin
import UserAdmin

class SellerAdmin(UserAdmin):
    pass
```

Now that we have written the admin classes, let's register them next.

Registering models

We need to write a register statement that will link an admin class to its corresponding model and automatically create the URL patterns that will pertain to that model. There are two ways to do this and they both do the exact same thing:

- The first is with a single statement that is written at the bottom of the document, placed right after any admin classes that have been written.
- The second is to wrap each admin class in a register decorator function.

Both will be demonstrated in the following examples but choose only the one that you like the most. Implementing both at the same time may cause errors.

Using a statement

Using a statement is easy; first we write the admin classes and then, at the bottom of the same `admin.py` file, write the register statement just like we have done for `Seller` in the following code block:

```python
# /becoming_a_django_entdev/chapter_6/admin.py
...
from django.contrib import admin
from django.contrib.auth.admin import UserAdmin
from ..chapter_3.models import Seller
...
class SellerAdmin(UserAdmin):
    pass
admin.site.register(Seller, SellerAdmin)
```

Here, we use the `admin.site.register(Model, ModelAdmin)` statement to register the admin classes. Write three more statements to register the `Vehicle`, `VehicleModel`, and `Engine` model classes to their corresponding admin classes.

Using a decorator

Using a decorator works just like when we used the `@property` model method decorator introduced in *Chapter 3, Models, Relations, and Inheritance*. Decorators wrap classes, written on the line before the class is declared, as is done on the `SellerAdmin` class here:

```
# /becoming_a_django_entdev/chapter_6/admin.py
...
from django.contrib
import admin
from ..chapter_3.models import (
    Engine,
    Seller,
    Vehicle,
    VehicleModel
)

@admin.register(Seller)
class SellerAdmin(UserAdmin):
    pass
```

Here, we are using the `@admin.register(Model)` decorator provided by Django. When used this way, this function takes in only one positional argument and that is the name of the model class we wish to link to that admin class. The admin class is derived from the class name that the decorator is being used on, in this case, the `SellerAdmin` class. Add this decorator to the three remaining admin classes and adjust the related model accordingly for each decorator.

Now that we have these models registered, when accessing the Django admin dashboard, you should now see a fourth section titled **CHAPTER_3** containing four items, as shown in the following screenshot:

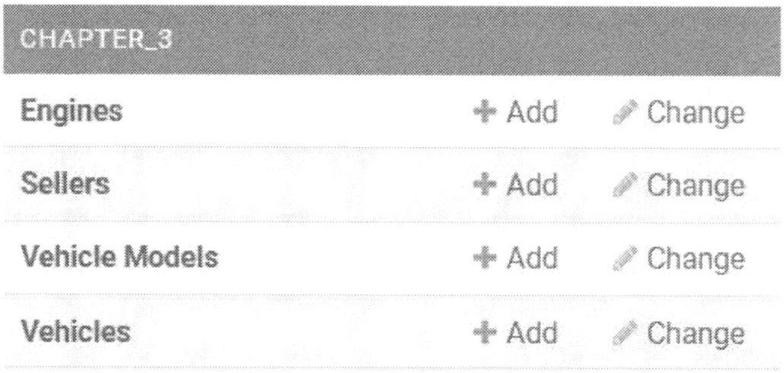

CHAPTER_3		
Engines	+ Add	Change
Sellers	+ Add	Change
Vehicle Models	+ Add	Change
Vehicles	+ Add	Change

Figure 6.3 – Django – registering models

Clicking any one of these will take you to what is called a **changelist view**, where a list or collection of all those objects is displayed. Clicking on any of those items would then take you to what is called a **change view**. Clicking on the **Add** button found on the changelist view page will take the user to what is called an **add view**, which is a form that creates a new instance of that model rather than editing an existing one. Similarly, deleting an object will take the user to what is called a **delete view** page for that object. Similar to how models and forms are each controlled using the fields and methods written in those classes, we can control admin classes the same way by defining certain variables known as options and custom methods. Let's discuss what those options are next.

Configuring admin class options

Django provides admin class options for customizing the Django admin site interface directly. In this section, we will go through some of the most important and widely used options and provide examples of how to use them. We don't have enough room to discuss them all in great detail.

For a complete breakdown of how to use any of the options available, visit the official Django documentation, found here: `https://docs.djangoproject.com/en/4.0/ref/contrib/admin/#modeladmin-options`.

The following options have been broken down into categories based on what view type they relate to (changelist view, change or add view, and just the add view).

> **Note**
> Before adding any of the options to your admin classes, remember to remove the `pass` statement that was previously written for that class as a placeholder.

Changelist view-related options

These options relate to an admin class on the changelist view page, such as those listed here:

- `http://localhost:8000/admin/chapter_3/engine/`
- `http://localhost:8000/admin/chapter_3/seller/`
- `http://localhost:8000/admin/chapter_3/vehicle_model/`
- `http://localhost:8000/admin/chapter_3/vehicle/`

Option – actions

The `actions` option relates to the checkbox that is found to the left of every item on a changelist view page. By default, Django automatically provides at least one action for every model that is created and registered; that action is the delete action. For example, navigate to the `Sellers` changelist view page at `http://localhost:8000/admin/chapter_3/seller/`, select the dropdown next to the **Action** label, and you will see only one option, the delete option, as shown in the following screenshot:

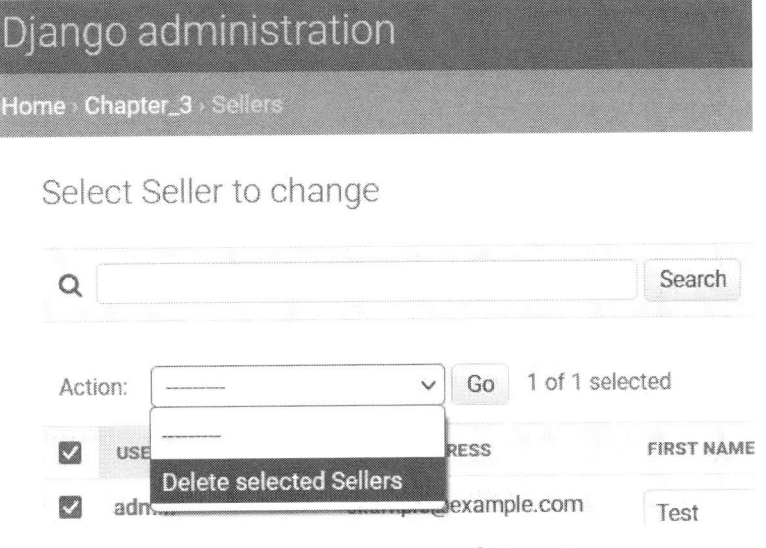

Figure 6.4 – Django – actions admin option

If we had 20 sellers in this list, we could delete all 20 of them at once by using this action, instead of having to do a lot of needless clicking around. Additional actions can be created for custom use. An example of where this can be used is if you have a set of pages, which can have a published or unpublished state, stored in a field within your table. A custom action could be created that can publish or unpublish all of the selected objects.

We won't be creating a custom action in these exercises because it would be a complicated task to discuss and goes beyond the scope of this book. Additionally, some of the actions that you might be thinking of, such as editing a field, can also be done using the `list_editable` option, which we will be discussing in the *Option – list_editable section*.

Django provides full documentation on how to create custom actions here: `https://docs.djangoproject.com/en/4.0/ref/contrib/admin/actions/`.

Option – actions_on_bottom

The `actions_on_bottom` option is used to display the **Action** dropdown that is shown in the previous subsection in *Figure 6.4*. By default, Django will set this value to `False`. If set to `True`, as is done to the `SellerAdmin` class in the following example, the **Action** dropdown will appear below the changelist results:

```
# /becoming_a_django_entdev/chapter_6/admin.py
...
class SellerAdmin(UserAdmin):
    ...
    actions_on_bottom = True
```

Option – actions_on_top

Similar to the `actions_on_bottom` option, the `actions_on_top` option will display the **Action** dropdown above the changelist results. By default, Django sets this value to `True`. We only need to write this if we wish to disable it above the changelist, but we can set it to `True` in the `SellerAdmin` class using the following example without triggering errors as well:

```
# /becoming_a_django_entdev/chapter_6/admin.py
...
class SellerAdmin(UserAdmin):
    ...
    actions_on_top = True
```

If both this option and the `actions_on_bottom` option are set to `True`, the **Action** dropdown will appear both above and below the changelist results.

Option – actions_selection_counter

The `actions_selection_counter` relates to the counter displayed to the right of the **Action** drop-down box. This option controls whether or not it should appear next to **Action**, as depicted in the following screenshot:

Figure 6.5 – Django – actions_selection_counter admin option

By default, Django will set this value to `True`. There is no need to write this option unless you want to disable this feature by setting its value to `False`. However, there is no harm in including this option with a value of `True`, as is done in the following example:

```
# /becoming_a_django_entdev/chapter_6/admin.py
...
class SellerAdmin(UserAdmin):
    ...
    actions_selection_counter = True
```

Option – list_display

The `list_display` option is used to show vertical columns on the changelist view page of a model. For example, navigate to the URL `http://localhost:8000/admin/chapter_3/seller/` and you'll see that the five columns that currently exist are `username`, `email`, `first_name`, `last_name`, and `is_staff`. Django will display the value of each field for each row that exists in that table.

If we want to adjust this list to display the custom fields that we added to the `Seller` model that do not exist in the `User` model, such as the **Business Name** and **Superuser Status** columns, the `SellerAdmin` class would look as in the following example:

```
# /becoming_a_django_entdev/chapter_6/admin.py
...
class SellerAdmin(UserAdmin):
    ...
    list_display = (
        'username',
        'email',
        'first_name',
        'last_name',
```

```
        'name',
        'is_staff',
        'is_superuser',
)
```

The five columns that existed before were already defined in the `list_display` option found in the `UserAdmin` class, which was used to construct the `SellerAdmin` class. Navigate back to the same URL at http://localhost:8000/admin/chapter_3/seller/ and you should now see the **Business Name** column third from last on the page and the **Superuser Status** column as the last column on the page because that is how they are positioned in the preceding list.

The `list_display` option can also be used in the form of a callable function, allowing you to write a method within that admin class to format the data displayed in that column. Just add the name of the custom method to this list just like any other field name when using a callable for this option.

Option – list_display_links

The `list_display_links` option is used to control which columns in the changelist results will navigate the user to the change view page of that object when clicked. By default, Django will make only the first column in this list clickable. If you want to make other columns editable, use this option.

On the `SellerAdmin` class, add the option as follows:

```
# /becoming_a_django_entdev/chapter_6/admin.py
...
class SellerAdmin(UserAdmin):
    ...
    list_display_links = (
        'username',
        'name',
    )
```

When using the `list_display_links` option, the `list_display` option must also be used. Only fields added to the `list_display` option can be added to this option. Also, if the `list_display_links` option is defined, Django will no longer make the first column clickable. For example, if we want to keep the first column clickable, that is, the **Username** column, as well as making the **Business Name** column clickable, we must specify both the `username` and `name` fields in this option. Also, they must be in the order in which they appear in the `list_display` option.

> **Note**
> If you are using the `list_editable` option, which we are about to discuss, those fields cannot be used in the `list_display_links` option, such as the `first_name` and `last_name` fields, which we will reserve for the `list_editable` example next.

Option – list_editable

The `list_editable` option is an option that allows us to specify what fields on the changelist view page will be editable from that page. This prevents the need to open up the change view for that particular object just to edit a single field. Additionally, only fields found in the `list_display` option can be included in the `list_editable` option. This is because the column must exist before we can edit it.

For example, if we want to make the `first_name` and `last_name` fields editable on the changelist view page, the `SellerAdmin` class would be written as follows:

```python
# /becoming_a_django_entdev/chapter_6/admin.py
...
from django.contrib.auth.admin
import UserAdmin

class SellerAdmin(UserAdmin):
    ...
    list_editable = (
        'first_name',
        'last_name',
    )
```

Now, navigate to the changelist view found at `http://localhost:8000/admin/chapter_3/seller/`. We can see the `first_name` and `last_name` fields now appear as an input box with a save button at the bottom of that list, as depicted in the following screenshot:

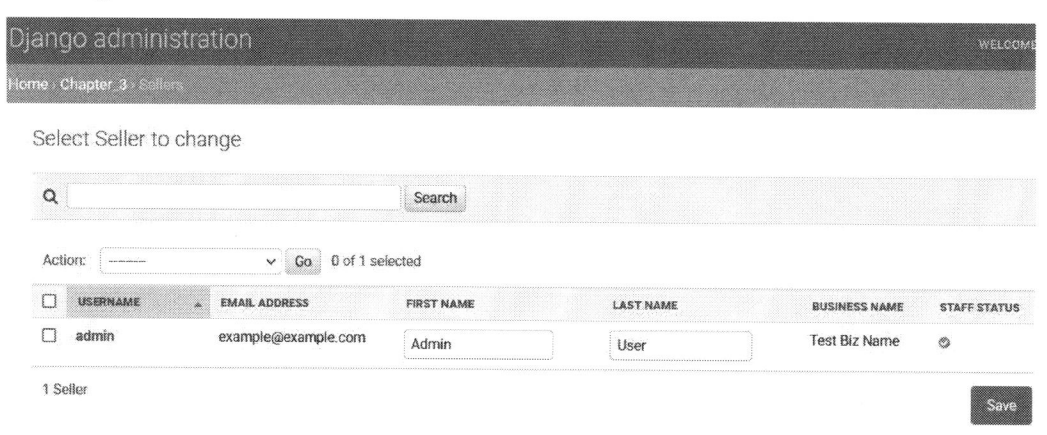

Figure 6.6 – Django – list_editable admin option

Option – list_filter

The `list_filter` option is a powerful tool that creates a box with a label titled **Filter** just to the right of the results on a changelist view page. The fields that are added to this option will tell Django to create a filter with a set of related choices derived from the values found in that QuerySet of results.

For example, if we want to override the default `list_filter` option that is found in the `UserAdmin` class and add the `Seller` model field called `name` as a filter, then we would write the `SellerAdmin` class as in the following example:

```
# /becoming_a_django_entdev/chapter_6/admin.py
...
class SellerAdmin(UserAdmin):
    ...
    list_filter = (
        'is_staff',
        'is_superuser',
        'is_active',
        'name',
        'groups'
    )
```

In the previous example, we just copied the `list_filter` option found in the `UserAdmin` class, located in the `django.contrib.auth.admin` library of Django. Then, we just modified that value to the desired value.

Now when we navigate back to the URL `http://localhost:8000/admin/chapter_3/seller/`, we see the **By Business Name** filter, as depicted in the following screenshot:

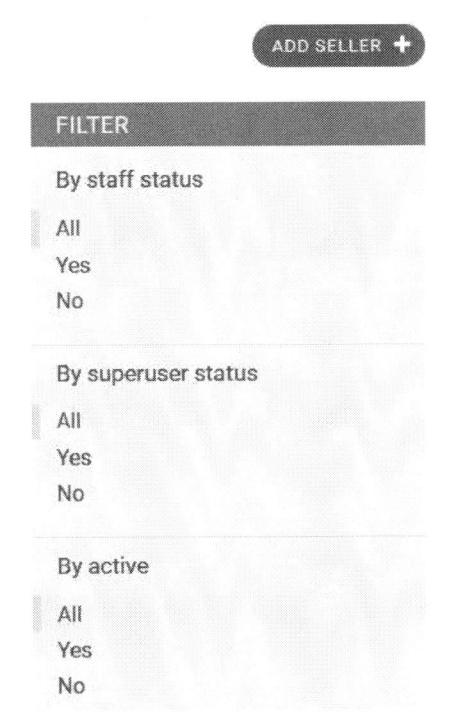

Figure 6.7 – Django – list_filter admin option

Option – list_per_page

The `list_per_page` option designates the number of items that we want to appear on a changelist view page. By default, Django will set this value to `100`. This can sometimes be too much for a user and so let's go ahead and practice setting this to a much more friendly number of, say, `20` on the `SellerAdmin` class by using the following example:

```
# /becoming_a_django_entdev/chapter_6/admin.py
...
class SellerAdmin(UserAdmin):
    ...
    list_per_page = 20
```

If you add more than 20 items to your tables, you will see a set of pagination buttons appear at the bottom of your changelist view page. When there are fewer than 20 items in total, no pagination buttons will appear since there is only one page of results.

> **Note**
> If you are using a third-party package or custom class instead of the default `django.core.paginator.Paginator` class used in Django, you can implement that custom paginator class by using the `paginator` admin option. Instructions on how this is done can be found here: https://docs.djangoproject.com/en/4.0/ref/contrib/admin/#django.contrib.admin.ModelAdmin.paginator/.

Option – ordering

The `ordering` option is done the same way as the `ordering` option in a model `Meta` class. This option accepts a list of fields that are ordered by the field specified when the page first loads.

For example, the default ordering option in the `UserAdmin` class is set to order by `username` in ascending order. Go ahead and add that to the `SellerAdmin` class by using the following example:

```python
# /becoming_a_django_entdev/chapter_6/admin.py
...
class SellerAdmin(UserAdmin):
    ...
    ordering = ('username',)
```

Here, we can add the subtract symbol, such as in `('-username',)`, to make it order in descending order, just like the model `Meta` class `ordering` option. Multiple fields can be added and Django will sort by the items in the order that they appear in this options list. Also, once the page loads, the user can opt to unsort or sort by another column if they press the action buttons in the table heading of those columns.

Option – preserve_filters

The `preserve_filters` option relates to how filters are applied when the user visits the changelist view page. By default, when a user decides to create, change, or edit an object for a model, when they are brought back to the changelist view page, the filters will be preserved. The only time we would actually have to use this option is when we want to disable this feature, making all filters reset whenever an add, change, or delete action has been performed.

To disable this feature, set the `preserve_filters` value to `False`, as is done in the following example:

```
# /becoming_a_django_entdev/chapter_6/admin.py
...
class SellerAdmin(UserAdmin):
    ...
    preserve_filters = False
```

Option – search_fields

The `search_fields` option enables a search bar on the changelist view page. One should already appear on the `Sellers` list because the `UserAdmin` class already defines this option for us. However, fields such as `name` are not currently searchable. Navigate to `http://localhost:8000/admin/chapter_3/seller/` and search for the **Biz** keyword and you should get no results.

Now, add the following code block to the `SellerAdmin` class, making the field labeled **Business Name** searchable:

```
# /becoming_a_django_entdev/chapter_6/admin.py
...
class SellerAdmin(UserAdmin):
    ...
    search_fields = (
        'username',
        'first_name',
        'last_name',
        'name',
        'email'
    )
```

Now, refresh the page and search for the same **Biz** keyword, and you will now see one result appear, `Seller` with a **Business Name** value of **Test Biz Name**. This data was provided in the `chapter_3` fixture.

Change/add view-related options

These options pertain to an admin class on the add or change view pages, such as those listed here:

- http://localhost:8000/admin/chapter_3/engine/add/
- http://localhost:8000/admin/chapter_3/engine/1/change/
- http://localhost:8000/admin/chapter_3/seller/add/
- http://localhost:8000/admin/chapter_3/seller/1/change/
- http://localhost:8000/admin/chapter_3/vehicle_model/add/
- http://localhost:8000/admin/chapter_3/vehicle_model/1/change/
- http://localhost:8000/admin/chapter_3/vehicle/add/
- http://localhost:8000/admin/chapter_3/vehicle/1/change/

Option – exclude

The `exclude` option can be thought of as the reverse of the `fields` option. This option will accept a list of fields that we wish to exclude from appearing on the form on the Django admin site. The fields added to the `exclude` option should not appear anywhere in the `fieldsets` or `add_fieldsets` option; otherwise, an error will be triggered. If a field exists in both the `fields` and `exclude` options, the field will be excluded.

For example, if we want to exclude the `first_name` field using the following code, we would also have to remove the `first_name` field everywhere it appears in the `fieldsets`, `add_fieldsets`, `list_display`, `list_editable`, `search_fields`, and `prepopulated_fields` options, as they have been written in previous and future examples:

```
# /becoming_a_django_entdev/chapter_6/admin.py
...
class SellerAdmin(UserAdmin):
    ...
    exclude = ('first_name',)
```

You may now remove this setting and reset the `first_name` field to its previous usage.

Option – fields

The `fields` option lets us explicitly state what fields to include in the admin form. Without declaring this field, Django will automatically include every field that exists for the model specified. However, the '`__all__`' value can also be used to explicitly state that all fields that exist in a related model shall be included.

We will not be including this option since we want all fields included in these forms. However, if we did want to specify only certain fields, that would be done using a list, where the name of each field in the model is separated by a comma:

```
# /becoming_a_django_entdev/chapter_6/admin.py
...
class SellerAdmin(UserAdmin):
    fields = ('username', 'password', 'first_name', 'last_name',)
```

In this example, only these four fields would appear on the change view page for the `Seller` object.

> **Note**
> The `fields` option cannot be combined with the `fieldsets` or `add_fieldsets` option and doing so will result in an error. However, the `fieldsets` and `add_fieldsets` options can be used together. On the `SellerAdmin` class, we can only use the `fieldsets` and `add_fieldsets` options because the `UserAdmin` parent class that was used to construct the `SellerAdmin` class already uses those options. In this case, the `exclude` option would be best used if we did not want to include specific fields. Also, if a field is not included in an admin class and is specified in any of the class options, then an error will be triggered.

Option – fieldsets

The `fieldsets` option is similar to the `fields` option in that it relates to customizing fields but it will group like fields together into designated categories that we create. Django will add HTML and special formatting to group these fields on the change and add view pages.

For example, because we extended the Django `User` model in *Chapter 3, Models, Relations, and Inheritance*, and are now using the `UserAdmin` class to construct the `SellerAdmin` class, we will need to write our own `fieldsets` option. We have to do this because Django will be using the `fieldsets` option as it was written in the `UserAdmin` class, which currently does not include the additional fields we created called `name` and `vehicles`. In order for the `name` and `vehicles` fields to appear on the change and add view pages, we need to add them to any fieldset group; otherwise, only the original `User` fields will appear.

Start by copying the original `fieldsets` option found in the `django.contrib.auth.admin` library of Django into your `SellerAdmin` class and modify the groups to now include the `name` and `vehicles` fields, as shown:

```
# /becoming_a_django_entdev/chapter_6/admin.py
...
class SellerAdmin(UserAdmin):
    fieldsets = (
        (None, {
            'classes': ('wide',),
            'fields': (
                'username',
                'password',
            ),
        }),
        (('Personal Info'), {'fields': (
            'first_name',
            'last_name',
            'name',
            'email',
        )}),
        (('Permissions'), {'fields': (
            'is_active',
            'is_staff',
            'is_superuser',
            'groups',
            'user_permissions',
        )}),
        (('Important Dates'), {'fields': (
```

```
                'last_login',
                'date_joined',
        )}),
        (('Vehicles'), {
            'description': ('Vehicles that this user is
selling.'),
            'fields': (
                'vehicles',
            ),
        }),
    )
```

This option accepts a list of tuples. Each tuple contains two items, the label of that fieldset or the value of None to display no label at all, as depicted in the first group previously. The second item is another list of tuples where that tuple either defines one or all of three available keys: `fields`, `description`, and `classes`. The `classes` key is used to give the container of that fieldset an HTML class name, as depicted in `'classes': ('wide',)`. The `description` key will add an optional description that is rendered above a field in the admin form as a `<p></p>` HTML object, as shown in the Vehicles group previously. The `fields` key will accept a list of fields separated by a comma to add the fields desired to that fieldset group. This is the one mandatory key.

Visit the change view for the seller named admin using the link `http://localhost:8000/admin/chapter_3/seller/1/change/`, and you should see five sections. The first section is not labeled and the other four are named in the order listed here:

- *No label displayed*
- **Personal Info**
- **Permissions**
- **Important Dates**
- **Vehicles**

The new fields are the ones labeled **Business Name** and **Vehicles**. We put the name field in the **Personal Info** group and gave the `vehicles` field its own group.

Option – filter_horizontal

The `filter_horizontal` option relates to the `ManyToMany` field called `vehicles`, which was created for the `Seller` model. Navigate to the change view page for any seller in the database, such as `http://localhost:8000/admin/chapter_3/seller/1/change/`, and you'll see the field labeled **Vehicles** is rendered as a single `<select multiple="">` HTML object. This can actually be difficult for some users to interact with, especially with the need to use the keyboard by either pressing the *Ctrl* button on Windows or the *Command* button on Mac to select multiple items for submission. Django provides a slick JavaScript-based user interface that can be applied to any `ManyToMany` fields.

For example, go ahead and apply the following option to the `SellerAdmin` class, converting the `vehicles` field to now using the horizontal JavaScript user interfaces:

```
# /becoming_a_django_entdev/chapter_6/admin.py
...
class SellerAdmin(UserAdmin):
    ...
    filter_horizontal = ('vehicles',)
```

Next, refresh the same change view page and you will see the vehicles now look as in the following screenshot, where the boxes are stacked side by side horizontally from one another:

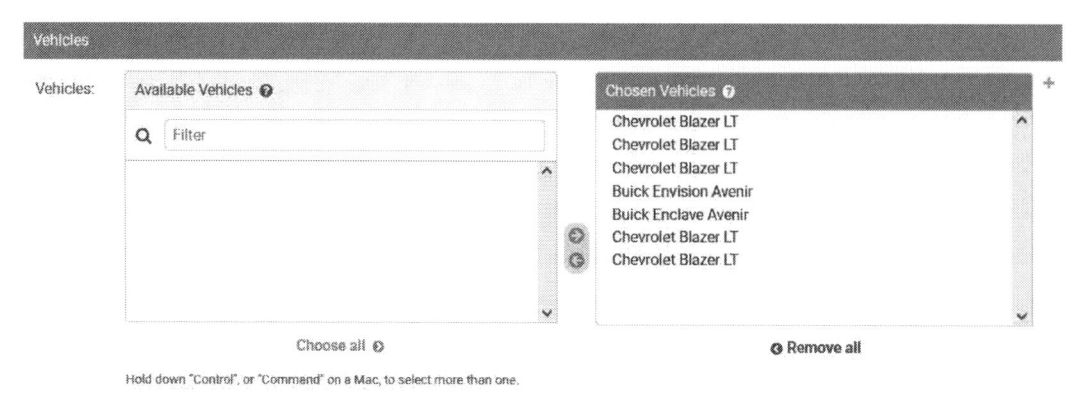

Figure 6.8 – Django – filter_horizontal admin option

Now, the user has more than one method of interacting with this field. They could still use the keyboard to do everything, they could use the mouse to do everything, or they could use a combination of both. Visually it is much more appealing and easier to see what is and is not selected. This even provides a search field to help filter results and trim the fat if there are too many available choices. The two boxes are used for selecting what is available on the left and moving it to the selected box on the right with controls that move items in either direction. Additional controls allow the user to select and move all items found in one box to the other box.

Option – filter_vertical

The `filter_vertical` option is exactly the same as the `filter_horizontal` option except it will stack the boxes vertically instead of horizontally next to each other. The top box will be the items available and the bottom box is used for the items selected.

Option – form

When creating a custom admin form, which we will do later in this chapter, the `form` option is used to point to the form class that we wish to use. If we don't use this setting, Django will dynamically create a `ModelForm` for the model that you have registered with that admin class.

Preparing ourselves for the section titled *Writing custom admin form classes* of this chapter, add the following option to the `EngineAdmin` class:

```
# /becoming_a_django_entdev/chapter_6/admin.py
...
class EngineAdmin(ModelAdmin):
    ...
    form = EngineForm
```

This option will link the admin class to an admin form that we will later call `EngineForm`.

> **Note**
> Until we actually create the `EngineForm` form, you may run into errors. To prevent those errors, you can either comment out this line of code and leave the `pass` statement under the `EngineAdmin` class or create the `EngineForm` class now and add the `pass` statement to that `EngineForm` class until we actually add code to it later in this chapter.

Option – inlines

The `inlines` option is an advanced feature allowing us to make child models editable from within the parent model's change view page as an inline formset display. This feature is considered advanced in that we need to write separate classes just to use and implement this option. These classes can be edited with options that customize the look and feel of those formsets. Each inline object starts with an `InlineModelAdmin` class. The two `InlineModelAdmin` subclasses that are used to render an inline formset are `StackedInline` and `TabularInline`. These two classes perform the same actions as the `InlineModelAdmin` class except that they render a different HTML template for each class. Additional form classes can even be created and used with these inline classes. Refer to the documentation found at https://docs.djangoproject.com/en/4.0/ref/contrib/admin/#inlinemodeladmin-objects, as well as the concepts provided in *Chapter 5, Django Forms*.

Both the `StackedInline` and `TabularInline` classes are used for the model to which a `ForeignKey` field is linked. In the vehicle objects, we can apply the inline option to the `EngineAdmin` and `VehicleModelAdmin` classes. For any `ManyToMany` fields, we will have to link them in a slightly different way.

Next, we will go over each of these classes and discuss briefly how they are used.

Class – InlineModelAdmin

The `InlineModelAdmin` class is the parent class that the two classes used to render inline formsets are constructed from. Every option and method of this class is available in those two child classes.

Many of the options and methods available to the `ModelAdmin` class are also available in the `InlineModelAdmin` class. Here is a full list of what is provided in the `InlineModelAdmin` class:

can_delete	get_min_num()
classes	get_queryset()
exclude	has_add_permission()
extra	has_change_permission()
fields	has_delete_permission()
fieldsets	has_module_permission()
filter_horizontal	max_num
filter_vertical	min_num
fk_name	model
form	ordering
formfield_for_choice_field()	prepopulated_fields
formfield_for_foreignkey()	radio_fields
formfield_for_manytomany()	raw_id_fields
formfield_overrides	readonly_fields
formset	show_change_link
get_extra()	template
get_fieldsets()	verbose_name
get_formset()	verbose_name_plural
get_max_num()	

A common option that we will be adding to all of the inline classes is `extra = 1`, which sets this value to `1` in order to show only one additional blank formset, allowing the user to dynamically add objects when they want to. If this value were set to, say `10`, then 10 additional blank formsets would appear. The default value is `3` and this is why we are going to override the default value in all of our classes to the value of `1`, providing a better user experience.

For a complete breakdown of how to use these options and methods, visit https://docs.djangoproject.com/en/4.0/ref/contrib/admin/#inlinemodeladmin-options.

Class – StackedInline

The `StackedInline` class is used to render inline formsets using the `/admin/edit_inline/stacked.html` template.

To practice using this option on the `EngineAdmin` class, add the following class to the `/chapter_6/admin.py` file, preferably placing all inline formset classes at the top of this document:

```
# /becoming_a_django_entdev/chapter_6/admin.py
...
from django.contrib.admin
import ..., StackedInline

class VehicleInline(StackedInline):
    model = Vehicle
    extra = 1
```

Next, add the following option to the `EngineAdmin` class, placed below all inline formset classes:

```
# /becoming_a_django_entdev/chapter_6/admin.py
...
class EngineAdmin(ModelAdmin):
    ...
    inlines = [VehicleInline,]
```

Now, navigate to the change view page of any of the engine objects, such as `http://localhost:8000/admin/chapter_3/engine/1/change/`. We can see that each vehicle that uses that particular engine can be edited from the edit engine page, as shown in the following screenshot:

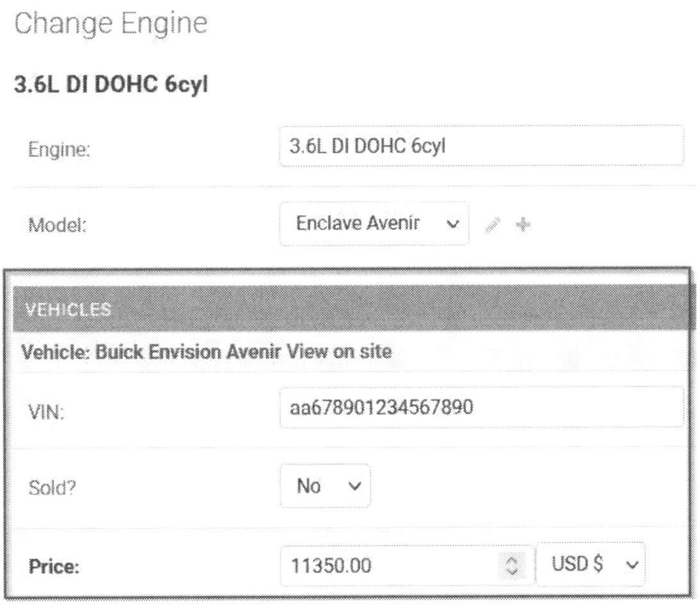

Figure 6.9 – Django – inlines admin option – StackedInline

The `StackedInline` class will display each field stacked one on top of the other, vertically, as shown in the previous screenshot.

Class – TabularInline

The `TabularInline` class is written and implemented in the exact same way as the previous `StackedInline` example except that the `VehicleInline` class is used, as shown in the following example:

```
# /becoming_a_django_entdev/chapter_6/admin.py
...
from django.contrib.admin
import ..., TabularInline

class VehicleInline(TabularInline):
    model = Vehicle
    extra = 1
```

Now, refresh the same page, `http://localhost:8000/admin/chapter_3/engine/1/change/`, and when rendered to the page, the fields will now display horizontally in neatly organized columns, as shown in the following screenshot:

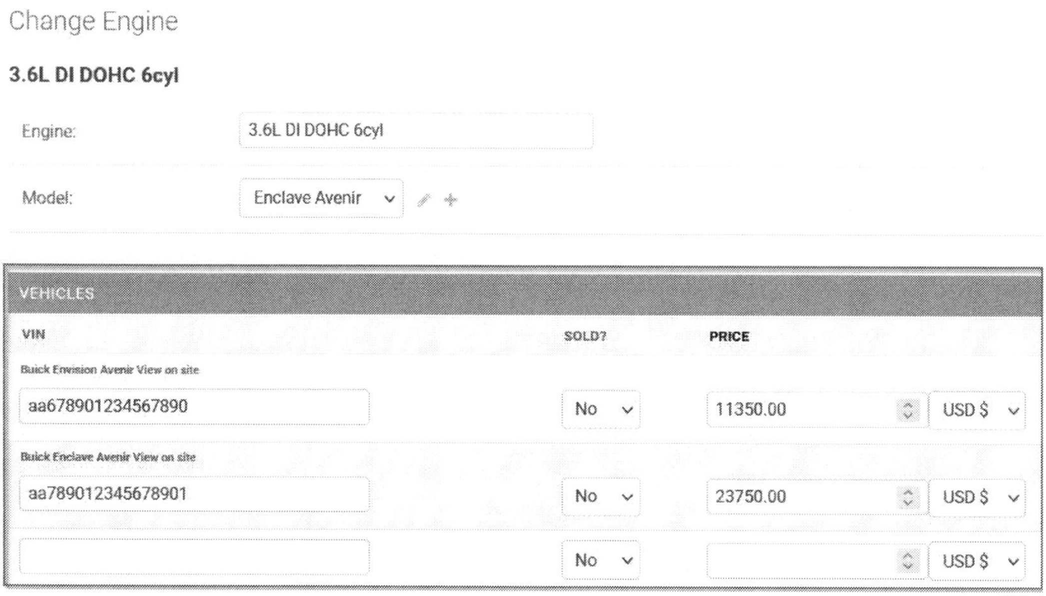

Figure 6.10 – Django – inlines admin option – TabularInline

ManyToMany field inlines

What would be the most useful and also make the most sense in the vehicle relations would be to link all of the vehicles that a seller is selling on the `Seller` change view page. If we write an inline class the same way we wrote an inline class for a `ForeignKey` field, now for a `ManyToMany` field relation, we would wind up getting an error. To prevent that error, write your inline class almost the same way that you implemented inline classes for related `ForeignKey` fields except now, you will add a `through` statement.

Create the following class, to be used on the `SellerAdmin` class, using either a `TabularInline` or `StackedInline` class as its constructor, and for the model, use the following `through` statement:

```
# /becoming_a_django_entdev/chapter_6/admin.py
...
from django.contrib.admin
import ..., TabularInline
```

```python
class VehiclesInline(TabularInline):
    model = Seller.vehicles.through
    extra = 1
```

Here, we are naming this class the plural `VehiclesInline`, with an *s*, instead of the first class that we wrote, called `VehicleInline`, as the naming convention. We are doing this to indicate that one is related to a `ManyToMany` field and the other is not. This naming convention is not mandatory; your naming convention can be anything you would like it to be, but this is helpful. We are linking the `model` option directly to the `Seller` model by the `vehicles` field, which is the `ManyToMany` field, using the `through` attribute.

In the `SellerAdmin` class, add the following `inlines` option:

```python
# /becoming_a_django_entdev/chapter_6/admin.py
...
class SellerAdmin(UserAdmin):
    inlines = [VehiclesInline,]
```

Now, navigate to the change view page for a seller at http://localhost:8000/admin/chapter_3/seller/1/change/, and we can see that the vehicles this seller is selling are now rendered the same as the previous inline formset exercises. One difference in using the `ManyToMany` fields is that they will render as related objects. They can be edited by clicking the pencil icon next to each item, where a pop-up window will appear, allowing the user to edit that item.

> **Tip**
> Remove the `vehicles` field from the `fieldsets`, `filter_horizontal`, and `filter_vertical` options for best results when implementing the vehicle inline fieldset.

Option – radio_fields

The `radio_fields` option is used on `ForeignKey`, `OneToOne` fields, and any `CharField` that is using a list of choices. By default, Django will render these fields as a `<select>` HTML object, where the user can select a single option from a drop-down list of choices. By adding a field to the `radio_fields` option, Django will render the choices as a set of HTML radio buttons, where the user has all the choices visually presented to them when they view this page. For fields with dozens or even hundreds of choices, this might not be the best option and is the reason why Django will default to a `<select>` box.

298   Exploring the Django Admin Site

Go ahead and add the `radio_fields` to the `VehicleAdmin` class, where we have two `ForeignKey` fields to play with. Apply this option to just one of those fields, the `engine` field, and leave the `vehicle_model` field as it is, just like in the following example. This way, when we view it on the page, we can see the differences between the two:

```
# /becoming_a_django_entdev/chapter_6/admin.py
...
from django.contrib import admin
from django.contrib.admin import ModelAdmin

class VehicleAdmin(ModelAdmin):
    radio_fields = {'engine': admin.HORIZONTAL,}
```

In the previous example, each key in the `radio_fields` option relates to the name of the field that we are converting from a `<select>` to a radio button. The value of that key takes in one of two choices, `admin.VERTICAL` or `admin.HORIZONTAL`. This value is used to display the radio button choices either vertically or horizontally on the page.

Now, navigate to the change view page for any of the vehicles, such as `http://localhost:8000/admin/chapter_3/vehicle/1/change/`, and see how the `vehicle_model` and `engine` fields differ, as depicted in the following screenshot, with a select box and radio button choices:

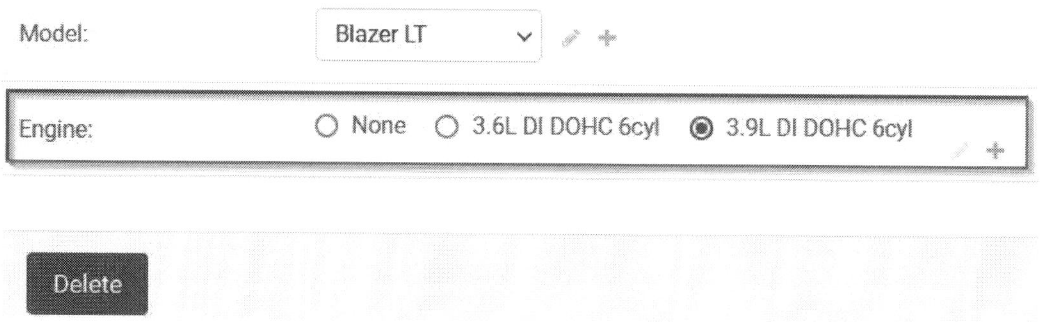

Figure 6.11 – Django – radio_fields admin option

Option – save_on_top

The `save_on_top` option is used to display a set of action buttons at the top of the change or add view pages. This is not the same as the `actions_on_bottom` or `actions_on_top` options, which only relate to the changelist view page. By default, Django sets this value to `False`, showing only action buttons at the bottom of the page. Setting this value to `True` means the buttons will appear both at the top and at the bottom of those pages.

For example, add the following option to the `SellerAdmin` class to show those buttons at the top and bottom of the change and add view pages:

```python
# /becoming_a_django_entdev/chapter_6/admin.py
...
class SellerAdmin(UserAdmin):
    ...
    save_on_top = True
```

Now, navigate to any of the change or add view pages, such as `http://localhost:8000/admin/chapter_3/seller/1/change/`, and we will see the action buttons appear both at the top and the bottom of this page.

Add view-related options

These options override the behavior of admin classes that only pertain to the add view and not the change view pages, such as those listed here:

- `http://localhost:8000/admin/chapter_3/engine/add/`
- `http://localhost:8000/admin/chapter_3/seller/add/`
- `http://localhost:8000/admin/chapter_3/vehicle_model/add/`
- `http://localhost:8000/admin/chapter_3/vehicle/add/`

Option – add_fieldsets

The `add_fieldsets` option does exactly what the `fieldsets` option does except these are fields that relate only to the add/create view form rather than the change view form. For example, navigate to `http://localhost:8000/admin/chapter_3/seller/add/` and you'll see that the Django `UserAdmin` class that the `SellerAdmin` class is constructed from only provides three fields, and then the remaining fields appear after we have created a new `Seller` object.

If we wanted to provide the `first_name`, `last_name`, `name`, and `email` fields, we would modify the `add_fieldsets` variable of the `SellerAdmin` class to look like the following example:

```python
# /becoming_a_django_entdev/chapter_6/admin.py
...
class SellerAdmin(UserAdmin):
    ...
    add_fieldsets = (
        (None, {
            'classes': ('wide',),
            'fields': (
                'username',
                'password1',
                'password2',
            ),
        }),
        (('Personal Info'), {'fields': (
            'first_name',
            'last_name',
            'name',
            'email',
        )}),
    )
```

In the preceding example, we see that writing and grouping fieldsets are written exactly the same as the `fieldsets` example was written earlier. Now, when we visit the same add `Seller` URL as before, `http://localhost:8000/admin/chapter_3/seller/add/`, we can see four additional fields, the four we included in the **Personal Info** fieldset previously.

Option – prepopulated_fields

The `prepopulated_fields` option tells a field(s) to listen for an event when the target field's value has changed and then updates those field values with the value of the target field. This is handy in situations where the user changes the value of a `title` field as the `slug` field will automatically populate with the same value. For example, in the `Seller` model, let's wire this up to listen for when the `first_name` and `last_name` fields change and then populate the `username` field value with a value derived from both of the `first_name` and `last_name` values.

For this example, apply the following option to the `SellerAdmin` class:

```
# /becoming_a_django_entdev/chapter_6/admin.py
...
class SellerAdmin(UserAdmin):
    ...
    prepopulated_fields = {
        'username': ('first_name', 'last_name',)
    }
```

In the preceding code, we can also apply additional fields just as we did with the `first_name` and `last_name` fields. Navigate to the add view page for the `Seller` model at `http://localhost:8000/admin/chapter_3/seller/add/` and begin typing within the `first_name` or `last_name` fields. You will see the `username` field auto-populate with the values that are typed. Spaces will be replaced with a dash and the value of the fields will display in the order in which they were written in the `prepopulated_fields` option. For example, `first_name` will appear before the `last_name` value based on how we wrote it previously.

Now that we have learned all about the different options and applied many of them to our admin classes, let's dive into the various admin class methods that we can use.

Adding admin class methods

Admin class methods allow us to add or change the default behavior of a `ModelAdmin` or `UserAdmin` class. Any of the options available in an admin class can have its value dynamically calculated by writing a method. Those methods use the `get_` naming convention and then the name of the option, as in `get_ordering()` or `get_form()`. Django also provides many built-in methods that add extra actions when something happens, such as when an object is saved or deleted using the `save_model()` or `delete_model()` methods.

Next, we will explore just some of these methods and also provide a demonstration using a dynamic value, specifically for the `form` option. That will prepare us to use a separate form class later in this chapter.

For a complete breakdown of how to use Django admin class methods, visit the official Django documentation here: `https://docs.djangoproject.com/en/4.0/ref/contrib/admin/#modeladmin-methods`.

Method – get_form()

The `get_form()` method is used to get the form class that will be used within an admin class. For example, in the following two exercises, one will check to see whether an object exists, then based on the result of that condition, we will serve one form class for the change view and another form class for the add view. In the other exercise, we will demonstrate showing one form for a superuser and another for a regular user.

> **Note**
>
> We have not created the `EngineForm`, `EngineSuperUserForm`, or `AddEngineForm` classes yet. Go ahead and create these classes with at least the `pass` statement in the `/chapter_6/forms.py` file to allow pages other than the engine change and add view ones to load without errors. After completing these exercises, your engine change and add view pages will error out even with the `pass` statement included. Please wait to load/reload the engine change or add view pages until we have completed the section titled *Writing custom admin form classes* of this chapter, which will add the necessary components to prevent errors when loading those pages.

Change/add view condition

In the `EngineAdmin` class, add the following `get_form()` method and remove or comment out the previous `form` option that we wrote earlier for this class, as depicted here:

```python
# /becoming_a_django_entdev/chapter_6/admin.py
from .forms import AddEngineForm, EngineForm
...
class EngineAdmin(ModelAdmin):
    ...
    #form = EngineForm

    def get_form(self, request, obj=None, **kwargs):
        if obj:
            return EngineForm
        else:
            return AddEngineForm
```

```
            return super(EngineAdmin, self).get_form(request, obj,
**kwargs)
```

As we can see in the preceding example, we replaced `form = EngineForm` with a method that performs a little bit of logic to serve up one of two different forms now. Using the pound symbol, we commented out the `form = EngineForm` line.

Superuser condition

Another use of this method is serving up one form if a user has superuser status and another if they do not, using the conditional statement shown here:

```
# /becoming_a_django_entdev/chapter_6/admin.py
from .forms
import ..., EngineSuperUserForm
...
class EngineAdmin(ModelAdmin):
    ...
    def get_form(self, request, obj=None, **kwargs):
        if obj:
            if request.user.is_superuser:
                return EngineSuperUserForm
            else:
                return EngineForm
        else:
            return AddEngineForm
```

The idea here is that we grant the superuser additional fields that a regular user cannot edit, such as permission rights and permission group settings.

> **Note**
> Even though we extended the Django `User` model as a seller, the currently logged-in seller will appear in the `request` dictionary as a `user` key, as in `request.user` shown in the previous code block.

Method – save_model()

The `save_model()` method is used to add actions before and/or after the object is saved in a change or add view. To add this method to the `EngineAdmin` class, include the code shown here:

```python
# /becoming_a_django_entdev/chapter_6/admin.py
...
class EngineAdmin(ModelAdmin):
    ...
    def save_model(self, request, obj, form, change):
        print(obj.__dict__)
        # Code actions before save here
        super().save_model(request, obj, form, change)
        # Code actions after save here
```

Here, we create the `save_model()` method with five positional arguments, those being `self`, `request`, `obj`, `form`, and `change`, in that order. These five arguments make relevant data available to use when writing logic within that method. The `change` argument has a value of either `True` or `False`. If the object being saved is from the add view page, the `change` value will be `False`; if the object is on the change view page, the `change` value will be `True`. The `super().save_model(request, obj, form, change)` line is what actually saves the object and this is the same as using a `Model.save()` operation. Actions above this line will take place before the object is saved. Actions written after this line take place after the object has been saved, actions such as sending an email or triggering a notification alert.

> **Tip**
> Using the `__dict__` property within the `print` statement shown previously will display a dictionary of keys and values available within that `obj`.

Method – delete_model()

The `delete_model()` method is used just like the `save_model()` method except for when an object is deleted and not saved. In the same `EngineAdmin` class, add the method shown here:

```python
# /becoming_a_django_entdev/chapter_6/admin.py
...
```

```
class EngineAdmin(ModelAdmin):
    ...
    def delete_model(self, request, obj):
        print(obj.__dict__)
        # Code actions before delete here
        super().delete_model(request, obj)
        # Code actions after delete here
```

Next, we will create and modify the custom admin form classes that we spoke about earlier in this chapter, in the subsection titled *Method – get_form()*.

Writing custom admin form classes

Admin forms can be created and used just like the standard form classes we discussed in *Chapter 5, Django Forms*. For admin form classes, we need to use the Django `ModelForm` class instead of the standard `Form` class found in the `django.forms` library, because the fields in these forms will link to model classes. Refer to the examples found in *Chapter 5, Django Forms*, to learn more about how to customize and change your form class behavior, for either a `Form` or `ModelForm` class. Here, we will demonstrate just initializing your admin forms and enabling all fields that exist, to allow any of the engine change and add view pages to load without the errors mentioned earlier.

Initializing an admin form

If you have not already done so, in the `chapter_6` app folder, create a file called `forms.py`. We need to create the three different form classes used in the previous examples of this chapter and call them `EngineForm`, `AddEngineForm`, and `EngineSuperUserForm`. Create them using the example provided here, except change the name `EngineForm` to the name of the class that you are writing and change the related model class for all three of the classes as well:

```
# /becoming_a_django_entdev/chapter_6/forms.py
...
from django.forms
import ..., ModelForm
from ..chapter_3.models
import Engine


class EngineForm(ModelForm):
```

```
    def __init__(self, *args, **kwargs):
        print('EngineForm Initialized')
        super(EngineForm, self).__init__(*args, **kwargs)

    class Meta:
        model = Engine
        fields = '__all__'
```

The least amount of code that is needed for a `ModelForm` class to work within admin classes can be achieved by providing the `__init__` method, initializing the form. In addition, we will need the `Meta` subclass with the `model` and `fields` options. On all three of these classes (`EngineForm`, `AddEngineForm`, and `EngineSuperUserForm`), give the `model` option a value of `Engine`, linking them all to the `Engine` model. For the `fields` option, provide a value of `'__all__'` to let Django create the fields for you based on the fields that have been written in the `Engine` model class. Unlike the admin classes that we wrote, we actually have to tell Django to use all or some fields in this class.

You are welcome to adjust the fields and/or add other options in order to customize the look and feel of each of these forms, allowing us to see how they differ from one another when they are rendered. Alternatively, you can use `print` statements in each form's `__init__` method, as was done previously, to let you know that the logic is working properly. If you visit any of the engine change or add view pages with the options provided in the *Configuring admin class options* section of this chapter, the page should now load without errors.

The engine change and add pages are listed here:

- Engine add view – `http://localhost:8000/admin/chapter_3/engine/add/`
- Engine change view – `http://localhost:8000/admin/chapter_3/engine/1/change/`

Next, let's discuss configuring user permissions within the Django admin site.

Using the Django authentication system

Django provides a very powerful authentication system to grant permission rights to users. By default, a superuser has the authority to do everything, which is why we had to create at least one superuser in *Chapter 2, Project Configuration*. That superuser is needed at all times within the Django system to maintain control of your site and your data. The superuser granted us the ability to take control of our system and establish user roles and groups for every other user in the system. Creating a user and superuser can be done via the command line using a Django management command or through the IDE, just like when we explored those subjects in *Chapter 2, Project Configuration*. It can also be done through the Django shell, as we did in *Chapter 3, Models, Relations, and Inheritance*, when we created and saved models using the Django shell. `user` and `Seller` are just other model objects that we create and save. Now that we have access to the Django admin site, we can also add users, or in our case, sellers, and edit their permissions using this interface.

Next, let's add a regular user to the system so that we can have at least one regular user and one superuser to compare and contrast their roles.

Adding a seller

Here, we will activate the Django shell, import the `Seller` model from the `chapter_3` app, and then proceed to create the new `Seller` object, which is a standard user:

1. Activate the Django shell in any terminal or command-line window, just as we did in *Chapter 3, Models, Relations, and Inheritance*. Once activated, import the `Seller` object, as shown:

   ```
   (virtual_env) PS > python3 manage.py shell
   >>> from becoming_a_django_entdev.chapter_3.models import Seller
   ```

   Django includes, in the `User` model, a `create_user()` method, used for easily creating a new user that does not have superuser rights. This method does the heavy lifting of encrypting the password for us, so all we have to do is provide the unencrypted password as a string.

2. Since we extended the Django `User` model into a `Seller` in *Chapter 3, Models, Relations, and Inheritance*, we will have to use the `create_user()` method on the `Seller` model, as is shown in the following code. Execute the following command, remembering the password that you used as you will need it to log into the Django admin site with that user:

```
>>> seller = Seller.objects.create_user('test', 'testing@example.com', 'testpassword', is_staff=True)
```

3. Now, exit the Django shell by executing the `exit()` command and run the project again by executing the `runserver` command, as shown:

```
>>> exit()
(virtual_env) PS > python3 manage.py runserver
```

Now, visit the `Seller` changelist view page here: `http://localhost:8000/admin/chapter_3/seller/`. You should see at least two results, as shown in the following screenshot:

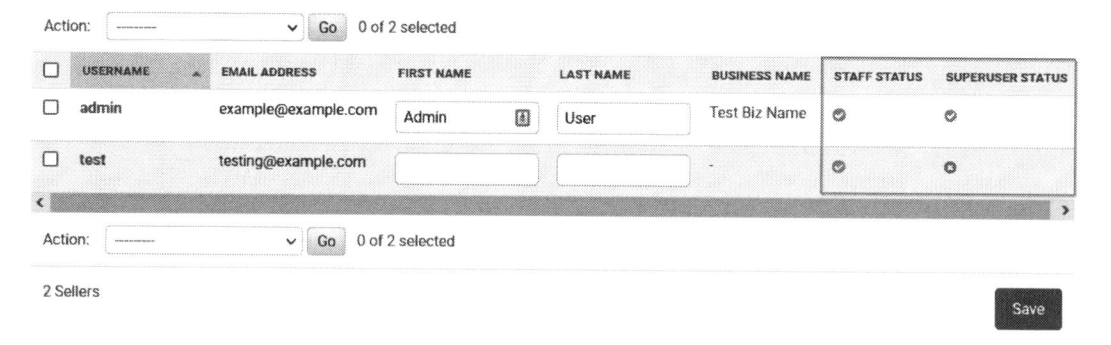

Figure 6.12 – Django – Seller's changelist view

As is depicted in the preceding screenshot, one result has a superuser status and the other, the one that we just created, does not. The **STAFF STATUS** column indicates whether or not the user has permission to log into the admin site, and by default, the `is_staff` value is set to `False` when using the `create_user()` method. This is why we had to explicitly set it to `True` in the preceding code example.

Now, log out of the admin site and then log back in, with the username as `test` and password as `testpassword`, and you should now see a message on your dashboard indicating that you do not have permission to view anything yet, as shown in the following screenshot:

Django administration

Site administration

You don't have permission to view or edit anything.

Figure 6.13 – Django – admin site test for Seller

This is expected behavior because we have not granted this user any permissions yet. Next, let's grant this user some permissions.

Granting permissions

To grant users permissions, we will be using the admin interface this time. Log out again and then log back in with the `admin` user or whatever name you may have given your superuser. Navigate to the change view of your `test` user at `http://localhost:8000/admin/chapter_3/seller/2/change/`, which should be ID number 2, unless you created more users on your own, then find the change view of the user ID that you are currently working with.

On this page, grant the `test` user the ability to change everything in the `chapter_3` app and leave everything else unselected, as shown:

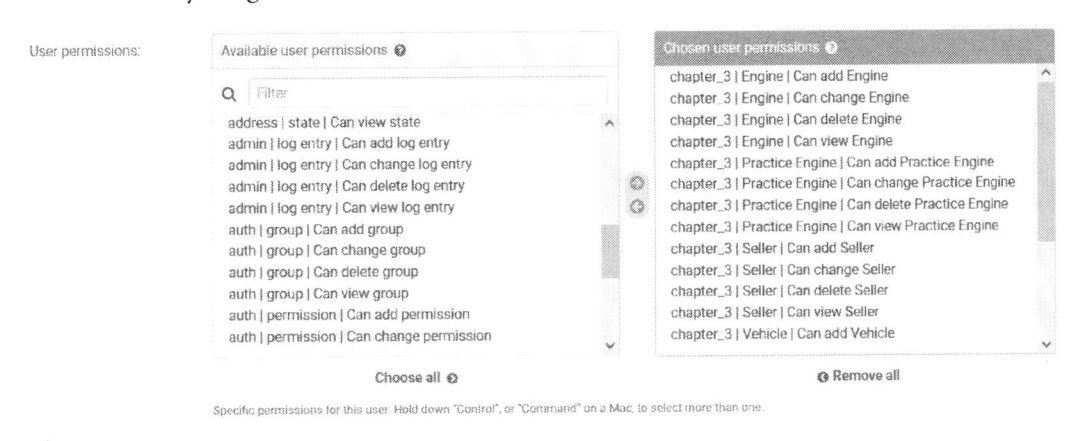

Figure 6.14 – Django – user permissions

Using the **Filter** input box shown in the previous screenshot, you can enter `chapter_3` to show only the relevant permissions for this task. Don't forget to save this user before proceeding. Log out and then log back in again, this time with the `test` user credentials. Now, we should see the models related to our vehicles, as depicted in the following screenshot:

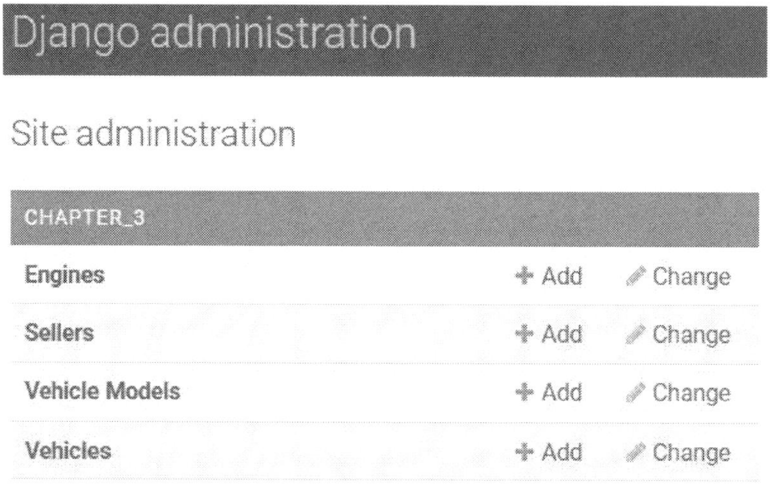

Figure 6.15 – Django – admin site test for Seller 2

Permissions can be granted on a per-group basis instead of navigating to each user and granting permissions one at a time.

> **Note**
> The `Sellers` object is now available to the `test` user. Navigating to the change view of any of the `Sellers` that exists while logged in as a standard user will show the permissions fields. To prevent this from happening, you can either limit only superusers to view and edit the `Seller` model objects or follow the steps depicted in the *Method – get_form()* subsection of this chapter to then add your own logic to the `SellerAdmin` class. That will only show the permission-related fields to superusers.

Permission groups

Permission groups are a way to add or remove users to or from a group by defining a set of permissions. A system with thousands of users would prove tedious to manage, not to mention how many inconsistencies it could result in, as we factor in human error.

Now, make sure you are logged out of the `test` user account, then log back in with the `admin` user account and navigate to the group add view page here: `http://localhost:8000/admin/auth/group/add/`. Then, create a new group called `test_group` and grant the same permissions to this group that were given to the `test` user in the previous exercise. Next, go back to the change view page of that `test` user, remove all the user permissions from before, and assign them to the `test_group` group instead. This `test` user will be given the same permissions as before. With this, you can create as many groups as you would like, assign users to each group as you desire, and customize rights to the needs of your project. Additional permissions can be given to users on an ad hoc basis by assigning them to a group and then giving them extra user-based permissions in addition to that group assignment.

Summary

We activated and customized the Django admin site for a project, otherwise known as the admin panel. This powerful tool helps us to get up and running with search, filter, sort, create, edit, and delete capabilities for all of the models that we choose to register on this site. With the concepts provided in this chapter, you should be able to make your admin panel a very useful tool that your users will enjoy.

With the authentication system that Django provides, many different types of users can all access and use the same site but have very different roles and uses. Each type of user could even be given entirely different templates and flows if we venture down the road of extending templates or building onto that templating system using the concepts provided in previous chapters.

In the next chapter, we will discuss sending emails, creating custom email templates, as well as creating PDF reports using the Django template language.

7
Working with Messages, Email Notifications, and PDF Reports

In this chapter, we will work with the Django messages framework, email notifications and templates, and PDF documents. In order for us to know that emails are actually being sent from our system and that they are rendered correctly in different email clients, we will be using a free third-party service to capture all of our outgoing emails. By capturing all outgoing emails, we can prevent development and test emails from being sent to people who should not be seeing them yet. We will use HTML, CSS, and the Django template language to create email and PDF report templates. Both will use context data just like how we passed context into templates in *Chapter 4, URLs, Views, and Templates*.

In this chapter, we will cover the following:

- Creating a test environment for capturing all emails sent by the app
- Using the Django messages framework to create flash messages and custom message levels
- Creating and sending HTML and/or plain text-formatted emails
- Creating template-based emails using HTML, CSS, and the Django template language
- Generating PDF documents using HTML, CSS, and the Django template language

Technical requirements

To work with the code in this chapter, the following tools will need to be installed on your local machine:

- Python version 3.9 – used as the underlying programming language for the project
- Django version 4.0 – used as the backend framework of the project
- pip package manager – used to manage third-party Python/Django packages

We will continue to work with the solution created in *Chapter 2, Project Configuration*. However, it is not necessary to use the Visual Studio IDE. The main project itself can be run using another IDE or run independently using a terminal or command-line window from within the project root folder, which is where the `manage.py` file resides. Whatever editor or IDE you are using, a virtual environment will also be needed to work with the Django project. Instructions for how to create a project and virtual environment can be found in *Chapter 2, Project Configuration*. You will need a database to store the data contained in your project. PostgreSQL was chosen for the examples in the previous chapter; however, any database type that you choose for your project can be used to work with the examples in this chapter.

We will not be using any data found in the `chapter_3` app data fixture but if that data is already loaded, don't worry! The exercises in this chapter will all use data that is obtained from forms that the user is interacting with and not data coming from within a database.

All of the code created in this chapter can be found in the GitHub repository for this book: `https://github.com/PacktPublishing/Becoming-an-Enterprise-Django-Developer`. The bulk of the code depicted in this chapter can be found in the `/becoming_a_django_entdev/becoming_a_django_entdev/chapter_7/` directory.

Check out the following video to see the *Code in Action*: `https://bit.ly/3OzpalD`.

Preparing for this chapter

Start by creating a new app in your project called `chapter_7` by following the steps discussed in *Chapter 2, Project Configuration*, in the subsection titled *Creating a Django app*. As discussed in that section, don't forget to change the value of the `name =` variable for your app class found in the `/becoming_a_django_entdev/becoming_a_django_entdev/chapter_7/apps.py` file to now point to the path where you installed your app. Be sure to also include this app in the `INSTALLED_APPS` variable found in the `settings.py` file as well.

In the main `urls.py` file of the site, add the following path, which points to the URL patterns of the app that we will be creating in this chapter:

```
# /becoming_a_django_entdev/urls.py
...
urlpatterns = [
    path(
        '',
        include('becoming_a_django_entdev.chapter_7.urls')
    ),
]
```

Copy the URL patterns, forms, fields, views, templates, CSS, and JavaScript files found in the `chapter_5` app directly into the newly created `chapter_7` app. This way, we can keep the exercises of each chapter separated, and the exercises of this chapter will build on the exercises of *Chapter 5, Django Forms*. In the code that you copied into this chapter's app, make sure you update all file/code references from `chapter_5/chapter-5` to `chapter_7/chapter-7` where needed.

Creating a Mailtrap account

In order to work with the email examples throughout this chapter, you will need an email testing service that will capture all emails being sent from the system being built, as we run the project locally. There are numerous different third-party services on the market today that all provide this solution. Each service varies in terms of the additional testing tools and features that they provide as well as the cost associated with that service. You are welcome to use a service other than the one chosen for this book. If you choose to do so, you will have to follow the instructions from that service in order to configure the settings for your project instead of the instructions found in this section.

316   Working with Messages, Email Notifications, and PDF Reports

For the purpose of demonstrating the exercises throughout this chapter, we will be using a completely free service called **Mailtrap**. No credit card is required to create an account with them and it's free for personal side projects. This is not a trial-based plan; it is free for a lifetime, or at least until Mailtrap changes its policies and procedures. Mailtrap also offers upgraded paid plans, which provide additional tools and support should you and your team decide to use this service, which would be particularly useful in multiple development environments and with large testing teams.

Follow these steps to create and set up your Mailtrap account:

1. Visit `https://mailtrap.io/register/signup` to create a new account. Follow the steps that they provide on their website.
2. To activate your account, you will need to go back to your email inbox and click the **Confirm My Account** button in the confirmation email that you will receive shortly after creating the account. Check your `Junk` folder if you do not see it in your inbox.
3. Once that is complete, log into your new account and you will be taken to **My Inbox**, with the first tab, **SMTP Settings**, selected.
4. Under the **Integrations** dropdown of the **SMTP Settings** tab, select the **Django** option. Here, it will provide you with four settings variables that will need to be added to the `settings.py` file of your project, as shown:

My Inbox

SMTP Settings | Email Address | Auto Forward | Manual Forward | Team Members

SMTP / POP3   Reset Credentials

Use these settings to send messages directly from your email client or mail transfer agent.

⚠ Don't disclose your username or password as this may result in your inbox getting filled up with spam.

Show Credentials ⌄

Integrations

[Django ⇅]

First start by adding the following to settings.py:

```
EMAIL_HOST = 'smtp.mailtrap.io'
EMAIL_HOST_USER = '...'
EMAIL_HOST_PASSWORD = '...'
EMAIL_PORT = '2525'
```

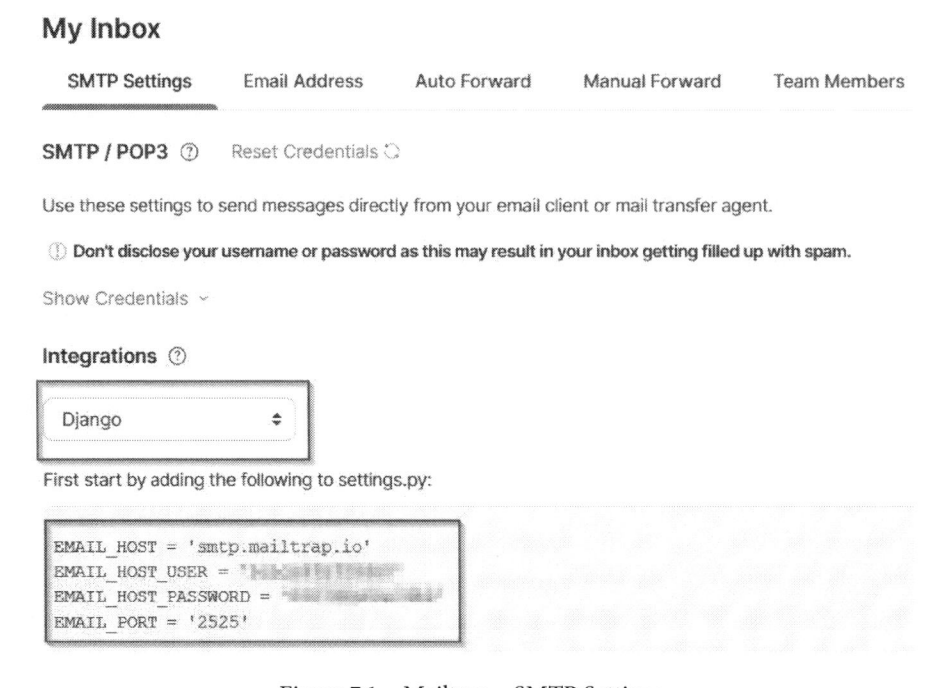

Figure 7.1 – Mailtrap – SMTP Settings

Add these variables, along with the credentials that were provided in your account, anywhere inside your `settings.py` file.

5. This step is optional. To separate these variables in a production environment, use the following conditional statement in your `settings.py` file. The values of each variable are also being kept within the `.env` file of a project:

```
# /becoming_a_django_entdev/settings.py
...
if DEBUG:
    EMAIL_HOST = os.getenv('EMAIL_HOST')
    EMAIL_HOST_USER = os.getenv('EMAIL_HOST_USER')
    EMAIL_HOST_PASSWORD = os.getenv('EMAIL_HOST_PASSWORD')
    EMAIL_PORT = os.getenv('EMAIL_PORT')
else:
    # Production Email Connection Settings
    Pass
```

Make sure to add the variables to your local `.env` file before running your project when using the preceding example.

> **Note**
>
> In order for Mailtrap to work with your project on Heroku, make sure you add the four email variables from your local `.env` file to the config variables of each Heroku app. For instructions on how to do this, refer to *Chapter 2, Project Configuration*, under the subsection titled *Remote variables*. You can use the same connection settings for each environment and they will all go to the same inbox.

That's it. Mailtrap is now configured and will intercept all emails being sent from your Django project. Let's move on to creating flash messages with the Django messages framework next.

Using the Django messages framework

Let's begin by introducing the **Django Messages Framework**, which is a framework used to provide session-based messages to the user. A **flash message** is a one-time notification message displayed directly to the user and is the kind of message that this framework creates. What we can do with this is render messages to the user anywhere we put the code inside our templates, whether that be in a modal popup or a message that drops down from the top of the page or comes up from the bottom of the page. It can even appear above or below a form that the user is submitting.

The `chapter_7 FormClassView` class will be the primary working class throughout this chapter, as it will be used primarily to trigger the actions we will be writing. We will be writing the methods to perform those actions in the corresponding `ContactForm` class used by that `FormClassView` class of the `chapter_7` app.

Before we start writing those classes, we will begin by enabling the Django messages framework next.

Enabling the Django messages framework

These settings will enable the Django messages framework. A project does not require this framework to operate. These settings can be removed if desired but are required to work with this chapter. It is likely that when you created your project, these settings were generated for you automatically. Double-check just to make sure.

In your `settings.py` file, make sure these settings and values exist:

```
# /becoming_a_django_entdev/settings.py
...
INSTALLED_APPS = [
    ...
    'django.contrib.sessions',
    'django.contrib.messages',
]
MIDDLEWARE = [
    ...
    'django.contrib.sessions.middleware.SessionMiddleware',
    'django.contrib.messages.middleware.MessageMiddleware',
]
TEMPLATES = [
    {
```

```
        ...
        'OPTIONS': {
            'context_processors': [
                ...
                'django.contrib.messages.context_processors.
  messages',
            ],
        },
    },
]
```

One important thing to remember in the preceding settings is that `SessionMiddleware` always comes before the `MessageMiddleware` entry in the `MIDDLEWARE` list. The same applies to the `INSTALLED_APPS` variable; make sure the `django.contrib.sessions` app comes before the `django.contrib.messages` app. The Django messages framework context processor shown under the `TEMPLATES` configuration is also needed to make your Django messages framework context available from within any of your templates. This means that you do not have to explicitly define a variable in the context of each page specifically for your messages. Instead, it will be available via the global context of your project automatically.

Next, we will discuss additional configuring/enabling of the Django messages framework.

Message storage backends

Storage backends are a way to store messages created throughout the life cycle of your app. This is set using the `MESSAGE_STORAGE` variable in the `settings.py` file.

The backend choices available for `MESSAGE_STORAGE` are listed here:

- `django.contrib.messages.storage.session.SessionStorage` – stores messages in the requests session and will require that the `django.contrib.sessions` app be included in the `INSTALLED_APPS` variable.

- `django.contrib.messages.storage.fallback.FallbackStorage` – this option uses the now-legacy `CookieStorage` first and then, when cookie data exceeds the 2,048-byte threshold, instead of deleting those older cookies, as is the default action of the `CookieStorage` option, new messages will instead be placed in `SessionStorage`. `CookieStorage` is no longer supported in Django 4.0 but is still available in the `django.contrib.messages.storage` library. It is unknown when this storage method will be removed completely.

- `django.contrib.messages.storage.base.BaseStorage` – Django provides this class as a way for developers to create their own storage systems. By itself, this will not work because this is an abstract class meant to be extended. This is considered an advanced topic beyond the scope of this book.

Let's go ahead and set this to use the `SessionStorage` option for now:

```
# /becoming_a_django_entdev/settings.py
...
MESSAGE_STORAGE = 'django.contrib.messages.storage.session.SessionStorage'
```

Message levels

Message levels indicate the different severity levels of a message. These levels have a variable name, a lowercase tag name, and a numeric value indicating the severity level, as shown in the following table:

Constant	Tag	Value	Used For...
DEBUG	Debug	10	These are intended to be used and seen only by developers and never shown in a production environment.
INFO	info	20	Informs the user of something minor.
SUCCESS	success	25	Informs the user that an action was successful.
WARNING	warning	30	Warns the user that proceeding could result in an error.
ERROR	error	40	Tells the user the action did result in an error.

By default, Django sets the `MESSAGE_LEVEL` variable to `INFO`; more specifically, Django sets this to a value of `20`. This means if we try to issue a `DEBUG`-related message, which has a value of `10`, it will never be rendered to the page. Some might think this is a bug in the Django framework; however, this is by intentional design. The reason is that in a production setting, we do not want those messages to appear anywhere to the user. Any custom message levels with a value below `20` would also not appear. Instead, we only want developers, and maybe the testers, to see that message in a development or local environment.

To enable `DEBUG`-related messages in your environment, the best way to do this is by once again utilizing the debug conditional in your `settings.py` file, as shown:

```
# /becoming_a_django_entdev/settings.py
...
from django.contrib.messages
import constants as messages
...
if DEBUG:
    MESSAGE_LEVEL = messages.DEBUG
else:
    pass
```

Here, we are explicitly defining the `MESSAGE_LEVEL` setting to include `DEBUG`-related messages while the project's `DEBUG` variable is set to `True`. If `DEBUG` is set to `False`, as is done in the `.env` file of the production environment, then it will use the default Django setting of `messages.INFO` for this variable. We could just leave the `else` condition out of the equation altogether; however, it was written as a placeholder for illustrative purposes.

Message tags

Message tags are the lowercase string representation of a message level. They are used for things such as a CSS class added to an HTML node that gets rendered in a template. You can use this class to style a message, such as giving each message level a different CSS color. In the `/becoming_a_django_entdev/chapter_7/static/chapter_7/css/site.css` file provided with the code of this book, there are CSS styles that do just that; they style each message level discussed in this chapter as a different color. Copy and paste these styles into your project to see the same colors depicted in these images within your browser.

In this example, let's change the tag for the `INFO` message from the original `info` to `information`, using the following example:

```
# /becoming_a_django_entdev/settings.py
...
from django.contrib.messages
import constants as messages
...
MESSAGE_TAGS = {
```

```
        messages.INFO: 'information',
}
```

In the preceding code, the `DEBUG`, `SUCCESS`, `WARNING`, and `ERROR` message tags will all continue to use their default message tag values because we did not include them in this list.

Custom message levels

Custom message levels are when we create our own message levels that are not one of the five defaults provided by Django. In the same `settings.py` file, go ahead and add three new variables with numeric values, as shown:

```
# /becoming_a_django_entdev/settings.py
...
MINOR = 50
MAJOR = 60
CRITICAL = 70

MESSAGE_TAGS = {
    messages.INFO: 'information',
    MINOR: 'minor',
    MAJOR: 'major',
    CRITICAL: 'critical',
}
```

Each new level is defined using those numeric values. They can be named anything that does not conflict with other settings variables. These values can be any number, such as 19 or 199, though it is best not to use any of the default values, such as 10, 20, 25, 30, or 40 because these values are being used by other levels, We also added those variables to the `MESSAGE_TAGS` variable because when we have events that create a new message, it will also need a message tag to add a CSS class to when rendering the HTML.

Now that the settings are configured for the Django messages framework, we can use that framework and create messages next.

Creating a message

Creating messages is very simple. For this exercise, let's modify the `post()` method found in the `FormClassView` class that we duplicated into the `chapter_7` app. Here, we will be adding the code that will create the message when the form is submitted. Django provides two ways to write a message, one way using the provided `add_message()` method and another by explicitly adding that message to one of the five default message levels.

The following steps demonstrate using both ways. Please use only one or the other:

1. In the `/chapter_7/views.py` file, add the `add_message()` statement and context highlighted in the following code block to the `FormClassView` class under the `if form.is_valid():` condition. Remember to comment out or delete the `return` statement found in this condition:

```python
# /becoming_a_django_entdev/chapter_7/views.py
...
from django.contrib import messages
from django.template.response import TemplateResponse
from django.views.generic.edit import FormView

class FormClassView(FormView):
    ...
    def post(self, request, *args, **kwargs):
        ...
        if form.is_valid():
            messages.add_message(
                request,
                messages.SUCCESS,
                'Your contact form submitted successfully'
            )
            context = {
                'title': 'FormClassView Page',
                'page_id': 'form-class-id',
                'page_class': 'form-class-page',
```

```
                        'h1_tag': 'This is the FormClassView Page 
Using ContactForm',
                        'form': form,
            }
        ...
```

2. Next, in the /chapter_7/views.py file, add the add_message() statement and context highlighted in the following code block to the FormClassView class under the else: condition. Remember to comment out or delete the return statement found in this condition and add the new return statement shown here:

```
# /becoming_a_django_entdev/chapter_7/views.py
...
class FormClassView(FormView):
    ...
    def post(self, request, *args, **kwargs):
        ...
        if form.is_valid():
            ...
        else:
            messages.add_message(
                request,
                messages.ERROR,
                'There was a problem submitting your contact form.<br />Please review the highlighted fields below.'
            )
            context = {
                'title': 'FormClassView Page - Please Correct The Errors Below',
                'page_id': 'form-class-id',
                'page_class': 'form-class-page errors-found',
                'h1_tag': 'This is the FormClassView Page Using ContactForm<br /><small class="error-msg">Errors Found</small>',
                'form': form,
            }
```

```
        return TemplateResponse(
            request,
            self.template_name,
            context
        )
    ...
```

3. This step is not required; it just shows an alternative way of writing and using the messages shown previously. Use the `Success` and `Error` level statements highlighted in the following code block as alternatives to the ones shown previously. Use only one or the other:

```
# /becoming_a_django_entdev/chapter_7/views.py
...
class FormClassView(FormView):
    ...
    def post(self, request, *args, **kwargs):
        ...
        if form.is_valid():
            messages.success(
                request,
                'Your contact form submitted successfully'
            )
            ...
        else:
            messages.error(
                request,
                'There was a problem submitting your contact form.<br />Please review the highlighted fields below.'
            )
    ...
```

Using either of the add message examples will perform the same add message action, whereas using both at the same time will result in the same message being added twice to your storage system. In the `post()` method depicted previously, we commented out the old redirect statement and are now defining a success and failure message on form submission, using the same condition as before to check whether the form is valid. The message itself can accept a string and that string can contain HTML, as depicted in the preceding failure message. If HTML does exist in your string, the message would have to use the `|safe` filter when working with messages in a template.

Next, let's go over the extra things we can do when creating a message.

Using a custom message level

If we want to use one of the custom message levels that we created, such as `CRITICAL`, then we can only use the `add_message()` method. We also need to import `settings` to access those variables, as depicted here:

```
# /becoming_a_django_entdev/chapter_7/views.py
from django.views.generic.edit
import FormView
...
from django.conf
import settings
class FormClassView(FormView):
    ...
    def post(self, request, *args, **kwargs):
        ...
        if form.is_valid():
            messages.add_message(
                request,
                settings.CRITICAL,
                'This is critical!'
            )
        ...
```

Messages are created in the same way, except `settings.LEVEL` is used instead of `messages.LEVEL`.

With extra tags

We can pass additional custom CSS classes for a message and that message only. This is done by adding that class(es) to the add message operation using the `extra_tags` attribute. For example, let's render our message with two classes, the `success` class, which gets added automatically, and an additional class called `bold` to then bolden the text that is rendered, using the following example:

```python
# /becoming_a_django_entdev/chapter_7/views.py
from django.contrib import messages
from django.views.generic.edit import FormView
from django.conf import settings
...
class FormClassView(FormView):
    ...
    def post(self, request, *args, **kwargs):
        ...
        if form.is_valid():
            messages.success(
                request,
                'Your contact form submitted successfully',
                extra_tags = 'bold'
            )
            ...
```

After completing the section of this chapter titled *Displaying messages*, when we load the page and then inspect the message, what we should see rendered to the screen when inspecting that particular element is both the CSS classes **bold** and **success**, as shown in the following screenshot:

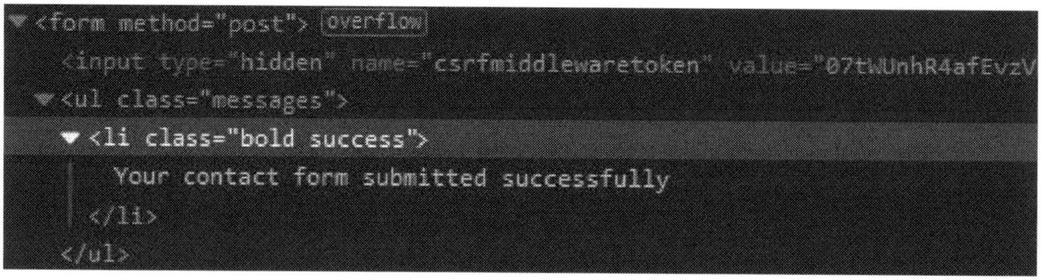

```
▼<form method="post"> overflow
    <input type="hidden" name="csrfmiddlewaretoken" value="07tWUnhR4afEvzV
  ▼<ul class="messages">
    ▼<li class="bold success">
        Your contact form submitted successfully
      </li>
    </ul>
```

Figure 7.2 – Django messages framework – extra_tags attribute

That fails silently

Creating a message that **fails silently** simply means creating a reusable app using the Django messages framework that does not require other developers using your app in a different project to actually have the Django messages framework enabled within their project. This means if they have disabled this framework or just do not have it enabled yet, the add message operations will not prevent their project from functioning properly.

To use this option, add the `fail_silently` attribute to your add message actions, as shown:

```python
# /becoming_a_django_entdev/chapter_7/views.py
from django.contrib import messages
from django.views.generic.edit import FormView
from django.conf import settings
...
class FormClassView(FormView):
    ...
    def post(self, request, *args, **kwargs):
        ...
        if form.is_valid():
            messages.success(
                request,
```

```
            'Your contact form submitted successfully',
    fail_silently=True
)
...
```

With the `fail_silently` attribute set to `True`, the application will run as normal, without errors that prevent the code from running. If the developer has disabled the Django messages framework and the `fail_silently` attribute is not included, then when running the application, that should trigger a flash message, where you will see a **MessageFailure** error, as shown:

MessageFailure at /chapter-7/form-class/

You cannot add messages without installing django.contrib.messages.middleware.MessageMiddleware

```
Request Method:     POST
Request URL:        http://www.localhost:8000/chapter-7/form-class/
Django Version:     3.2.9
Exception Type:     MessageFailure
Exception Value:    You cannot add messages without installing django.contrib.messages.middleware.MessageMiddleware
Exception Location: C:\...\Repo\becoming_a_django_entdev\virtual_env\lib\site-packages\django\contrib\messages\api.py, line 29, in add_message
Python Executable:  C:\...\Repo\becoming_a_django_entdev\virtual_env\Scripts\python.exe
Python Version:     3.9.9
```

Figure 7.3 – Django messages framework – fail_silently attribute

In the next section, we will render our messages into a template as HTML.

Displaying messages

In order for messages to actually be seen by the user, we need to add some code to a Django template. Using the `/chapter_7/templates/chapter_7/form-class.html` file, which the `chapter_7 FormClassView` class uses as its template, add the following code to the top of the HTML `<form>` object found inside that template:

```
# /becoming_a_django_entdev/chapter_7/templates/chapter_7/form-class.html
...
{% block body_content %}
    ...
    <form method="post">
        {% csrf_token %}

        {% if messages %}
            <ul class="messages">
                {% for message in messages %}
                    <li{% if message.tags %} class="{{ message.
```

```
      tags }}"{% endif %}>
                      {{ message|safe }}
                </li>
            {% endfor %}
        </ul>
    {% endif %}
    ...
```

All other code in this file can be left as is. Here, we use a simple conditional statement checking whether any messages exist in the storage system for this request. If they do, a `<ul>` list is created and then iterated through every message that exists, creating each one as a separate `<li>` item within that list. The message itself is using the `|safe` filter, allowing it to render HTML that can exist in the message string.

Visit the URL `http://www.localhost:8000/chapter-7/form-class/` and submit the form. Either the valid or invalid message will display, depending on whether or not you actually triggered a validation error with that form, as shown in the following screenshot:

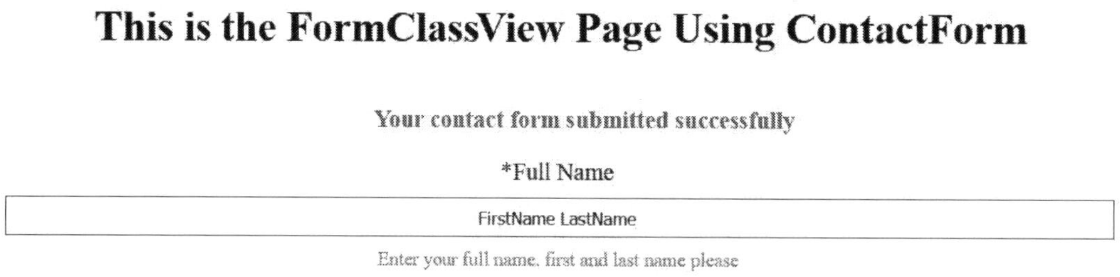

This is the FormClassView Page Using ContactForm

Your contact form submitted successfully

*Full Name

| FirstName LastName |

Enter your full name, first and last name please

Figure 7.4 – Django messages framework – displaying messages

The preceding message is displayed within the browser in green, if you are using the CSS classes provided by the book.

Now that we have enabled the Django messages framework and added several messages to one of our view classes, let's practice sending an email notification instead of displaying a flash message next.

Configuring email notifications

This section will help us to build actual email notifications instead of flash messages. We will write our logic to trigger the send email action in the same `FormClassView` class where we added messages inside the `post()` method. We will be utilizing the Mailtrap account that we created at the beginning of this chapter to capture all emails that are sent by our project. If you have not already done so, please create an account with Mailtrap and configure that connection in your `settings.py` file. Without doing so, you will have difficulty executing the code throughout this section.

There are three MIME types that exist for emails, as follows:

- **Plain text** – `text/plain`
- **Rich text** – `application/rtf`
- **HTML** – `text/html`

While there are three MIME types, only two are used by Django when sending emails: plain text and HTML. Rich text emails are treated as HTML emails because they contain HTML markup.

As plain text emails

Plain text emails are just like they sound; they are just text and nothing else. We will be creating a method that prepares and then actually sends the email inside of the `ContactForm` class that we are using. The method that triggers the sending of an email can technically be placed in any class or any file. Follow these steps to create yours:

1. In the `ContactForm` class that was duplicated into the `/chapter_7/forms.py` file, add a new method called `send_email()` using the following code:

    ```
    # /becoming_a_django_entdev/chapter_7/forms.py
    ...
    from django.core.mail
    import EmailMessage
    ...
    class ContactForm(Form):
        ...
        def send_email(self, request):
            data = self.cleaned_data
            msg_body = 'Hello World'
    ```

```
        email = EmailMessage(
            subject = 'New Contact Form Entry',
            body = msg_body,
            from_email = 'no-reply@example.com',
            reply_to = ['no-reply@example.com'],
            cc = [],
            bcc = [],
            to = [data['email_1']],
            attachments = [],
            headers = {},
        )

        email.content_subtype = 'plain'
        email.send()
```

This method will handle all of the busy work involved in actually formatting and sending the email. Of course, this is a basic `text/plain` email consisting of only the phrase **Hello World**, defined in the `msg_body` variable. The `email.content_subtype` statement is where we are telling Django that we want to format this email as a plain text email. We also imported and used the `EmailMessage` class from the `django.core.mail` library, used to structure the email and format headers pertaining to that email. Django also provides simpler method-based functions, such as `send_mail()` or `send_mass_mail()`, among a small handful of other methods. We will focus on just the `EmailMessage` class, as it will encompass every aspect of what we need to achieve in this chapter. To learn more about all of the email methods that Django provides, visit the official documentation, found here: https://docs.djangoproject.com/en/4.0/topics/email/.

Because we are keeping this example extremely basic, we are only defining the `subject`, `body`, `from_email`, `reply_to`, and `to` attributes. Data is accessed by using `self.cleaned_data` and here we assign the value of the field named `email_1` to be the value of the `to` attributes list, as in the recipient's email address. If you are sending the email to multiple addresses, separate each email address with a comma in that list with no spaces.

2. In the `FormClassView` class found in the /chapter_7/views.py file, leave everything as is, relating to the sending of messages in that view class. To actually send the email, add the following line of code to the post() method, as depicted here:

```python
# /becoming_a_django_entdev/chapter_7/views.py
from django.template.response import TemplateResponse
...
class FormClassView(FormView):
    ...
    def post(self, request, *args, **kwargs):
        form = self.form_class(request.POST)
        ...
        form.send_email(request)
        return TemplateResponse(
            request,
            self.template_name,
            context
        )
```

Here, we are placing the send email operation just above the `return` statement and below the conditional statement that checks whether the form is valid. We are not separating the send operation for valid and invalid form submissions at this time.

3. Now, visit the URL http://www.localhost:8000/chapter-7/form-class/ and submit the form, in either a valid or invalid state. The page should refresh without programming errors. You should now see your email in the inbox of your Mailtrap account, found at https://mailtrap.io/inboxes/, as depicted in the following screenshot:

Figure 7.5 – Mailtrap – plain text email

You will also notice that the email is displayed under the **Text** tab found on this screen. The **HTML** tab is inactive; we cannot click to open it. This is because HTML is not available for this email, as it was formatted as `text/plain`.

As HTML emails

Configuring an HTML or rich text email is fairly easy. Using the same example from the previous section, *As plain text emails*, all that is needed to convert to an HTML email is to change two lines of code. The first line of code is to change the `msg_body` variable to equal `'<b>Hello World</b>'`. This way, we can actually pass in HTML to see whether it is working or not. The second is to change the value of `email.content_subtype` to equal `'html'`, and that's it!

Now, visit the same URL, `http://www.localhost:8000/chapter-7/form-class/`, and submit the form. This time, when you visit your Mailtrap inbox at `https://mailtrap.io/inboxes/`, you should see the **Hello World** text in bold, as depicted in the following screenshot:

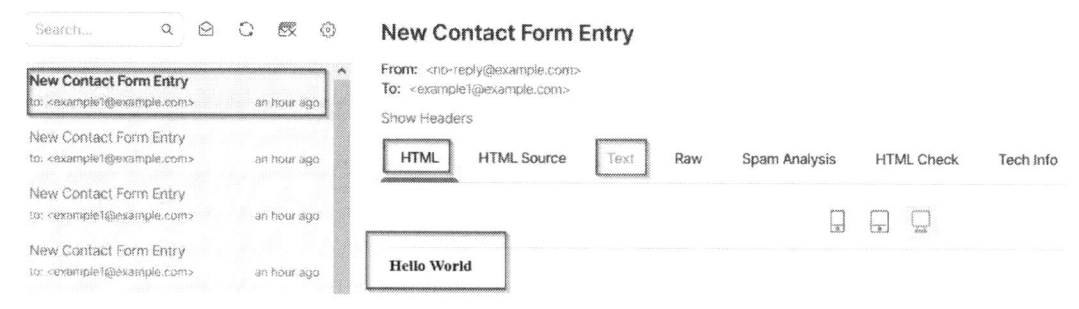

Figure 7.6 – Mailtrap – HTML email

In the preceding screenshot, you will also see that the email is now displayed in the **HTML** tab and not the **Text** tab this time. This is because we formatted the email as a `text/html` MIME type with no text fallback provided, meaning only HTML is available for this email. Clicking on the **Tech Info** tab will reveal other detailed information about your email. In this tab, you can verify the actual content type. Check if the value of the Content-Type has a MIME type that equals **text/html; charset=utf-8**.

> **Note**
> The value of `'html'` is used for both rich text- and HTML-formatted emails. They will both be sent as `text/html`. This is because we cannot explicitly tell Django to use `'application/rtf'` for rich text emails. Django just assumes rich text emails are HTML because they contain HTML markup.

As HTML emails with a plain text alternative

HTML emails that have plain text alternatives are used for email clients that have difficulty rendering the HTML-formatted version of the email or or if spam blockers only display text first. We need to use the Django-provided `EmailMultiAlternatives` class instead of the `EmailMessage` class to do this. `EmailMultiAlternatives` is an extension of the `EmailMessage` class, meaning that all of the methods and attributes available in the `EmailMessage` class are still available for us to use in this class, plus more. When using this class, what we do is format the email as `text/html` and then use the new `attach_alternative()` method available in the `EmailMultiAlternatives` class with that alternative email formatted as `text/plain`.

Use the same code as in the *As HTML emails* subsection and make the following highlighted changes:

```python
# /becoming_a_django_entdev/chapter_7/forms.py
...
from django.core.mail import (
    EmailMessage,
    EmailMultiAlternatives
)
...
class ContactForm(Form):
    ...
    def send_email(self, request):
        data = self.cleaned_data
        msg_body = '<b>Hello World</b>'

        email = EmailMultiAlternatives(
            subject = 'New Contact Form Entry',
            body = msg_body,
            from_email = 'no-reply@example.com',
            reply_to = ['no-reply@example.com'],
            cc = [],
            bcc = [],
            to = [data['email_1']],
            attachments = [],
```

```
        headers = {},
    )

    email.content_subtype = 'html'
    email.attach_alternative(
        'Hello World',
        'text/plain'
    )
    email.send()
```

In the preceding example, we just replaced the `EmailMessage` class with the new `EmailMultiAlternatives` class. Then, we added the `email.attact_alternative()` action statement, which formats a brand-new email as `text/plain` using the text that we provided, `Hello World`, and attaches that new plain text-formatted email to the original HTML email. We do this instead of using the `attachment` attribute of the `EmailMessage` class because we are actually restructuring the content type of the email to now be a `multipart/alternative` MIME type instead of either the `text/html` or `text/plain` MIME types.

That's it; you now have an email that is both HTML and plain text. Let's verify this. Visit the same URL, `http://www.localhost:8000/chapter-7/form-class/`, and submit the form. This time, when you visit your Mailtrap inbox at `https://mailtrap.io/inboxes/`, you should see the **Hello World** text in bold and also see the **Text** tab is now highlighted and clickable, as shown:

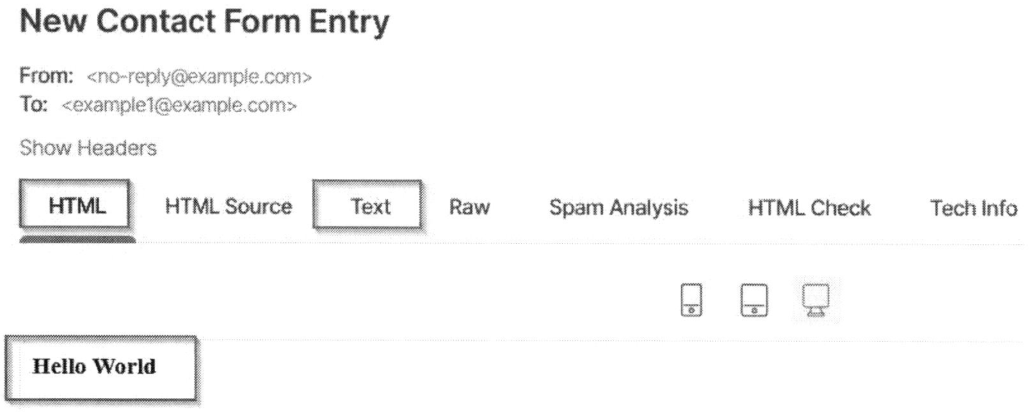

New Contact Form Entry

From: <no-reply@example.com>
To: <example1@example.com>

Show Headers

| HTML | HTML Source | Text | Raw | Spam Analysis | HTML Check | Tech Info |

Hello World

Figure 7.7 – Mailtrap – HTML and plain text email

Clicking on the **Text** tab will show you the plain text format that is available. The primary format is HTML and the fallback will be plain text. The order of the content types can be reversed in this example. When we click on the **Tech Info** tab, we will now see that **Content-Type** is displaying **multipart/alternative**, as shown:

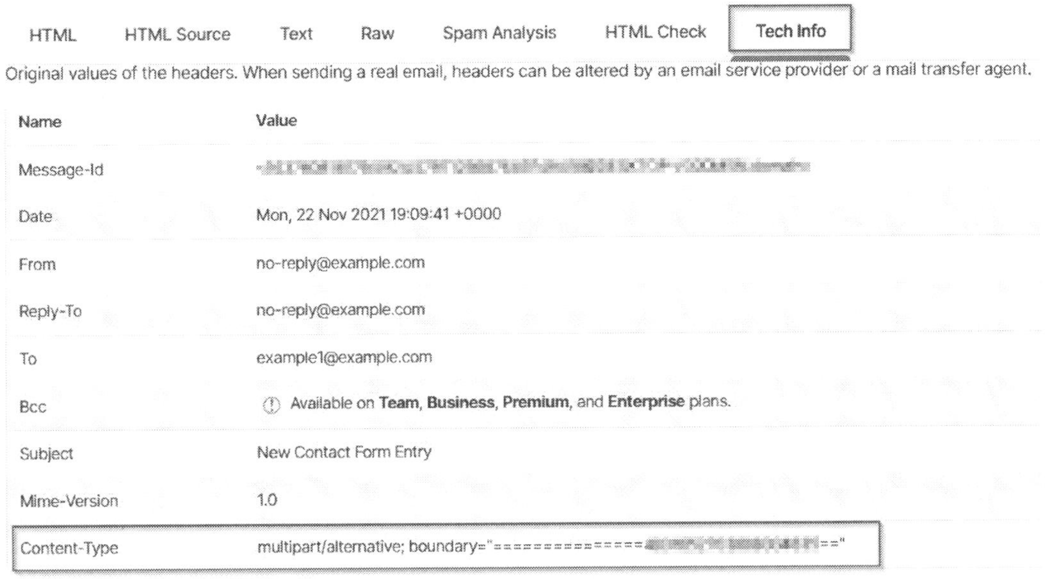

Figure 7.8 – Mailtrap – multipart/alternative

With file attachments

Sending an email with a file attachment is also very easy. Django's `EmailMessage` class provides a method called `attach_file()`, which easily lets us attach a file by passing in the two positional arguments of that method, the path of the file and an optional MIME type. For this next exercise, copy the example PDF document that has been provided along with the code of this book in the `/becoming_a_django_entdev/chapter_7/static/chapter_7/pdf/` directory, called `example.pdf`. Copy that file into the same directory as your project before following this example, or create a dummy PDF file of your own.

In this next example, we will continue with the last example we just completed in the *As HTML emails with a plain text alternative* section, and attach the `example.pdf` document to that email. The Django documentation depicts using the `attach_file()` method with a path written as `email.attach_file('static/chapter_7/pdf/example.pdf')`. This is how a path will be defined when using this method in many Django projects. However, due to using the `whitenoise` package, we will have to import the `settings.py` file and use the `STATIC_ROOT` variable, as shown:

```
# /becoming_a_django_entdev/chapter_7/forms.py
...
from django.conf import settings
...
class ContactForm(Form):
    ...
    def send_email(self, request):
        ...
        email.attach_file(settings.STATIC_ROOT + '/chapter_7/pdf/example.pdf')
        email.send()
```

> **Note**
>
> When using the `STATIC_ROOT` variable in combination with the `whitenoise` package, we now have to run the `collectstatic` Django management command for that file to be found when we run the project locally. This doesn't need to be done in every Django project but in ours, it must. To do so, first stop your project from running. In a terminal or command-line window, this can be done by pressing *Ctrl + C* on Windows or *Cmd + C* on a Mac with your keyboard. Then, execute the following commands. When prompted to do so, type the word `yes` and press *Enter* when it asks whether you are sure:
>
> `(virtual_env) python manage.py collectstatic`
>
> `(virtual_env) python manage.py runserver`
>
> This is a built-in Django command that will collect static files from all apps loaded into your project and place a copy of them into the `STATIC_ROOT` of your project, which is defined as the `/becoming_a_django_entdev/staticfiles/` folder that we have ignored in our Git repository.

That's it. Now, if you visit the same URL, `http://www.localhost:8000/chapter-7/form-class/`, and submit the form, this time when you visit your Mailtrap inbox at `https://mailtrap.io/inboxes/`, you should see the attached file in the top right-hand corner of that email, as shown:

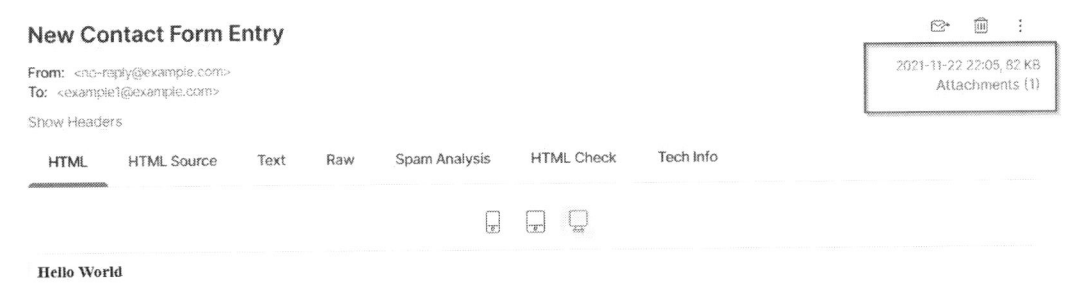

Figure 7.9 – Mailtrap – PDF attachment

Mailtrap will let you click on this document to open and view it or download it. Open the document to see it working properly.

That fail silently

Developers can write reusable apps containing actions that send emails and have them fail silently just as we did when using the Django messages framework. This means that a project won't error out when a developer has installed your app but has not configured a connection to an email client yet. Django provides this option as an attribute of the `send()` method of the `EmailMessage` or `EmailMultiAlternatives` class.

To activate the `fail_silently` option on the send email examples that we just wrote, add the following attribute to the existing `send()` action, as shown:

```python
# /becoming_a_django_entdev/chapter_7/forms.py
...
class ContactForm(Form):
    ...
    def send_email(self, request):
        ...
        email.send(fail_silently=True)
```

This prevents the `email.send()` action from displaying an error message when this code is executed.

> **Note**
> Django also provides this option when using the `send_mail()` and `send_mass_mail()` methods mentioned earlier. To learn more, visit https://docs.djangoproject.com/en/4.0/topics/email/.

Now that we have a better understanding of how emails are being sent in Django, let's go ahead and create our own email templates to let us custom-tailor them for our clients.

Writing custom email templates

Writing HTML as a string in Python can get really messy. We can write the body contents, such as `'<b>Hello World</b>'`, as a `.html` template file instead. That will allow us to organize multiple email templates into the `/templates/emails/` directory of the `chapter_7` app. Programming work can also be shared among developers in this way. Email templates can also be used for plain text-formatted emails, placing only the text without any HTML code inside of that `.html` file. While that may not sound appealing for plain text emails, this does have its benefits when working among a large team of developers. Let's begin with the simplest template using only plain text emails.

Django provides the `get_template()` method, found in the `django.template.loader` library. This method will be used for all the email template examples in the following subsections.

For plain text emails

Follow these steps to create a template for a plain text email:

1. In the `ContactForm` class that we have been working with, modify the `send_email()` method to now be the following code:

    ```
    # /becoming_a_django_entdev/chapter_7/forms.py
    ...
    from django.template.loader
    import get_template
    ...
    class ContactForm(Form):
        ...
    ```

```python
def send_email(self, request):
    data = self.cleaned_data
    template = get_template(
        'chapter_7/emails/plain_text_format.html'
    )
    msg_body = template.render()

    email = EmailMessage(
        subject = 'New Contact Form Entry',
        body = msg_body,
        from_email = 'no-reply@example.com',
        reply_to = ['no-reply@example.com'],
        cc = [],
        bcc = [],
        to = [data['email_1']],
        attachments = [],
        headers = {},
    )

    email.content_subtype = 'plain'
    email.send(fail_silently = True)
```

In the preceding code, we imported the `get_template()` method and used it to construct the template variable, which points to the `/chapter_7/emails/plain_text_format.html` file.

2. Now, go ahead and create that file in that same directory within your `/chapter_7/templates/` folder. Inside that file, just add the text `Hello World` and nothing else. If you place any HTML in this file, it will be rendered as a string within the plain text body content of that email and will not be rendered as HTML.

3. Now, visit the same URL, `http://www.localhost:8000/chapter-7/form-class/`, and submit the form. This time, when you visit your Mailtrap inbox at `https://mailtrap.io/inboxes/`, you should see that the **HTML** tabs are disabled, leaving only the **Text** tab to view your email. This also indicates that the process was successful, as shown in the following screenshot:

New Contact Form Entry

From: <no-reply@example.com>
To: <example1@example.com>

Show Headers

HTML   HTML Source   **Text**   Raw   Spam Analysis   Tech Info

```
Hello World
```

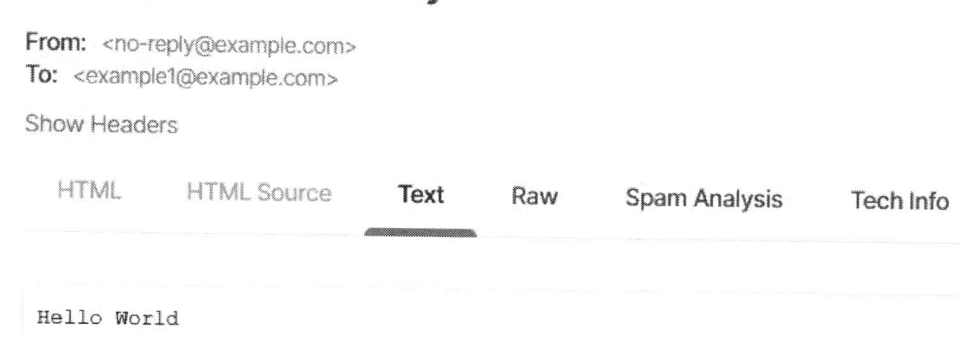

Figure 7.10 – Mailtrap – plain text template

For HTML emails

Writing HTML templates is done in the same way as how we loaded a template for the plain text example previously. Only the following alterations are needed:

1. First, we load a new file called `html_format.html` and change `content_subtype` back to `'html'`, as is highlighted here:

```python
# /becoming_a_django_entdev/chapter_7/forms.py
...
from django.template.loader
import get_template
...
class ContactForm(Form):
    ...
    def send_email(self, request):
        data = self.cleaned_data
        template = get_template(
            'chapter_7/emails/html_format.html'
        )
        msg_body = template.render()
```

```python
            email = EmailMessage(
                subject = 'New Contact Form Entry',
                body = msg_body,
                from_email = 'no-reply@example.com',
                reply_to = ['no-reply@example.com'],
                cc = [],
                bcc = [],
                to = [data['email_1']],
                attachments = [],
                headers = {},
            )

            email.content_subtype = 'html'
            email.send(fail_silently = True)
```

2. Now, create the `html_format.html` file in your `/chapter_7/templates/chapter_7/emails/` directory. Inside this file, place the following code, where we actually have to format the document like an HTML page, in addition to providing the marked-up `Hello World` text:

```html
# /becoming_a_django_entdev/chapter_7/templates/
chapter_7/emails/html_format.html
<!DOCTYPE html>
<html lang="en" xmlns="http://www.w3.org/1999/xhtml">
    <head>
        <meta charset="utf-8" />
        <title>Hello World</title>
    </head>
    <body>
        <b>Hello World</b>
    </body>
</html>
```

In this template, you can format your HTML `<head>` and `<body>` content as desired. It might even be wise to include responsive email and browser/client-supported syntax within this document to make sure it renders properly on every device. Your email test client will usually provide documentation to help you with stuff like that.

3. Now, visit the same URL, `http://www.localhost:8000/chapter-7/form-class/`, and submit the form. This time, when you visit your Mailtrap inbox at `https://mailtrap.io/inboxes/`, you should see that the **HTML** tab is now enabled and the **Text** tab is disabled. Again, this indicates that the process was successful, as depicted here:

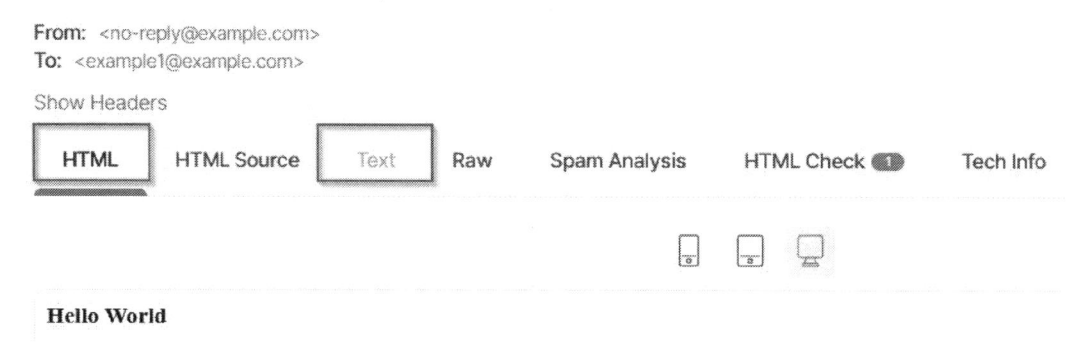

Figure 7.11 – Mailtrap – HTML template

Providing template context

Using template-based emails can become even more useful when we introduce dynamic content into the equation. To do this, we need to send context into the `template.render()` statement. By doing this, we can even pass the form data that was already defined as the `data` variable directly into the template, accessing form field values within that template.

In this next exercise, we will render a template that also displays exactly what the user typed for each field of that form. Follow these steps to do just that:

1. In the `send_email()` method of `ContactForm`, make the following highlighted changes:

```
# /becoming_a_django_entdev/chapter_7/forms.py
...
from django.template.loader
```

```python
import get_template
...
class ContactForm(Form):
    ...
    def send_email(self, request):
        data = self.cleaned_data
        template = get_template('chapter_7/emails/new_contact_form_entry.html')
        context = {'data': data}
        msg_body = template.render(context)

        email = EmailMessage(
            subject = 'New Contact Form Entry',
            body = msg_body,
            from_email = 'no-reply@example.com',
            reply_to = ['no-reply@example.com'],
            cc = [],
            bcc = [],
            to = [data['email_1']],
            attachments = [],
            headers = {},
        )

        email.content_subtype = 'html'
        email.send(fail_silently = True)
```

2. Now, create a new file called new_contact_form_entry.html in your /chapter_7/templates/chapter_7/emails/ directory and place the following code inside that file:

```
# /becoming_a_django_entdev/chapter_7/templates/
chapter_7/emails/new_contact_form_entry.html
{% load static %}
<!DOCTYPE html>
<html lang="en" xmlns="http://www.w3.org/1999/xhtml">
    <head>
        <meta charset="utf-8">
        <title>Contact Form Submitted</title>
```

```html
        </head>
        <body>
            <center>
                <h1>New Contact Form Entry</h1>
                <h2>The field contents are listed below</h2>
                <ul>
                    <li>Full Name: {{ data.full_name }}</li>
                    <li>Email Field Example 1: {{ data.email_1 }}</li>
                    <li>Email Field Example 2: {{ data.email_2 }}</li>
                    <li>Email Field Example 3: {{ data.email_3 }}</li>
                    <li>Conditionally Required Field: {{ data.conditional_required }}</li>
                    <li>Multiple Emails Field: {{ data.multiple_emails }}</li>
                    <li>Message: {{ data.message }}</li>
                </ul>
            </center>
        </body>
</html>
```

In this template, you can use any of the tags and filters that come standard with the Django template language, such as writing conditional statements to check whether a field value equals a specific value. This means you could write a loop to automatically loop through all of the fields that exist in your `data` variable and then use the provided field labels instead of those custom labels depicted previously. You can also load `static` and/or custom `templatetags` using the load tag depicted previously, as with any other Django template.

3. Now, visit the same URL, `http://www.localhost:8000/chapter-7/form-class/`, and submit the form. This time, when you visit your Mailtrap inbox at `https://mailtrap.io/inboxes/`, you should see the values of each field inside the new email, as depicted here:

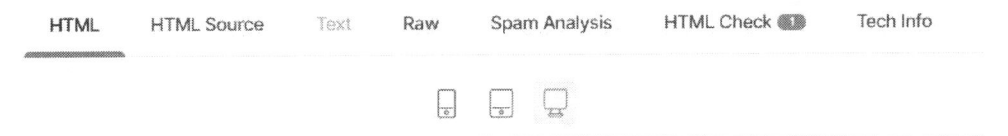

Figure 7.12 – Mailtrap – template context

Next, let's add a new action that creates a PDF document in the same spot where we are triggering our send email actions.

Generating PDF reports

Django relies on the support of third-party packages in order to generate PDF documents. Their own documentation even suggests using the `reportlab` package; however, any third-party package that provides PDF support can be used. When using anything other than `reportlab`, refer to that package's documentation for instructions on how to use that package. The `reportlab` package even provides sample PDF invoices, reports, catalogs, and more for developers to get started quickly and easily, that is, if they are using the paid Plus version of the `reportlab` package. The Plus version requires the `rlextra` package, which is not available to the public. To learn more about what this service and package can provide, visit their documentation at `https://www.reportlab.com/dev/docs/`.

For the exercises throughout this section, we will be using the `xhtml2pdf` package instead, which is also free but a bit simpler and easier to use when working with template-based PDFs. We will keep to the same idea of creating a separate `.html` file for the content of each static or dynamic PDF.

348   Working with Messages, Email Notifications, and PDF Reports

Add the `xhtml2pdf` package to your `requirements.txt` file and install it into your virtual environment or run the following command:

```
(virtual_env) pip install xhtml2pdf
```

> **Tip**
> In all packages that I have worked with, I found that some have difficulty rendering complex HTML tables consistently. I would recommend avoiding tables altogether, or if you need to structure data as a table, do so with a simple structure to prevent rendering discrepancies and errors during document creation.

Now that we have installed a tool that generates PDF documents, let's practice using it.

As template-based PDFs

Here, we will be using the same Django template language to build what we will call **PDF templates**.

Follow these steps to create your template:

1. Create a new method called `generate_pdf()` in the `ContactForm` class and include the following code:

   ```python
   # /becoming_a_django_entdev/chapter_7/forms.py
   ...
   from django.conf import settings
   from django.http import HttpResponse
   from django.template.loader import get_template
   from xhtml2pdf import pisa
   ...
   class ContactForm(Form):
       ...
       def generate_pdf(self, request):
           dest = open(settings.STATIC_ROOT + '/chapter_7/pdf/test.pdf', 'w+b')
   ```

```
            template = get_template('chapter_7/pdfs/pdf_
template.html')
            html = template.render()
            result = pisa.CreatePDF(
                html,
                dest = dest,
            )
            return HttpResponse(result.err)
```

Here, we import the `pisa` library from within the `xhtml2pdf` package and use the `CreatePDF()` method. We are also using the Python `open()` method to specify the destination folder and filename of the document that we want to create. We are using the same `STATIC_ROOT` variable that we used before, most likely due to the `whitenoise` package in our project stack. The file being created will be located in the `/becoming_a_django_entdev/staticfiles/chapter_7/pdf/` directory. Then, we are setting the `result` variable to equal the result of running the `CreatePDF()` method where we pass in the rendered HTML template as the content of that PDF. Additional information is available in the documentation, found here: https://xhtml2pdf.readthedocs.io/en/latest/format_html.html.

> **Note**
> Since we are creating this file, there is no need to run the `collectstatic` command as we had to before.

2. Next, in the `post()` method of the `FormClass_View` class, where we wrote our `send_email()` action, let's add the `generate_pdf()` operation just below that statement, as shown and highlighted here:

```
# /becoming_a_django_entdev/chapter_7/views.py
from django.template.response
import TemplateResponse
from django.views.generic.edit
import FormView
...
class FormClass_View(FormView):
    ...
    def post(self, request, *args, **kwargs):
```

```
            form = self.form_class(request.POST)
            ...
            form.send_email(request)
            form.generate_pdf(request)
            return TemplateResponse(
                request,
                self.template_name,
                context
            )
```

3. Next, in the `pdf_template.html` file that we are specifying as the template used for the body content of the PDF, add the following code:

```
# /becoming_a_django_entdev/chapter_7/templates/
chapter_7/pdfs/pdf_template.html
<!DOCTYPE html>
<html>
    <head></head>
    <body>
        <div id="header_obj"><h1>Header</h1></div>
        <div id="footer_obj">
            &copy;Footer - Page <pdf:pagenumber> of <pdf:pagecount>
        </div>
        <div class="body-content">
            <h2>Hello World</h2>
            {% lorem 50 p %}<pdf:pdf-next-page />{% lorem 50 p %}
        </div>
    </body>
</html>
```

Here, we are writing standard HTML code to create the content of the PDF. The preceding example creates a reusable and repeatable header and footer on every page of the document. We also use special vendor-specific tags to tell us things such as the current page or the total page count of the document, such as what is used in the footer of the document, `<pdf:pagenumber>` and `<pdf:pagecount>`. We also use the Django-provided `{% lorem %}` template tag, which generates 50 paragraphs worth of Latin text, using the `50 p` values that we are passing into that function. The Latin text, represented as **Lorem Ipsum**, is used only to illustrate what happens when there is more than one page worth of content without actually writing that content.

4. The `size` attribute is used to specify the HTML document size that we want to specify the physical size and orientation of the PDF document. Next, use the `@page` and `@frame` CSS objects to format your PDF document:

```css
# /becoming_a_django_entdev/chapter_7/templates/
chapter_7/pdfs/pdf_template.html
...
    <head>
        <style>
            @page {
                size: a4 portrait;
                @frame header_frame {
                    -pdf-frame-content: header_obj;
                    top: 50pt; left: 50pt;
                    width: 512pt; height: 40pt;
                }
                @frame content_frame {
                    top: 90pt; left: 50pt;
                    width: 512pt; height: 632pt;
                }
                @frame footer_frame {
                    -pdf-frame-content: footer_obj;
                    top: 772pt; left: 50pt;
                    width: 512pt; height: 20pt;
                }
            }
            #header_obj { color: darkblue; text-align: center; }
```

```
                .body-content { color: black; text-align:
left; }
                #footer_obj { color: green; text-align:
right; }
            </style>
        </head>
    ...
```

The `-pdf-frame-content` attribute is used to map the `@frame` object to the actual `<div>` with an ID attribute that matches the value specified. This must be `<div>` and not a `<header>` or `<footer>` HTML object or else your content will not render properly.

5. Now, visit the same URL, `http://www.localhost:8000/chapter-7/form-class/`, and submit the form. This time, you should see a new file called `test.pdf` in your `/becoming_a_django_entdev/staticfiles/chapter_7/pdf/` directory. When opening that document, you should see about eight pages worth of randomly generated Latin text, and on every page, you should see the same header and footer, as depicted in the following screenshot:

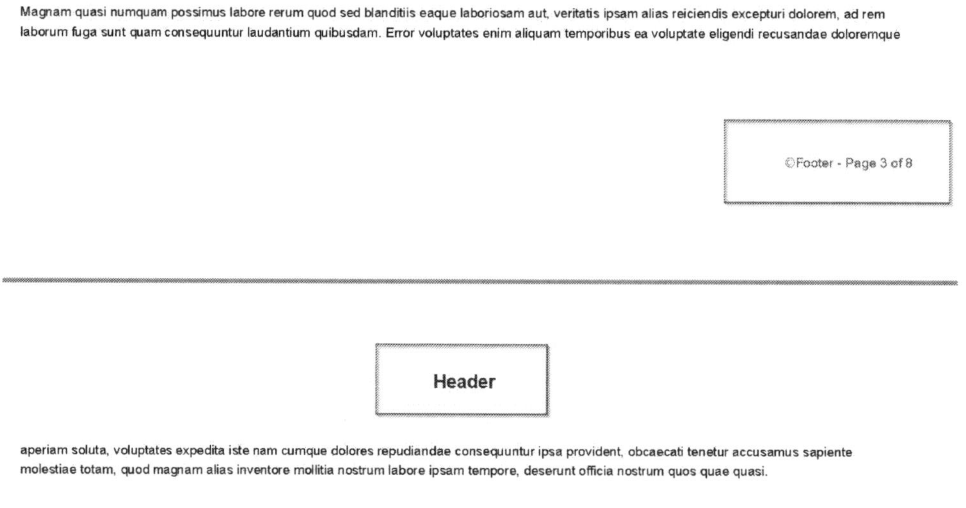

Magnam quasi numquam possimus labore rerum quod sed blanditiis eaque laboriosam aut, veritatis ipsam alias reiciendis excepturi dolorem, ad rem laborum fuga sunt quam consequuntur laudantium quibusdam. Error voluptates enim aliquam temporibus ea voluptate eligendi recusandae doloremque

©Footer - Page 3 of 8

Header

aperiam soluta, voluptates expedita iste nam cumque dolores repudiandae consequuntur ipsa provident, obcaecati tenetur accusamus sapiente molestiae totam, quod magnam alias inventore mollitia nostrum labore ipsam tempore, deserunt officia nostrum quos quae quasi.

Figure 7.13 – xhmtl2pdf – static PDF

> **Tip**
> When opening this document to see what it looks like, particularly on Windows, you must close this document before submitting your form again, triggering it to generate a new document. You may run into permission errors stating that another person or application is already using that file if you don't.

Let's add context to the PDF templates next.

Adding context

Let's pass the contents of the form field values into that PDF as context. This method does not always need to live in a form class; the same also applies to the `send_email()` method. They can live in a view or model class or even exist as a standalone utility method that can be used anywhere.

For now, modify the previous example to pass in context using the following steps:

1. In the same `generate_pdf()` method of the `ContactForm` class, make the changes highlighted here:

    ```
    # /becoming_a_django_entdev/chapter_7/forms.py
    ...
    from django.conf import settings
    from django.template.loader import get_template
    from xhtml2pdf import pisa
    ...
    class ContactForm(Form):
        ...
        def generate_pdf(self, request):
            data = self.cleaned_data
            context = { 'data': data }
            dest = open(settings.STATIC_ROOT + '/chapter_7/pdf/test_2.pdf', 'w+b')

            template = get_template(
                'chapter_7/pdfs/pdf_template.html'
            )
            html = template.render(context)
            result = pisa.CreatePDF(
                html,
                dest = dest,
    ```

```
        )

        return HttpResponse(result.err)
```

2. Next, in the same /chapter_7/pdfs/pdf_template.html file, add the following highlighted code between the two existing lines of code, as shown:

```
# /becoming_a_django_entdev/chapter_7/templates/
chapter_7/pdfs/pdf_template.html
...
        <div class="body-content">
            <h2>Hello World</h2>
            <h3>The field contents are listed below</h3>
            <ul>
                <li>Full Name: {{ data.full_name }}</li>
                <li>Email Field Example 1: {{ data.email_1 }}</li>
                <li>Email Field Example 2: {{ data.email_2 }}</li>
                <li>Email Field Example 3: {{ data.email_3 }}</li>
                <li>Conditionally Required Field: {{ data.conditional_required }}</li>
                <li>Multiple Emails Field: {{ data.multiple_emails }}</li>
                <li>Message: {{ data.message }}</li>
            </ul>
            {% lorem 50 p %}<pdf:pdf-next-page />{% lorem 50 p %}
        </div>
...
```

The same code written in the *Providing template context* subsection of this chapter is used.

3. Now, visit the same URL, `http://www.localhost:8000/chapter-7/form-class/`, and submit the form. You should see a new file called `test_2.pdf` in the `/becoming_a_django_entdev/staticfiles/chapter_7/pdf/` directory on your local machine. When you open that file, there should still be eight pages worth of content. On the first page only, there will be a list containing the content of the form that we just passed into that PDF template, as depicted here:

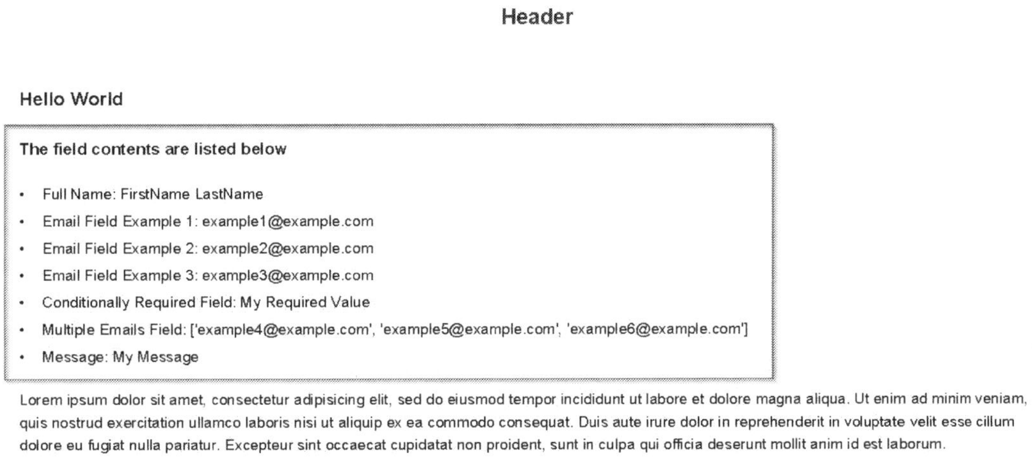

Header

Hello World

The field contents are listed below

- Full Name: FirstName LastName
- Email Field Example 1: example1@example.com
- Email Field Example 2: example2@example.com
- Email Field Example 3: example3@example.com
- Conditionally Required Field: My Required Value
- Multiple Emails Field: ['example4@example.com', 'example5@example.com', 'example6@example.com']
- Message: My Message

Lorem ipsum dolor sit amet, consectetur adipisicing elit, sed do eiusmod tempor incididunt ut labore et dolore magna aliqua. Ut enim ad minim veniam, quis nostrud exercitation ullamco laboris nisi ut aliquip ex ea commodo consequat. Duis aute irure dolor in reprehenderit in voluptate velit esse cillum dolore eu fugiat nulla pariatur. Excepteur sint occaecat cupidatat non proident, sunt in culpa qui officia deserunt mollit anim id est laborum.

Figure 7.14 – xhmtl2pdf – dynamic PDF

Now that we know how to build PDF templates and generate PDF documents, we can present data in a very clean and structured way that makes using these a valuable reporting tool.

Summary

With the skills gained after completing the exercises found in this chapter, you can now create and send messages, notifications, and reports of various types. We now know how to use the Django messages framework to serve up flash messages every time a page loads or reloads. We can create and send emails of various content types and even use an email test client account to capture those emails, indicating that they are actually working. We even installed a package and began building our own PDF reports.

Use any combination of these tools to add value to your project. Flash messages, email notifications, and report generating concepts all help to keep users informed and engaged with your application. Always remember that too much information can overwhelm a user, such as having thousands of email notifications flooding their inbox. Use them wisely!

The Django messages framework offers a wide range of tools that can create flash messages for users. With a little bit of creativity, the Django messages framework can be used with **Asynchronous JavaScript and XML** (**AJAX**) to serve up messages that act more like a **Single-Page App** (**SPA**). In the next chapter, *Chapter 8, Working with the Django REST Framework*, we will discuss what the Django REST framework is and how it can be used to work with AJAX requests.

Part 3 – Advanced Django Components

In this part, you will be introduced to more advanced components of the Django framework. While the Django REST Framework is a completely separate package, it is a dependency that is made specifically to extend onto the Django framework, allowing us to build an API. You will learn about how the REST framework is used in a Django environment and how it can be used in combination with the Django template language. This part will also introduce packages used to test classes and methods found throughout a Django project, allowing developers to write custom test scripts. Lastly, you will learn about how to optimize database queries and manage data within a project.

This part comprises the following chapters:

- *Chapter 8, Working with the Django REST Framework*
- *Chapter 9, Django Testing*
- *Chapter 10, Database Management*

8
Working with the Django REST Framework

This chapter will focus on working with an **Application Programming Interface** (**API**). An API is actually a set of tools and communication protocols working to allow two different applications to communicate with each other effectively; it is what acts as the middleman between two systems. A **REST API** adopts the design principles set forth in a **Representational State Transfer** (**REST**) software architecture and is most commonly used with web-based applications. Every time we mention the word API in this chapter, we are really referring to a REST API as they are technically slightly different but usually interpreted as the same thing.

Django itself relies on third-party packages to work with an existing API or to create an API yourself. A common Python package that is available is called the `requests` package. The `requests` package is used to send and receive requests to and from an existing API found on the server side. More information about this package can be found here: https://pypi.org/project/requests/. On the other hand, a JavaScript-based framework, such as React, AngularJS, or Vue.js, to name a few, will all perform these requests on the client side, within the user's browser. There is no right or wrong way to communicate with an API, in terms of choosing tools that operate on the client versus the server side. Those decisions are made as a result of the technical requirements obtained for your project. We won't actually be using the `requests` package or any of the client-side JavaScript-based frameworks; instead, we will focus on just the **Django REST framework**, which is used to build a model-based API for the models we previously created.

The Django REST framework is licensed as open source, allowing developers to use it within their commercial or private applications. It is used to construct APIs based on the models of a Django project, where endpoints execute HTTP requests that perform **Create, Read, Update, and Delete** (**CRUD**) operations. This means it is used to serialize and deserialize related models of a Django project into JSON format, commonly used in web-based APIs. When using the Django REST framework, there is no need to use the pip `requests` package, but it won't hurt either if you use this package in combination with the framework, which is sometimes done in projects. This chapter will focus entirely on using the Django REST framework to create an API for all of the vehicle models that we created in *Chapter 3, Models, Relations, and Inheritance*. We will be serializing those models and registering URL patterns, which are the API endpoints, to views and viewsets that we write. We will also be using routers to generate some of those URL patterns for us, based entirely on the data that exists in our database tables.

In this chapter, we will cover the following:

- Installing and configuring the Django REST framework
- Serializing related models of a project
- Using the browsable API, a tool provided by the Django REST framework
- Creating SPA-style pages
- Creating custom API endpoints
- Performing API requests using token authentication measures

Technical requirements

To work with the code in this chapter, the following tools will need to be installed on your local machine:

- Python version 3.9 – used as the underlying programming language for the project
- Django version 4.0 – used as the backend framework of the project
- pip package manager – used to manage third-party Python/Django packages

We will continue to work with the solution created in *Chapter 2, Project Configuration*. However, it is not necessary to use the Visual Studio IDE. The main project itself can be run using another IDE or run independently using a terminal or command-line window from within the project root folder, which is where the `manage.py` file resides. Whatever editor or IDE you are using, a virtual environment will also be needed to work with the Django project. Instructions for how to create a project and virtual environment can be found in *Chapter 2, Project Configuration*. You will need a database to store the data contained in your project. PostgreSQL was chosen for the examples in the previous chapter; however, any database type that you choose for your project can be used to work with the examples in this chapter.

We will also be using data that is in the form of a Django fixture, provided in *Chapter 3, Models, Relations, and Inheritance*, in the subsection titled *Loading the chapter_3 data fixture*. Make sure the `chapter_3` fixture is loaded into your database. If this has already been done, then you may skip the next command. If you have already created the tables found in *Chapter 3, Models, Relations, and Inheritance*, and have not loaded that fixture yet, then run the following command, after activating your virtual environment:

```
(virtual_env) PS > python manage.py loaddata chapter_3
```

All of the code created in this chapter can be found in the GitHub repository for this book: https://github.com/PacktPublishing/Becoming-an-Enterprise-Django-Developer. The bulk of the code depicted in this chapter can be found in the `/becoming_a_django_entdev/becoming_a_django_entdev/chapter_8/` directory.

Check out the following video to see the *Code in Action*: https://bit.ly/3Ojocdx.

Preparing for this chapter

Start by creating a new app in your project called `chapter_8` by following the steps discussed in *Chapter 2, Project Configuration*, in the subsection titled *Creating a Django app*. As discussed in that section, don't forget to change the value of the `name` = variable for your app class found in the `/becoming_a_django_entdev/becoming_a_django_entdev/chapter_8/apps.py` file to now point to the path where you installed your app. Be sure to also include this app in the `INSTALLED_APPS` variable found in the `settings.py` file as well.

In the main `urls.py` file of the site, add the following path, which points to the URL patterns of this chapter that we will be creating:

```python
# /becoming_a_django_entdev/urls.py
...
urlpatterns = [
    path(
        '',
        include(
            'becoming_a_django_entdev.chapter_8.urls'
        )
    ),
]
```

Installing the Django REST framework

To install the Django REST framework in any Django project and enable the bare-minimum settings needed to begin working with it, follow these steps:

1. Add the `djangorestframework`, `markdown`, and `django-filter` packages to your `requirements.txt` file and install them in your virtual environment using your IDE or command line. You can also run the following individual `pip` commands. Use the first of the following commands to activate your virtual environment:

   ```
   PS C:\Projects\Packt\Repo\becoming_a_django_entdev>
   virtual_env/Scripts/activate
   (virtual_env) PS > pip install djangorestframework
   (virtual_env) PS > pip install markdown
   (virtual_env) PS > pip install django-filter
   ```

There is no need to run the Django migration commands when installing these three packages as no additional tables will be created by them.

2. Next, in your `settings.py` file, add the following app to the `INSTALLED_APPS` list. Then, add the `REST_FRAMEWORK` dictionary, including the `DjangoModelPermissionsOrAnonReadOnly` permission class shown here:

```
# /becoming_a_django_entdev/settings.py
INSTALLED_APPS = [
    ...
    'rest_framework',
]
REST_FRAMEWORK = {
    'DEFAULT_PERMISSION_CLASSES': [
        'rest_framework.permissions.
            DjangoModelPermissionsOrAnonReadOnly'
    ],
}
```

This permission class allows us to check for model-based CRUD rights and allows anonymous users to only view or read items. For a complete breakdown of the over half-dozen other permission classes, visit https://www.django-rest-framework.org/api-guide/permissions/. We will only be working with one permission class throughout this chapter.

3. You will need to register the URL patterns related to this framework's authentication mechanisms. In your `/chapter_8/urls.py` file, add the following `include` pattern, along with a home page and Django admin site links for this chapter, as shown:

```
# /becoming_a_django_entdev/chapter_8/urls.py
from django.contrib import admin
from django.urls import include, path
from django.views.generic import TemplateView

urlpatterns = [
    path('admin/', admin.site.urls),
    path(
        '',
        TemplateView.as_view(
```

```
                template_name = 'chapter_8/index.html'
            )
        ),
        path('api-auth/', include('rest_framework.urls'))
    ]
```

4. We also need to include the admin site URLs just like we did in *Chapter 6, Exploring the Django Admin Site*, for this chapter. If you have already placed this include statement in the main `urls.py` file of your project, then you do not need to include it again in the `chapter_8` app.

Now, the Django REST framework is installed and ready to use in your project. Currently, we have no API URLs except for the authentication URLs that come with this framework. Currently, those authentication URLs don't provide us with anything to do. You can navigate to the login page just to see whether it loads properly by visiting the URL `http://localhost:8000/api-auth/login/`. If you log in with your superuser account, there will currently be nothing to display and it will show you a **404 Page not found** message.

> **Note**
>
> The reason we enabled the Django admin site URL patterns for the `chapter_8` app is to be able to log into the Django admin site with a superuser account and authenticate a user when working with some of the exercises in this chapter. For those exercises, if you are not logged in, you will find a message in your results stating **Authentication credentials were not provided**. For other exercises toward the end of this chapter, you will not need to be logged into the Django admin site; authentication will be performed by using token-based authorization measures.

To begin using this framework and creating new API endpoints, we will start by creating a serializer class for each of the models created in *Chapter 3, Models, Relations, and Inheritance*.

Serializing objects

Creating an API starts with creating a serializer class and then creating a view, in particular a `ModelViewSet` view class. Serializing objects means converting a model object into JSON format to represent the data of that object. The last thing we need to do is create URL patterns that map to the view classes that we wrote; this will be done using URL routers. These URL patterns are considered your API endpoints.

One thing to note in this section is that we need to create serializers for all models that relate to other models when using related fields. This is why the following exercises will show examples for all four models of the `chapter_3` app. This has to be done in order to ensure that we do not get errors when using the Browsable API, which we will introduce later in this chapter, and when performing API requests. This means if you have multiple `Seller` that have been assigned a `Group` or `Permission`, that `Group` and/or `Permission` object will also have to be serialized. Remember, the `Seller` object replaced the default `User` object found in the `django.contrib.auth.models` library when we changed the `AUTH_USER_MODEL` setting to now equal `'chapter_3.Seller'` in *Chapter 3, Models, Relations, and Inheritance*. Examples for serializing the `Group` or `Permission` objects are not shown because there is only one `Seller` provided in the `chapter_3` data fixture, as shown:

```
134        "model": "chapter_3.seller",
135        "pk": 1,
136        "fields": {
137          "password": "pbkdf2_sha256$260000$SojQSyHvGi47z
138          "last_login": null,
139          "is_superuser": true,
140          "username": "admin",
141          "first_name": "Admin",
142          "last_name": "User",
143          "email": "example@example.com",
144          "is_staff": true,
145          "is_active": true,
146          "date_joined": "2021-08-31T05:05:40.367Z",
147          "name": "Test Biz Name",
148          "groups": [],
149          "user_permissions": [],
150          "vehicles": [ 1, 2, 3, 4, 5, 6, 7 ]
151        }
```

Figure 8.1 – chapter_3 data fixture – Seller object

The `Seller` here is not assigned to a `Group` or `Permission`, so as a result, we should not experience errors in the following exercises. Instead, that `Seller` has the `is_superuser` field set to `true`, which allows us to perform all of the CRUD operations when logged into the Django admin site.

> **Note**
>
> If you experience errors, either delete all but the `Seller` data shown previously or it is recommended to just create the additional serializers, viewsets, and routers for the `Group` and `Permission` objects. Follow the same code format that is used in the following examples. The same applies to the `ContentType` object found in the `django.contrib.contenttypes.models` library. This will be needed if you have a `depth` property defined in the `Meta` subclass of that serializer class, more specifically, if `depth` is set to a value of 2 or greater. We will discuss what this property does soon.

Next, let's begin writing our serializer and learn more about the classes that are available to use.

The serializer classes

The `rest_framework.serializers` library provides us with five classes, as follows:

- `Serializer` – used when nesting `ManyToManyField`, `ForeignKey`, and `OneToOneField` relationships.

- `ModelSerializer` – used to create serializers with fields that map directly to fields of models found in your project.

- `HyperlinkedModelSerializer` – used to do everything the `ModelSerializer` class does, except it will generate a clickable link to each related object when viewed in the Browsable API, instead of displaying those objects as a numeric ID.

- `ListSerializer` – used to serialize multiple objects in one request and is often used by Django when `Serializer`, `ModelSerializer`, or `HyperlinkedModelSerializer` has been initialized with the `many=True` attribute defined.

- `BaseSerializer` – provided to allow developers the ability to create their own serialization and deserialization styles. This is similar to how the `BaseStorage` class is used in the Django messages framework, as discussed in *Chapter 7, Working with Messages, Email Notifications, and PDF Reports*, in the subsection titled *Message storage backends*.

Begin by following these steps to create a `ModelSerializer` class for each model created in *Chapter 3, Models, Relations, and Inheritance*, the `Engine`, `Vehicle`, `VehicleModel`, and `Seller` models:

1. Create a new file in your /becoming_a_django_entdev/chapter_8/ folder called `serializers.py`. Inside this file, add the following imports:

    ```
    # /becoming_a_django_entdev/chapter_8/serializers.py
    from rest_framework.serializers import ModelSerializer
    from ..chapter_3.models import (
        Seller,
        Vehicle,
        Engine,
        VehicleModel
    )
    ```

2. In this file, add the `EngineSerializer` class shown here:

    ```
    # /becoming_a_django_entdev/chapter_8/serializers.py
    ...
    class EngineSerializer(ModelSerializer):
        class Meta:
            model = Engine
            fields = '__all__'
    ```

3. In this file, add the `VehicleModelSerializer` class shown here:

    ```
    # /becoming_a_django_entdev/chapter_8/serializers.py
    ...
    class VehicleModelSerializer(ModelSerializer):
        class Meta:
            model = VehicleModel
            fields = '__all__'
    ```

4. In this file, add the `VehicleSerializer` class shown here:

    ```
    # /becoming_a_django_entdev/chapter_8/serializers.py
    ...
    class VehicleSerializer(ModelSerializer):
        class Meta:
    ```

```
            model = Vehicle
            fields = '__all__'
```

5. In this file, add the `SellerSerializer` class shown here:

```
# /becoming_a_django_entdev/chapter_8/serializers.py
...
class SellerSerializer(ModelSerializer):
    class Meta:
        model = Seller
        fields = '__all__'
```

You might notice that the preceding classes resemble some of the classes used in the exercises found in previous chapters. Here, we defined the fields using the '`__all__`' value but we can provide a list of only the fields needed and the order in which we need them, as was done with the form classes of *Chapter 5*, *Django Forms*.

The Meta subclass

The `Meta` subclass provides additional options, similar to how we customized the `Meta` subclasses in the models written for *Chapter 3*, *Models, Relations, and Inheritance*. For a complete breakdown of all the `Meta` class options available and anything about serializers in general, visit https://www.django-rest-framework.org/api-guide/serializers/. Other options include the following:

- `model` – used to specify the model class to map that serializer to.
- `fields` – used to specify what fields, or all fields, to include in that serializer.
- `validators` – used to add validation when performing a create or update operation. Similar to how form validation was used in *Chapter 5*, *Django Forms*, Django will rely on any constraints set at the database level first, and then it will check for validation applied at the serializer level. More information about serializer validators can be found here: https://www.django-rest-framework.org/api-guide/validators/.
- `depth` – used to represent related objects as nested JSON instead of using the numeric ID up to the depth specified. The default value for this option is `0`.
- `read_only_fields` – used to specify the fields that are read-only at the serializer level.
- `extra_kwargs` – used to specify extra keyword arguments on specific fields within that serializer.

- `list_serializer_class` – used to specify a custom `ListSerializer` that was created using the `ListSerializer` class. This is done when you need to modify the behavior of the `ListSerializer` class, such as performing custom validation on the entire set, for example, comparing values of nested objects versus performing field-level validation.

Now that we have serializer classes to work with, we need to create a view class for them. We can do that with the `ModelViewSet` class provided by the Django REST framework.

The viewset classes

Instead of creating views/methods for each CRUD operation, the Django REST framework offers a class that combines them all into one. It starts by creating a view class within the `views.py` file, similar to what we did in *Chapter 4, URLs, Views, and Templates*, except they are constructed using one of the following viewset classes. The Django REST framework provides the following four viewset classes:

- `GenericViewSet` – includes methods that perform certain operations, commonly used for creating APIs that are not model-based.

- `ModelViewSet` – this class includes all of the methods needed to perform CRUD operations and is intended to map directly to the models of your project.

- `ReadOnlyModelViewSet` – only provides read actions and all other methods will not be provided. This viewset is also intended to work with the models of your project.

- `ViewSet` – used by developers to create custom viewsets similar to how the `BaseSerializer` and `BaseStorage` classes were used. This class does not provide any actions and those methods will have to be created by the developer in order to use this class.

Follow these steps to prepare your viewset classes:

1. In your `/chapter_8/views.py` file, add the following imports:

    ```
    # /becoming_a_django_entdev/chapter_8/views.py
    from rest_framework.permissions import IsAuthenticated
    from rest_framework.viewsets import ModelViewSet
    from .serializers import (
        EngineSerializer,
        SellerSerializer,
        VehicleSerializer,
    ```

```
        VehicleModelSerializer
)
from ..chapter_3.models import (
    Engine,
    Seller,
    Vehicle,
    VehicleModel
)
```

2. In that same file, add the following `EngineViewSet` class, as shown:

```
# /becoming_a_django_entdev/chapter_8/views.py
...
class EngineViewSet(ModelViewSet):
    queryset = Engine.objects.all().order_by('name')
    serializer_class = EngineSerializer
    permission_classes = [IsAuthenticated]
```

3. In that same file, add the following `VehicleModelViewSet` class, as shown:

```
# /becoming_a_django_entdev/chapter_8/views.py
...
class VehicleModelViewSet(ModelViewSet):
    queryset = VehicleModel.objects.all().order_by(
        'name'
    )
    serializer_class = VehicleModelSerializer
    permission_classes = [IsAuthenticated]
```

4. In that same file, add the following `VehicleViewSet` class, as shown:

```
# /becoming_a_django_entdev/chapter_8/views.py
...
class VehicleViewSet(ModelViewSet):
    queryset = Vehicle.objects.all().order_by('price')
    serializer_class = VehicleSerializer
    permission_classes = [IsAuthenticated]
```

5. In that same file, add the following `SellerViewSet` class, as shown:

```
# /becoming_a_django_entdev/chapter_8/views.py
...
class SellerViewSet(ModelViewSet):
    queryset = Seller.objects.all()
    serializer_class = SellerSerializer
    permission_classes = [IsAuthenticated]
```

In each class depicted, we define only three properties for each of those classes, the `queryset`, `serializer_class`, and `permission_classes` properties. In the preceding examples, we are only using the `all()` method to search for all records within that table. Instead of using the `all()` method, the `filter()` and `get()` functions can also be used to look up specific records. The `serializer_class` property is used to map your view to the serializer class that we constructed in the previous subsection; it maps to the model class that we are performing the query on. The `permission_classes` property is used to define the permissions for that request. Permissions differ from the authentication token that we will discuss toward the end of this chapter. Permissions ensure the user who is accessing the system is allowed to perform those specific CRUD operations on the model in question. These are the only three properties available and only the first two are required when using a `ModelViewSet` or `GenericViewSet` class; the last is optional. You can also customize these using a callable method or even override the default action methods yourself. To learn more about viewsets, visit https://www.django-rest-framework.org/api-guide/viewsets/.

Next, let's configure those URL routers to map to the viewsets that we just created. These will be the API endpoints of your project.

Using URL routers

URL routers are used as a way to prevent developers from having to write individual URL patterns for each of the CRUD operations pertaining to each model in your API. That can get very complicated after a while and the Django REST framework provides these URL routers as a means to automatically generate each endpoint for you.

Follow these steps to configure your routers:

1. In your /chapter_8/urls.py file, add the following `import` statements:

    ```
    # /becoming_a_django_entdev/chapter_8/urls.py
    ...
    from rest_framework import routers
    from .views import (
        EngineViewSet,
        SellerViewSet,
        VehicleViewSet,
        VehicleModelViewSet
    )
    ```

2. In that same file, add the following `router` and `register` statements:

    ```
    # /becoming_a_django_entdev/chapter_8/urls.py
    ...
    router = routers.DefaultRouter()
    router.register(r'engines', EngineViewSet)
    router.register(r'sellers', SellerViewSet)
    router.register(r'vehicles', VehicleViewSet)
    router.register(
        r'vehicle-models',
        VehicleModelViewSet
    )
    ```

3. In that same file, include the following `include` path for your routers:

    ```
    # /becoming_a_django_entdev/chapter_8/urls.py
    ...
    urlpatterns = [
        ...
        path('chapter-8/', include(router.urls)),
        path('api-auth/', include('rest_framework.urls')),
    ]
    ```

The `include(router.urls)` path shown previously is placed between the `api-auth` path and below your admin and home page paths. A router variable is defined for each model using the `routers.DefaultRouter()` class provided by the Django REST framework. Each `router.register()` function creates a set of URL patterns for that model. For example, where the `engines` path is shown in this URL, `http://localhost:8000/chapter-8/engines/`, that is what is defined in the first parameter of the first register function, as `r'engines'`. The router generated a set of URL patterns, one for each object in that table, which gets added to your `urlpatterns` list using the `path('chapter-8/', include(router.urls))` path. Adding `chapter-8` to this `path()` function is where we are telling Django to prefix `http://localhost:8000/chapter-8/` for every path created using this set of routers.

That's it; you now have a very basic API to use with the four models created in *Chapter 3, Models, Relations, and Inheritance*. To test your API and see the data that would be sent and received in each request, we will use the Browsable API next, which is provided with the Django REST framework.

Using the Browsable API

The Browsable API is a built-in tool that allows for easy browsing and testing of your API. It allows us to read and view data in JSON and API format. This section will teach us how to use and access this tool. When we added the `chapter-8` path to the URL routers in the previous section, we activated that path as what is called the **API root**, which provides all of the URLs available in your API, with some exceptions. Visit `http://localhost:8000/chapter-8/` to see these URLs, as depicted here:

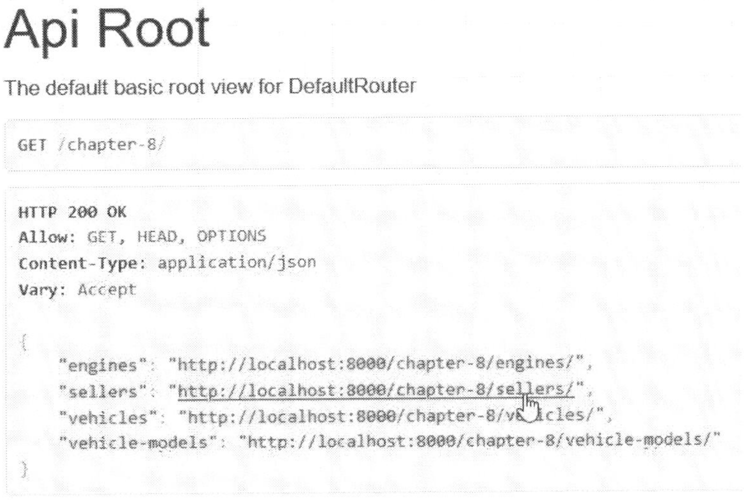

Api Root

The default basic root view for DefaultRouter

```
GET /chapter-8/
```

```
HTTP 200 OK
Allow: GET, HEAD, OPTIONS
Content-Type: application/json
Vary: Accept

{
    "engines": "http://localhost:8000/chapter-8/engines/",
    "sellers": "http://localhost:8000/chapter-8/sellers/",
    "vehicles": "http://localhost:8000/chapter-8/vehicles/",
    "vehicle-models": "http://localhost:8000/chapter-8/vehicle-models/"
}
```

Figure 8.2 – The Browsable API – API root

When building custom API endpoints, as we will do later in this chapter, you will likely not see them displayed in your API root. You'll see that the serializers for the groups, permissions, and content types have all been included with the code of this book. There is a dropdown at the top right of every main router path that we created, to switch between the two formats, API and JSON, as shown in the following screenshot:

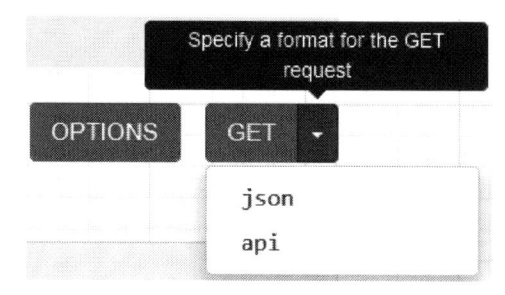

Figure 8.3 – The Browsable API – GET formats

If using `HyperlinkedModelSerializer` to construct your serializer classes, each object will be displayed as a clickable URL versus an ID that is not clickable. The hyperlinked version is shown in the following screenshot, when visiting the main URL path that the router created for the `Seller` model at `http://localhost:8000/chapter-8/sellers/`:

Figure 8.4 – The Browsable API – Sellers list

To view the same results as in the preceding screenshot, just change `ModelSerializer` to `HyperlinkedModelSerializer` in all of your serializer classes. Also, change your `SellerSerializer` class to exclude the fields shown in the following code in order to prevent an error indicating an incorrectly configured `lookup_field`, which is an advanced topic that goes beyond the scope of this book to resolve:

```
# /becoming_a_django_entdev/chapter_8/serializers.py
...
from rest_framework.serializers import (
    HyperlinkedModelSerializer,
    ModelSerializer
)
class SellerSerializer(HyperlinkedModelSerializer):
    class Meta:
        model = Seller
        #fields = '__all__'
        exclude = ['groups', 'user_permissions']
```

On each of the routers registered in the previous subsection, the main URL, such as the `http://localhost:8000/chapter-8/sellers/` link shown previously, will allow you to perform a create operation (a `POST` request) using the form at the bottom of that page. Just viewing this page performs a read operation (a `GET` request). A **detail page**, such as `http://localhost:8000/chapter-8/sellers/1/`, includes a form at the bottom of that page that will allow you to perform `PUT`, `PATCH`, and `DELETE` operations for the object being viewed, as shown here:

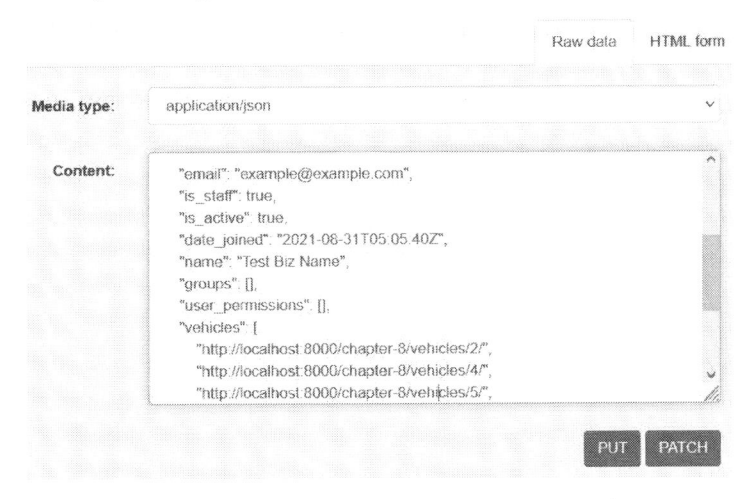

Figure 8.5 – The Browsable API – Sellers detail

By default, Django will show the **Raw data** tab that is shown in the preceding screenshot. The **HTML form** tab will only allow **PUT** operations. The **Delete** button is found at the top of this page, not where the **PUT** and **PATCH** buttons are located in the preceding screenshot. If you are logged into the Django admin site using a `Seller` that does not have superuser status, then that user/seller must have group or individual permission-level access granted in order to perform any of the CRUD operations on that model object. If a user/seller only has permission to do one thing and not the other, such as update but not delete or create and not update, then only those action buttons will appear. If you do not see any of the action buttons where you would expect to see them, double-check your permission settings for that user.

Now that we have a working API and have explored how to use the Browsable API, let's build pages that change content without needing to reload or redirect that page.

Building SPA-like pages

Single-Page App (**SPA**) pages are web pages where content gets updated within containers/nodes rather than reloading or redirecting the page to display that data. Usually, some of the work of the server is offloaded to the client's browser to perform these requests and/or render the HTML, usually with JavaScript or jQuery. When an event is triggered, such as the clicking of a button or submission of a form, JavaScript is used to obtain the data from the server and then render that content onto the page, wherever we want it to display.

In this exercise, we will use the API endpoint of the `Seller` created by the router, at `http://localhost:8000/chapter-8/sellers/1/`, to render JSON as a string within a container found in the body of a query page. The query page is just a standard page that uses JavaScript to communicate with an API endpoint.

Creating the view

In this subsection, we will build the view to handle a page where the user can enter a number relating to the ID of a `Seller` that they want to query. This will be known as the `GetSellerView` class and it will be used as the backbone for the remaining two exercises of this chapter.

To get started, take the following step:

1. Open the /chapter_8/views.py file and add the following GetSellerView class:

```python
# /becoming_a_django_entdev/chapter_8/views.py
...
from django.template.response import TemplateResponse
from django.views.generic import View
...
class GetSellerView(View):
    template_name = \
        'chapter_8/spa_pages/get_seller.html'

    def get(self, request, *args, **kwargs):
        context = {}
        return TemplateResponse(
            request,
            self.template_name,
            context
        )
```

In the preceding example, we are constructing a class-based view the same as we did in *Chapter 4, URLs, Views, and Templates*. The only thing we are doing differently here is we are not including the post() method; we only provided the get() method. Since we are not working with form submissions. The call-to-action button will be controlled using JavaScript as a button of type='button' and not type='submit'. There is no need to use the post() method when that is done. Also, we are creating a standard Django view class and not a REST API view class because this page is only used to communicate with API endpoints and not to serve as an API endpoint itself.

Now, let's create the template to format the HTML that gets rendered to the page.

Building the template

The previous subsection constructed the view for this exercise. This subsection will create the template that is used in our exercise.

Follow these steps to create your template:

1. Create the `get_seller.html` template file in the `/chapter_8/templates/chapter_8/spa_pages/` folder.

2. Earlier, in *Chapter 4, URLs, Views, and Templates*, we created a file called `/chapter_4/templates/chapter_4/base/base_template_1.html`. We will repurpose that file for this chapter. Go ahead and copy this file and any related template files, into your `chapter_8` app. Related template files include the header, footer, JavaScript, and CSS files that are referenced inside the `base_template_1.html` file. Place them in the `templates` and `static` directories in the same subfolders that you copied them from and then rename any mention of `chapter_4` and `chapter-4` to now reference `chapter_8` and `chapter-8` inside those files. You can always copy the `chapter_8` JavaScript, CSS, and template files found in the code of this book.

3. Next, in the `get_seller.html` file that you created in *step 1*, add the following code shown:

```
# /becoming_a_django_entdev/chapter_8/templates/chapter_8/spa_pages/get_seller.html
{% extends 'chapter_8/base/base_template_1.html' %}
{% load static %}
...
{% block body_content %}
    <form>
        <div class="field-box input-box">
            <label for="seller-id">Seller ID:</label>
            <div class="form-group">
                <input id="seller-id" type="text" />
                <span class="help-text">Please enter
                    the ID of the seller you want to
                        lookup</span>
            </div>
        </div>
        <button type="button" id="get-sellers" onclick
            ="$gotoSPA_Page()">
```

```
                    Get Seller Details</button>
        </form>

        <div id="details">
            <p>!!! No Details to Display !!!</p>
        </div>
{% endblock %}
```

4. This page is pretty simple. All we are doing is creating an input field of `type="text"` and then a button of `type="button"`. We gave the button an `onclick` attribute that fires off a JavaScript function called `$gotoSPA_Page()`. There is a `<div>` container with an attribute of `id="details"`, which contains a paragraph of text, indicating that there is nothing to display at this time.

The idea here is that we will replace all of the content of the `<div id="details">` container with the contents of what is received from the API request. A `<form>` container is not necessary for this particular setup; it has been added only to conform to the same CSS styles and HTML node structuring that was written in previous chapters. It is acceptable to deviate from this structure and create your own. Please use the preceding structure for the purpose of demonstrating this exercise.

Next, let's add the JavaScript responsible for performing an API request. We will be performing this action on the client side and not on the server side.

Writing the JavaScript

We don't need much JavaScript, just one small function that utilizes the native JavaScript `fetch()` function. This is almost identical to the jQuery `.ajax()` function, but it does differ slightly. The `fetch()` function differs in that it won't send `cross-origin` headers, the default mode is set to `no-cors`, and the `.ajax()` function sets the default mode to `same-origin`. That could be important depending on your project's requirements. The result of the request will then be displayed in the container with the CSS ID attribute of `details`, better known as the `details` container.

If you copied your JavaScript file from `chapter_4`, that file should be blank right now. Take the following steps to prepare your JavaScript. If you copied this file from `chapter_8` found in the code of the book, make sure to comment out all but the following code:

1. In your `/chapter_8/static/chapter_8/js/site-js.js` file, add the following code:

   ```
   # /becoming_a_django_entdev/chapter_8/static/chapter_8/js/site-js.js
   function $gotoSPA_Page() {
       const input = document.getElementById(
           'seller-id'
       );
       const container = document.getElementById(
           'details'
       );
       const id = input.value;
       var url = `/chapter-8/sellers/${id}/`;
   }
   ```

2. In the same `$gotoSPA_Page()` function, add the `fetch()` method just below your constants and variables, as shown:

   ```
   # /becoming_a_django_entdev/chapter_8/static/chapter_8/js/site-js.js
   function $gotoSPA_Page() {
       ...
       fetch(url, {
           method: 'GET',
           headers: {
               'Content-Type': 'application/json',
       }}).then(response => {
           return response.json();
       }).then(data => {
           container.innerHTML = JSON.stringify(data);
       });
   }
   ```

This is the `$gotoSPA_Page()` function that we configured in the previous subsection to execute when the `onclick` action of the **Get Seller Details** button is triggered. That's it! This is all the JavaScript that we need to complete a single task of retrieving an individual record from a database, using the API that we created.

In the preceding code, we wrote three constants, one called `input` to target the `input` field node and another called `container` to target the `details` container node. The third, called `id`, is used to capture the `value` of the input field at the time that this function is executed. The `url` variable is used to construct a string using the `value` of the `input` field as the keyword argument of that path converter. In JavaScript, this is known as concatenating strings, and because we are doing this, you need to make sure the backtick character (`` ` ``) is used instead of a single-quote character (`'`). They look almost identical; if you are just glancing at the preceding code, be careful. Here, we are telling that `url` variable to point to the URL created by the router of the `Seller` API.

The `fetch()` function accepts the `url` variable as the first positional argument of that function, which is a required argument. We then pass in additional optional arguments, such as the method that accepts these values (`GET`, `POST`, `PUT`, `PATCH`, and `DELETE`). All we want to demonstrate for now is retrieving the data, so we will use the `GET` method in this exercise. The headers argument is sometimes used to specify `'Content-Type'`; in this case, it is set to `'application/json'`. The method and headers shown previously are the defaults to using the `fetch()` function. They are not needed for the read operation since they are the default values but they are provided for illustrative purposes.

The `fetch()` function also uses the two `then()` methods shown previously; they each return a promise as a response object in JSON format. In simple terms, a promise is an object that consists of a state and a result. The second `then()` method uses the returned promise as the `data` variable, which we then use by writing a simple statement to place that `data` into the `details` container. We use the `JSON.stringify()` method to convert that JSON object into a readable format, particularly a string placed inside that container. Without using the `JSON.stringify()` function, we would only see a single object printed to the screen in brackets, which won't make much sense to us when we are looking at it. We will see screenshots of this in action in the subsection titled *First demo* of this chapter.

Currently, all we are doing is printing the string of JSON into the `<div>` container. We are not creating HTML nodes and/or CSS styles for those nodes. This is where you would have to either write additional JavaScript to do that for you manually or use the power of a JavaScript-based framework. Let's finish this exercise to see it working first, and then we will show you how to render that HTML and CSS on the server side, in the section titled *Writing custom API endpoints* of this chapter.

Using the async and await keywords

Traditional JavaScript is synchronous and single-threaded. It will run one process after the other and if one process gets hung up on, say, an API request where the server takes a long time to respond, then processes that take place after will hang up too. The problem is that a page can become unresponsive when this occurs. Asynchronous JavaScript allows functions to run side by side while other functions might be waiting for a response from the server. A `then()` function returning a promise is already an asynchronous function and is the reason why we gravitated toward using the `fetch()` function. JavaScript provides the `async` and `await` keywords, which make using and working with asynchronous functions a little bit easier, especially when your code begins to grow beyond these basic usage examples.

Take the following step to modify your JavaScript.

Make the highlighted changes in the following code block to your `$gotoSPA_Page()` function from the previous example:

```
# /becoming_a_django_entdev/chapter_8/static/chapter_8/js/site-js.js
function $gotoSPA_Page() {
    ...
    fetch(url, {
        method: 'GET',
        headers: {
            'Content-Type': 'application/json',
        }
    }).then(async(response) => {
        return await response.json();
    }).then(async(data) => {
        const thisData = await data;
        container.innerHTML = JSON.stringify(
            thisData
        );
    });
}
```

The variable and constants are still needed. They are left unchanged and are represented by the previous three-dot notation. We now have enough to almost run our project and demonstrate this exercise in action. We just need to map a URL pattern to the view we create next.

Mapping the URL pattern

Now, we are going to wire up the view that we created to a URL pattern, listening for the `/chapter-8/get-seller/` path.

Take the following step to configure your URL pattern.

In your `/chapter_8/urls.py` file, add the following path to the `urlpatterns` list:

```python
# /becoming_a_django_entdev/chapter_8/urls.py
from .views import ..., GetSellerView
...
urlpatterns = [
    ...
    path(
        'chapter-8/get-seller/',
        GetSellerView.as_view(),
        name = 'get-seller'
    ),
]
```

You also need to import the `GetSellerView` class to map to the preceding pattern.

Next, let's demonstrate this code in action.

First demo

To demonstrate the code depicted in the *Building SPA-like pages* exercise, follow these steps:

1. Navigate to the get seller page at `http://localhost:8000/chapter-8/get-seller/`, and it should look similar to the following screenshot:

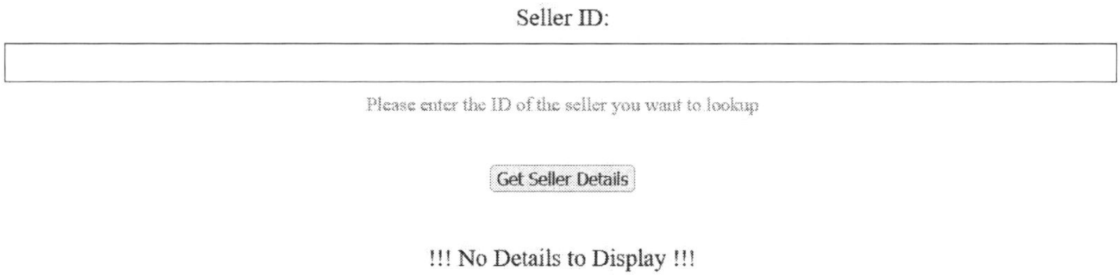

Seller ID:

Please enter the ID of the seller you want to lookup

Get Seller Details

!!! No Details to Display !!!

Figure 8.6 – Get seller page

384   Working with the Django REST Framework

2. Next, enter the number 1 into the input field shown in the preceding screenshot, relating to the ID of the first `Seller` in your database. Then, click the button labeled **Get Seller Details**.

3. To witness what is happening, in any major browser, right-click and select **Inspect element** or press *F12* on your keyboard. When that window opens, navigate to the **Network** tab if it didn't already navigate there for you. Here, you can watch each request that is performed in your browser as you press the preceding button. It is in this tab that you can see that your page is not reloading or redirecting in any way. Instead, you will see that it is just performing API requests. You can view the details of each request, such as what errors you are receiving, if any. You can navigate to the **Console** tab to view additional details about the JavaScript that is being executed, such as displaying any `console.log()` messages or errors that occur during runtime. If this action was successful, you should see the words **!!! No Details to Display !!!** replaced with the results of the request, as shown in the following screenshot:

> Get Seller Details
>
> {"url":"http://localhost:8000/chapter-8/sellers/1/","password":"pbkdf2_sha256$260000$SojQSyHvGi47zJh4moC5S6$vsWMBnbsHNyaY+gSWU9wzS1cc46tKPyt5y/XOoSgWJA=","last_login":"2021-11-30T17:39:50.308917Z","is_superuser":true,"username":"admin","first_name":"Admin","last_Biz Name","groups":[],"user_permissions":[],"vehicles":["http://localhost:8000/chapter-8/vehicles/2/","http://localhost:8000/chapter-8/vehicles/4/","http://localhost:8000/chapter-8/vehicles/5/","http://localhost:8000/chapter-8/vehicles/6/","http://localhost:8000/chapter-8/vehicles/7/","http://localhost:8000/chapter-8/vehicles/1/","http://localhost:8000/chapter-8/vehicles/3/"]}

Figure 8.7 – Get seller results – JSON.stringify()

> **Tip**
> You will need to have the **Network** tab opened at all times in order for data to be logged into this tab. Open this tab and then refresh the page to get accurate results as you perform these actions.

4. Now, look at the Network tab again, and you should see that we have two **/chapter-8/get-seller/** requests displayed in that list, as shown here:

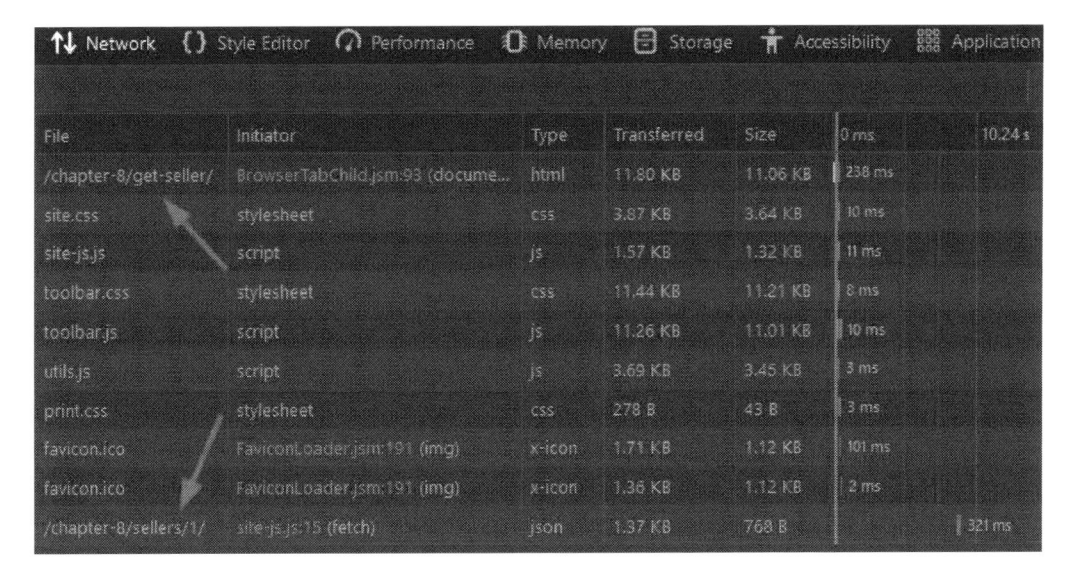

Figure 8.8 – Get seller page – Network tab

The first request, at the top of this list, was initiated by the browser when the user first loaded the page at `http://localhost:8000/chapter-8/get-seller/`. The second **request, /chapter-8/sellers/1/** at the very bottom of this list, shows that the initiator was the `site-js.js` file, which is the file where we wrote the `$gotoSPA_Page()` function. The last column shows the time it took to perform each request. All of the files in between are other assets, such as CSS and JavaScript files used by other apps in your project.

> **Note**
> There is no need to worry if you do not see these files; it just means they have not been loaded for one reason or another.

5. Next, remove the `JSON.stringify()` function used in the `$gotoSPA_Page()` function and just use the `thisData` variable instead. Then, refresh this page and perform the query one more time. What we should see is a single object, as shown here:

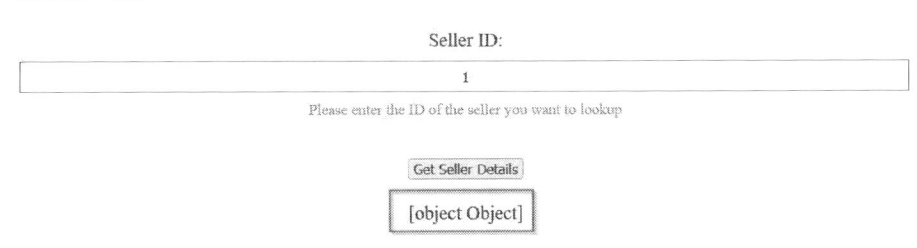

Figure 8.9 – Get seller results – standard

6. It is here that we can see why we had to use the `JSON.stringify()` function. Without this function, we can see the object is depicted as **[object Object]**, which is not very helpful.

Now that we have the client side of our API up and running, let's explore how to return rendered HTML instead of a string representation of the JSON object that is returned.

Writing custom API endpoints

Creating our own API endpoints is just as easy as writing another URL pattern. This section will teach us how to write our own API endpoints and practice sending preformatted HTML back to the client. You do not need to create all custom API endpoints to return preformatted HTML but we will practice doing that. Preformatting HTML only works well if the app communicating with your API does not need to restructure or restyle the HTML in any way after it has been received. This means the server/developer needs to know exactly how the client will use the data that it receives. No more JavaScript will be needed other than what was already written in the `$gotoSPA_Page()` function of the previous exercise. We will reuse that same function and just alter one or two things before we move forward. We will create a new view class and add permission logic to secure that endpoint from unwanted users accessing the API.

Let's begin working on this exercise in the same order as the previous exercise, starting with the view.

Creating the view

Follow these steps to create your `APIView` class:

1. In your `/chapter_8/views.py` file, add the `import` statements shown here:

    ```
    # /becoming_a_django_entdev/chapter_8/views.py
    ...
    from django.shortcuts import render
    from ..chapter_3.models import ..., Seller
    from rest_framework.permissions import IsAuthenticated
    from rest_framework.views import APIView
    ...
    ```

2. In that same file, create the `GetSellerHTMLView` class and `get()` method, as shown:

```python
# /becoming_a_django_entdev/chapter_8/views.py
...
class GetSellerHTMLView(APIView):
    permission_classes = [IsAuthenticated]
    template_name = 'chapter_8/details/seller.html'

    def get(self, request, format=None, id=0, *args,
        **kwargs):
        if request.user.is_authenticated and
            request.user.has_perm
                ('chapter_3.view_seller'):
            try:
                seller = Seller.objects.get(id=id)
            except Seller.DoesNotExist:
                seller = None
        else:
            seller = None

        context = {'seller': seller,}

        return render(
            request,
            self.template_name,
            context = context
        )
```

Here, the new `GetSellerHTMLView` class mimics the `GetSellerView` class that we created in the previous exercise, except now it uses the `APIView` class, provided by the Django REST framework. We only need to specify the `get()` method in this class as well; there is no need for the `post()` method since we are not working with form objects. We are only creating a view that handles the GET API method at this time, to view/read an object. The template we are mapping to this view is the `/chapter_8/templates/chapter_8/details/seller.html` file, which we will create in the next subsection. We need to pass `id=0` into the `get()` method, as is highlighted in the preceding code, in anticipation for how we will write the URL pattern for this API endpoint. We have to explicitly set `id=0` in the `get()` method since we are using the `APIView` class. If you are inheriting the regular `View`, `FormView`, `CreateView`, `UpdateView`, or `DeleteView` classes, you would only have to write `id` without the `=0` part. The same applies to the `format=None` argument, which is only needed when working with `APIView` classes and not regular `View` classes.

This approach is reliant on a user logged into your system, by accessing the currently logged-in user with the `request.user` object. Users outside your organization, who do not have access to the Django admin site, would have to use an authorization token to log in, which will be discussed later in this chapter. Even though we changed the AUTH_USER_MODEL setting in *Chapter 3, Models, Relations, and Inheritance*, to use the `Seller` model instead of the Django `User` model, we can still access the current user in the `request` object by using `request.user`. You do not have to use `request.seller`; in fact, that will result in an error. When using the `is_authenticated` property of that user, we can determine whether the user is actually logged in with an active session.

The `has_perm()` method is used to check the permissions of that user. In this case, we are checking whether the user has read/view permissions on a `Seller` model object using `'chapter_3.view_seller'`. If the user is authenticated and has the correct permissions, we are performing a query to look up the `Seller` object being searched by using the ID provided. If the user is not authenticated, then we are setting the `seller` variable to `None`, which we will use to compare whether or not it has a value within the template file.

That `seller` variable then gets passed into the `context` of the template being used, so that we can access its data. Also, we need to wrap the query statement in a `try/except` block, which is necessary to prevent runtime errors when the user searches for a `Seller` that does not exist. With the `try/except` block, we can set the value of `seller` to `None`, allowing the program to continue to run without errors. When used in the template, it will indicate that the search returned nothing.

We are using the `render()` method provided by the `django.shortcuts` library instead of the `TemplateResponse` class that we have been using up to now. This is because we want to return only a snippet of HTML and not an entire HTML page, with all of the bells and whistles that a page may have.

Now that the view is created, let's construct the template that uses that `seller` object as context.

Building the template

Follow these steps to prepare your template:

1. Create a file called `seller.html` in the `/chapter_8/templates/chapter_8/details/` directory.
2. Inside that file, add the following code:

    ```
    # /becoming_a_django_entdev/chapter_8/templates/
    chapter_8/details/seller.html
    {% load static %}

    <h1>Seller Details</h1>

    {% if seller %}
        <h2>{{ seller.first_name|safe }} {{
            seller.last_name|safe }}</h2>
        <h3>{{ seller.name|safe }}</h3>

        {% if seller.vehicles %}
            <ul>
                {% for vehicle in seller.vehicles.all %}
                    <li>{{ vehicle.fullname }}</li>
                {% endfor %}
            </ul>
        {% endif %}
    {% else %}
        <p>
            <b>No Seller to Display</b><br />
            <em>or you <b>DO NOT</b> have permission</em>
    ```

```
            </p>
        {% endif %}
```

Note that we are not extending any another template in this file. All we are doing is displaying simple text objects as a component of a page and not the page in whole. A conditional statement compares whether or not the `seller` object has a value, using the `{% if seller %}` statement. If no `seller` object exists, text is rendered showing the message **No Seller to Display**. If a `seller` does exist, then another conditional statement compares whether or not the `seller` has any `vehicles`, using the `{% if seller.vehicles %}` statement. If `vehicles` do exist, we iterate through all of the vehicle objects using the `{% for vehicle in seller.vehicles.all %}` statement. It is important that you add `.all` to the end of this statement; otherwise, you will receive errors. This is how you access any nested list of objects found in a single object within the Django template language. We use the `fullname` property method created in *Chapter 3, Models, Relations, and Inheritance*, to print the full name of the vehicle as an `<li>` HTML node object.

Now that we have our template, let's move on to modify the `$gotoSPA_Page()` function created in the previous exercise.

Modifying the JavaScript

Change the `url` variable in the existing `$gotoSPA_Page()` function to point to the new endpoint, which we will write in the next subsection as `` `/chapter-8/seller/${id}/` ``, as in a singular `seller` in contrast to the plural `sellers` that we used in the previous exercise.

Take the following step to modify your JavaScript function.

In the `$gotoSPA_Page()` function, make the following highlighted changes:

```
# /becoming_a_django_entdev/chapter_8/static/chapter_8/js/site-js.js
function $gotoSPA_Page() {
    ...
    var url = `/chapter-8/seller/${id}/`;

    fetch(url, {
        method: 'GET',
        headers: {
            'Content-Type': 'application/json',
```

```
    }}).then(async(response) => {
        return await response.text();
    }).then(async(data) => {
        container.innerHTML = await data;
    });
}
```

In the preceding code, we are still using the `async` and `await` keywords but you are not required to do so. The first three constants of the `$gotoSPA_Page()` function, `container`, `input`, and `id`, are left untouched and are represented by the preceding three-dot notation.

That's it; now all we have to do is create the URL pattern that will act as the API endpoint being used.

Mapping the URL pattern

Take the following step to map your URL pattern.

In your `/chapter_8/urls.py` file, add the following highlighted pattern, keeping the `get-seller` path that we previously wrote:

```
# /becoming_a_django_entdev/chapter_8/urls.py
from .views import (
    ...,
    GetSellerView,
    GetSellerHTMLView
)
...
urlpatterns = [
    ...
    path(
        'chapter-8/get-seller/',
        GetSellerView.as_view(),
        name = 'get-seller'
    ),
    path(
        'chapter-8/seller/<int:id>/',
        GetSellerHTMLView.as_view(),
```

```
        name = 'seller-detail'
    ),
]
```

We will still need that first URL pattern because it is the page that triggers the API request, containing the **Get Seller Details** button.

That should be it. Now, let's see what this looks like in action.

Second demo

To demonstrate this in action, follow these steps:

1. Make sure you are currently logged into the Django admin site at `http://localhost:8000/admin/`, with your superuser account.

2. Then, navigate to the get seller page at `http://localhost:8000/chapter-8/get-seller/` and it should look the same as before, in *Figure 8.6*, in the previous exercise.

3. Enter the number 1 into the input field on this page and then click the **Get Seller Details** button. Since you have superuser status, you should see the formatted HTML get injected into the `details` container found on this page, as is also shown here:

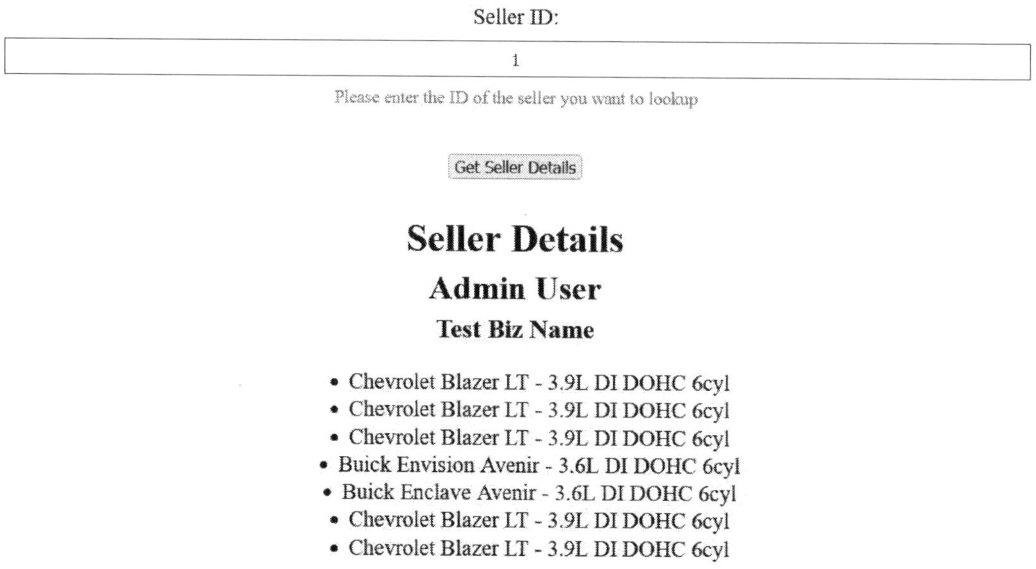

Seller ID:

| 1 |

Please enter the ID of the seller you want to lookup

Get Seller Details

Seller Details
Admin User
Test Biz Name

- Chevrolet Blazer LT - 3.9L DI DOHC 6cyl
- Chevrolet Blazer LT - 3.9L DI DOHC 6cyl
- Chevrolet Blazer LT - 3.9L DI DOHC 6cyl
- Buick Envision Avenir - 3.6L DI DOHC 6cyl
- Buick Enclave Avenir - 3.6L DI DOHC 6cyl
- Chevrolet Blazer LT - 3.9L DI DOHC 6cyl
- Chevrolet Blazer LT - 3.9L DI DOHC 6cyl

Figure 8.10 – Get seller page – custom API endpoint

If you have the Network tab of your browser tools open, you will also see that this action was performed without reloading or redirecting your page. You can style this to look exactly as you need it. For this example, we just used simple HTML nodes with minimal styling and formatting to demonstrate this exercise.

4. Next, add or create a new superuser account using the Django admin site at `http://localhost:8000/admin/chapter_3/seller/`. This can also be done through the command line just as we did in *Chapter 2, Project Configuration*.

5. In a different browser or incognito window, log in with the new superuser that you just created.

6. Next, navigate to the original superuser's edit page, found here: `http://localhost:8000/admin/chapter_3/seller/1/change/`. This is the user with the username `admin` and an ID of `1`.

7. In the **Permissions** section of this page, uncheck the **Superuser status** checkbox, restricting that user from doing anything. Leave the **Active** and **Staff status** checkboxes enabled. Make sure the **Chosen user permissions** box has nothing selected, as shown here:

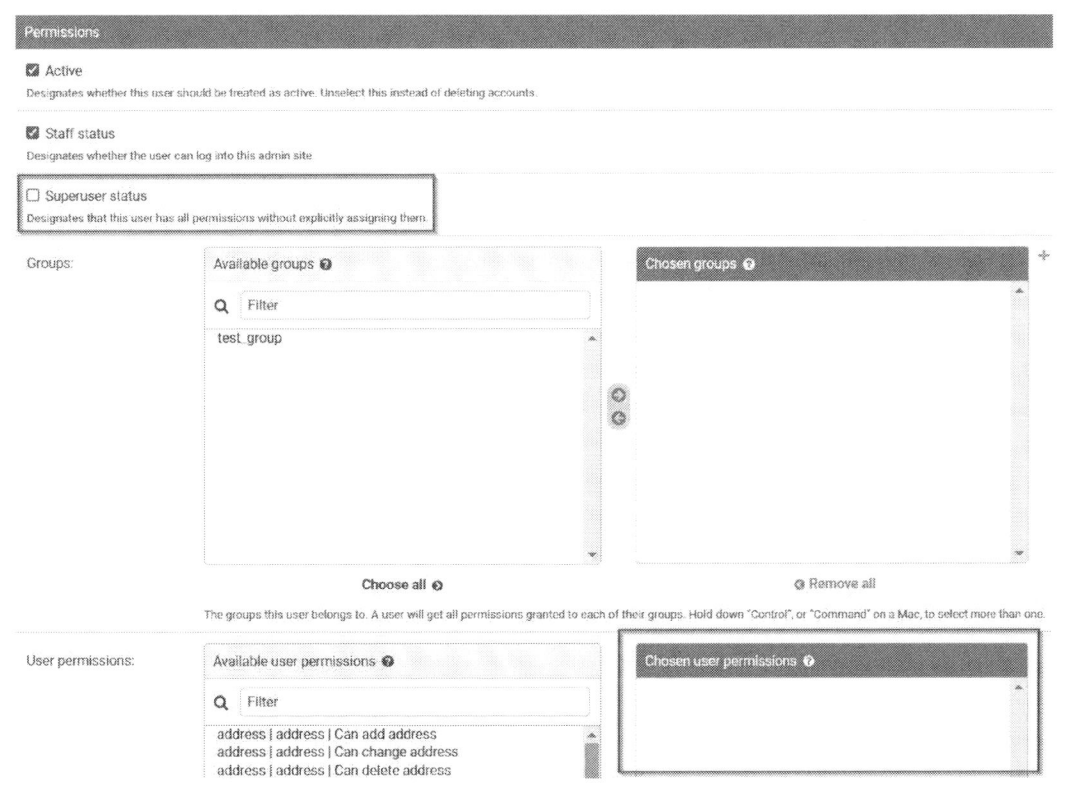

Figure 8.11 – Editing superuser permissions

8. In your first browser, where you are already logged in as `Seller` with the username of `admin`, navigate to `http://localhost:8000/chapter-8/get-seller/` in a different tab or refresh the existing tab if it is still open.

9. Enter the number 1 into the input field and then click the **Get Seller Details** button again. It should say that you do not have permission, as depicted in the following screenshot:

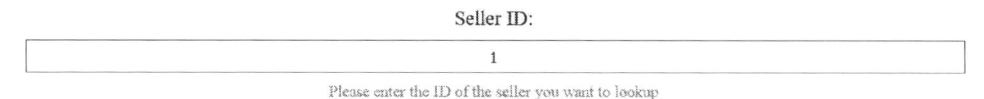

Seller ID:

| 1 |

Please enter the ID of the seller you want to lookup

Get Seller Details

Seller Details

No Seller to Display
*or you **DO NOT** have permission*

Figure 8.12 – Get seller page – permission restricted

10. This is because we removed the original permission for this user. The preceding message is the HTML that we wrote in the `/chapter_8/details/seller.html` template, specifically in the condition that checks whether the `seller` object has a value.

11. To ensure that the `seller` object has no value as a result of a permission issue and not because of a non-existent query, you can write `print()` statements in your code to provide that indicator for you. Go back to the other browser window that is open at `http://localhost:8000/admin/chapter_3/seller/1/change/`, where you are logged in with the new superuser created for this exercise, and edit the `admin` user one more time.

12. Go ahead and give that user the **chapter_3 | Seller | Can view Seller** permission, as depicted in the following screenshot:

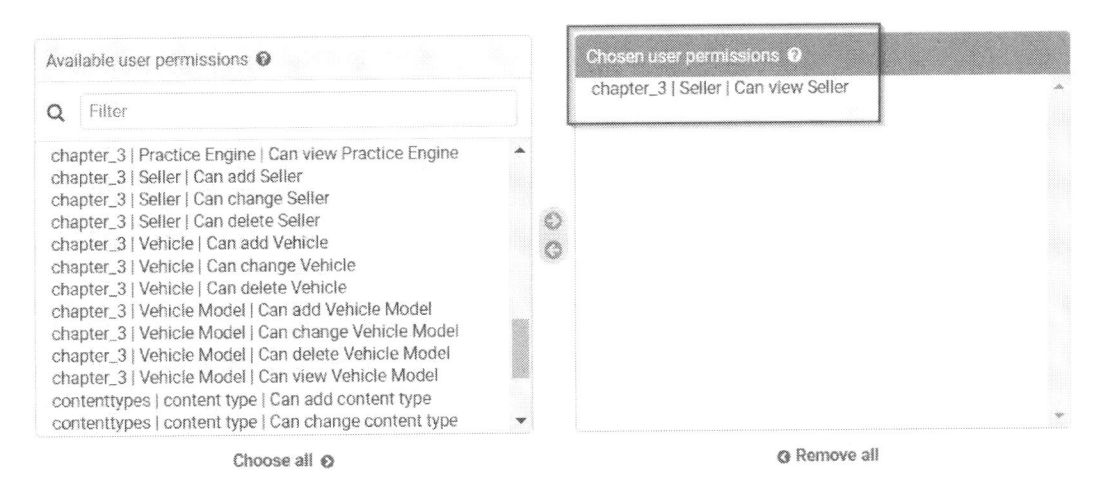

Figure 8.13 – Editing superuser permissions – view Seller

By doing this, we are giving this user the exact permission that we are checking for in the `GetSellerHTMLView` class. Remember to click the **Save** button at the bottom of this page before proceeding.

13. In your first browser, on the get seller page at `http://localhost:8000/chapter-8/get-seller/`, make sure you are still logged in with the original `admin` user and click the **Get Seller Details** button one more time. Here, we will see the same results that we saw before in *Figure 8.9*.

This exercise demonstrated how to use the Django template language to preformat HTML that is being returned in an API `GET` request. As we discovered working with this exercise, we actually need a user who is already logged into the Django admin site of the site before performing this operation. Without being logged in, this approach will not work. This is controlled by the **Staff status** checkbox, under the **Permissions** section when editing a user, which grants that user the ability to access the Django admin site. With the **Staff status** checkbox left unchecked, a user cannot access your system and thus, will not be able to use any of the permissions in the permission system.

> **Note**
> Switch your original superuser, with the username `admin`, back to its original settings, with the **Staff status** and **Superuser status** checkboxes enabled and the individual permissions and group permissions all removed. Make sure this is done and that you are logged in with this user before proceeding to the next exercise.

If you need to build an API that doesn't grant users access to your Django admin site, then authentication tokens will be needed. In the next exercise, we will use authentication tokens in combination with the Django REST framework to achieve this task.

Authenticating with tokens

In this exercise, we will be treating the API that we built earlier in this chapter as if it is now an API provided by a third party. Pretend for a moment that you did not build your API and we will practice authenticating by using a security token. Token security will be used in addition to the individual model permissions as we did in the previous exercise. This will be done whether you grant a user access to the Django admin site or not. That also means we will create a new user/seller for this exercise and then restrict that user's access to the Django admin site for demonstration purposes.

We will follow the same steps as the previous two exercises next.

Project configuration

This exercise requires a little bit of configuration inside the project's `settings.py` file before we can get started with the same steps as before.

Follow these steps to configure your project:

1. In your `settings.py` file, add the following app to your `INSTALLED_APPS` list, as well as the highlighted additions to the `REST_FRAMEWORK` setting, as shown:

    ```python
    # /becoming_a_django_entdev/settings.py
    INSTALLED_APPS = [
        ...
        'rest_framework',
        'rest_framework.authtoken',
    ]

    REST_FRAMEWORK = {
        'DEFAULT_AUTHENTICATION_CLASSES': (
            'rest_framework.authentication.TokenAuthentication',
            'rest_framework.authentication.SessionAuthentication',
        ),
        'DEFAULT_PERMISSION_CLASSES': [
    ```

```
            'rest_framework.permissions.
                DjangoModelPermissionsOrAnonReadOnly'
        ],
    }
```

The `rest_framework.authtoken` app is already installed in your virtual environment, so you do not have to install any additional `pip` packages. It comes standard when installing the `djangorestframework` package but does not get enabled in your project with just the basic settings needed for this framework. If we actually intend to use it, we have to add the two authentication classes shown previously to the `REST_FRAMEWORK` setting, telling the Django REST framework to use token authentication with all of its `APIView` classes. This means that tokens will be needed for any custom endpoints that we create using that `APIView` class, as well as all of the endpoints created using the `router` method from earlier in this chapter.

Endpoints created using the `router` method are all constructed using the `APIView` class. Adding the `SessionAuthentication` class means that we will enable the ability for users to log into the Django admin site to test that endpoint using the Browsable API. Without it, you will see a message indicating you are not authenticated. We will also leave the `DjangoModelPermissionsOrAnonReadOnly` permission class in the settings shown previously to continue to check for model-level permissions.

Please also make sure you are following proper Python indentation. There is not enough room to display that properly in the code shown previously.

2. Now that we have added new packages to our `settings.py` file for this project, we will need to run the following migrate command:

   ```
   (virtual_env) PS > python3 manage.py migrate
   ```

3. Next, make sure that you are logged into the Django admin site with your `admin` user and navigate to `http://localhost:8000/admin/chapter_3/seller/add/`, to create a new user/seller with the username `test`. You may already have a test user from a previous chapter. If so, just delete that user and recreate it for this exercise. This time, leave the **Staff status** and **Superuser status** checkboxes unchecked. Give that new user only one permission, the same **chapter_3 | Seller | Can view Seller** permission that we used before.

4. Next, navigate to the URL `http://localhost:8000/admin/authtoken/tokenproxy/` and add a new token for the user you just created. This can also be done in your command-line window or terminal by executing the following command:

```
(virtual_env) PS > python manage.py drf_create_token test
```

5. Copy the token key that was created for that user and save it for later, in Notepad or something.

Next, we will proceed in the same order as we did for the last two exercises.

Creating the view

Now, we need to create a new view class for this exercise. It will be used for a new endpoint that we will add to the API before we treat it like someone else built it for us. This endpoint will only return standard JSON data and will not return the preformatted HTML that we practiced doing in the previous exercise. JSON is what is traditionally returned in API requests.

Follow these steps to prepare your view class:

1. In your `/chapter_8/views.py` file, add the following highlighted `import` statement and the `GetSellerWithTokenView` class shown:

    ```
    # /becoming_a_django_entdev/chapter_8/views.py
    ...
    from django.http import JsonResponse
    from rest_framework.permissions import IsAuthenticated
    from rest_framework.views import APIView
    from .serializers import SellerSerializer
    from ..chapter_3.models import ..., Seller
    ...
    class GetSellerWithTokenView(APIView):
        permission_classes = [IsAuthenticated]
    ```

2. Inside that same `GetSellerWithTokenView` class, add the following `get()` method and conditional statement:

    ```
    # /becoming_a_django_entdev/chapter_8/views.py
    ...
    class GetSellerWithTokenView(APIView):
    ```

```python
    ...
    def get(self, request, format=None, id=0, *args,
        **kwargs):
        seller = None
        req_user = request._user

        if req_user.has_perm('chapter_3.view_seller'):
            perm_granted = True

            try:
                seller = Seller.objects.get(id=id)
            except Seller.DoesNotExist:
                pass
        else:
            perm_granted = False
```

3. Inside that same get() method, add the following context, serializer, new_context, and return statements below what you just added to that method:

```python
# /becoming_a_django_entdev/chapter_8/views.py
...
class GetSellerWithTokenView(APIView):
    ...
    def get(self, request, format=None, id=0, *args,
        **kwargs):
        ...
        context = {
            'request': request,
            'seller': seller,
        }

        seller = SellerSerializer(
            seller,
            context = context
        )

        new_context = {
```

```
                'seller': seller.data,
            'perm_granted': perm_granted
        }

        return JsonResponse(new_context)
```

> **Note**
> When using the `JsonResponse()` object to return data as formatted JSON in your endpoint in this way, your endpoint will not be readily available in the Browsable API tool. If you wish for it to be accessible via that tool, use `Response()` instead. Keep in mind that it may alter the way developers work with the returned data.

In the preceding class, we are following the same logic format as was used in the `GetSellerHTMLView` class, written in the previous exercise. We added a property called `permission_classes`, which uses the `IsAuthenticated` class. This is needed to work with token authentication. We added an additional query to the `get()` method. The logic here is that we are using two items added to the request headers when the request is sent, using the `fetch()` JavaScript function. Those two headers are `HTTP_AUTHORIZATION` and `HTTP_USER`, which we will soon add to our JavaScript function.

The `request._user` item is used to look up the user associated with that `request`, whether the user is logged into the Django admin site or is passed into the request via the `HTTP_USER` header, that being the `test` user created for this exercise, the user we will associate with the API request. We are looking up that user to compare individual model permissions using the same `has_perm()` method from the previous exercise. If the API request user is found, then we are performing the same logic as before to check whether that user has permission to view a `seller` object. This time, we removed the `is_authenticated` property from that conditional statement, as we are now relying on this class's token authentication. If you granted your `test` user the ability to view a `seller` object, the logic continues to look up the `seller` with the ID provided in that input field, the same as before. If your `test` user is not granted the ability to view a `seller` object, then the `perm_granted` context item will return `False`, to provide an indicator in the data being returned to us.

The context was broken up into two different items, shown in *step 3*, because the request is needed in the context when using `SellerSerializer`. Then, we are removing that request from the final context being returned as `JsonResponse()`.

Building the template

This exercise does not require a brand-new template. It will be returning only JSON and is not following the preformatted HTML example.

Modifying the JavaScript

We will be using the same JavaScript example provided in the *Modifying the JavaScript* subsection under the *Writing custom API endpoints* section.

Take the following step to modify your JavaScript for this exercise.

In the same JavaScript file, make the following highlighted changes to your existing `$gotoSPA_Page()` function:

```
# /becoming_a_django_entdev/chapter_8/static/chapter_8/js/site-js.js
function $gotoSPA_Page() {
    ...
    var url = `/chapter-8/sellertoken/${id}/`;

    fetch(url, {
        method: 'GET',
        headers: {
            'Content-Type': 'application/json',
            'Authorization': 'Token your_token',
            'User': 'test'
    }}).then(async(response) => {
        return await response.text();
    }).then(async(data) => {
        container.innerHTML = await data;
    });
}
```

In this example, we are leaving the first three constants, `container`, `input`, and `id`, the same as they have been written in previous examples and represented by the preceding three-dot notation. We are changing the `url` variable to point to a new path that we will create shortly, `` `/chapter-8/sellertoken/${id}/` ``. The rest of the `fetch()` function is left the same as before, where we are returning the result as preformatted HTML instead of JSON. The only thing different is that we are adding the `'Authorization'` and `'User'` items to the `headers` of this request. The value of the `'Authorization'` item is the value of the token that was created, the one you were asked to copy earlier; paste that in place of the preceding `your_token` shown. The value of the `'User'` item is the username of the new user/seller that you just created, the one assigned to the token that you are providing.

> **Note**
> Tokens should *never* be kept in a JavaScript file, as is done in the preceding example. An explanation for why this is done in the preceding example is provided in the subsection titled *Third demo* at the end of this exercise.

Mapping the URL pattern

We are almost done! We just need to map the endpoint that we are communicating with to our new view class.

Take the following step to map your URL pattern.

In your `/chapter_8/urls.py` file, add the following path. You can leave the other paths that have already been created, as depicted:

```
# /becoming_a_django_entdev/chapter_8/urls.py
from .views import ..., GetSellerView, GetSellerHTMLView,
    GetSellerWithTokenView
...
urlpatterns = [
    ...
    path(
        'chapter-8/get-seller/',
        GetSellerView.as_view(),
        name = 'get-seller'
    ),
    path(
        'chapter-8/seller/<int:id>/',
```

```
            GetSellerHTMLView.as_view(),
            name = 'seller-detail'
    ),
    path(
        'chapter-8/sellertoken/<int:id>/',
        GetSellerWithTokenView.as_view(),
        name = 'seller-token-detail'
    ),
]
```

That's it; let's demonstrate this code in action next.

Third demo

Follow these steps to see this in action:

1. Open a new incognito window and navigate to `http://localhost:8000/chapter-8/get-seller/`. The reason I am asking you to open an incognito window is to ensure that you are not logged into the Django admin site with any user for this test run. You can also navigate to `http://localhost:8000/admin/` to double-check, making sure that you are not logged in.

2. Next, enter the number 1 into the input field and click the **Get Seller Details** button. If everything is successful, you should now see the `seller` data in JSON format, including the extra `perm_granted` context that we passed in, as shown in the following screenshot:

Seller ID:

```
1
```

Please enter the ID of the seller you want to lookup

Get Seller Details

{"seller": {"url": "http://localhost:8000/chapter-8/sellers/1/", "password": "pbkdf2_sha256$320000$ND2TqVsrMvvFsoYfRdBDua$/GFviMELhen("last_login": "2022-02-03T16:27:02.309956Z", "is_superuser": true, "username": "admin", "first_name": "Admin", "last_name": "User", "email": "example@example.com", "is_staff": true, "is_active": true, "date_joined": "2021-08-31T05:05:40Z", "name": "Test Biz Name", "groups": [], "user_permissions": [], "vehicles": ["http://localhost:8000/chapter-8/vehicles/2/", "http://localhost:8000/chapter-8/vehicles/4/", "http://localhost:8000/chapter-8/vehicles/5/", "http://localhost:8000/chapter-8/vehicles/6/", "http://localhost:8000/chapter-8/vehicles/7/", "http://localhost:8000/chapter-8/vehicles/1/", "http://localhost:8000/chapter-8/vehicles/3/"]}, "perm_granted": true}

Figure 8.14 – Get seller page – custom API endpoint with token auth

You could also add `print()` statements to your code to verify if and when each condition is actually met. Additional `print()` statements and comments providing details have been included with the code of this book.

> **Note**
> You will see hyperlinked vehicles in the preceding example if you are inheriting the `HyperlinkedModelSerializer` class in your serializers. If you are still using the `ModelSerializer` class, only numeric IDs will be displayed.

3. If you were not successful or you enter an incorrect token in your JavaScript file, then you will see an **Invalid token** message returned to you. Go ahead and enter an invalid token into the `fetch()` function just to see the **Invalid token** message display, and then refresh your get seller page, enter the number 1 into the input field again, and click the **Get Seller Details** button. The invalid token message should look something as in the following screenshot:

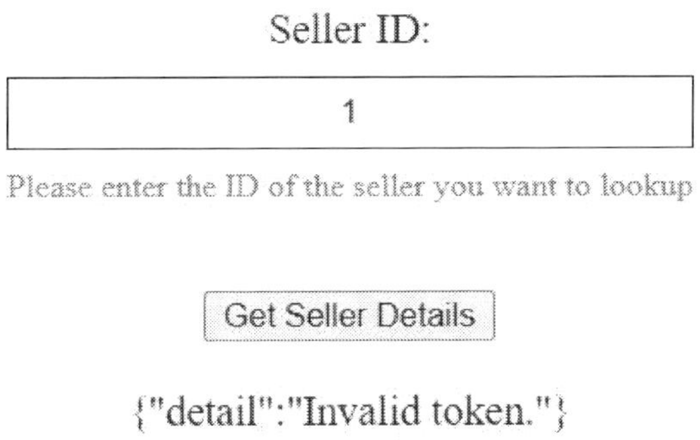

Seller ID:

[1]

Please enter the ID of the seller you want to lookup

[Get Seller Details]

{"detail":"Invalid token."}

Figure 8.15 – Get seller page – invalid token

> **Important Note**
>
> In a real-world example, the token should *never* be kept directly in the JavaScript file or even a Python file, if you are using the `requests` package. Instead, you should consider creating an additional API endpoint that utilizes the built-in token generator called `obtain_auth_token`, as discussed here: https://www.django-rest-framework.org/api-guide/authentication/#generating-tokens. The token generator works by accepting a username and password that is attached to the headers of the first API request and then receives a newly created token in return. Then, a second API request is used to execute the action desired by attaching the token received from the first request to the second request's headers. The Django REST framework does the rest of the work to authenticate that request using the credentials provided. The examples provided in this exercise are intended only to demonstrate how to perform requests after the token has already been received. The approach of generating tokens requires the use and knowledge of signals, which goes beyond the scope of this book.

If using the double-request approach as noted in the preceding information box, you can now let developers of third-party apps communicate with your API without needing to create user accounts. However, you can still create a user in your system for that third-party user in order to keep using the granular permission levels of your system as was done throughout this exercise. The path you take is determined by the requirements of your project.

Summary

The examples provided throughout this chapter demonstrate a simple way to construct and work with your newly created API, in a variety of ways! If you want to give your app an SPA-like feel, the simplest implementation is to use the vanilla JavaScript `fetch()` function or the jQuery `ajax()` function. Instead of writing your own actions with either of these two functions, you could settle upon using a JavaScript-based framework, such as React, AngularJS, or Vue.js, just to name a few. The JavaScript-based frameworks can format and style your HTML on the client side. One of the template-based approaches provided in this chapter also demonstrates how this work can be transferred from the client side onto the server side. This provides you with numerous tools in your toolbox, in regard to building and working with an API.

We also learned how to work with authentication tokens and discovered that we can still work with tokens when formatting HTML on the server side. However, the token approach does require additional, more advanced topics of Django and security measures before being able to fully implement that approach on a live site. The Django REST framework is intended to be the backend of an API and is designed to work with any frontend that a team settles upon.

In the next chapter, we'll explore how to test our project and make sure what has been written does actually work. To do that, we will explore how to write automated test scripts, and then install a new package that provides even more tools, as well as learning how to use them.

9
Django Testing

This chapter is dedicated to testing and debugging a Django project. Django has a wide range of test classes built into its framework that are used to write automated test scripts. As we build each app and/or component of a project, we can run one command at any time to ensure that every component still works as it should. This is great for **regression testing**, which means testing a new or changed component, making sure that it does not affect the intended behavior of existing components or the entire system as a whole. For most of what we will cover in this chapter, we do not need to install any third-party packages. The last thing we will cover is the **Django Debug Toolbar (DjDT)**, which does require us to install a third-party package to use.

In this chapter, we will cover the following topics:

- Writing automated test scripts
- Creating unit test cases
- Testing view classes and their get and post methods
- Testing view classes that require user authentication
- Testing Django REST API endpoints
- Installing the DjDT, a tool used for debugging

Technical requirements

To work with the code in this chapter, the following tools will need to be installed on your local machine:

- Python version 3.9 – used as the underlying programming language for the project
- Django version 4.0 – used as the backend framework of the project
- pip package manager – used to manage third-party Python/Django packages

We will continue to work with the solution created in *Chapter 2*, *Project Configuration*. However, it is not necessary to use the Visual Studio IDE. The main project itself can be run using another IDE or run independently using a terminal or command-line window from within the project root folder, which is where the `manage.py` file resides. Whatever editor or IDE you are using, a virtual environment will also be needed to work with the Django project. Instructions for how to create a project and virtual environment can be found in *Chapter 2*, *Project Configuration*. You will need a database to store the data contained in your project. PostgreSQL was chosen for the examples in the previous chapters; however, any database type that you choose for your project can be used to work with the examples in this chapter.

We will also be using data that is in the form of a Django fixture, provided in *Chapter 3*, *Models, Relations, and Inheritance*, in the subsection titled *Loading the chapter_3 data fixture*. Make sure the `chapter_3` fixture is loaded into your database. If this has already been done, then you may skip the next command. If you have already created the tables found in *Chapter 3*, *Models, Relations, and Inheritance*, and have not loaded that fixture yet, then run the following command, after activating your virtual environment:

```
(virtual_env) PS > python manage.py loaddata chapter_3
```

All of the code created in this chapter can be found in the GitHub repository for this book: https://github.com/PacktPublishing/Becoming-an-Enterprise-Django-Developer. The bulk of the code depicted in this chapter can be found in the /becoming_a_django_entdev/becoming_a_django_entdev/chapter_9/ directory.

Check out the following video to see the *Code in Action*: https://bit.ly/3yh0tW6.

Preparing for this chapter

Start by creating a new app in your project called `chapter_9` by following the steps discussed in *Chapter 2, Project Configuration*, in the subsection titled *Creating a Django app*. As discussed in that section, don't forget to change the value of the `name =` variable for your app class found in the `/becoming_a_django_entdev/becoming_a_django_entdev/chapter_9/apps.py` file to now point to the path where you installed your app. Be sure to also include this app in the `INSTALLED_APPS` variable found in the `settings.py` file as well.

In the main `urls.py` file of the site, add the following two paths:

```
# /becoming_a_django_entdev/urls.py
...
urlpatterns = [
    path(
        '',
        include(
            'becoming_a_django_entdev.chapter_9.urls'
        )
    ),
    path(
        '',
        include(
            'becoming_a_django_entdev.chapter_8.urls'
        )
    ),
]
```

These point to the Chapter 9 URL patterns that we will be creating for this chapter and includes all of the URL patterns that we created for *Chapter 8, Working with the Django REST Framework*. We will need the API endpoints that we created in the previous chapter for some of the REST API test exercises. Make sure the Chapter 9 URLs take precedence over the other by placing them first in this list.

In your `/chapter_9/urls.py` file, you should add the following paths. These paths were used in the exercises in *Chapter 4, URLs, Views, and Templates*:

```
# /becoming_a_django_entdev/chapter_9/urls.py
from django.urls import path, register_converter
from django.views.generic import TemplateView
```

```python
from ..chapter_4.converters import YearConverter
from ..chapter_4.views import (
    practice_year_view,
    VehicleView
)

register_converter(YearConverter, 'year')
urlpatterns = [
    path(
        '',
        TemplateView.as_view(
            template_name = 'chapter_9/index.html'
        )
    ),
    path(
        'my_year_path/<year:year>/',
        practice_year_view,
        name = 'year_url'
    ),
    path(
        'vehicle/<int:id>/',
        VehicleView.as_view(),
        name = 'vehicle-detail'
    ),
]
```

Instead of including all of the URLs from *Chapter 4, URLs, Views, and Templates*, we are only providing you with the ones that are needed. The reason behind this is that in *Chapter 4, URLs, Views, and Templates*, we discussed several variations of writing the same paths for learning purposes. To prevent confusion, only the variation of the URL patterns that are needed to satisfy the type of tests that we are about to perform is included in the preceding code.

Copy the `index.html` file from the code of the book found in the `/chapter_9/templates/chapter_9` directory into your project in the same directory. Also, copy the `chapter_9` CSS and JavaScript files from the code of the book into your project.

> **Note**
> If you cloned the entire repository of code provided with this book and the DjDT is already turned on/enabled, please disable it before running any of the test cases that we will soon create. Look for the **Turn Off/Comment Out For the First Half of Chapter 9** comments throughout the settings and URL files. That tool will be discussed after working through some test cases.

Next, let's discuss what automated testing is in Django and how it is used.

Understanding automated testing in Django

Automated testing is helpful for a number of reasons. Developers use it when refactoring old components that need to be modified. Test scripts are used to regression test older components to see whether they were affected negatively by any new additions. Django offers several test classes that are an extension of the standard Python library called `unittest`. You can learn more about this package here: https://docs.python.org/3/library/unittest.html. The Django test classes are all found in the `django.test` library. The most commonly used class is `TestCase`.

The following list depicts all of the test classes that are available in the `django.test` library:

- **SimpleTestCase** – this is the smallest test possible, extending the Python `unittest` library. This class will not interact with a database.
- **TransactionTestCase** – this test extends the `SimpleTestCase` class and allows for database transactions.
- **TestCase** – this test extends the `TransactionTestCase` class and includes features that allow for better interactions with a database. It is the most commonly used test class.
- **LiveServerTestCase** – this test extends the `TransactionTestCase` class and allows the use of test clients other than the test client provided by Django, such as Appium, Cypress, Selenium, Serenity, or any of the dozens of other ones available. It will actually spin up a live Django server in the background to run the test and then destroy that server upon completion.
- **SeleniumTestCase** – this test extends the `LiveServerTestCase` class. This class is built specifically for using the Selenium test framework as the test client due to how popular it is.

Writing test classes is just like writing any other Python class. They must consist of at least a test method, and they usually contain a `setUp()` method, but this method is not required. Test methods have the word `test_` prepended to their name, for example, `test_one()` and `test_two()`. The `setUp()` method is used to prepare your environment and/or database for any of the test methods in that class. If a class has more than one test method, an object created in one test method will not be accessible in the other test method. If you need an object in both test methods of a class, you need to place that logic in the `setUp()` method.

Test classes may also have a `tearDown()` method, which will perform any cleanup tasks necessary after a test has been performed and before moving on to the next test. `tearDown()` is not used very often seeing as Django will automatically destroy any servers and databases created during the test after the test has completed. Other methods are available as well and you can learn more about them here: https://docs.djangoproject.com/en/4.0/topics/testing/tools/.

> **Tip**
> Selenium is a third-party library of tools that simulates actual browsers, allowing you to run automated tests in many different browser types and versions. It is not necessary to perform basic/standard test cases and this is considered an advanced topic beyond the scope of this book. To learn more about Selenium, visit https://www.selenium.dev/, https://pypi.org/project/selenium/, and https://django-selenium.readthedocs.io/en/latest/.

Every time a new app is created in Django, such as when all of the chapter apps were created prior to this chapter, you may have noticed that a `tests.py` file was automatically created for you in that app directory. This file is created whether you are using the IDE or command line to create the new app. We have just been disregarding this file as it served no purpose to us, until now. The code in this chapter will live almost entirely within the `tests.py` file. If you are using the Visual Studio IDE, you may have also noticed that it created a `SimpleTest(TestCase)` class in your `tests.py` file. Apps created through the command-line window or terminal will not have created this class for you. Go ahead and comment this out or delete it before proceeding so that we only see the results pertaining to the test(s) at hand.

Now that we have a better understanding of how tests are performed, let's dive in and begin testing next.

Getting started with unit testing

Unit testing is the act of testing the smallest components possible, such as logic statements, for example, 1 + 1 equals 2. That is what the `SimpleTest` class that the Visual Studio IDE created for us is actually testing for. These can be utility methods, conditional or comparison statements, Django models, forms, email messages, and so on.

Let's practice writing a simple test script and then write another to include our models.

Basic unit test script

In this exercise, we will write a very basic test class that executes two different test methods. These tests will not interact with a database and are only used to compare `True` and `False` statements. The class as a whole can be used as a boilerplate when creating new test classes and modified as needed.

Follow these steps:

1. In your `/chapter_9/tests.py` file, add the structure of the class, as shown:

    ```python
    # /becoming_a_django_entdev/chapter_9/tests.py
    from django.test import SimpleTestCase

    class TestingCalibrator(SimpleTestCase):
        def setUp(self):
            pass

        def tearDown(self):
            pass

        def test_pass(self):
            '''Checks if True == True, Value set to
                True'''
            self.assertTrue(True)

        def test_fail(self):
            '''Checks if False == False, Value set to
                True'''
            self.assertFalse(True)
    ```

The `test_pass(self)` method is used to compare whether `True` actually equals `True` when `True` is passed into the function; it is intended to be a successful test. The `test_fail(self)` method is used to compare whether `False` equals `False` when `True` is passed into the function; it is intended to produce a failure.

2. Now, in your command-line window or terminal, navigate to your project's root directory and activate your virtual environment but do not run the project at this time. Instead, execute the Django test command depicted in the following code, which will only execute the tests found in your `chapter_9` app:

```
(virtual_env) PS > python manage.py test becoming_a_
django_entdev.chapter_9
```

If everything runs as intended in this exercise, it should tell you in your command-line window that two tests were performed and which one failed, as shown:

```
Found 2 test(s).
System check identified no issues (0 silenced).
F.
============================================================
FAIL: test_fail (becoming_a_django_entdev.chapter_9.
tests.TestingCalibrator)
Checks if False == False, Value set to True
------------------------------------------------------------
Traceback (most recent call last):
  File "C:\Projects\Packt\Repo\becoming_a_django_entdev\
becoming_a_django_entdev\chapter_9\tests.py", line 49,
in test_fail
    self.assertFalse(True)
AssertionError: True is not false
------------------------------------------------------------
Ran 2 tests in 0.001s

FAILED (failures=1)
Destroying test database for alias 'default'...
```

On the third line in the preceding output, it printed `F..`. The capital `F` represents one test was a failure and the period represents one test was a success. It then prints each of the tests that failed below that line. For each test that it prints out, Django includes the comment written for that test case, such as `'''Checks if False == False, Value set to True'''`. Make use of the triple double-quote or single-quote comment notation to include helpful information when your test does fail. It then provides traceback information, indicating the cause and location of the error or failure. You can also include `print()` statements within these test methods if you want to provide additional information regarding a particular test.

> **Tip**
> To run the tests for all of the apps included in your project, run the following command:
> `(virtual_env) PS > python manage.py test`
>
> Also, if you break your single-line double-quote or single-quote comment into a multiline comment, only the first line of that comment will appear in your command-line window.

Now, comment out or delete the `TestingCalibrator` class before moving on to the next exercise.

Testing Django models

In this exercise, we will use the `TestCase` class because we will be connecting to a database. The database that the test client spins up for us will not affect any of the data found in all local or remote databases. Follow these steps:

1. In your `/chapter_3/models.py` file, make sure the (8, 'Jeep') value exists in the MAKE_CHOICES list of choices:

    ```
    # /becoming_a_django_entdev/chapter_3/models.py
    ...
    MAKE_CHOICES = (
        ...
        (8, 'Jeep'),
        ...
    )
    ```

2. In your /chapter_9/tests.py file, add the following import statements:

```python
# /becoming_a_django_entdev/chapter_9/tests.py
from django.test import ..., TestCase
from djmoney.money import Money
from ..chapter_3.models import (
    Engine,
    Seller,
    Vehicle,
    VehicleModel
)
```

3. In that same file, add the following class and setUp() method:

```python
# /becoming_a_django_entdev/chapter_9/tests.py
...
class ModelUnitTestCase(TestCase):
    def setUp(self):
        model = VehicleModel.objects.create(
            name = 'Grand Cherokee Laredo 4WD',
            make = 8
        )
        engine = Engine.objects.create(
            name = '3.6L FI FFV DO',
            vehicle_model = model
        )
        vehicle = Vehicle.objects.create(
            vin = 'aa890123456789012',
            sold = False,
            price = Money(39875, 'USD'),
            make = 8,
            vehicle_model = model,
            engine = engine
        )
        seller = Seller.objects.create_user(
            'test',
            'testing@example.com',
            'testpassword',
```

```
                is_staff = True,
                is_superuser = True,
                is_active = True,
                name = 'Chapter 9 Seller 1'
            )
            seller.vehicles.set([vehicle])
```

4. In that same `ModelUnitTestCase` class, add the following test method:

```
# /becoming_a_django_entdev/chapter_9/tests.py
...
class ModelUnitTestCase(TestCase):
    ...
    def test_full_vehicle_name(self):
        vehicle_1 = Vehicle.objects.get(
            vin = 'aa890123456789012'
        )
        self.assertEqual(
            vehicle_1.full_vehicle_name(),
            'Jeep Grand Cherokee Laredo 4WD - 3.6L FI
                FFV DO'
        )
```

The preceding `setUp(self)` method will create a `VehicleModel`, `Engine`, `Vehicle`, and `Seller` model object that we imported from the `chapter_3` app. The `setUp()` method creates these objects before any of the test cases in that class are executed. We create each related object as a variable and then use that variable to assign as the related object of the next object that we create. The `Seller` object uses the same `create_user()` method that was introduced in *Chapter 6, Exploring the Django Admin Site*, to create a new `Seller` with the hashed password and date fields formatted for us. We created only one test, called `test_full_vehicle_name()`, which looks up the vehicle that was created upon setup by the vin field value specified. It uses the `full_vehicle_name()` method that we created in *Chapter 3, Models, Relations, and Inheritance*, to return to us the custom-formatted name of that newly created vehicle. The expected value is `Jeep Grand Cherokee Laredo 4WD - 3.6L FI FFV DO`, which is in the format `{{ make }} {{ model }} - {{ engine }}`. If the resulting value does not match that value, the test will fail.

5. Now, execute the run test command shown here:

```
(virtual_env) PS > python manage.py test becoming_a_
django_entdev.chapter_9
```

If you commented out all the other tests prior to this one, you should see the results shown here:

```
Found 1 test(s).
Creating test database for alias 'default'...
System check identified no issues (0 silenced).
.
----------------------------------------------------------
Ran 1 test in 0.229s

OK
Destroying test database for alias 'default'...
```

6. Go ahead and change the expected value found in the `self.assertEqual()` function of *step 4* previously to something that doesn't exist, and then rerun your test command one more time. Now, you should see a failure message, as depicted here:

```
Found 1 test(s).
Creating test database for alias 'default'...
System check identified no issues (0 silenced).
F
==========================================================
FAIL: test_full_vehicle_name
----------------------------------------------------------
Traceback (most recent call last):
  File "C:\Projects\Packt\Repo\becoming_a_django_entdev\
becoming_a_django_entdev\chapter_9\tests.py", line 88,
in test_full_vehicle_name
    self.assertEqual(vehicle_1.full_vehicle_name(),
'Jeep Grand Cherokee Laredo 4WD - 3.6L FI FFV DO
asdfasdfas') # Incorrect Value
AssertionError: 'Jeep Grand Cherokee Laredo 4WD - 3.6L FI
FFV DO' != 'Jeep Grand Cherokee Laredo 4WD - 3.6L FI FFV
DO asdfasdfas'
- Jeep Grand Cherokee Laredo 4WD - 3.6L FI FFV DO
```

```
+ Jeep Grand Cherokee Laredo 4WD - 3.6L FI FFV DO
asdfasdfas
?
+++++++++++
----------------------------------------------------------
Ran 1 test in 0.227s

FAILED (failures=1)
Destroying test database for alias 'default'...
```

Go ahead and comment out the `ModelUnitTestCase` class before proceeding to the next exercise. Now that we have an understanding of how to write simple test cases and cases that test model CRUD actions, next, we will test a custom view class that was written in *Chapter 4, URLs, Views, and Templates*.

Testing HTTP view requests

In this section, we will expand on the basic test cases that we previously wrote to include HTTP view requests. When testing view classes, whether they are a method-based view or a class-based view, they will both use the same `TestCase` class that we have been using so far.

In the following subsections, we will perform two tests, one for a method-based view and the other for a class-based view.

Testing method-based views

In this exercise, we will test the `practice_year_view()` method, written in *Chapter 4, URLs, Views, and Templates*. What we are comparing in this test is whether the response code that gets returned equals the value of `200`, which means a successful response.

Follow these steps to create your test case:

1. In your `/chapter_9/tests.py` file, add the following `YearRequestTestCase` class and methods:

   ```
   # /becoming_a_django_entdev/chapter_9/tests.py
   ...
   from django.contrib.auth.models import AnonymousUser
   from django.test import ..., RequestFactory, TestCase
   from ..chapter_4.views import practice_year_view
   ```

```python
class YearRequestTestCase(TestCase):
    def setUp(self):
        self.factory = RequestFactory()

    def test_methodbased(self):
        request = self.factory.get(
            '/my_year_path/2022/'
        )
        request.user = AnonymousUser()
        response = practice_year_view(request, 2022)
        self.assertEqual(response.status_code, 200)
```

This test uses a `RequestFactory()` object saved as the `self.factory` variable. It then uses that factory to construct an actual `request` object. The path that we want to test is passed into the `self.factory.get()` method as `/my_year_path/2022/`. Since we are not requiring authentication within `practice_year_view()`, we are setting the `request.user` object to an `AnonymousUser()` class object provided in the `django.contrib.auth.models` library. The response is constructed using the `practice_year_view(request, 2022)` method. Here, we pass in the `request` object and the value of the year keyword argument that we are attempting to access. The last line checks whether `response.status_code` actually equals a value of `200`.

2. Next, run the following test command for the `chapter_9` app test cases:

```
(virtual_env) PS > python manage.py test becoming_a_
django_entdev.chapter_9
```

If successful, you should see the following message:

```
Found 1 test(s).
Creating test database for alias 'default'...
System check identified no issues (0 silenced).
.
----------------------------------------------------------------------
Ran 1 test in 0.003s

OK
Destroying test database for alias 'default'...
```

Go back to *step 1* and change all instances of the year 2022 to 12 (found in two spots), and then rerun your test command. You should see the failure/error message shown here:

```
Found 1 test(s).
Creating test database for alias 'default'...
System check identified no issues (0 silenced).
E
==========================================================
ERROR: test_methodbased (becoming_a_django_entdev.
chapter_9.tests.YearRequestTestCase)
Checks if the path http://localhost:8000/my_year_
path/2022/ actually exists and returns a 200 response code
(Valid)
----------------------------------------------------------
Traceback (most recent call last):
  File "C:\Projects\Packt\Repo\becoming_a_django_entdev\
becoming_a_django_entdev\chapter_9\tests.py", line 115,
in test_methodbased
    response = practice_year_view(request, 12)
  File "C:\Projects\Packt\Repo\becoming_a_django_entdev\
becoming_a_django_entdev\chapter_4\views.py", line 37,
in practice_year_view
    raise Http404('Year Not Found: %s' % year)
django.http.response.Http404: Year Not Found: 12
----------------------------------------------------------
Ran 1 test in 0.004s

FAILED (errors=1)
Destroying test database for alias 'default'...
```

This test case failed because of the condition that we wrote in the `practice_year_view()` method in *Chapter 4, URLs, Views, and Templates*, which checks to make sure the user enters a year greater than or equal to 1900. You will also see that instead of printing an F or period for this test, it printed the capital letter E, which stands for error. The error versus a failure is a result of the custom parameters that we are checking for, meaning the URL pattern is correct but the view itself performs additional logic that triggers the page-not-found error.

Go ahead and comment out the `YearRequestTestCase` class before proceeding to the next exercise.

Let's test a class-based view in the next section.

Testing class-based views

In this exercise, we will test the `VehicleView` class, written in *Chapter 4, URLs, Views, and Templates*. We will be loading the `chapter_3` data fixture instead of creating objects in the `setUp()` method, as we have done in the `ModelUnitTestCase` class. We already performed a test to see whether creating objects was a success. We can save time and effort now by just loading a fixture for all other tests that we write.

Follow these steps to create your test case:

1. In your `/chapter_9/tests.py` file, add the `VehicleRequestTestCase` class and methods, as shown:

    ```
    # /becoming_a_django_entdev/chapter_9/tests.py
    ...
    from django.contrib.auth.models import AnonymousUser
    from django.test import ..., RequestFactory, TestCase
    from ..chapter_4.views import ..., VehicleView

    class VehicleRequestTestCase(TestCase):
        fixtures = ['chapter_3']

        def setUp(self):
            self.factory = RequestFactory()

        def test_classbased(self):
            request = self.factory.get('/vehicle/1/')
            request.user = AnonymousUser()
            response = VehicleView.as_view()(request, 1)
            self.assertEqual(response.status_code, 200)
    ```

    We still need the `RequestFactory()` object and `AnonymousUser()` as we used before, because the `VehicleView` class does not require authentication as well. We created the response object for this test using `VehicleView.as_view()(request, 1)`. It looks similar to a URL pattern mapping to a view class, using the `.as_view()` method, found in any `urls.py` file. We again check to see whether `response.status_code` equals a value of `200`, indicating success.

2. Now, run the test command shown in the following code and you should once again see a successful test:

   ```
   (virtual_env) PS > python manage.py test becoming_a_
   django_entdev.chapter_9
   ```

3. Now, change the number 1 found in *step 1* in `'/vehicle/1/'` and (`request`, 1) to 99. This number represents the index of the vehicle that we are trying to access, an index that should not currently exist. Then, rerun your `test` command and you should see the following message:

   ```
   Found 1 test(s).
   Creating test database for alias 'default'...
   System check identified no issues (0 silenced).
   E
   ======================================================
   ERROR: test_classbased (becoming_a_django_entdev.
   chapter_9.tests.VehicleRequestTestCase)
   Checks if the path http://localhost:8000/vehicle/1/ actually
   exists and returns a 200 response code (Valid)
   ------------------------------------------------------
   Traceback (most recent call last):
     File "C:\Projects\Packt\Repo\becoming_a_django_entdev\
   becoming_a_django_entdev\chapter_4\views.py", line 68,
   in get
       vehicle = Vehicle.objects.get(id=id)
     File "C:\Projects\Packt\Repo\becoming_a_django_entdev\
   virtual_env\lib\site-packages\django\db\models\manager.py",
   line 85, in manager_method
       return getattr(self.get_queryset(), name)(*args,
   **kwargs)
     File "C:\Projects\Packt\Repo\becoming_a_django_entdev\
   virtual_env\lib\site-packages\django\db\models\query.py",
   line 439, in get
       raise self.model.DoesNotExist(
   becoming_a_django_entdev.chapter_3.models.Vehicle.
   DoesNotExist: Vehicle matching query does not exist.
   ```

```
During handling of the above exception, another exception
occurred:

Traceback (most recent call last):
  File "C:\Projects\Packt\Repo\becoming_a_django_entdev\
becoming_a_django_entdev\chapter_9\tests.py", line 143,
in test_classbased
    response = VehicleView.as_view()(request, 99)
  File "C:\Projects\Packt\Repo\becoming_a_django_entdev\
virtual_env\lib\site-packages\django\views\generic\base.
py", line 69, in view
    return self.dispatch(request, *args, **kwargs)
  File "C:\Projects\Packt\Repo\becoming_a_django_entdev\
virtual_env\lib\site-packages\django\views\generic\base.
py", line 101, in dispatch
    return handler(request, *args, **kwargs)
  File "C:\Projects\Packt\Repo\becoming_a_django_entdev\
becoming_a_django_entdev\chapter_4\views.py", line 70,
in get
    raise Http404('Vehicle ID Not Found: %s' % id)
django.http.response.Http404: Vehicle ID Not Found: 99
-------------------------------------------------------
Ran 1 test in 0.062s

FAILED (errors=1)
Destroying test database for alias 'default'...
```

You'll notice, inside the preceding traceback message, that it indicates that an object with that ID was not found. The bottom of your traceback is where you will likely find your answer as to what caused the problem to occur, but that is not always the case. This is because we have less than 10 vehicle items found in the `chapter_3` fixture.

Comment out the `VehicleRequestTestCase` class before proceeding to the next exercise.

Now that we have learned how to test request responses and load data fixtures into a test case, let's build on that by adding authentication measures next.

Testing authenticated view requests

In this section, we will be building on the same request test cases that we just built to remove the `AnonymousUser` class and perform our own authentication, requiring only permitted users. We have a few view classes that we wrote in *Chapter 8, Working with the Django REST Framework*, that require user authentication. Let's create test scripts that allow us to authenticate with an actual user when performing an automated test. This is where loading the `chapter_8/urls.py` file when preparing for this chapter comes into play. Django provides a class called `Client` found in the `django.test` library that lets us perform user authentication when testing a view class.

In the following subsection, we will implement the `Client` class when performing authentication.

Using the Client() class

In this exercise, we will test the custom API endpoint written in *Chapter 8, Working with the Django REST Framework*, in the `GetSellerHTMLView` class. This is the class we wrote to query a seller by ID and return preformatted HTML instead of the expected JSON, from a traditional API endpoint. What we will be testing for is whether or not the `seller` context object has the business name that is expected for the ID that we are looking up. When using the `Client` class, the `RequestFactory` class is no longer needed, and neither is the `AnonymousUser` class.

Follow these steps to implement your own authentication:

1. In your `/chapter_9/tests.py` file, add the `SellerClientTestCase` class and `setUp()` method shown here:

   ```
   # /becoming_a_django_entdev/chapter_9/tests.py
   ...
   from django.test import ..., Client, TestCase
   from ..chapter_3.models import ..., Seller

   class SellerClientTestCase(TestCase):
       fixtures = ['chapter_3']

       def setUp(self):
           self.user = Seller.objects.get(id=1)
           self.client = Client()
           self.client.login(
   ```

```
            username = self.user.username,
            password = 'mynewpassword'
        )
```

We first set the `self.user` value to equal a single `Seller`. The ID provided is the number 1, relating to the first superuser created with the username of `admin`. This is the only seller object that has been provided in the `chapter_3` fixture for you. Next, we set the `self.client` value to be a newly created `Client()` object. The last line of the `setUp(self)` method is where we simulate logging into the system. We use `self.user.username` to grab the username of the `Seller` that we queried. Do not use `self.user.password` as the password; instead, use the unhashed password as a string manually written into the code. This is because there is no way to retrieve the unhashed password of a user and that is by design for security reasons.

> **Note**
>
> When writing your own test cases, it would be wise to keep test user credentials stored in a `.env` file and imported into your project as a `settings.py` variable, which can then be referenced instead of hardcoding the password, as was done previously.

2. In that same `SellerClientTestCase` class, add the following test method:

```
# /becoming_a_django_entdev/chapter_9/tests.py
...
class SellerClientTestCase(TestCase):
    ...
    def test_get(self):
        response = self.client.get(
            '/chapter-8/seller/1/'
        )
        self.assertEqual(response.status_code, 200)
        seller = response.context['seller']
        self.assertEqual(seller.name, 'Test Biz Name')
```

In the preceding `test_get(self)` method, we created the response object using `self.client.get()`. Inside that method, we are passing in the path that we are testing, of `http://localhost:8000/chapter-8/seller/1/`. We are performing two checks instead of one within this test case; the first checks whether `response.status_code` actually equals `200`, to indicate success. The other checks whether or not the seller's business name is what is expected for the object that we are looking up, that being `Test Biz Name`.

This is why we are creating the lowercase `seller` variable, which grabs the `seller` from the context returned with the request. It is also important that we add the `self.assertEqual(response.status_code, 200)` statement before we create the lowercase `seller` variable. If we do not have a successful response for any reason, the `seller` object will obviously not exist and so the test will fail. When that happens, it could point you in the wrong direction as to what the real problem could be.

3. Now, run the following `test` command and you should once again see a successful test:

   ```
   (virtual_env) PS > python manage.py test becoming_a_
   django_entdev.chapter_9
   ```

4. Next, change the `password` value found in *step 1* to an incorrect password, such as mynewpassword1, which will force a failed response. Rerun your `test` command and you should see the following message:

   ```
   Found 1 test(s).
   Creating test database for alias 'default'...
   System check identified no issues (0 silenced).
   F
   ==========================================================
   FAIL: test_get (becoming_a_django_entdev.chapter_9.
   tests.SellerClientTestCase)
   Tests a custom-built REST-API Endpoint using the Client()
   class.
   ----------------------------------------------------------
   Traceback (most recent call last):
     File "C:\Projects\Packt\Repo\becoming_a_django_entdev\
   becoming_a_django_entdev\chapter_9\tests.py", line 171,
   in test_get
       self.assertEqual(response.status_code, 200)
   ```

```
AssertionError: 401 != 200
----------------------------------------------------------
Ran 1 test in 0.356s

FAILED (failures=1)
Destroying test database for alias 'default'...
```

We can see the reason why a failure occurred is due to **AssertionError: 401 != 200**. A **401** response means an unauthorized response, which means the requested resource does not have valid authentication credentials and access will not be granted.

5. Change your password back to the correct password of `mynewpassword` and then, returning to *step 2*, change the business name in the last line to something incorrect, such as `Test Biz Name1`.

6. Rerun the `test` command one more time and now you should see the following failed message:

```
Found 1 test(s).
Creating test database for alias 'default'...
System check identified no issues (0 silenced).
F
==========================================================
FAIL: test_get (becoming_a_django_entdev.chapter_9.
tests.SellerClientTestCase)
Tests a custom-built REST-API Endpoint using the Client()
class.
----------------------------------------------------------
Traceback (most recent call last):
  File "C:\Projects\Packt\Repo\becoming_a_django_entdev\
becoming_a_django_entdev\chapter_9\tests.py", line 175,
in test_get
    self.assertEqual(seller.name, 'Test Biz Name1')
AssertionError: 'Test Biz Name' != 'Test Biz Name1'
- Test Biz Name
+ Test Biz Name1
?              +
----------------------------------------------------------
Ran 1 test in 0.561s
```

```
FAILED (failures=1)
Destroying test database for alias 'default'...
```

This also indicates that we achieved a **200** successful response code seeing that this is the second assertion that failed and not the first one.

You may now comment out the `SellerClientTestCase` class before proceeding to the next exercise. Now that we have a better understanding of how to add authentication measures to our test cases, we will test Django REST API endpoints with authentication next.

Testing Django REST API endpoints

This section will introduce writing test cases that test Django REST framework endpoints. When testing any REST API endpoints created using the Django REST framework, we need to use the `APITestCase` class provided by the `rest_framework.test` library. We also should use the `APIClient()` class provided by that same library when requiring authentication, instead of using the `Client()` class as we did before.

In the following exercises, we will create one test class that performs two tests: the first will create an engine object and the other will update an object.

Creating an object test case

This test will use the `POST` request method to send data to the `http://localhost:8000/chapter-8/engines/` endpoint and create an engine object in the database. Since we are loading a data fixture that contains only two engine objects with the IDs 1 and 2, we should expect the new object to be created at index 3, but your results may vary. We will refer back to this in the *Updating an object test case* subsection.

Follow these steps to create your test case:

1. In your `/chapter_9/tests.py` file, add the following `EngineAPITestCase` class, the `setUp()` method, and the `import` statement:

    ```
    # /becoming_a_django_entdev/chapter_9/tests.py
    ...
    from rest_framework.test import APITestCase, APIClient

    class EngineAPITestCase(APITestCase):
        fixtures = ['chapter_3']

        def setUp(self):
    ```

```python
        self.user = Seller.objects.get(id=1)
        self.client = APIClient()
        self.client.login(
            username = self.user.username,
            password = 'mynewpassword'
        )
```

The structure of the preceding class follows a very similar pattern to what was done in the subsection titled *Using the Client() class*. Here, we set the value of `self.client` to use the `rest_framework.test` library-provided `APIClient` class. Login is done the same as before, in the `self.client.login()` declaration.

2. In that same `EngineAPITestCase` class, add the following `test_post()` method:

```python
# /becoming_a_django_entdev/chapter_9/tests.py
...
class EngineAPITestCase(APITestCase):
    ...
    def test_post(self):
        response = self.client.post(
            '/chapter-8/engines/',
            {'name': 'New Engine'},
            format = 'json'
        )

        self.assertEqual(response.status_code, 201)
        self.assertEqual(response.data['name'], 'New Engine')
```

For the response object, instead of using `self.client.get()`, we are using `self.client.post()` because we want to send information to the test client server. Inside is the data we are sending, noting that the last argument is the format of the data, which is set to JSON format in this example. We then check the `response.status_code` value, this time to see whether it equals `201` and not `200`. A `201` response code indicates that an object was created successfully. The last line checks whether the data that was returned to us, which is the object that was created, has the engine name that we expect. In this case, the new engine name we are expecting is `New Engine`.

3. Now, run the following `test` command and you should once again see a successful test:

   ```
   virtual_env) PS > python manage.py test becoming_a_
   django_entdev.chapter_9
   ```

4. Next, go back to *step 1* and add an incorrect password, such as `mynewpassword1`, and then run your `test` command again. You should see the following message:

   ```
   Found 1 test(s).
   Creating test database for alias 'default'...
   System check identified no issues (0 silenced).
   F
   ======================================================
   FAIL: test_post (becoming_a_django_entdev.chapter_9.
   tests.EngineAPITestCase)
   Checks if it returns a 201 response code (Created).
   ------------------------------------------------------
   Traceback (most recent call last):
     File "C:\Projects\Packt\Repo\becoming_a_django_entdev\
   becoming_a_django_entdev\chapter_9\tests.py", line 203,
   in test_post
       self.assertEqual(response.status_code, 201)
   AssertionError: 401 != 201
   ------------------------------------------------------
   Ran 1 test in 0.363s

   FAILED (failures=1)
   Destroying test database for alias 'default'...
   ```

We can see in this test that we are being warned of `AssertionError: 401 != 201` and not `200` this time. You can `achieve` the same by changing the expected value of the engine name and you will see it warn you of that assertion.

Next, let's add to this class to allow us to test updating an object.

Updating an object test case

This test will use the `PUT` request method to send data to the `http://localhost:8000/chapter-8/engines/1/` endpoint, a specific engine object to update within the database.

Follow these steps to update your class for this test case:

1. Inside the same `EngineAPITestCase` class, add the following `test_put()` method:

   ```
   # /becoming_a_django_entdev/chapter_9/tests.py
   ...
   from rest_framework.test import APITestCase, APIClient

   class EngineAPITestCase(APITestCase):
       ...
       def test_put(self):
           response = self.client.put(
               '/chapter-8/engines/1/',
               {'name': 'My Changed Engine Name'},
               format = 'json'
           )

           self.assertEqual(response.status_code, 200)
           self.assertEqual(
               response.data['name'],
               'My Changed Engine Name'
           )
   ```

   Please leave the `setUp()` and `test_post()` methods as they are. In the preceding `test_put()` method, we are using the `self.client.put()` method to create the response object. The data that we are sending is in the same JSON format. Note that in the preceding example, we are specifying the path as `'/chapter-8/engines/1/'`, which refers to the first engine object with an ID index of `1`. That object is being inserted into the dummy database that gets created through the `chapter_3` fixture that is still being used in this class. We once again are checking that `response.status_code` equals `200`, success. We don't need to check for `201` because nothing is being created currently, only updated. We then check to make sure that the expected object's name equals `My Changed Engine Name`.

2. Now, run the following test command and you should see that both tests are a success:

   ```
   (virtual_env) PS > python3 manage.py test becoming_a_django_entdev.chapter_9
   ```

3. To demonstrate how creating an item in one test cannot be retrieved from another test within the same class, change the ID of 1 to 3 within the `test_put()` method, as in `'/chapter-8/engines/3/'`.

   When we created an object in the `test_post(self)` method, you might expect the newly created object to have had an ID index of 3 since the `chapter_3` fixture only has two objects. The reason we won't find the new object to update that object is that when the `test_post(self)` method is complete, anything created during that operation gets destroyed upon completion.

4. Rerun your `test` command and now you should see the failure message shown here:

```
Found 2 test(s).
Creating test database for alias 'default'...
System check identified no issues (0 silenced).
.F
======================================================
FAIL: test_put (becoming_a_django_entdev.chapter_9.
tests.EngineAPITestCase)
Checks if it returns a 200 response code (Success).
------------------------------------------------------
Traceback (most recent call last):
  File "C:\Projects\Packt\Repo\becoming_a_django_entdev\
becoming_a_django_entdev\chapter_9\tests.py", line 219,
in test_put
    self.assertEqual(response.status_code, 200)
AssertionError: 404 != 200
------------------------------------------------------
Ran 2 tests in 1.037s

FAILED (failures=1)
Destroying test database for alias 'default'...
```

The reason we are seeing a failure is that Django does not keep objects created between other test cases within the same test class. Django will keep a counter of the last object ID created, which means if or when a test case completes and an object gets destroyed, the counter will continue to count. This could make for a frustrating time testing and, as such, is the reason we are loading a fixture, so that we know for sure that the ID is what it should be for the object that we are testing.

Now that we have a better understanding of how automated testing works in Django, let's introduce the DjDT next, a powerful set of tools that helps developers to debug during development.

Using the DjDT

The DjDT is a third-party package that integrates a set of configurable panels that display debug information in real time to the developer. Other third-party packages can be installed to add additional panels to this toolbar. With that in mind, you could also build your own panels too. We will only be installing the DjDT package by itself and then explaining each of its most common features, guiding you through using it, interpreting what it is showing you. To learn more about all of its capabilities, visit https://pypi.org/project/django-debug-toolbar/ and https://django-debug-toolbar.readthedocs.io/en/latest/.

Installing the DjDT

To get started with installing the DjDT, follow these steps:

1. Add the `django-debug-toolbar` package to your `requirements.txt` file and install it into your virtual environment via that file or run the following `pip` command, making sure your virtual environment is already active:

    ```
    PS C:\Projects\Packt\Repo\becoming_a_django_entdev> virtual_env/Scripts/activate
    (virtual_env) PS > pip install django-debug-toolbar
    ```

2. In your `settings.py` file, add the following items to your `INSTALLED_APPS` list:

    ```
    # /becoming_a_django_entdev/settings.py
    ...
    INSTALLED_APPS = [
        ...
        'debug_toolbar',
        ...
    ]
    ```

3. In the same `settings.py` file, add the following middleware to the top of your `MIDDLEWARE` list:

```
# /becoming_a_django_entdev/settings.py
...
MIDDLEWARE = [
    'debug_toolbar.middleware.DebugToolbarMiddleware',
    ...
]
...
```

The `debug_toolbar` app and the `MIDDLEWARE` item should be the only new items that you are adding to this file.

4. The `django.contrib.staticfiles` app, the `INTERNAL_IPS` list, and the `STATIC_URL` variable should have already been added in *Chapter 2, Project Configuration*, when we created and configured the project for the first time. Note that they are required for this toolbar to work. Should you be working on a project of your own that does not follow the `settings.py` specifications of this book, make sure that these items are included:

```
# /becoming_a_django_entdev/settings.py
...
INTERNAL_IPS = [
    '127.0.0.1',
]

INSTALLED_APPS = [
    ...
    'django.contrib.staticfiles',
    'debug_toolbar',
    ...
]

STATIC_URL = '/staticfiles/'
...
```

5. Next, you will need to import the URL patterns relative to this third-party app. To make sure this toolbar can be used in all chapters throughout this book, in your main `urls.py` file, add the following `include` pattern:

```python
# /becoming_a_django_entdev/urls.py
...
from django.urls import ..., include, re_path
...
if settings.DEBUG:
    ...
    import debug_toolbar

    urlpatterns = [
        re_path(
            r'^__debug__/',
            include(debug_toolbar.urls)
        ),
    ] + urlpatterns
```

Note that in the preceding example, we are placing the import under the `settings.DEBUG` conditional statement, checking whether our environment is the `DEBUG` environment. We don't ever want this toolbar to appear in a production or production-like test environment, such as staging. The development environment is usually acceptable.

That's it; by now, this toolbar should be installed and working properly. Next, let's discuss making an adjustment to work with our remote environments.

Adjusting DjDT settings

Any of the panels that you are about to learn about have behavioral settings that can be defined in your `settings.py` file. A common example of this is how we need to use the `SHOW_TOOLBAR_CALLBACK` setting to allow us to see the DjDT in a Heroku environment. To learn more about all of the settings available, visit https://django-debug-toolbar.readthedocs.io/en/latest/configuration.html#debug-toolbar-config.

Follow these steps to activate this setting:

1. In the `settings.py` file, add the following code:

   ```
   # /becoming_a_django_entdev/settings.py
   ...
   def show_toolbar(request):
       return True

   if os.getenv('SHOW_TOOLBAR_CALLBACK') == 'True':
       DEBUG_TOOLBAR_CONFIG = {
           'SHOW_TOOLBAR_CALLBACK': show_toolbar,
       }
   ```

   We have to use a callable and a variable in the `.env` file because using the DEBUG_TOOLBAR_CONFIG dictionary and running your automated Django test command locally will result in an error due to the DjDT package. Using either the toolbar or the Django testing commands separately will be fine without the preceding code, but when used together, this code is required.

2. To show this toolbar in your Heroku-hosted environments, set the following value to `True` in your `.env` file. Refer to the subsection titled *Remote variables* found in *Chapter 2, Project Configuration*:

   ```
   # .env
   SHOW_TOOLBAR_CALLBACK=True
   ```

3. Leave this value as `False` in your local environment.

Now, let's use this toolbar.

How to use the DjDT

Make sure your virtual environment is activated and then take the following steps to use the DjDT:

1. Run your project using the following command, or you can use the IDE, as discussed in *Chapter 2, Project Configuration*:

   ```
   PS C:\Projects\Packt\Repo\becoming_a_django_entdev> virtual_env/Scripts/activate
   (virtual_env) PS > python3 manage.py runserver
   ```

438   Django Testing

2. In your browser, navigate to your home page at `http://localhost:8000/` and you should see the classic home page image with the **Chapter 9** subtitle and now, a tab in the top right of the window, as shown in the following screenshot, with the arrow pointing to it:

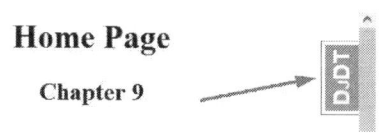

Figure 9.1 – DjDT – tab

3. Click on this toolbar to open it and see what mysteries behold, as shown in the following screenshot:

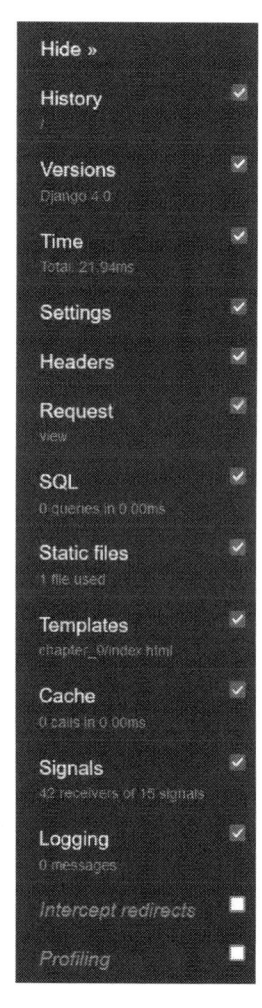

Figure 9.2 – DjDT – opened

Each item in this toolbar can be clicked on to expand it even further. The following subsections give you a breakdown of what each panel actually shows you.

History

The **History** panel shows us a list of every request that was made within this browser tab. Every time you refresh the page or navigate to a new path within your site, that information will be logged within this panel. For each item within this panel, there is a **Switch** button. When that button is clicked, debug information will update in the other tabs relative to that request, highlighted with arrows in the following screenshot:

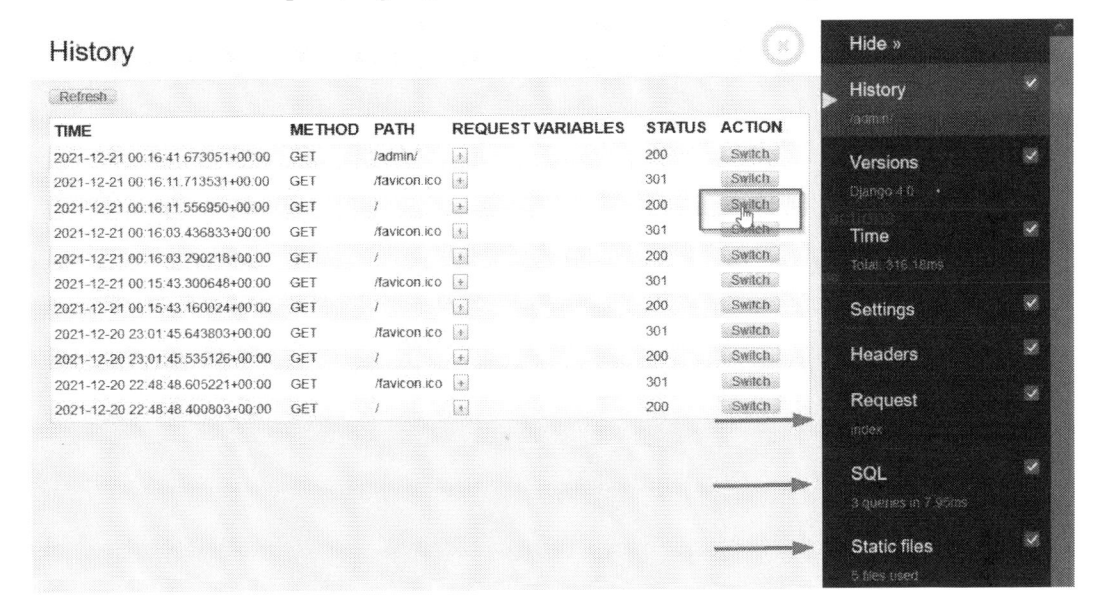

Figure 9.3 – DjDT – History tab

When you click the **Switch** button, your page won't actually update to that page that is in your browser's history; only the data displayed in your debug toolbar gets updated. That allows you to see what changed from one request to another. The preceding screenshot shows how I refreshed the home page five times before navigating to the Django admin site. The Django admin site URL patterns should have been imported when we imported the `chapter_8` app URL patterns in preparation for this chapter. In this example, I am actually logged into my admin panel, showing in the **SQL** tab that there are three queries, then when I switch to one of the home page URLs, the **SQL** tab updates to tell me I now have two queries. I'll explain what these queries mean in the *SQL* subsection that follows. For now, you can at least see how this data is changing.

Versions

The **Versions** panel displays the version number of Django, Python, and all related third-party packages that have been installed in your software stack. It is a quick and easy way to share what is needed in a visually appealing way with your clients and developers. Remember the `requirements.txt` file is shared with developers to automate the installation of the required packages and versions of your project. The following screenshot shows what this tab looks like, verifying that we are indeed using Django 4.0:

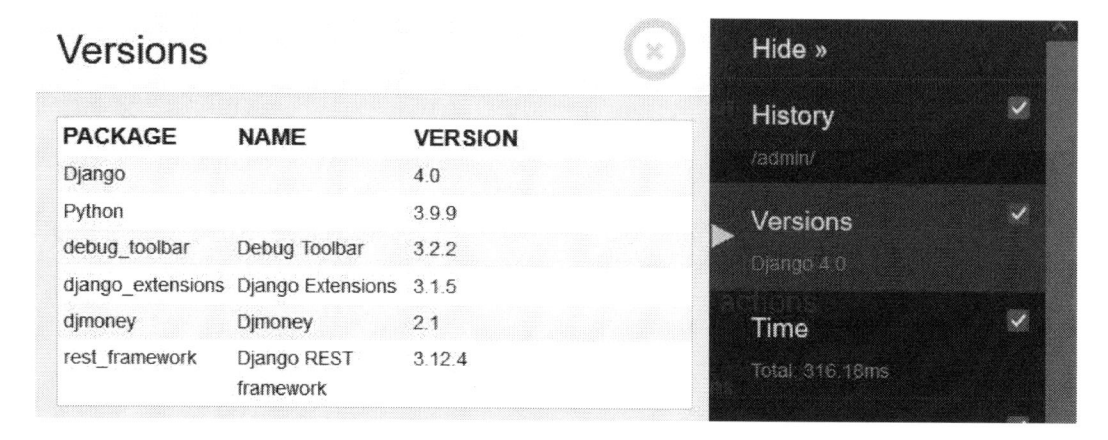

Figure 9.4 – DjDT – Versions tab

Time

The **Time** tab only displays the time it took to execute the current request. It doesn't actually open a new panel like the first two tabs. It's just a placeholder tab that displays useful information.

Settings

The **Settings** panel displays a list of all of your `settings.py` variables and their computed values. This is handy if you have methods calculating values, or if you are linking many different `settings.py` files together from other packages that override or change the values in your parent file, they can all be viewed from here. The following screenshot shows you what that looks like:

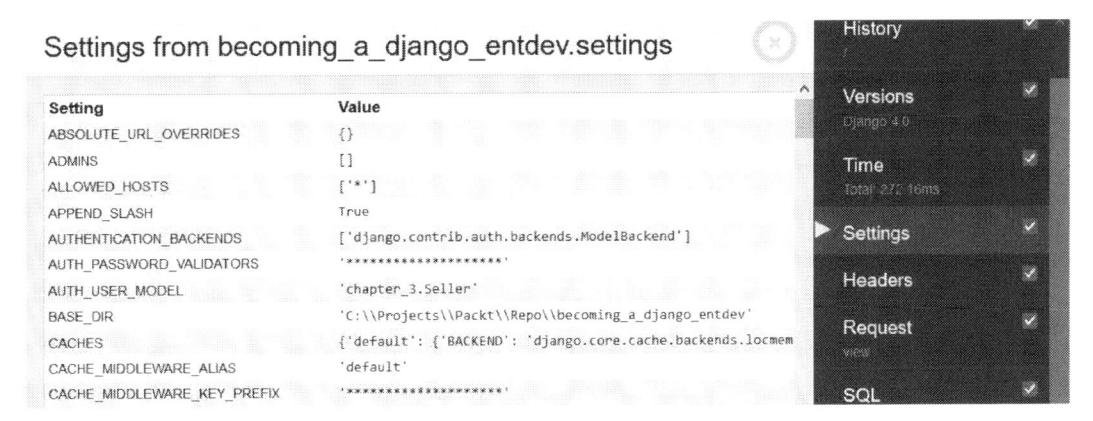

Figure 9.5 – DjDT – Settings tab

Headers

The **Headers** panel displays all of the information pertaining to your HTTP request and response headers. It also displays your WSGI or ASGI environment variables at the bottom of this panel. This can be very helpful when you are working with API endpoints and you need to make sure the information in your request and response headers is as what you would expect it to be. The following screenshot shows you what this looks like:

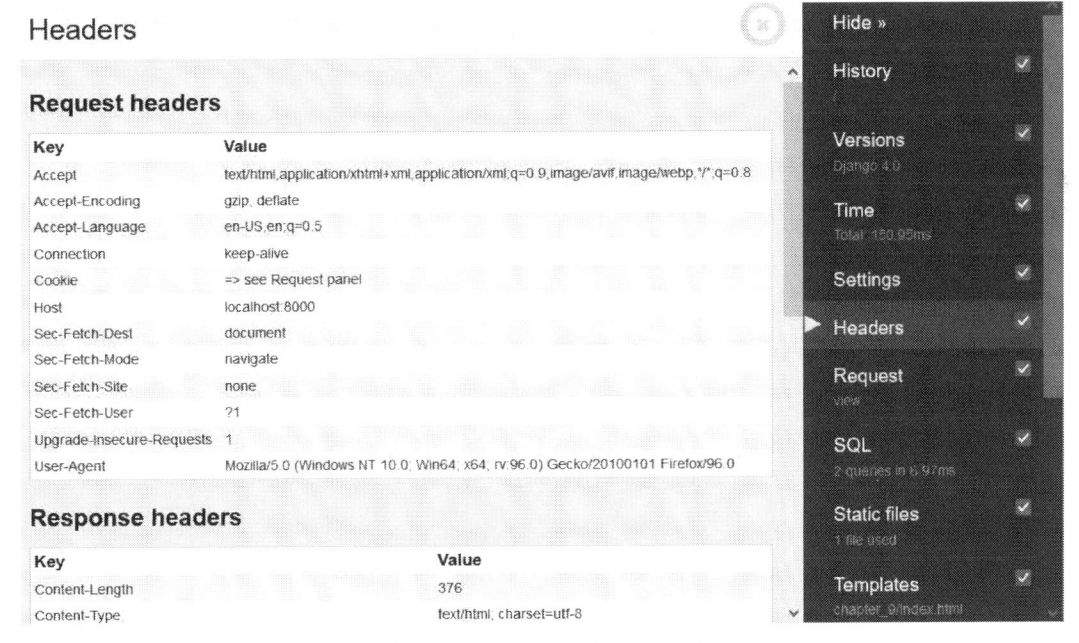

Figure 9.6 – DjDT – Headers tab

Request

The **Request** panel shows you all of the data related to your request, such as keyword arguments and cookie and session data. This tab is very useful for checking to make sure this information is what it is expected to be. The following screenshot shows what this panel looks like:

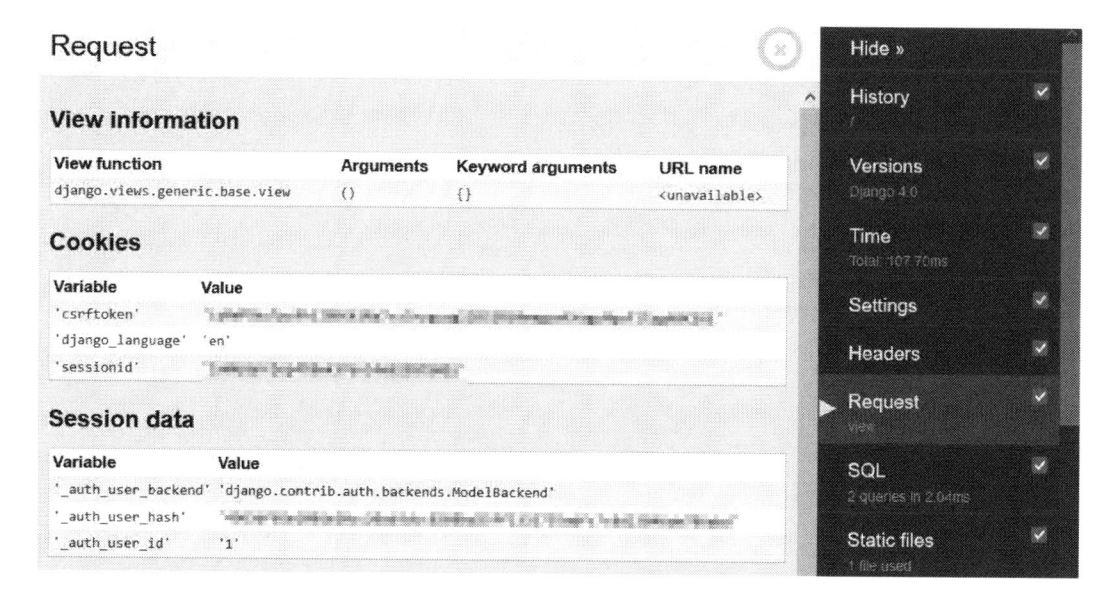

Figure 9.7 – DjDT – Request tab

SQL

The **SQL** panel shows you a very detailed and broken-down look of what each query is doing, as well as showing you all of the queries involved in a particular request. For example, if you are visiting the home page while not logged into the Django admin site, the **SQL** tab will tell you there are zero queries, as depicted in *Figure 9.2*. However, if you are logged into the Django admin site and are visiting the home page, you should see at least two queries under the **SQL** tab. When you click on this tab, you will see what those two queries are, as shown in the following screenshot:

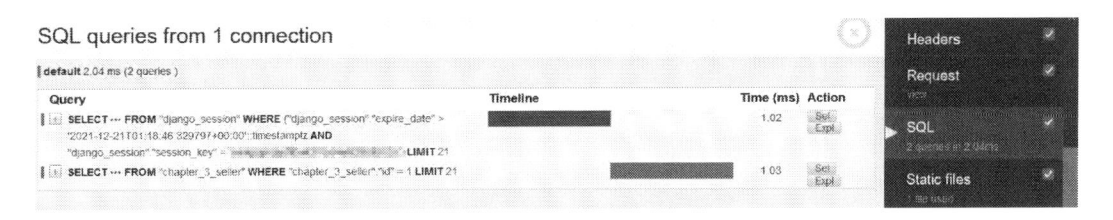

Figure 9.8 – DjDT – SQL tab

Here, we can see the first query establishes a session for the current request and then queries the object of the user logged into the system. That user object is a `Seller` model object because of how we extended the `User` model in *Chapter 3, Models, Relations, and Inheritance*. Each query also has a **Sel** and **Expl** button, which provide other details about that query. Clicking the plus sign, found to the left of any one of these queries expands even more, giving you information about that query, including traceback information, as shown:

Figure 9.9 – DjDT – SQL tab expanded

Static files

The **Static files** panel displays all of the apps installed that actually contain static files. The middle section lists all of the static files related to the current request. You can actually click on them to open and view them in the current or a new tab. The last section in this panel displays a list of all of the static files found in all of the apps that are installed. This can sometimes be helpful if you are comparing a static file that overrides the same static file of another app, you can see which one is used and which ones are ignored. The following screenshot shows you what this panel looks like:

Figure 9.10 – DjDT – Static files tab

Here, we can see that the only static file being used on this page is the `home_page.jpg` file. Since the `index.html` file is not extending the `base_template_1.html` file, we don't have any CSS or JavaScript files used on this page; they do not get loaded. Should you activate the DjDT and go back to previous chapters, you will likely see those additional assets because we were using the `base_template_1.html` file. Any debug tools, such as CSS and JavaScript files related to the DjDT, will not be shown in the middle section. The idea is that those are debug-related assets and we don't need to know that on the page that we are debugging. Should you inspect a page using your browser tools, you will see assets related to the DjDT; they will not appear in production.

Templates

The **Templates** panel displays information related to the templates used and the context that is available. The middle section displays all of the templates. If you had partial HTML files using includes or extends, each one of those templates would appear in this list in the order that they are used. When you click on the **Toggle context** arrow, shown in the following screenshot, it will display a list of all of the context variables and their values related to that file:

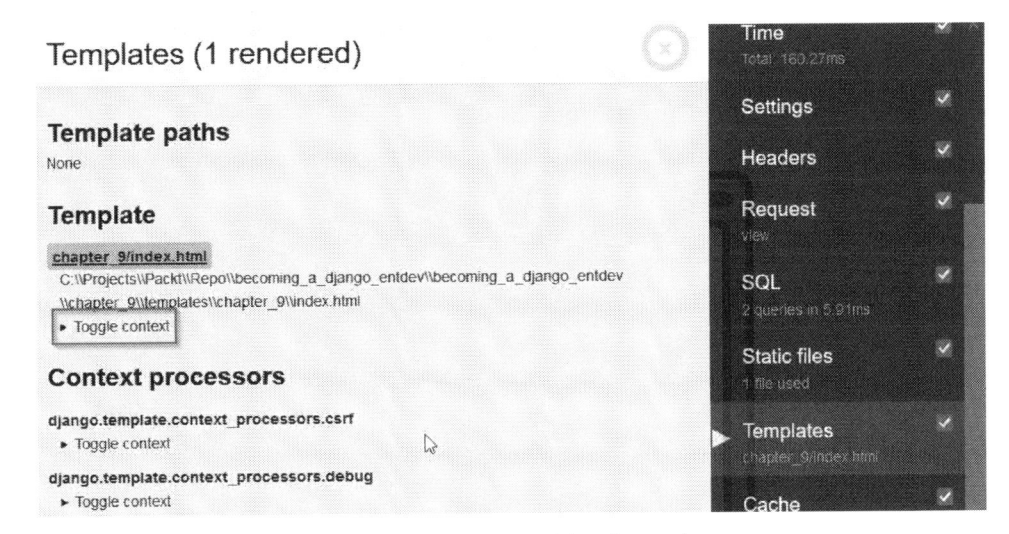

Figure 9.11 – DjDT – Templates tab

The following screenshot depicts what clicking the **Toggle context** button looks like, showing us the context available in that particular template or partial file:

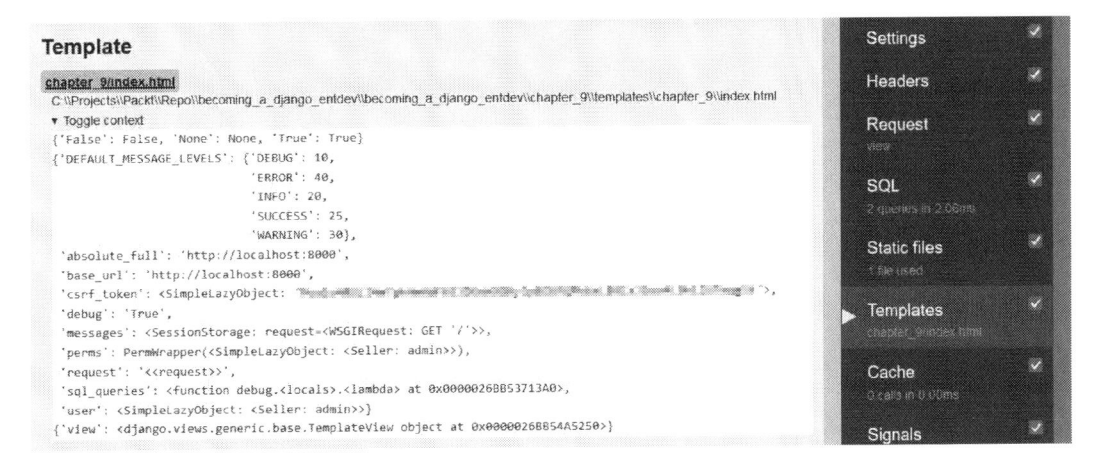

Figure 9.12 – DjDT – Templates tab showing context

At the bottom of this panel is where all of the context processors are located. You can view the context available in each of the context processors available.

Cache

The **Cache** panel displays all of the cached objects involved with this page. This is if you are using tools that help enhance the performance of your database. This is considered an advanced topic beyond the scope of this book.

> **Note**
> The DjDT publisher also notes in their own documentation that this panel is incompatible with Django's per-site caching.

Signals

The **Signals** panel displays the notifiers and receivers within an application that are communicating with each other. These can be closely compared to what **WebSocket** is. This is also considered an advanced topic beyond the scope of this book.

Logging

The **Logging** panel is a quick and easy way to view logs in Django. Similar to the Django messages framework, introduced in *Chapter 7, Working with Messages, Email Notifications, and PDF Reports*, Django allows the use of the standard Python `logging` library. Before showing how this panel looks, let's wire up an actual log to view. As with the Django messages framework, the logging system has different levels of messages. The default minimum log level is `WARNING` but you can show `DEBUG`- and `INFO`-level logs the same way, either by setting it in your `settings.py` file or by declaring it inline where your log is set, as we are going to do in the following steps. To learn more about all of the capabilities of using the logging system, visit https://docs.djangoproject.com/en/4.0/topics/logging/ and https://docs.python.org/3/library/logging.html.

Take the following steps to practice using the logging system:

1. In your /chapter_4/views.py file, add the following log statements at the beginning of the existing practice_year_view():

   ```
   # /becoming_a_django_entdev/chapter_4/views.py
   ...
   import logging

   def practice_year_view(request, year):
       logger = logging.getLogger(__name__)
       logger.setLevel(logging.INFO)
       logger.info('The Requested Year Is: %s' % year)
       ...
   ```

   The first two lines lower the logging level to show all INFO-level logs and higher, allowing us to use the logger.info() method to create the log message. Otherwise, the lowest level we could use by default would be the logger.warning() level method. The log message we are expecting to see should be The Requested Year Is: 2022 when visiting the URL.

2. Now, navigate to http://localhost:8000/my_year_path/2022/ in your browser and expand the debug toolbar. Open the **Logging** tab and now you should see the log that we created, as depicted in the following screenshot:

Log messages

Level	Time	Channel	Message	Location
INFO	07:43:26 12/20/2021	becoming_a_django_entdev.chapter_4.views	The Requested Year Is: 2022	C:\Projects\Packt\Repo\becoming_a_django_entdev \becoming_a_django_entdev\chapter_4\views.py:38

Figure 9.13 – DjDT – Logging tab

Intercept redirects

The **Intercept redirects** checkbox is used to display an intermediary page whenever a redirect is performed to display information about that redirect, before the browser is updated with the redirected page.

Profiling

The **Profiling** checkbox enables the gathering of extra data on page load. It is a detailed analysis of memory and CPU processes taking place. Each process is broken down into the smallest measurements possible. By default, this checkbox is left unchecked. An example of what this looks like is shown in the following screenshot:

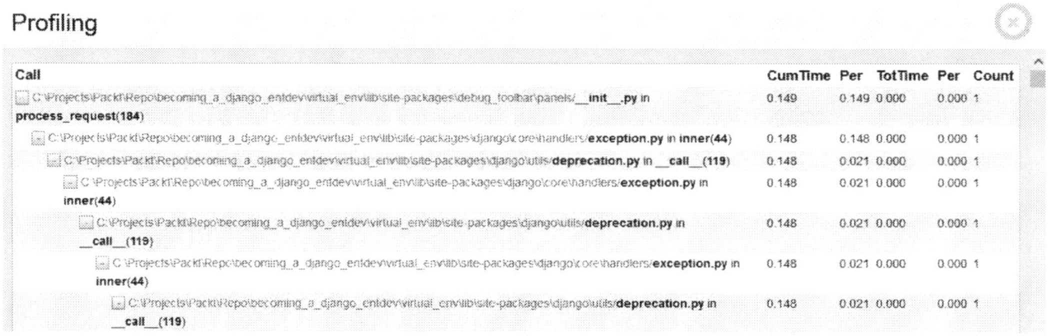

Figure 9.14 – DjDT – Profiling tab

We now have a deeper understanding of all of the tabs available within the DjDT and what they are used for. This now adds a wealth of tools to our toolbox to help us make world-class applications with ease.

Summary

By now, we have developed a solid understanding of how automated testing in Django is performed. We wrote several test cases that test many of the exercises done in previous chapters. We practiced writing test cases that simulate success and others that deliberately trigger a failure to better understand what is happening. We even discovered how to write test cases that work with the Django REST framework. After we worked with automated testing, we then installed what I would consider the most powerful tool of them all, the DjDT. The DjDT is used for real-time debugging of developers' code as they write that code and run their projects locally.

In the next chapter, we will learn how to use the DjDT to monitor performance as we learn how to optimize database queries.

10
Database Management

In programming, the subject of database management encompasses a broad spectrum of subcategories. Many of those categories were already introduced in earlier chapters, such as in *Chapter 2*, *Project Configuration*, when we discussed the concept of using a database management tool, or in *Chapter 3*, *Models, Relations, and Inheritance*, when we explored the concept of model managers. While these subjects can be considered topics of this chapter, they were introduced in earlier chapters to better fit what that chapter's subject matter was discussing or to serve as a tool that was suited to the exercises in those earlier chapters. The Django fixtures that were introduced and used in *Chapter 3*, *Models, Relations, and Inheritance*, can also be considered a database management tool and will finally be covered in more depth in this chapter.

Django fixtures are used to import and export data found in a database that is connected to a Django project. The `chapter_3` data fixture that was provided and used throughout every chapter prior to this chapter helped to demonstrate those exercises by providing the necessary test/dummy data for you. We will cover how to export data, creating our own data fixtures for projects and developers to use. We will also explain in a little more depth the import process that we have been using and the options that are available.

In this chapter, we will explore other methods of executing queries that enhance the overall performance of your system. The two methods commonly used are `select_related()` and `prefetch_related()`, which are known in Django as **performance boosters**. We will practice using these performance boosters on queries made to the `Vehicle` and `Seller` model class data that exists in our database. We will use the **Django Debug Toolbar (DjDT)** introduced in *Chapter 9, Django Testing*, to monitor how the performance changes.

In this chapter, we will cover the following:

- Exporting data into a data fixture
- Importing data from a data fixture
- Boosting query performance using the `select_related()` method
- Boosting query performance using the `prefetch_related()` method
- Boosting query performance using the `Prefetch()` class

Technical requirements

To work with the code in this chapter, the following tools will need to be installed on your local machine:

- Python version 3.9 – used as the underlying programming language for the project
- Django version 4.0 – used as the backend framework of the project
- pip package manager – used to manage third-party Python/Django packages

We will continue to work with the solution created in *Chapter 2, Project Configuration*. However, it is not necessary to use the Visual Studio IDE. The main project itself can be run using another IDE or run independently using a terminal or command-line window from within the project root folder, which is where the `manage.py` file resides. Whatever editor or IDE you are using, a virtual environment will also be needed to work with the Django project. Instructions for how to create a project and virtual environment can be found in *Chapter 2, Project Configuration*. You will need a database to store the data contained in your project. PostgreSQL was chosen for the examples in the previous chapter; however, any database type that you choose for your project can be used to work with the examples in this chapter.

We will also be using data that is in the form of a Django fixture, provided in *Chapter 3, Models, Relations, and Inheritance*, in the subsection titled *Loading the chapter_3 data fixture*. Make sure the `chapter_3` fixture is loaded into your database. If this has already been done, then you may skip the next command. If you have already created the tables found in *Chapter 3, Models, Relations, and Inheritance*, and have not loaded that fixture yet, then run the following command, after activating your virtual environment:

```
(virtual_env) PS > python manage.py loaddata chapter_3
```

All of the code created in this chapter can be found in the GitHub repository for this book: https://github.com/PacktPublishing/Becoming-an-Enterprise-Django-Developer. The bulk of the code depicted in this chapter can be found in the /becoming_a_django_entdev/becoming_a_django_entdev/chapter_10/ directory.

Check out the following video to see the *Code in Action*: https://bit.ly/3zYgbqd.

Preparing for this chapter

Start by creating a new app in your project called `chapter_10` by following the steps discussed in *Chapter 2, Project Configuration*, in the subsection titled *Creating a Django app*. As discussed in that section, don't forget to change the value of the `name =` variable for your app class found in the /becoming_a_django_entdev/becoming_a_django_entdev/chapter_10/apps.py file to now point to the path where you installed your app. Be sure to also include this app in the `INSTALLED_APPS` variable found in the `settings.py` file as well.

In the main `urls.py` file of the site, add the following path, which points to the URL patterns of this chapter that we will be creating:

```
# /becoming_a_django_entdev/urls.py
...
urlpatterns = [
    path(
        '',
        include(
            'becoming_a_django_entdev.chapter_10.urls'
        )
    ),
]
```

Next, copy the `/chapter_10/urls.py` file from the code provided with this book into your project in the same directory.

In the following exercises, we will use the DjDT that was introduced in *Chapter 9, Django Testing*, to monitor performance. Please make sure that you have installed the DjDT in your project before proceeding. Instructions can be found in the subsection titled *Installing the DjDT* of that chapter.

Now that we have created the app for this chapter, let's start by creating our own data fixtures.

Exporting data into a data fixture

A **data fixture** is considered a collection of files that contain data objects related to the models in your application. This really refers to a directory of files that Django searches in for data; by default, that is the `fixtures` folder found in every Django app. This directory can also be changed by modifying the `settings.py` variable called `FIXTURE_DIRS`, but this is not necessary if you intend to use the default directory and behavior. Django fixture files can be written in JSON, JSONL, XML, or YAML file formats. This means you can easily export data from other systems if that data is exported into one of these formats, even if that other system is not a Django project. Keep in mind that the table structure of the objects must match exactly if you wish to do a clean export from an old system and import into a new system.

Usually, there is a great deal of data parsing involved when exporting from an older legacy system and importing into the newly updated system. The other option is to use one or a combination of many command options when exporting or importing data to prevent errors when data structures do not align. Sometimes, using the options provided is not enough to accomplish what needs to be done to your data. **Parsing data** is the process of transforming data from one format or data type to another. We sometimes have to parse data because a newer system changes the data structure and/or constraints that were set on the old data structures. When that happens, we sometimes get errors during the import. Sometimes, data imports fine but at runtime, your users experience odd behavior as a result of improperly formatted data found within your database. We will only cover using the options provided in this chapter; if data in your system is so complex that it needs to be parsed, you will have to look into writing your own Python script to transform your data as needed.

Let's practice using the Django `dumpdata` management command next.

Using the dumpdata command

The `dumpdata` management command is the opposite of the `loaddata` command that we have been using to import the `chapter_3` fixture data. It is used to export data from a database connected to your Django project into a data fixture. By default, Django will export data fixtures into JSON format, but you can specify a different format by using the `--format` option when running the `dumpdata` command.

We will start by just dumping the tables of all applications in our project using the `-o` or `--output` option to place a fixture in the `chapter_10` app directory, in order to keep the chapter exercises nicely organized. Every `dumpdata` exercise in this chapter will use the `--output` option for this reason; it is not a required option.

More information about these options and other options that are not covered can be found here: https://docs.djangoproject.com/en/4.0/ref/django-admin/#dumpdata.

Before proceeding with this exercise, make sure you have data in your database, whether you added it manually or imported it from the `chapter_3` app. We will export all existing data into a `chapter_10` data fixture folder for practice, by following these steps:

1. Make sure you are inside your project's root directory, the same folder where your `manage.py` file is located. Then, open your command-line window or terminal and activate your virtual environment, but do not run your project at this time.

2. Create a new folder called `fixtures` in your `/becoming_a_django_entdev/chapter_10/` directory using the following command:

   ```
   (virtual_env) PS > mkdir becoming_a_django_entdev/chapter_10/fixtures
   ```

3. Execute the `dumpdata` command using the `-o` output option to place the dumped data into a file called `chapter_10.json` inside the folder we just created:

   ```
   (virtual_env) PS > python manage.py dumpdata -o becoming_a_django_entdev/chapter_10/fixtures/chapter_10.json
   ```

If you were successful, you should now see a new file called `chapter_10.json` in your `/becoming_a_django_entdev/chapter_10/fixtures/` folder, as shown in the following screenshot, using the **Solution Explorer** in the Visual Studio IDE:

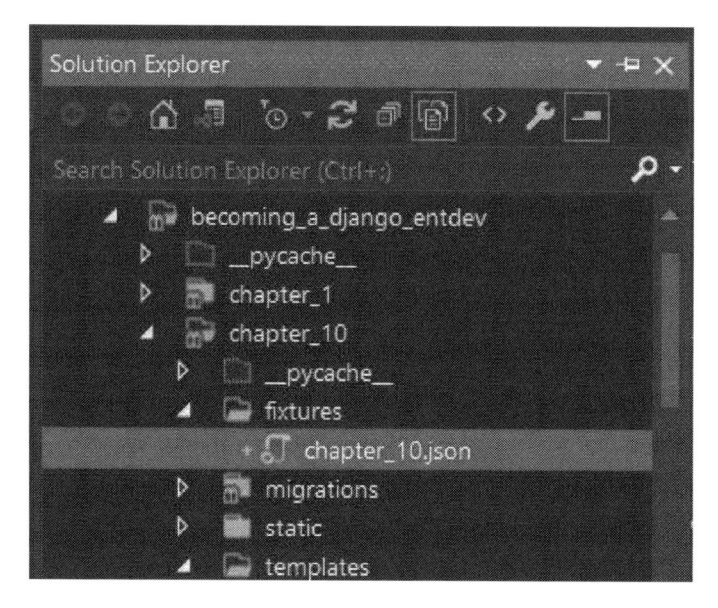

Figure 10.1 – Dumping all data with the dumpdata command

The reason we had to create the `fixtures` folder first is that the `dumpdata` command will fail if we specify a folder that does not exist. The actual `.json` file doesn't have to exist, Django will create that file for you. Keep in mind that if your `.json` file does already exist and you run the `dumpdata` command specifying that file as the output option, then all the data in your existing fixture file will be overwritten and lost.

Inside the `chapter_10.json` file that was created, you will notice that it is in minified file format. You are welcome to format that document into something readable. In Visual Studio, you can right-click inside your document and select **Format Document** to do that. You can also copy and paste that data into an online formatting tool, such as my favorite, https://jsonlint.com/. Formatting the document is not necessary but it is helpful if you want to read the data objects and/or edit them directly in that file.

You'll also notice that inside the `chapter_10.json` file that was created, you will have data for every app of your project, including the `auth`, `authtoken`, and `chapter_3` data tables and any Django-related data tables, such as the `admin` and `contenttypes` tables. This is far more information than what was provided to you in the `chapter_3.json` data fixture. Odds are, you won't need to include information such as the `admin.logentry` and `contenttypes.contenttype` objects, as they usually cause conflicts when importing that data into a different system.

In the next subsection, we will practice exporting only the tables found in a specific application of a project by specifying the `app_name` and/or `model_name` of what data we want to include.

Exporting a specific application

When using the `dumpdata` command without specifying any application, just like we did in the previous exercise, Django will export data from all tables in all applications of a project. There is no option syntax for doing this; if there was, it would be in `dumpdata {{ app_name }}` or `dumpdata {{ app_name.model_name }}` format, without the curly brackets of course.

To specify an app or table, follow these steps:

1. Make sure you are inside your project's root directory, the same folder where your `manage.py` file is located. Then, open a command-line window or terminal and activate your virtual environment, but do not run your project at this time.

2. Execute the following `dumpdata` command, which will specify all of the tables found only in the `chapter_3` application:

   ```
   (virtual_env) PS > python manage.py dumpdata chapter_3 -o becoming_a_django_entdev/chapter_10/fixtures/chapter_3_models.json
   ```

   Now, what should have been created for us is a single file called `chapter_3_models.json` in the `/chapter_10/fixtures/` folder. It should contain data for only the `vehiclemodel`, `engine`, `vehicle`, and `seller` tables. All of the other data that we saw in the previous fixture file will no longer be found in this new file.

3. Inside that file, format the data so that you can read what is found in it. If you are using Visual Studio, right-click inside your document and select **Format Document** or copy and paste the data into the online tool found at https://jsonlint.com/. Your data should look similar to that in the following screenshot:

```
[
    {
        "model": "chapter_3.seller",
        "pk": 1,
        "fields": {
            "password": "pbkdf2_sha256$320000$ND2Tq...",
            "last_login": "2021-12-21T01:18:39.905Z",
            "is_superuser": true,
            "username": "admin",
            "first_name": "Admin",
            "last_name": "User",
            "email": "example@example.com",
            "is_staff": true,
            "is_active": true,
            "date_joined": "2021-08-31T05:05:40Z",
            "name": "Test Biz Name",
            "groups": [
            ],
            "user_permissions": [
            ],
            "vehicles": [
                2,
                4,
                5,
                6,
                7,
                1,
                3
            ]
        }
    },
```

Figure 10.2 – Dump chapter_3 app dumpdata command

By default, all related objects are displayed using the foreign key of that related object. We can see this with all seven of the related Vehicle objects, represented as a list of the numbers 1 through 7 in the preceding screenshot. The order depends on the default ordering of that model.

> **Note**
> JSON exports don't always follow the same or logical order. Your results may vary. In the preceding screenshot, each object that was exported includes its original primary key, represented as the "pk" field. We can remove this using the --natural-primary option, which we will soon discuss.

4. To practice exporting only a specific table, use the following command to export the `Seller` model data, by specifying `chapter_3.seller` as the source:

   ```
   (virtual_env) PS > python manage.py dumpdata chapter_3.
   seller -o becoming_a_django_entdev/chapter_10/fixtures/
   chapter_3_sellers.json
   ```

   Use the same dot notation to specify other models and/or other applications if you want extra practice.

Next, let's practice exporting everything again, as we did in the first exercise. This time, we will use the `--exclude` option to exclude apps that we do not want to be included.

Using the --exclude option

The `--exclude` or `-e` option is used to tell Django to exclude a particular app or model from the given inclusion of a `dumpdata` command. In this exercise, we will perform the same dump-everything operation that we performed earlier in the subsection titled *Using the dumpdata command* of this chapter and exclude all of the Django-related tables. We want to produce the same results as in the *Exporting a specific application* subsection, by using the `--exclude` option rather than telling Django what to include.

Follow these steps to perform your `--exclude` operation:

1. Make sure you are inside your project's root directory, the same folder where your `manage.py` file is located. Then, open a command-line window or terminal and activate your virtual environment, but do not run your project at this time.

2. Execute the following `dumpdata` command, which excludes the following applications:

   ```
   (virtual_env) PS > python manage.py dumpdata -e
   contenttypes -e sessions -e authtoken -e auth -e admin
   -o becoming_a_django_entdev/chapter_10/fixtures/
   chapter_10_exclude.json
   ```

   > **Note**
   > Keep in mind that all the `dumpdata` commands in this chapter are very long single-line commands. Anything broken down onto a new line is likely separated by a single space, as is the case with the preceding command.

Options can also be written using an equals character, such as `-e=app_name` or `--exclude=app_name`.

The contents of the newly created `chapter_10_exclude.json` file should match the contents of the `chapter_3_models.json` file that we created in the previous subsection, titled *Exporting a specific application*. This is because we technically performed the same action, except the first time we told Django what to include, and the second time, we told Django what to exclude. Compare your files' output to see the results.

Next, let's practice exporting data as something other than the default JSON format.

Using the --format option

The `--format` option is used to tell Django to output the data into the format specified. The four types that we can specify when exporting data are JSON, JSONL, XML, and YAML. The default is JSON if this option is not specified.

Follow these steps to export your data in every format type possible, one format for each step:

1. Make sure you are inside your project's root directory, the same folder where your `manage.py` file is located. Then, open a command-line window or terminal and activate your virtual environment, but do not run your project at this time.

2. Execute the following `dumpdata` command, which dumps the `Sellers` objects as XML:

    ```
    (virtual_env) PS > python manage.py dumpdata chapter_3.seller --format xml -o becoming_a_django_entdev/chapter_10/fixtures/chapter_3_sellers.xml
    ```

3. Execute the following `dumpdata` command, which dumps the `Sellers` objects as JSONL:

    ```
    (virtual_env) PS > python manage.py dumpdata chapter_3.seller --format jsonl -o becoming_a_django_entdev/chapter_10/fixtures/chapter_3_sellers.jsonl
    ```

4. To work with YAML formats, you need to install the `pip` package called `pyyaml`. Add this package to your `requirements.txt` file and install it from that file or run the following command to install this package manually into your virtual environment:

    ```
    (virtual_env) PS > pip install pyyaml
    ```

5. Execute the following `dumpdata` command, which dumps the `Sellers` objects as YAML:

   ```
   (virtual_env) PS > python manage.py dumpdata chapter_3.
   seller --format yaml -o becoming_a_django_entdev/
   chapter_10/fixtures/chapter_3_sellers.yaml
   ```

You should now have three more `chapter_3_sellers` files, one in each format: `.xml`, `.jsonl`, and `.yaml`. Open each of these documents to view how the data is represented in each format and how they differ from the default `.json` format.

Next, let's practice removing the primary key, the `"pk"` field, when exporting data into a fixture using the `--natural-primary` option.

Using the --natural-primary option

The `--natural-primary` option is used to generate a fixture that does not include the `"pk"` field for each object that is exported. This is helpful if you have a system that already has data and you need to append data to the existing data. Say the primary key was included; it could conflict with an existing object that has that same primary key but is not the same object. This could potentially result in lost or changed data that produces undesirable results.

Follow these steps to use the `--natural-primary` option:

1. Make sure you are inside your project's root directory, the same folder where your `manage.py` file is located. Then, open a command-line window or terminal and activate your virtual environment, but do not run your project at this time.

2. Execute the following `dumpdata` command, specifying the `seller` table found in the `chapter_3` application:

   ```
   (virtual_env) PS > python manage.py dumpdata chapter_3.
   seller --natural-primary -o becoming_a_django_entdev/
   chapter_10/fixtures/chapter_3_sellers_natural_primary.
   json
   ```

   A new file called `chapter_3_sellers_natural_primary.json` should have been created in your `/chapter_10/fixtures/` folder.

3. Inside that file, format the data so that you can read what is found in it. If you are using Visual Studio, right-click inside your document and select **Format Document** or copy and paste the data into the online tool found here: https://jsonlint.com/.

Now, what you should see is the same exact data as in the previous subsection except all of the `"pk"` fields have been removed from your data, as shown:

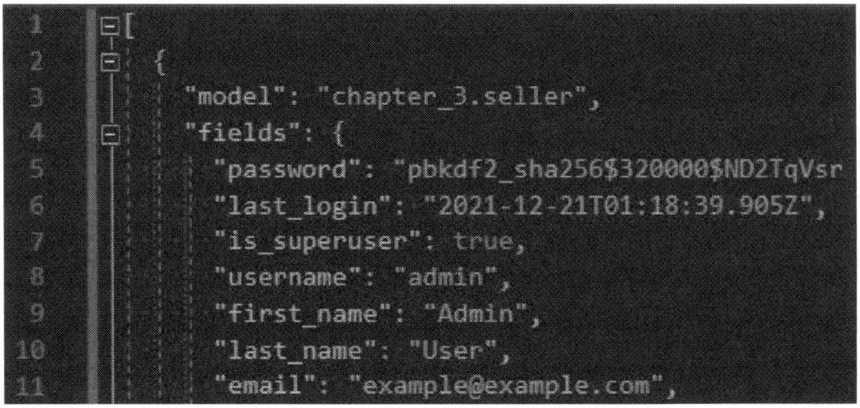

Figure 10.3 – dumpdata --natural-primary option

You should also still be seeing the numeric foreign key values for all `Vehicles` of your `Sellers`, as shown earlier in *Figure 10.2*. This could prove problematic if we are dumping all data using the `--natural-primary` option. What could happen is a vehicle gets created in your new database with its own primary key that doesn't equal the foreign key specified. To overcome that problem, we should also use the `--natural-foreign` option, which we will discuss next.

Using the --natural-foreign option

The `--natural-foreign` option will print out a string representation of all related objects rather than the numeric foreign key value of that object. We also need to write a new model class method on all of our related objects in order to format and structure the string representation of that object when used in this way. The output can differ from the `__str__()` method that we covered in *Chapter 3, Models, Relations, and Inheritance*.

Follow these steps to add a new model method to your `Vehicle` model and then export your `Seller` data again using the `--natural-foreign` option:

1. Inside your existing `/chapter_3/models.py` file, in the existing `Vehicle` model class, add the following `natural_key()` method:

   ```
   # /becoming_a_django_entdev/chapter_3/models.py
   from django.db import models
   ...
   class Vehicle(models.Model):
       ...
       def natural_key(self):
           return self.full_vehicle_name()
   ```

   This method is reliant on the existing `full_vehicle_name()` method created in *Chapter 3*, *Models, Relations, and Inheritance*, in the subsection titled *Custom model method*. Please make sure that method exists in your `Vehicle` model class before proceeding with the next steps.

2. Make sure you are in your project root directory, the same folder where your `manage.py` file is located. Then, open a command-line window or terminal and activate your virtual environment, but do not run your project at this time.

3. Execute the following `dumpdata` command, specifying all of the tables found in the `chapter_3` application:

   ```
   (virtual_env) PS > python manage.py dumpdata chapter_3.seller --natural-foreign -o becoming_a_django_entdev/chapter_10/fixtures/chapter_3_sellers_natural_foreign.json
   ```

   A new file called `chapter_3_sellers_natural_foreign.json` should have been created in your `/chapter_10/fixtures/` folder.

4. Inside that file, format the data so that you can read what is found in it. If you are using Visual Studio, right-click inside your document and select **Format Document** or copy and paste the data into the online tool found here: `https://jsonlint.com/`.

What you should see now is something similar to the following screenshot, where the vehicles list is no longer represented by numbers; it now shows the string returned by the `natural_key()` method that we created:

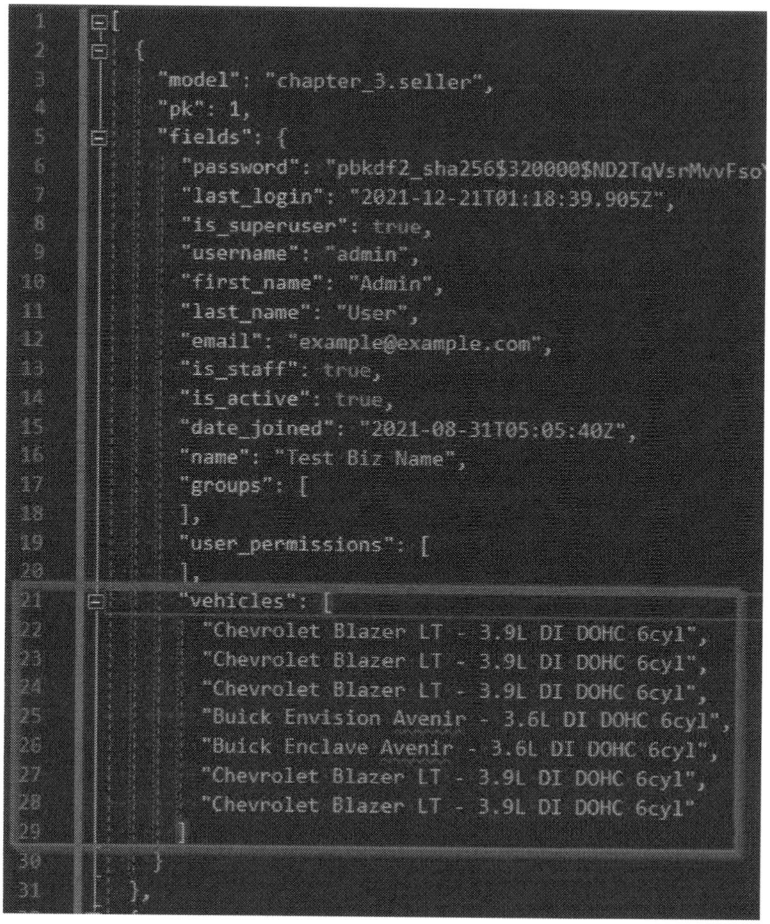

Figure 10.4 – dumpdata --natural-foreign option

If you see duplicate string entries, as you do in the proceeding screenshot, this is because the natural key string representation uses data from models that happen to have the exact same value in this case, even though they're different objects. You may want to go back and configure the `natural_key()` method to return something more unique.

You are welcome to create a `natural_key()` method for every model that exists in the `chapter_3` app and then rerun any combination of these commands over again for practice. Inside the `/chapter_10/fixtures/` folder of the code provided with this book are many different fixture documents that have been pre-generated for you, all using the initial data provided in the `chapter_3.json` fixture file. Inside the `/chapter_10/readme.md` file, you can find a list of commands that extend the examples provided in this chapter. Each of the commands provided generates a different `chapter_10` fixture file.

> **Note**
> You can combine options, such as combining `--natural-foreign --natural-primary` within a single command. Doing so would produce the results found in *Figure 10.4* without the `"pk"` field present.

Next, let's practice importing data with the `loaddata` Django management command.

Importing data from a data fixture

Importing data from a fixture is done using the `loaddata` Django management command. As long as data exists in one of the four file formats, JSON, JSONL, XML, or YAML, it can be imported using this command. Data can be imported even if it was not exported from a Django project. The `loaddata` management command does not have as many options as the `dumpdata` command uses but they do share most of the same options.

We have been using this command throughout most of this book to ensure that we have test data available when working with the exercises of previous chapters. Instead of going through examples of how to use this command in depth, we will briefly remind ourselves how it is used and then describe each of the options that are available and what they are used for.

Using the importdata command

Follow these steps to practice loading the `/chapter_10/fixtures/chapter_3_sellers.json` fixture file that we created earlier in this chapter. If we are successful, we should see no change in our data because we are importing the same data, overwriting itself. You can practice changing field values and/or adding new objects to your file before importing if you wish to see data change in your database management tool:

1. Make sure you are inside your project's root directory, the same folder where your `manage.py` file is located. Then, open a command-line window or terminal and activate your virtual environment, but do not run your project at this time.

2. Execute the following `loaddata` command, telling Django to load only the `chapter_3_sellers.json` fixture:

   ```
   (virtual_env) PS > python manage.py loaddata chapter_3_sellers.json
   ```

   > **Note**
   >
   > In the previous section, we created many different fixture formats, all with the same name, `chapter_3_sellers`, and different file extensions. Because of this, you will have to include the file extension when executing your command. If you are using anything other than JSON file formats, don't forget to always include the `--format` option. If you do not have multiple file formats that share the same name, it is not necessary to include the file extension when using the `loaddata` command.

Each of the options available and what they are used for are listed here:

- `--app` – used to tell Django to search for the fixture file in only the app directory specified using this option, versus having Django search in every app directory. This is sometimes important if you have two fixture files with the same name that exist in two different Django app directories.

- `--database` – tells Django to use a database that is configured in your `settings.py` file that is not the default database specified. Django uses the name you provide to identify that database in your `settings.py` file. This can also be used with the `dumpdata` command.

- `--format` – used to tell Django to use a format other than the default JSON format when importing the data file provided.

- `--exclude, -e` – used to tell Django to omit the `app_name` or `model_name` provided from the data that you are importing.

- `--ignorenonexistent, -i` – used to omit specific fields or models that may have been removed since the time the fixture file was created.

Let's begin working with performance boosters next.

Using the select_related() method

The `select_related()` method is used as a performance booster on queries pertaining to all related `ForeignKey` and `OneToOneField` relationships. This method is primarily used for obtaining the data of single objects that relate to a parent object. This method will not work on `ManyToManyField` relationships. On the SQL level, this method generally uses a left outer join to look up related data. To learn more about the `select_related()` method in its entirety, visit https://docs.djangoproject.com/en/4.0/ref/models/querysets/#select-related.

Here, we will monitor the performance of a page that displays a list of vehicles and the details about each vehicle, including related field data. Use the following subsections to create the required view class, template, and URL pattern to demonstrate this concept in action.

Creating the view

Follow these steps to create your `VehicleView` class:

1. In your `/chapter_10/views.py` file, add the following `VehiclesView` class and `import` statements:

    ```python
    # /becoming_a_django_entdev/chapter_10/views.py
    from django.http import Http404
    from django.template.response import (
        TemplateResponse
    )
    from django.views.generic import View
    from ..chapter_3.models import Vehicle

    class VehiclesView(View):
        template_name = 'chapter_10/vehicles.html'
    ```

    In this view class, we are telling Django to use the `/chapter_10/vehicles.html` file as the template, which we will create soon.

2. Add the following `get()` method to your `VehiclesView` class:

    ```python
    # /becoming_a_django_entdev/chapter_10/views.py
    ...
    class VehiclesView(View):
        ...
    ```

```python
def get(self, request, *args, **kwargs):
    try:
        vehicles = Vehicle.objects.all()
    except Vehicle.DoesNotExist:
        raise Http404('No Vehicles Found')

    return TemplateResponse(
        request,
        self.template_name,
        {'vehicles': vehicles}
    )
```

To explain what this `get()` method is doing, we are performing an `all()` query on the `Vehicle` model object. If no vehicles are found, we then raise an `Http404` not-found response. If vehicles are found, we then return a `TemplateResponse` with the vehicles QuerySet provided as context into the template that is rendered.

> **Note**
>
> The query performed in the `get()` method is not currently performance boosted. Jump ahead to the subsection titled *First demo* of this chapter to see the performance-boosted query.

Let's build the template next.

Building the template

Follow these steps to create your vehicles list template file:

1. Create a file called `vehicles.html` in the `/chapter_10/templates/chapter_10/` directory. Inside this file, add the following code:

    ```html
    # /becoming_a_django_entdev/chapter_10/templates/
    chapter_10/vehicles.html
    {% load static chapter_4 %}

    <html lang="en" xmlns="http://www.w3.org/1999/xhtml">
        <head>
            <title>All Vehicles Page</title>
        </head>
    ```

```
        <body style="text-align:center"
            class="chapter_10">
            <h1>All Vehicles</h1>
        </body>
</html>
```

The `{% load %}` tag imports the `templatetags` file that we created in *Chapter 4, URLs, Views, and Templates*, in the subsection titled *Custom tags and filters*. If you do not have the `chapter_4.py` file created at this time, just remove `chapter_4` from the `{% load %}` tag in the preceding code block and remove `|vehicle_make` shown in the code block in *step 2*.

2. In that same file, just before the closing `</body>` tag, add the following conditional and `for` loop, which will populate your page with the information shown for each `vehicle` in the `vehicles` QuerySet:

```
# /becoming_a_django_entdev/chapter_10/templates/
chapter_10/vehicles.html
...
        <body ...>
            ...
            {% if vehicles %}
                {% for vehicle in vehicles %}
                    <br />
                    <p>VIN #: {{ vehicle.vin }}</p>
                    <p>Price: {{ vehicle.price }}</p>
                    <p>Make: {{ vehicle.make|vehicle_make }}</p>
                    <p>Model: {{ vehicle.vehicle_model }}</p>
                    <p>Engine: {{ vehicle.engine }}</p>
                    <p>Is Sold? {{ vehicle.sold }}</p>
                    <br /><hr />
                {% endfor %}
            {% endif %}
        </body>
...
```

The preceding conditional statement will check to see whether there are any vehicles in the `vehicles` QuerySet object. Even though we are doing this with the try/except statement in the view class, it is still good practice to do this in the template just in case there are no exception handlers set in the view class/method to check for when an object is not found. We are displaying all of the field data that exists for each object. The `Engine` and `VehicleModel` data shown in the preceding code block are the related objects that we will monitor our performance on.

Let's map the URL pattern that we need next.

Mapping the URL pattern

Follow these step to map the URL pattern that we will be using to access this test page:

1. In your `/chapter_10/urls.py` file, add the following path to the `urlpatterns` list:

    ```
    from django.urls import path
    from .views import VehiclesView

    urlpatterns = [
        ...
        path(
            'all-vehicles/',
            VehiclesView.as_view(),
            name = 'all-vehicles'
        ),
    ]
    ```

The path that we just mapped to the `VehiclesView` class will point to the URL `http://localhost:8000/all-vehicles/`.

Next, let's inspect the performance of the vehicles listing page with the DjDT.

First demo

Follow these steps to view the vehicles listing page and inspect its database query performance with the DjDT:

1. Make sure your project is running in your virtual environment and navigate to the URL `http://localhost:8000/all-vehicles/`. If you are using the data provided with the `chapter_3` app fixture, you should see at least seven sets of vehicles, each separated by a solid horizontal line.

2. Open the DjDT and look at the **SQL** section. You should see at least **15 queries**, as shown in the following screenshot:

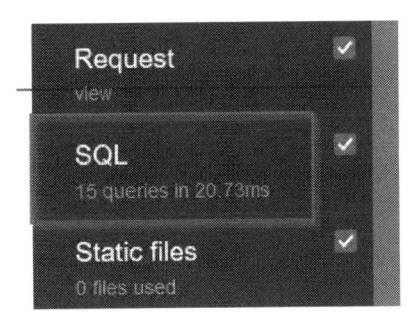

Figure 10.5 – Query without the select_related() method

3. Now, in your `/chapter_10/views.py` file, under the `get()` method of the `VehiclesView` class, change your query to the one highlighted in the following snippet, where we are adding the `select_related()` method to the query that we last used:

```python
# /becoming_a_django_entdev/chapter_10/views.py
...
class VehiclesView(View):
    ...
    def get(self, request, *args, **kwargs):
        try:
            vehicles=Vehicle.objects.select_related(
                'vehicle_model',
                'engine'
            ).all()
        ...
```

Inside the `select_related()` method, we are telling Django to grab the related `vehicle_model` and `engine` field data.

4. Refresh the page at `http://localhost:8000/all-vehicles/` and inspect the **SQL** section of the DjDT one more time. This time, you should only see at least **1 query**, as shown in the following screenshot:

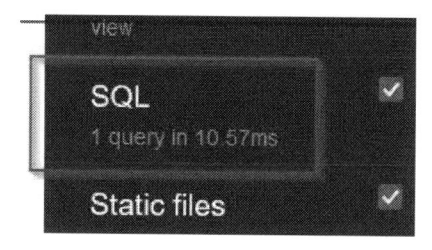

Figure 10.6 – Query with the select_related() method

As we can see, with this particular set of data, we were able to shave about 14 SQL query operations off of this search task. This also shaved off 10.16 ms from the original time that it took. While 10.16 ms may seem very small, remember, we only have about a dozen records that pertain to this particular dataset; imagine the difference in a dataset with a few hundred thousand records. The time adds up.

When we open the **SQL** tab to see what is going on, we can see that this one SQL query that was performed used a series of `LEFT OUTER JOIN` operations to obtain all related objects.

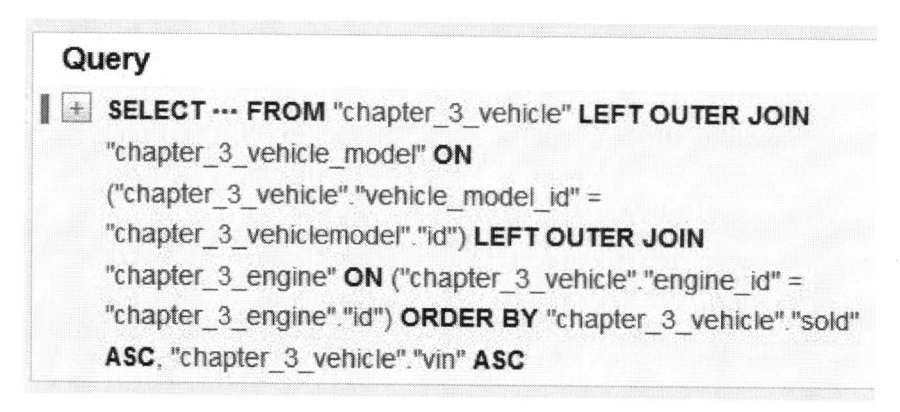

Figure 10.7 – Inspecting the select_related() query

Let's see what the `prefetch_related()` method does next.

Using the prefetch_related() method

The `prefetch_related()` method is used as a performance booster on queries pertaining to `ManyToManyField` relationships. This method can also be used for `ForeignKey` and `OneToOneField` relationships and allows for forward and backward lookups, as we will soon practice doing. On the SQL level, this method will generally use a WHERE or INNER JOIN statement to perform lookup operations. Unlike the `select_related()` method, the `prefetch_related()` method will perform a separate SQL query for each of the related sets of objects. For example, if we looked up a `Seller` and wanted the related `Vehicles` and their related `VehicleModel` and `Engine` objects, then Django would perform four separate queries to look up all the related data. To learn more about the `prefetch_related()` method in its entirety, visit https://docs.djangoproject.com/en/4.0/ref/models/querysets/#prefetch-related.

The following are two exercises, related to the *vehicles view* and the *sellers view*, to practice using the `prefetch_related()` method in different ways.

Vehicles view

In this exercise, we will modify the existing `VehiclesView` class that we created in the *Using the select_related() method* section of this chapter. What we did in that exercise was created a page that displayed all of the vehicles that are in our system and then performance boosted how we looked up the related `VehicleModel` and `Engine` objects. Using the `prefetch_related()` method, we will look up the related `Seller` object to display who is selling that particular vehicle.

Use the following subsections to prepare your template for this demonstration. The view and URL pattern will remain the same as before.

Checking the view

Leave your existing `VehiclesView` class the same as before, where it is using the performance-boosted query from the last demonstration, as follows:

```python
# /becoming_a_django_entdev/chapter_10/views.py
...
        Vehicles = Vehicle.objects.select_related(
            'vehicle_model',
            'engine'
        ).all()
...
```

We will modify this soon, but we first want to monitor how displaying the `seller` object in the template will change the performance-boosted query that we have now.

Modifying the template

Follow these steps to modify your vehicles list template:

1. In your /chapter_10/vehicles.html file, add the following highlighted code, just above the `<br /><hr />` line and below your last `vehicle` detail item:

   ```
   # /becoming_a_django_entdev/chapter_10/templates/
   chapter_10/vehicles.html
   ...
           {% if vehicles %}
               {% for vehicle in vehicles %}
                   ...
                   <p>Is Sold? {{ vehicle.sold }}</p>
                   {% for seller in vehicle.
                       vehicle_sellers.all %}
                       {{ seller.username }}
                   {% endfor %}
                   <br /><hr />
               {% endfor %}
           {% endif %}
   ...
   ```

2. It is important to note that the name used to access a `seller`, as in `vehicle_sellers` in `vehicle.vehicle_sellers.all`, is set on the `vehicles` field of the `Seller` model class, using the `related_name` argument. Make sure, in your /chapter_3/models.py file, under the `Seller` model class, that the `vehicles` field is using the arguments and values highlighted in the following snippet:

   ```
   # /becoming_a_django_entdev/chapter_3/models.py
   ...
   class Seller(AbstractUser):
       ...
       vehicles = models.ManyToManyField(
           Vehicle,
           verbose_name = 'Vehicles',
           related_name = 'vehicle_sellers',
   ```

```
                related_query_name = 'vehicle_seller',
                blank = True,
            )
```

> **Note**
> If the value of a `related_name` or `related_query_name` argument of a field on a model class ever changes, you will need to rerun your Django migration commands once again to reflect those changes in your database.

Let's see how this changes our performance now.

Second demo

Follow these steps to see how these changes affect the output of the **SQL** tab in the DjDT:

1. Make sure your project is running in your virtual environment and navigate to or refresh the URL `http://localhost:8000/all-vehicles/` one more time.

2. Inspect the **SQL** section of the DjDT one more time and you should no longer see **1 query** as we saw before with the `select_related()` method. Instead, we are now seeing at least **8 queries**, as shown in the following screenshot:

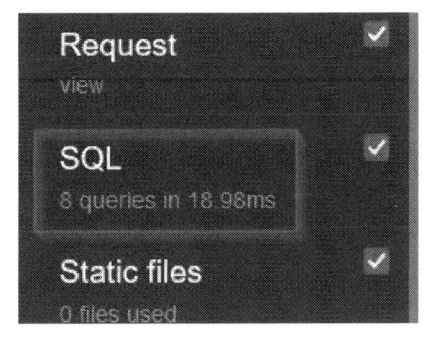

Figure 10.8 – Query with the select_related() method showing related seller

We are seeing seven extra queries in our search now, one extra for each seller that relates to all seven of the vehicles found.

3. In your `/chapter_10/views.py` file, in the same `VehiclesView` class, change the query to the one shown in the following code snippet:

```
# /becoming_a_django_entdev/chapter_10/views.py
...
        Vehicles = Vehicle.objects.prefetch_related(
    'vehicle_sellers'
```

```
).select_related(
    'vehicle_model',
    'engine'
).all()
...
```

We just added the `prefetch_related('vehicle_sellers')` method to the query that we had before, keeping the previous `select_related()` operation. Make sure you are following proper Python indentation where this is used. There is limited room to display this properly in the preceding example.

4. Refresh the URL `http://localhost:8000/all-vehicles/` one more time and inspect the **SQL** section of the DjDT one more time. You should now see at least **2 queries**, as shown in the following screenshot:

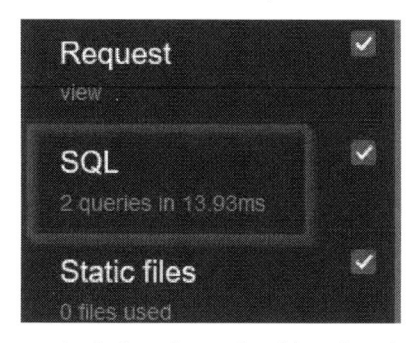

Figure 10.9 – Query using both the select_related() and prefetch_related() methods

If we inspect the **SQL** tab even further by clicking on it, we can see that Django performed the same **LEFT OUTER JOIN** lookup from before, and then the `prefetch_related()` method added the **INNER JOIN** and **WHERE** lookup, as shown in the following screenshot:

```
Query
  SELECT ··· FROM "chapter_3_vehicle" LEFT OUTER JOIN
    "chapter_3_vehicle_model" ON
    ("chapter_3_vehicle"."vehicle_model_id" =
    "chapter_3_vehiclemodel"."id") LEFT OUTER JOIN
    "chapter_3_engine" ON ("chapter_3_vehicle"."engine_id" =
    "chapter_3_engine"."id") ORDER BY "chapter_3_vehicle"."sold"
    ASC, "chapter_3_vehicle"."vin" ASC
  SELECT ··· FROM "chapter_3_seller" INNER JOIN
    "chapter_3_seller_vehicles" ON ("chapter_3_seller"."id" =
    "chapter_3_seller_vehicles"."seller_id") WHERE
    "chapter_3_seller_vehicles"."vehicle_id" IN (2, 4, 5, 6, 7, 1, 3)
    ORDER BY "chapter_3_seller"."name" ASC
```

Figure 10.10 – Inspecting both the select_related() and prefetch_related() queries

We can see from before that Django was performing an additional lookup for each of the `vehicle_sellers` objects that it was seeking to display the username of, on your page. That was how we wound up with eight queries after adding the `{% for seller in vehicle.vehicle_sellers.all %}` loop to the `/chapter_10/vehicles.html` template file. When we added the `prefetch_related()` method to the query operation in the `VehiclesView` class, it just added one extra lookup operation that retrieved all seven of the `vehicle_sellers` objects that pertain to this dataset, resulting in the two queries that we have now and reducing the excess. Adding more field lookups and using context in multiple places within your template file can sometimes increase your query count.

Next, let's apply the `prefetch_related()` method to a sellers listing page and see how it behaves following a lookup in the opposite direction of how we used it here.

Sellers view

In this exercise, we will create a new URL pattern, view class, and template that will display a list of sellers and the related vehicles that they are selling.

Use the following subsections to create the required view class, template, and URL pattern needed to build the sellers listing page.

Creating the view

Follow these steps to create your `SellersView` class:

1. In your `/chapter_10/views.py` file, add the following `SellersView` class and `import` statements:

    ```
    # /becoming_a_django_entdev/chapter_10/views.py
    from django.http import Http404
    from django.template.response import (
        TemplateResponse
    )
    from django.views.generic import View
    from ..chapter_3.models import Seller, Vehicle

    class SellersView(View):
        template_name = 'chapter_10/sellers.html'
    ```

    In this view class, we are telling Django to use the `/chapter_10/sellers.html` file as the template, which we will create soon. We are also using the same imports as before and then adding the `Seller` model class as a new import.

2. Add the following `get()` method to your `SellersView` class:

    ```
    # /becoming_a_django_entdev/chapter_10/views.py
    ...
    class SellersView(View):
        ...
        def get(self, request, *args, **kwargs):
            try:
                sellers = Seller.objects.all()
            except Seller.DoesNotExist:
                raise Http404('No Sellers Found')

            return TemplateResponse(
                request,
                self.template_name,
                {'sellers': sellers}
            )
    ```

The `get()` method is structured the same as the `VehiclesView` class. The only difference is that we are using the `Seller` model class to perform a query on. Again, this query is not currently performance boosted; we will do that after we take a measurement of this query operation.

Let's build the template next.

Building the template

Follow these steps to build the sellers listing page template:

1. Create a file called `sellers.html` in the `/chapter_10/templates/chapter_10/` directory. Inside this file, add the following code:

    ```
    # /becoming_a_django_entdev/chapter_10/templates/
    chapter_10/sellers.html
    {% load static chapter_4 %}

    <html lang="en" xmlns="http://www.w3.org/1999/xhtml">
        <head>
            <title>All Sellers Page</title>
            <style type="text/css">
                ...Found With the Code of this Book...
            </style>
        </head>

        <body style="text-align:center"
            class="chapter_10">
            <h1>All Sellers</h1>
        </body>
    </html>
    ```

    The `{% load %}` tag imports the `templatetags` file that we created in *Chapter 4, URLs, Views, and Templates* in the subsection titled *Custom tags and filters*. If you do not have the `chapter_4.py` file created at this time, just remove `chapter_4` from the `{% load %}` tag in the preceding code block and remove `|vehicle_make` where it is shown in *step 3*.

    The code of this book also provides additional CSS class styles. You can find those styles in the same file found with the code of this book and copy and paste them into your document to view these objects in a more organized way. This is not a necessary step to proceed.

2. Just before the closing `</body>` tag, add the following conditional and `for` loop, which will populate your page with the information for each `seller` in the `sellers` QuerySet:

```
# /becoming_a_django_entdev/chapter_10/templates/
chapter_10/sellers.html
...
    <body ...>
        ...
        {% if sellers %}
            {% for seller in sellers %}
                <p>First Name: {{ seller.first_name }}</p>
                <p>Last Name: {{ seller.last_name }}</p>
                <p>Username: {{ seller.username }}</p>
                <p>Business Name: {{ seller.name }}</p>
                <p>Email: {{ seller.email }}</p>
                <p>Last Login: {{ seller.last_login }}</p>
                <p>Date Joined: {{ seller.date_joined
                    }}</p>
                <p>Is Staff? {{ seller.is_staff }}</p>
                <p>Is Active? {{ seller.is_active
                    }}</p>
                <p>Is Superuser? {{
                    seller.is_superuser }}</p>
                <br /><hr /><br />
            {% endfor %}
        {% endif %}
    </body>
...
```

3. Just after the **Is Superuser** paragraph and before the `<br /><hr /><br />` code snippet line, insert the following conditional and `for` loop:

```
# /becoming_a_django_entdev/chapter_10/templates/
chapter_10/sellers.html
...
                {% for seller in sellers %}
                    ...
```

```django
                        <p>Is Superuser? {{
                            seller.is_superuser }}</p>

                    {% if seller.vehicles.all %}
                        <h2>Seller Vehicles</h2>

                        {% for vehicle in seller.
                            vehicles.all %}
                            <div class="vehicle-box">
                                <p>VIN #: {{ vehicle.vin
                                    }}</p>
                                <p>Price: {{ vehicle.price
                                    }}</p>
                                <p>Make: {{ vehicle.make
                                    |vehicle_make }}</p>
                                <p>Model: {{ vehicle.
                                    vehicle_model }}</p>
                                <p>Engine: {{
                                    vehicle.engine }}</p>
                                <p>Is Sold? {{ vehicle
                                    .sold }}</p>
                            </div>
                        {% endfor %}
                    {% endif %}

                    <br /><hr /><br />
                {% endfor %}
...
```

The logic here is pretty much the same as the vehicles listing page that we previously built. We added an additional layer of looping inside the `sellers` loop that loops through the `vehicles` related to each `seller`.

Let's map the URL pattern that we will need next.

Mapping the URL pattern

Take the following step to map the URL pattern that we will be using to access this listing page.

In your `/chapter_10/urls.py` file, add the following path to your `urlpatterns` list:

```python
from django.urls import path
from .views import SellersView, VehiclesView

urlpatterns = [
    ...
    path(
        'all-sellers/',
        SellersView.as_view(),
        name = 'all-sellers'
    )
]
```

The path that we just mapped to the `SellersView` class will point to the URL `http://localhost:8000/all-sellers/`.

Let's inspect the performance of the sellers listing page with the DjDT next.

Third demo

Follow these steps to view the sellers listing page and inspect its database query performance with the DjDT:

1. Make sure your project is running in your virtual environment and navigate to the URL `http://localhost:8000/all-sellers/`. If you are using the data provided with the `chapter_3` app fixture, you should see at least one set of `seller` data and seven `vehicles` for the first `seller`.

   If you have been following along with this book, you should have about three `sellers` in your database as a result of the exercises performed in previous chapters. Only one seller was provided in the `chapter_3` fixture. For the performance results shown in the following steps, assume that you have three `sellers` and seven `vehicles`, as your actual data may vary.

2. Open the DjDT and look at the **SQL** tab. You should see at least **19 queries**, as shown in the following screenshot:

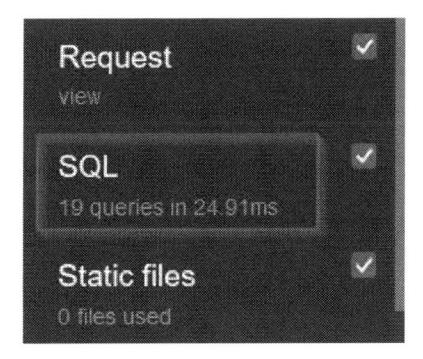

Figure 10.11 – Sellers list page not performance boosted

There are so many queries being executed because Django is looking up each vehicle and each related `vehicle_model` and `engine` over and over again. The conditional that we wrote `{% if seller.vehicles.all %}`, checking if `vehicles` exist, and also added a single query to the page performance.

3. Now, in your `/chapter_10/views.py` file, under the `get()` method of the `SellersView` class, change the query to the one highlighted in the following code snippet, where we are adding the `prefetch_related()` method to what we had before:

```python
# /becoming_a_django_entdev/chapter_10/views.py
...
class SellersView(View):
    ...
    def get(self, request, *args, **kwargs):
        try:
            sellers = Seller.objects.prefetch_related(
    'vehicles',
    'vehicles__vehicle_model',
    'vehicles__engine'
).all()
            ...
```

Inside the `prefetch_related()` method, we are telling Django to grab the related `vehicles` and then, in a separate action, the related `vehicle_model` and `engine` of each `vehicle` object. Whenever we need to specify other related fields, as we are doing in the preceding code block, we use a double underscore, __, to navigate up or down in a set of relationships. Please make sure you are following proper Python indentation where this is used. There is limited room to display this properly in the example shown previously.

4. Refresh the URL `http://localhost:8000/all-sellers/` one more time and inspect the **SQL** tab of the DjDT one more time. You should now see at least **4 queries**, as shown in the following screenshot:

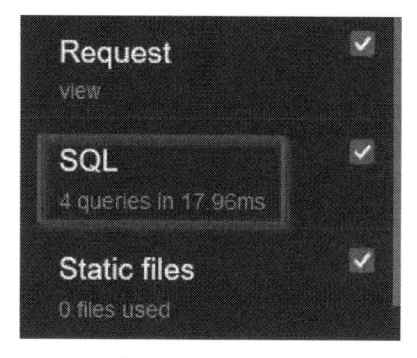

Figure 10.12 – Sellers list page performance boosted

We also saved 6.95 ms of time using the performance-boosted method with this query lookup task. If we inspect the **SQL** tab even further by clicking on it, we can see that Django performed one query for the `Seller` objects, one for the `Vehicle` objects, one for the `VehicleModel` objects, and the last for the `Engine` objects. Django used a combination of WHERE clauses and INNER JOIN operations to retrieve the related data.

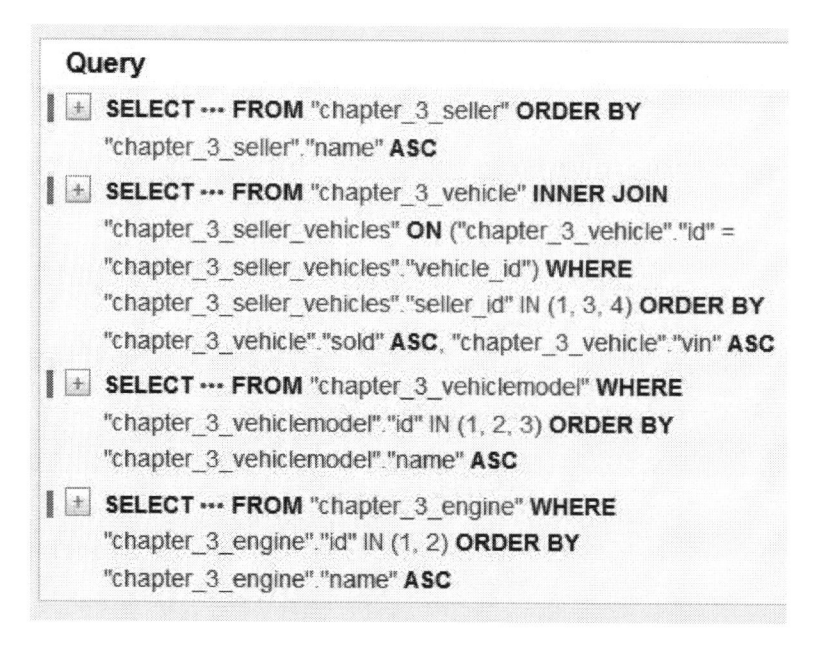

Figure 10.13 – Inspecting the Sellers list page queries

Django also provides a `Prefetch()` class that can be used to perform even more complex queries with performance-boosted capabilities. Next, let's use this class to perform advanced filtering of the `vehicles` that relate to a `seller`.

Using the Prefetch() class

The `Prefetch()` class that is provided in the `django.db.models` library is used to control how a `prefetch_related()` operation is performed. For instance, we will use it to filter and show only `vehicles` that are of the `VehicleModel` that equals `"Blazer LT"`. We can also prefetch all related objects when performing filters in this way. To learn about how to use this class in depth, visit https://docs.djangoproject.com/en/4.0/ref/models/querysets/#prefetch-objects.

Use the following subsections to prepare your view class and template for this demonstration. The URL pattern will remain the same as the demonstration found in the *Sellers view* subsection of this chapter.

Modifying the view

Follow these steps to modify your existing `SellersView` class for this next exercise:

1. In your `/chapter_10/views.py` file, add the following `import` statement, preferably before the existing `import` statements:

    ```
    # /becoming_a_django_entdev/chapter_10/views.py
    from django.db.models import Prefetch
    ...
    ```

2. In the `SellersView` class found inside this file, change your query statement to the one shown in the following code snippet:

    ```
    # /becoming_a_django_entdev/chapter_10/views.py
    ...
    class SellersView(View):
        ...
            sellers = Seller.objects.prefetch_related(
                Prefetch(
                    'vehicles',
                    to_attr = 'filtered_vehicles',
                    queryset = Vehicle.objects.filter(
    ```

```
                            vehicle_model__name =
                                'Blazer LT'
    )
                ),
            'filtered_vehicles__vehicle_model',
            'filtered_vehicles__engine'
        ).all()
...
```

Please make sure you are following proper Python indentation where this is used. There is limited room to display this properly in the preceding example.

We are writing our query statement similar to what we wrote before. What we did differently this time is placed the `Prefetch()` class inside the `prefetch_related()` method, as the first argument of that method. The `Prefetch()` class accepts three arguments itself. The first is the lookup argument, which is usually a field but it can also be used to traverse relationships upstream and downstream using the double underscore, __, in the string. The second and third arguments are optional and do not have to be in the exact order. The `to_attr` argument is used to store the resulting QuerySet as a list of objects with the name specified as its value. The QuerySet argument is used to perform a specific query on the subset of those items. In the preceding example, we performed the `filter()` operation, searching only for vehicles with a `vehicle_model__name` of "Blazer LT".

After the `Prefetch()` class, in the same `prefetch_related()` method that we are using previously, we added two more field lookups, those being the `filtered_vehicles__vehicle_model` and `filtered_vehicles__engine` objects. This will prefetch the related objects pertaining to the custom filtered list that we just created.

Next, we need to modify our existing template file in order to work with the `filtered_vehicles` list of objects.

Modifying the template

Follow these step to modify your existing sellers listing template file to work with the `filtered_vehicles` list that was created:

1. In your existing `/chapter_10/sellers.html` file, change the two lines where `seller.vehicles.all` is used to now say `seller.filtered_vehicles`, as shown:

    ```
    # /becoming_a_django_entdev/chapter_10/templates/chapter_10/sellers.html
    ```

```
            {% for seller in sellers %}
            ...
            {% if seller.filtered_vehicles %}
                <h2>Seller Vehicles</h2>

                {% for vehicle in
                    seller.filtered_vehicles %}
                ...
                {% endfor %}
            {% endif %}

            <br /><hr /><br />
        {% endfor %}
...
```

That's all that we need to modify. Let's see how this affected our performance next.

Fourth demo

Follow these steps to view the sellers listing page and inspect its database query performance using the `Prefetch()` class approach to how a query operation is performed:

1. Refresh the URL `http://localhost:8000/all-sellers/` in your browser.
2. Open the DjDT and look at the **SQL** tab. You should see at least **4 queries**, as shown in the following screenshot:

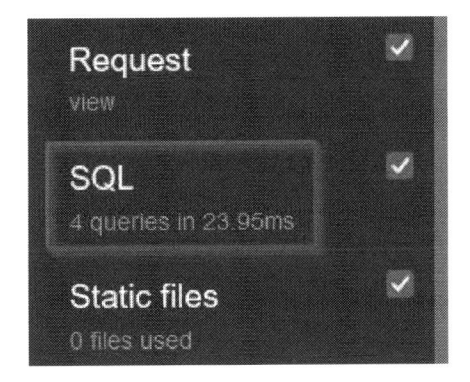

Figure 10.14 – Sellers list page using the Prefetch class

This should also be the same number of queries that we saw in our previous example, shown in *Figure 10.12*. The only difference in this dataset is that we see five `vehicles` under the first `seller` on the page, whereas before, we had seven `vehicles` shown. The results only display the **Blazer LT** vehicles now, as shown in the following screenshot:

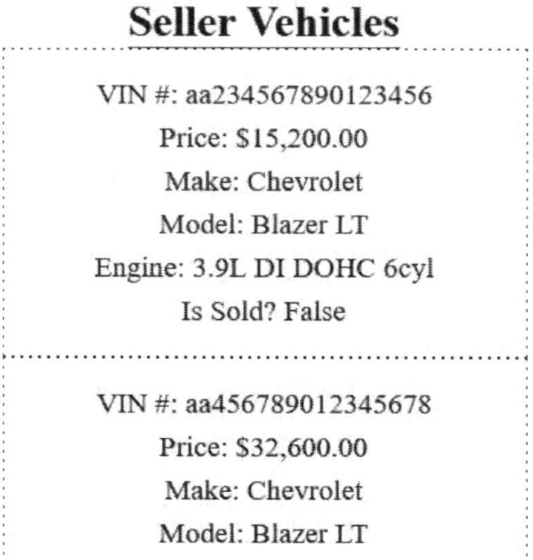

Seller Vehicles

VIN #: aa234567890123456

Price: $15,200.00

Make: Chevrolet

Model: Blazer LT

Engine: 3.9L DI DOHC 6cyl

Is Sold? False

VIN #: aa456789012345678

Price: $32,600.00

Make: Chevrolet

Model: Blazer LT

Figure 10.15 – Sellers list page using the Prefetch class results

While the number of results may differ, the number of queries that are executed remains the same. With this approach, we can define a very granular search query that is performance boosted.

Summary

We were able to conclude our journey in how to use Django to build enterprise-level systems by learning how to import and export data and apply performance-boosting tricks to all query operations. Knowing how to work with data is just as important as building the data siloes that they reside in. When you are working with existing systems, there is always the need to export the existing data from an old system and import that data into your new system. We now know how that is done. We can also combine this knowledge with the skills learned in *Chapter 2, Project Configuration*, in the subsection titled *Heroku database push/pull operations* to work with data in your remote testing and production environments as well. Use each tool as needed to perform different tasks throughout your project's life cycle.

The performance-boosting methods that were introduced in this chapter are intended to be applied to any query operation. Refer to the topics discussed throughout *Chapter 3, Models, Relations, and Inheritance*, to learn more about how to structure your data and perform other query operations. In that same chapter, you can also apply performance boosters where queries are made inside of model managers.

There is a wealth of knowledge, tips, and tricks that relate to the world of Django that were not covered in this book. I hope you enjoyed learning what you have read and practiced so far and I hope that you continue on your journey to learn even more. Use the links, resources, and references to packages and tools scattered throughout this book to expand your learning beyond what has been given to you. Feel free to reach out to me via any of the contact methods provided if you have questions, would like to point out an error in this book, or share a compliment. While I dedicated a lot of time and energy to writing this book and checking and then re-checking my work, we are all human and mistakes are bound to slip through the cracks. I would also love to hear about what marvels you created as a result of reading this book. Thank you all for taking the time to read this!

Index

Symbols

.gitignore file
   creating 79, 80
@property decorator 131
{% url %} template tag
   using 189, 190

A

absolute URLs
   context processor, creating 192-194
   resolving 192
   resolving, within model class 197, 198
   resolving, with request object 195-197
add view 276
add view-related options
   about 299
   add_fieldsets option 299, 300
   prepopulated_fields option 300, 301
admin classes, writing
   ModelAdmin class, using 272
   UserAdmin class, using 273
admin class methods
   adding 301
   delete_model() method 304, 305
   get_form() method 302
   save_model() method 304

admin class options
   change/add view-related options 286
   changelist view-related options 277
   configuring 276
advanced deployment 41
aggregate() 148, 149
aggregation functions
   about 148
   reference link 148
all() method 146
Amazon Selling Partner API (SP-API) 13
Amazon Web Services (AWS) 27
annotate() method 150
ANSI SQL Compliance 89
API root 373
Application Programming Interface (API)
   about 359
   Open APIs 13
   Partner APIs 13
   Private APIs 13
   types 12
arguments 107
artifact 21
as_p 242
as_table 243
as_ul 243

Asynchronous Server Gateway
    Interface (ASGI) 204
async keyword
  using 382
Atom
  about 52
  URL 52
authenticated view requests
  testing 425
  testing, with Client() class 425-427
automated testing
  in Django 411, 412
automatic deployment
  enabling 36, 37
await keyword
  using 382

B

basic model classes
  extending 133, 134
basic Python scripts
  running 139, 140
Behavioral Diagraming 19
Black
  URL 12
branches
  configuring 39-41
Browsable API
  using 373-376
buildpack 29
build scripts 42
business requirements 15

C

change/add view-related options
  about 286
  exclude option 286
  fieldsets option 287, 289
  fields option 287
  filter_horizontal option 290, 291
  filter_vertical option 291
  form option 291
  inlines option 292
  radio fields option 297, 298
  save_on_top option 299
changelist view 276
changelist view-related options
  about 277
  actions_on_bottom option 278
  actions_on_top option 278
  actions option 277
  actions_selection_counter option 279
  list_display_links option 280, 281
  list_display option 279, 280
  list_editable option 281, 282
  list_filter option 282
  list_per_page option 283
  ordering option 284
  preserve_filters option 284
  search_fields option 285
change view 276
chapter_3 data fixture
  loading 145
class-based views
  extending 203
  testing 422-424
  using 199-202
class diagram 20
Client() class
  using 425-429

Index 491

command line
  using 59, 60
complex views
  asynchronous views 204
  class-based views 199-202
  working with 199
conditional responses
  working with 182, 183
containerization 43
containers
  about 43
  repository 43
Content Management System (CMS) 8
context 158
context processor
  creating 192-194
  data, using in template 194, 195
Continuous Integration (CI) tools 37
CreateView class
  about 248
  configuring 248-252
custom admin form classes
  admin form, initializing 305, 306
  writing 305
custom API endpoints
  JavaScript, modifying 390, 391
  second demo 392-396
  template, building 389, 390
  URL pattern, mapping 391, 392
  view, creating 386-389
  writing 386
custom email templates
  for HTML emails 342-344
  for plain text emails 340-342
  template context, providing 344-347
  writing 340
Customer Relationship
    Management (CRM) 8

custom field class
  using 232, 233
custom form fields
  creating 229
custom message levels
  about 322
  using, to create message 326
custom path converters
  about 174
  creating 174, 175
custom repositories 35
custom tags and filters
  creating 210-212

D

data
  saving 141-143
Database Functions
  reference link 126
database indexing 125
database tables
  dropping 134, 135
data fixture
  about 452
  data, exporting into 452
  data, importing from 463
data integrity 17
data parsing 452
data warehousing 87
db_table 127, 128
decorator
  @property 131
  about 129, 131
  using 129
delete view 276
deployment 27

492 Index

deployment diagram
  about 21
  artifact 21
  device 21
  node 21
detail page 375
detail page/view 105
development tools
  integrated development
    environments (IDE) 53, 54
  selecting 51
  text editor 52
device 21
Django
  automated testing 411, 412
  features 10, 11
  need for 10
django-address field
  reference link 113
Django admin site
  activating 270
  admin classes, writing 272
  logging into 271, 272
  models, registering 274
  URL 271
  using 269
Django app
  activating 82, 83
  command line, using 82
  creating 81
  IDE, using 81, 82
Django, authentication system
  permission groups 310
  permissions, granting 309, 310
  seller, adding 307-309
  using 307
django-ckeditor
  reference link 113

djangocms-text-ckeditor
  reference link 113
Django database
  settings, using 84
  types 84
Django database, types
  MariaDB 87
  MySQL 86
  Oracle 87, 88
  PostgreSQL 89
  SQLite 85
  SQL Server 88
Django Debug Toolbar (DjDT)
  about 407
  installing 434-436
  performance of sellers listing
    page, inspecting 480-483
  performance of vehicles listing
    page, inspecting 469, 470
  settings, adjusting 436, 437
  usage 437, 439
  using 434
  Vehicles view, demo 473-475
Django Debug Toolbar (DjDT), panel
  Cache panel 446
  Headers panel 441
  History panel 439
  Intercept redirects checkbox 447
  Logging panel 446, 447
  Profiling checkbox 448
  Request panel 442
  Settings panel 440
  Signals panel 446
  SQL panel 442, 443
  Static files panel 444
  Templates panel 445, 446
  Time tab 440
  Versions panel 440

Django documentation, on working
    with Apache web server
  reference link 27
django-extensions package
  installing, on existing Django project 23
django-image-cropping
  reference link 113
Django media files 78
Django messages framework
  enabling 318, 319
  using 318
Django models
  testing 415-419
django-money fields
  reference link 113
django-phone-field
  reference link 113
Django REST API endpoints
  object test case, creating 429-431
  object test case, updating 431-434
  testing 429
Django REST framework
  authentication tokens 396
  Browsable API, using 373-376
  installing 362-364
  serializer class, creating 364, 365
  URL routers, using 371-373
  viewset classes 369-371
Django REST framework,
       authentication tokens
  JavaScript, modifying 401, 402
  project configuration 396-398
  template, building 401
  third demo 403-405
  URL pattern, mapping 402, 403
  view, creating 398-400

Django shell
  basic Python scripts, running 139, 140
  chapter_3 data fixture, loading 145
  data, saving 141-143
  SECRET_KEY variable,
       generating 140, 141
  using 138
Django static files 77, 78
Django template language 10
django.test library
  test classes 411
Django User model
  extending 136-138
Docker containers 43
Document Object Model (DOM) 221
domain forwarding 44
Domain Name System (DNS) 44-46
Don't Repeat Yourself (DRY) 10, 132, 181
dumpdata command
  --exclude option, using 457, 458
  --format option, using 458, 459
  --natural-foreign option, using 460-463
  --natural-primary option,
       using 459, 460
  specific application, exporting 455-457
  using 453-455
dynamic inline formsets 262-264

E

Eclipse
  PyDev with 54, 55
Eclipse IDE 54
ECMAScript 11
email notifications
  as HTML emails 334
  as HTML emails, with plain
       text alternative 335-337

    as plain text emails 331-334
    configuring 331
    that fail silently 339, 340
    with file attachments 337-339
  enterprise
    building 6
  Enterprise Application Software (EAS) 6
  Enterprise Asset Management (EAM) 8
  Enterprise Content Management (ECM) 8
  Enterprise Information System (EIS) 9
  enterprise-level applications
    selecting, reasons 6, 7
  Enterprise Resource Planning (ERP) 9
  enterprise systems
    Customer Relationship Management 8
    Enterprise Asset Management (EAM) 8
    Enterprise Content
      Management (ECM) 8
    Enterprise Information System (EIS) 9
    Enterprise Resource Planning (ERP) 9
    Supply Chain Management 9
    types 7
  Entity Relationship Diagram (ERD) 20, 22
  environment file
    creating 73
    local variables 74, 75
    remote variables 75, 76
  environments
    managing, in Heroku 34, 35
  error page templates 212, 213
  extra tags
    messages, creating 327, 328

F

  field arguments
    about 107, 108
    reference link 221

  Field class 230-232
  field constraints 107
  field options 107
  field validators
    reference link 225
  field widgets
    reference link 223
  filter() method 147, 148
  flash message 318
  flowcharts 25
  Form class
    about 218
    creating 218, 219
    ModelForm 219
  FormClassView
    about 234
    configuring 235-237
  form fields
    arguments 220, 221
    using 219, 220
    validators 223-225
    widgets 222, 223
  forms
    cleaning 225
    clean() method 228, 229
    clean_{{ your_field_name }}
      () method 226, 227
    model, linking to 247
    rendering, in templates 240-242
    types 218
  formset factory
    about 256
    creating 256-258
  forms in templates, render form
    as_p 242
    as_table 243
    as_ul 243

Index 495

demo 246, 247
template_name, using 244-246
form view
   about 234
   classes 234
   HTTP request methods 237
   working with 234
form view, classes
   reference link 234
functional requirements 15

G

get_form() method
   about 302
   superuser condition 303
   view condition, changing/
      adding 302, 303
get() method 147, 237-239
GitHub 35
Git repository
   initializing 32, 33
Git settings
   configuring 32, 33
Git workflows
   reference link 40
Graphical Processing Unit (GPU) 53
Graph Models
   about 23
   plugin, reference link 24
Gulp
   reference link, for installation guide 19
Gulp Command-Line Utility (CLI) 19

H

Heroku
   buildpack 29

environments, managing 34, 35
   URL 28
Heroku CLI
   about 92, 93
   using 30, 31
Heroku dashboard 91, 92
Heroku database
   push/pull operations 100, 101
Heroku environments
   configuring 30
Heroku Git repository
   cloning 34
Heroku plan
   configuring 28
   creating 28
Homebrew 4
hosting 27
HTTP Host Header Attacks 72
HTTP request methods
   about 237
   get() method 237-239
   post() method 239, 240
HTTP view requests
   class-based views, testing 422-424
   method-based views, testing 419-421
   testing 419
Hypertext Transfer Protocol
      (HTTP) server 27

I

immutable object
   versus mutable object 122, 123
importdata command
   using 463, 464
include() function 168, 169
indexes options 125, 126
inheritance 132, 203, 204

inline formsets
  about 256
  adding 256
  formset factory 256
  rendering, in template 260-262
  using, in view class 258-260
inlines option
  about 292
  InlineModelAdmin class 292, 293
  ManyToMany field inlines 296, 297
  StackedInline class 294, 295
  TabularInline class 295, 296
integrated development
      environments (IDE)
  about 53, 54
  port, setting manually 67
  project, running/activating 66, 67
  PyDev, with Eclipse 54, 55
  PyDev, with PyCharm 55
  PyDev, with Visual Studio 55, 56
  using 57, 58, 63-65
iTerm2 5

J

JavaScript
  writing 379-381
JSONLint
  URL 454

K

Keyword Arguments (kwargs)
  about 160
  using, in views 178-181
knowledge base 9

M

Mailtrap
  account, creating 315-317
  URL 316
many-to-many field relationship 121, 122
many-to-one relationship 117-120
MariaDB 87
Markdown language 32
Markdown language, to style
      README documents
  reference link 32
markup language 32
masking 44
media files
  configuring, with static ()
      function 162, 163
message levels 320, 321
messages
  creating 323-326
  creating, that fails silently 328, 329
  creating, with custom message level 326
  creating, with extra tags 327, 328
  displaying 329, 330
message storage backends 319, 320
message tags 321, 322
meta options
  about 124
  db_table 127, 128
  indexes 125, 126
  ordering 124, 125
  reference link 124
  verbose_name 124
  verbose_name_plural 124
Meta subclass
  about 368, 369
  using 124

method-based views
  testing 419-421
model
  linking, to forms 247
model class
  absolute URLs, resolving within 197-199
model classes
  model field validator 115
  standard field types 106, 107
  third-party field type 112, 113
  writing 105
model field relationships
  field arguments 117, 118
  ForeignKey, field type 119, 120
  ManyToManyField, field type 121, 122
  mutable object, versus immutable
    object 122, 123
  working with 117
model field validator
  about 115
  setting 115, 116
ModelForm
  creating 219
model, linking to form
  CreateView 248-252
  UpdateView 252-255
model manager
  reference link 151
  writing 151-153
model metadata 124
model method
  about 129
  custom model methods 130, 131
  __str__() method 130
  reference link 129
  using 129
  writing 129

model registration, Django admin site
  decorator, using 275, 276
  statement, using 274
  ways 274
models
  about 103
  extending 132
  linking, to views and models 184-186
mutable object
  versus immutable object 122, 123
MySQL 86

N

NGINX
  about 27
  reference link, for installation manual 27
Nicepage
  URL 18
node 21
Node.js
  URL 19
Node Package Manager (NPM) 19
Notepad++
  about 52
  URL 52

O

Object-Relational Mapping (ORM) 105
objects 103
object test case
  creating 429-431
  updating 431-434
Online Transaction Processing (OLTP) 87
Open APIs 13
Oracle Database 87, 88
ordering option 124, 125

P

Partner APIs 13
path 158
path converters
  custom path converters 174, 175
  re_path() function 175, 176
  using 172, 173
path () function 163-168
path functions
  about 160
  include() functions 168-170
  path() function 163-168
  static() function 161
PDF reports
  as template-based PDFs 348-352
  generating 347, 348
PDF templates
  context, adding 353-355
PgAdmin tool
  local database, creating 93
  remote database, creating 94-96
  using 93
pipeline 42
PIP Python Package Manager 5
Platform as a Service (PaaS) 28
PostgreSQL 89
PostgreSQL, for Heroku
  environment connection, settings 96, 97
  initial table structures, building 97
  installing 90
  local installation 90, 91
  preparing 90
  remote data migrations 99, 100
  remote installation 91-93
post() method 239, 240
PowerShell 5

Prefetch class
  demo 485, 486
  sellers listing template file,
    modifying 484, 485
  using 483
prefetch_related() method
  using 471
Private APIs 13
process file (Procfile)
  creating 76, 77
project
  decision making 16-18
  designing 14
  interpretation 18, 19
  planning 14
  requirements gathering 14, 15
  research and discovery 15, 16
  visualization 18, 19
project configuration
  about 71
  Django media files 78
  Django settings.py file 71-73
  Django static files 77, 78
  environment file, creating 73
  .gitignore file, creating 79, 80
  Procfile, creating 76, 77
pull requests 42
PyCharm
  about 55
  download link 55
PyDev
  download link 55
  with Eclipse 54, 55
PyPI
  about 12
  URL 12

Python
  about 4
  need for 10
  URL 4
Python Enhancement Proposal 8 (PEP-8) style guide 12
Python Package Index (PyPI) library
  reference link 12

Q

Q object
  about 118
  reference link 118, 148
Quality Assurance (QA) phases 14
queries
  aggregate() 148, 149
  aggregates 148
  all() method 146
  annotate() method 150
  filter() method 147, 148
  get() method 147
  performing 146

R

README file 32
regression testing 407
Relational Database Management System (RDBMS) 85
remote data migrations 99, 100
remotes
  configuring 37, 38
re_path() function 175, 176
REpresentational State Transfer (REST) framework 11
request object
  absolute URLs, resolving with 195-197
rest_framework.serializers library
  classes 366
reverse APIs 37
reverse() function
  using 187, 189
Role Playing 15
root URLconf 160

S

SECRET_KEY variable
  generating 140, 141
Secure Sockets Layer (SSL) 97
select_related() method
  reference link 465
  using 465
sellers listing page template
  building 477-479
Sellers view
  about 475
  creating 476, 477
  demo 480-483
  URL pattern, mapping 480
SellersView class
  modifying 483, 484
serializer class
  about 366-368
  creating 364, 365
  Meta subclass 368, 369
settings.py file 71-73
simple views (method-based view)
  using 176-178
Single-Page App (SPA) pages
  building 376
  code, demonstrating 383-385
  JavaScript, writing 379-381
  template, building 378, 379

URL pattern, mapping 383
view, creating 376, 377
Single-Page App (SPA) pages, JavaScript
async keyword, using 382
await keyword, using 382
Single-Page App (SPA) website 11
Software Development Life
   Cycle (SDLC) 34
SQLite 85
SQL Server 88, 89
standard field types
about 106, 107
adding 108-112
field arguments 107, 108
standard PostgreSQL settings.py 89, 90
state diagram 26
static files
activating, with static()
   function 161, 162
static() function
about 161
media files, configuring with 162, 163
static files, activating with 161, 162
Structural Diagraming 19
Structured Query Language (SQL) 105
Sublime Text
about 53
URL 53
suffix 158
Supply Chain Management (SCM) 9

T

table structures
building 97
createsuperuser 99
IDE, using 98
makemigrations and migrate 98
template
custom tags and filters 210
error page templates 212, 213
filters 209
forms, rendering 240-242
inline formsets, rendering 260-262
tags 205-209
working with 204
template_name
using 244-246
text editor
about 52
Atom 52
Notepad++ 52
Sublime Text 53
ThemeForest
URL 18
third-party field type
about 112, 113
adding 113-115
tickets 42
Top-Level Domains (TLD) 44
tracking 39
trailing slashes
processing 191, 192

Index 501

U

Unified Modeling Language (UML)
  diagram types 19, 20
unit testing
  basic test class 413-415
  working with 413
update_or_create() method
  using 143, 144
UpdateView class
  about 252
  configuring 252-255
URL configuration 160
URL dispatcher 160
URL pattern
  conditional responses, working
    with 182, 183
  configuring 160
  kwargs, using in views 178-181
  managing 176
  mapping 383
  models, linking to views and
    templates 184, 185
  path converters, using 172-175
  path functions 160
  redirecting 170, 171
  simple views (method-based
    view), using 176-178
URL routers
  using 371-373
URLs
  patterns, naming 186, 187
  resolving 186
  reverse() function, using 187-189
  trailing slashes, processing 191, 192
  {% url %} template tag, using 189, 190

use case diagram 26
User-Generated Content (UGC) 162
User Observation 15

V

validator functions
  reference link 115
Vehicle Identification Number (VIN) 108
vehicles listing page
  performance, inspecting 469, 470
vehicles list template file
  checking 472
  creating 466-468
Vehicles view
  about 471
  checking 471, 472
  demo 473-475
VehiclesView class
  URL pattern, mapping 468
VehicleView class
  creating 465, 466
verbose_name 124
verbose_name_plural 124
view class
  inline formsets, using 258-260
views
  kwargs, using 178-181
  models, linking to 184-186
viewset classes 369-371
virtual environment
  about 43
  command line, using 67, 68
  creating 60, 61
  IDE, using 63-65
  requirements.txt file(s),
    configuring 62, 63

virtual environment, with command line
  activating 69
  port, setting manually 70
  project, running 70
Visual Studio 55, 56
Visual Studio Code 56

W

webhook 37
web hosting 27
Web Server Gateway Interface
      (WSGI) 204
widget argument 222, 223
Windows users
  note 101, 102
Write Everything Twice (WET) 181

Packt.com

Subscribe to our online digital library for full access to over 7,000 books and videos, as well as industry leading tools to help you plan your personal development and advance your career. For more information, please visit our website.

Why subscribe?

- Spend less time learning and more time coding with practical eBooks and Videos from over 4,000 industry professionals
- Improve your learning with Skill Plans built especially for you
- Get a free eBook or video every month
- Fully searchable for easy access to vital information
- Copy and paste, print, and bookmark content

Did you know that Packt offers eBook versions of every book published, with PDF and ePub files available? You can upgrade to the eBook version at packt.com and as a print book customer, you are entitled to a discount on the eBook copy. Get in touch with us at customercare@packtpub.com for more details.

At www.packt.com, you can also read a collection of free technical articles, sign up for a range of free newsletters, and receive exclusive discounts and offers on Packt books and eBooks.

Other Books You May Enjoy

If you enjoyed this book, you may be interested in these other books by Packt:

Web Development with Django

Ben Shaw | Subhash Sundaravadivelu | Bidhan Mondal | Bharath Chandra K S | Saurabh Badhwar | Andrew Bird | Chris Guest

ISBN: 978-1-83921-250-5

- Create a new application and add models to describe your data
- Use views and templates to control behavior and appearance
- Implement access control through authentication and permissions

Python Microservices Development – 2nd edition

Simon Fraser | Simon Fraser

ISBN: 978-1-80107-630-2

- Explore what microservices are and how to design them
- Configure and package your code according to modern best practices
- Identify a component of a larger service that can be turned into a microservice
- Handle more incoming requests, more effectively
- Protect your application with a proxy or firewall

Packt is searching for authors like you

If you're interested in becoming an author for Packt, please visit `authors.packtpub.com` and apply today. We have worked with thousands of developers and tech professionals, just like you, to help them share their insight with the global tech community. You can make a general application, apply for a specific hot topic that we are recruiting an author for, or submit your own idea.

Share Your Thoughts

Now you've finished *Becoming an Enterprise Django Developer*, we'd love to hear your thoughts! Scan the QR code below to go straight to the Amazon review page for this book and share your feedback or leave a review on the site that you purchased it from.

`https://packt.link/r/1801073635`

Your review is important to us and the tech community and will help us make sure we're delivering excellent quality content.

Printed in Great Britain
by Amazon